The Known, the Unknown, and the Unknowable in Financial Risk Management

The Known, the Unknown, and the Unknowable in Financial Risk Management

Measurement and Theory Advancing Practice

Francis X. Diebold
Neil A. Doherty
Richard J. Herring, editors

PRINCETON UNIVERSITY PRESS

Princeton and Oxford

Copyright © 2010 by Princeton University Press
Published by Princeton University Press, 41 William Street,
Princeton, New Jersey 08540
In the United Kingdom: Princeton University Press, 6 Oxford Street,
Woodstock, Oxfordshire OX20 1TW

Library of Congress Cataloging-in-Publication Data

The known, the unknown, and the unknowable in financial risk management:
measurement and theory advancing practice / Francis X. Diebold, Neil A.
Doherty, and Richard J. Herring, editors.
     p. cm.
  Includes bibliographical references and index.
  ISBN 978-0-691-12883-2 (hbk. : alk. paper) 1. Financial risk management.
2. Risk management. I. Diebold, Francis X., 1959– II. Doherty, Neil A.
III. Herring, Richard.
  HD61.K598 2010
  658.15'5—dc22   2009041544

British Library Cataloging-in-Publication Data is available

This book has been composed in Minion Pro

Book design by Marcella Engel Roberts

Printed on acid-free paper. ∞

press.princeton.edu

Printed in the United States of America

10   9   8   7   6   5   4   3   2   1

CONTENTS

PREFACE

∙ ∙

This book provides a variety of glimpses into the successes and failures of various parts of modern financial risk management. However, it is not our intent—indeed it is not logically possible—to provide a *survey* of the known, the unknown, and the unknowable (**KuU**). Instead, we aim to provide illustrations of a **KuU**-based *perspective* for conceptualizing financial risks and designing effective risk management strategies. Sometimes we focus on **K**, and sometimes on **U**, but most often our concerns *blend* aspects of **K** and **u** and **U**. Indeed, **K** and **U** are extremes of a smooth spectrum, with many of the most interesting and relevant situations interior.

The contributions gathered here emphasize a tripartite reality. First, financial risk measurement and theory, depending on context, range from highly developed to woefully inadequate. Second, financial risk measurement and theory, in any particular context, are typically not equally well developed. Finally, financial risk measurement and/or theory, in many important contexts, may *never* be well developed: although some financial phenomena are amenable to statistical or mathematical quantification, many are not. Our focus, then, is on quantitative risk measurement *and its limits*, including risk mitigation and management in murky real-world environments (contractual, organizational, policy-making, etc.) characterized by large doses of the unknown and the unknowable.

A generous Sloan Foundation grant to the Wharton Financial Institutions Center fueled the research program distilled in this volume. Both Wharton and Sloan are well aware that just as measurement beneficially disciplines theory, so too do practitioners beneficially discipline academics. Hence, we aspired to blend the two, and a series of two conferences proved a stimulating and effective vehicle. The first meeting took place in Philadelphia, with additional generous support from the Oliver Wyman Institute, and featured a series of panel discussions by top practitioners in financial policy-making, banking, venture capital, insurance, and asset management. Top academics attended and used the perspectives and issues raised to inform their chapters-in-progress commissioned for this volume. We turned the tables at a second meeting in Boston a year later, at which the academics presented their chapters-in-progress and practitioners offered lively commentary.

Several factors have contributed to the volume's development. First, already mentioned but worth repeating, the Sloan Foundation and Oliver Wyman Institute provided generous financial support. Second, the team at Princeton University Press, especially Peter Dougherty, Seth Ditchik, and Tim Sullivan, provided valuable guidance. Finally, a variety of colleagues provided important additional intellectual and administrative input, including Geoffrey Boisi, Sid Browne, Nathan Carr, Janie Chan, Mark Chandler, H. Rodgin Cohen, Esq., Sir Andrew Crockett, John Drzik, Brian Duperreault, Brenda Gavin, Lawrence R. Klein, Ugur Koyluoglu, Andrew Metrick, Michael Mussa, Stan Raatz, Charles S. Sanford, Anthony Santomero, Myron Scholes, Hemant Shah, J. Michael Steele, and Ralph Verni.

We apologize in advance for the many errors of commission and omission that surely remain. Despite such errors, we hope that the volume's individual and collective contents will help expand the frontiers of financial risk management, providing snapshots of current best practice and its limitations, and pushing us toward future progress.

Philadelphia
2009

The Known, the Unknown, and the Unknowable in Financial Risk Management

1. Introduction

Francis X. Diebold, Neil A. Doherty, and Richard J. Herring

Successful financial risk management requires constant grappling with the known, the unknown and the unknowable ("*KuU*"). But think of *KuU* as more than simply an acronym for "the known, the unknown, and the unknowable"; indeed, we think of it as a *conceptual framework*. We believe that "*KuU* thinking" can promote improved decision making—helping us to recognize situations of *K* and *u* and *U* and their differences, using different tools in different situations, while maintaining awareness that the boundaries are fuzzy and subject to change.

Perhaps the broadest lesson is recognition of the wide applicability of *KuU* thinking, and the importance of *each* of *K* and *u* and *U*. *KuU* thinking spans all types of financial risk, with the proportion of *uU* increasing steadily as one moves through market, credit, and operational risks. In addition, *KuU* thinking spans risk measurement and management in all segments of the financial services industry, including investing, asset management, banking, insurance, and real estate. Finally, *KuU* thinking spans both the regulated and the regulators: regulators' concerns largely match those of the regulated (risk measurement and management), but with an extra layer of concern for systemic risk.

1.1. KNOWLEDGE AS MEASUREMENT, AND KNOWLEDGE AS THEORY

Knowledge is both measurement and theory. Observed or measured facts about our world have no meaning for us outside our ability to relate them to a conceptual model. For example, the numerous stones we find with what appear to be reverse images of animals and plants would be unremarkable if it were not for their place in our intellectual model of the world we live in. Without the evolutionary theories associated with Darwin, the fossil record would be no more than a collection of pretty stones. And, indeed, without the pretty stones, Darwin may not have conceived his theory.

When we speak of knowledge, there is no bright line that separates our measurements from our theories. Though we may see the deficit at one, or the other, end of the spectrum, knowledge joins phenomenological observations with conceptual structures that organize them in a manner meaningful to our wider human experience. We would argue, for example, that both of the following assertions are true:

> When you can measure what you are speaking about, and express it in numbers, you know something about it; but when you cannot measure it, when you cannot express it in numbers, your knowledge is of a meager and unsatisfactory kind: it may be the beginning of knowledge, but you have scarcely, in your thoughts, advanced to the stage of science. Lord Kelvin (*Popular Lectures and Addresses*, 1891–1894)

> The whole machinery of our intelligence, our general ideas and laws, fixed and external object, principles, persons and gods, are so many symbolic, algebraic expressions. They stand for experience, experience which we are incapable of retaining and surveying in its multitudinous immediacy. We should flounder hopelessly, like the animals, did we not keep ourselves afloat and direct our course by these intellectual devices. Theory helps us to bear our ignorance of fact. George Santayana (*The Sense of Beauty*, 1896).

Thus, if we talk of what is known and what is unknown, we may be referring to the presence or absence of data to corroborate our theories, or to the inability of our theories to provide meaning to the curious phenomena we observe and measure.

For this volume, we have adopted the taxonomy of knowledge used in a famous article by Ralph Gomory (1995). Gomory classifies knowledge into the known, the unknown, and the unknowable, for which we adopt the acronym *KuU*. As applied to knowledge-as-measurement and knowledge-as-theory, we envision the *KuU* paradigm roughly as follows.

Knowledge as Measurement. The knowledge-as-measurement approach focuses on measuring possible outcomes with associated probabilities.

1. *K* refers to a situation where the probability distribution is completely specified. For example, the distribution of automobile or life insurance claims for an insurance company is more or less known. This is Frank Knight's (1921) definition of *risk*—both outcomes and probabilities are known.

2. *u* refers to a situation where probabilities cannot be assigned to at least some events. The systemic risk to financial systems and terrorism risk might fall into this category. This is Knight's definition of *uncertainty*—events are known but probabilities are not.

3. *U* refers to a situation where even the events cannot be identified in advance—neither events nor probabilities are known. Once they occur, they enter the domain of *u*. Retrospectively, the surge of asbestos claims for long-standing injury (real or imagined) is an example, as, indeed, are many legal actions caused by innovative legal theories.

Knowledge as Theory. The knowledge-as-theory approach focuses on the conceptual model that helps us to understand the underlying structure of the phenomenon of interest.

1. *K* refers to a situation where the underlying model is well understood. We may refer to this as a paradigm. This is not to say that the model is correct, only that experts are in broad agreement. For example, scientific models of evolution based on Darwin refer to a situation of scientific knowledge. We may not agree on all the details, but there is almost universal agreement among scientists on the broad structure. We might say there is "knowledge" on the broad principles of corporate governance, or risk-neutral options pricing. Thus, in short, *K* refers to successful *theory*.

2. *u* refers to a situation where there are competing models, none of which has ascended to the status of a paradigm. Credit risk management and operations risk management fall into this category. Other examples might include the performance of markets and financial institutions in emerging economies. If *K* refers to theory, then *u* refers to *hypothesis* or, more weakly, *conjecture*.

3. *U* refers to a situation with no underlying model (or no model with scientific credibility). This does not mean that we cannot conceivably form hypotheses, and even theory, in the future. But until some conceptual model is constructed, we cannot understand certain phenomena that we observe. Indeed, we may not even to be able to identify the phenomena because, in the absence of hypotheses or theory, it never occurs to us to look! For example, we would never look for black holes

unless we had a theory about how matter behaves under extreme gravitational forces.

The two taxonomies are complementary. For example, the inability to specify the tail of a distribution might be due both to the absence of data and to deficiencies of statistical theory. Thus, innovations such as extreme value theory can lead to upgrading of knowledge (from U to u or from u to K) under both taxonomies. As another illustration, the absence of a theory for a yet-to-be-identified phenomenon is hardly surprising and the emergence of such events will generate an interest in both measurement and theory.

The various authors in this volume generally adopt the *KuU* framework (not surprisingly, as we did bully them gently toward a common terminology), though most use it to address knowledge-as-measurement issues, and some modify the framework. For example, Richard Zeckhauser notes that, as regards measurement, we could otherwise describe *KuU* as *risk*, *uncertainty*, and *ignorance*. Similarly, Howard Kunreuther and Mark Pauly use the alternative *ambiguity* in a similar manner to our *u* and Knight's *uncertainty*. However, the most common chomping at the *KuU* bit was in insisting that we look at informational asymmetries. For example, Ken Scott looks at corporate governance in *KuU* terms, driven partly by informational (and skill) differences between managers and owners. Similarly, Zeckhauser observes that some investors have informational and skill advantages over others and then examines how uninformed investors, who recognize their inferior status, form strategies to benefit from the higher returns that can be earned from the knowledge and skills they lack.

A related theme that arises in some of the chapters is that the language used by different stakeholders depends on what is important to them. Clive Granger in particular notes that risk means different things to different people. Most particularly, many people think mostly of the downside of risk because that is what worries them. Thus, he emphasizes downside measures of risk, many of which (such as the various value at risk measures) have become increasingly important in risk management. Similarly, Scott notes that the conflict of interest that lies behind corporate governance is partly due to the fact that different stakeholders emphasize different parts of the distribution; undiversified managers may be more focused on downside risk than diversified shareholders.

1.2. *KuU* LESSONS FOR FINANCIAL MARKETS AND INSTITUTIONS

Here we highlight several practical prescriptions that emerge from *KuU* thinking, distilling themes that run through subsequent chapters. That we will treat *K* first is hardly surprising. Indeed, the existing risk management literature focuses almost exclusively on *K*, as summarized, for example, in the well-known texts of Jorion (1997), Doherty (2000), and Christoffersen (2003), and emphasized in the Basel II capital adequacy framework, which employs probabilistic methods to set minimum capital requirements.

Perhaps surprisingly in light of the literature's focus on K, however, we ultimately focus more on situations of u and U here and throughout. The reason is simple enough: reflection (and much of this volume) makes clear that a large fraction of real-world risk management challenges falls largely in the domain of u and U. Indeed, a cynic might assert that, by focusing on K, the existing literature has made us expert at the least-relevant aspects of financial risk management. We believe that K situations are often of relevance, but we also believe that u and U are of equal or greater relevance, particularly insofar as many of the "killer risks" that can bring firms down lurk there.

1.2.1. INVEST IN KNOWLEDGE

Although life is not easy in the world of K, it is easier in K than in u, and easier in u than in U. Hence, one gains by moving leftward through KuU toward knowledge, that is, from U to u to K. The question, then, is how to do it: How to invest in knowledge? Not surprisingly given our taxonomy of knowledge as measurement and knowledge as theory, two routes emerge: better measurement and better theory. The two are mutually reinforcing, moreover, as better measurement provides grist for the theory mill, and better theory stimulates improved measurement.

Better Measurement. Better measurement in part means better data, and data can get better in several ways. One way is more precise and timely measurement of previously measured phenomena, as, for example, with increased survey coverage when moving from a preliminary GDP release through to the "final" revised value.

Second, better data can correspond to intrinsically *new* data about phenomena that previously did not exist. For example, exchange-traded house price futures contracts have recently begun trading. Many now collect and examine those futures prices, which contain valuable clues regarding the market's view on the likely evolution of house prices. But such data could not have been collected before—they did not exist. Chapters like Bardhan and Edelstein's sweeping chronicle of KuU in real estate markets call to mind many similar such scenarios. Who, for example, could collect and analyze mortgage prepayment data before the development of mortgage markets and associated prepayment options?

Third, better data can arise via technological advances in data capture, transmission, and organization. A prime example is the emergence and increasingly widespread availability of ultra-high-frequency (trade-by-trade) data on financial asset prices, as emphasized in Andersen et al. (2006). In principle, such data existed whenever trades occurred and could have been collected, but it was the advent and growth of electronic financial markets—which themselves require huge computing and database resources—that made these data available.

Finally, and perhaps most importantly, better financial data can result from new insights regarding the determinants of risks and returns. It may have always been possible to collect such data, but until the conceptual breakthrough, it seemed pointless to do so. For example, traditional Markowitz risk-return thinking emphasizes only return mean and variance. But that approach (and its extension, Sharpe's celebrated CAPM) assumes that returns are *Gaussian* with *constant variances*. Subsequent generations of theory naturally began to explore asset pricing under more general conditions, which stimulated new measurement that could have been done earlier, but wasn't. The resulting explosion of new measurement makes clear that asset returns—particularly at high frequencies—are highly non-Gaussian and have nonconstant variances, and that both important pitfalls and important opportunities are embedded in the new worldview. Mandelbrot and Taleb, for example, stress the pitfalls of assuming normality when return distributions are in fact highly fat-tailed (badly miscalibrated risk assessments), while Colacito and Engle stress the opportunities associated with exploiting forecastable volatility (enhanced portfolio performance fuelled by volatility timing).

Thus far, we have treated better measurement as better data, but what of better tools with which to summarize and ultimately understand that data? If better measurement sometimes means better data, it also sometimes means better statistical/econometric models—the two are obviously not mutually exclusive. Volatility measurement, for example, requires not only data but also models. Crude early proxies for volatility, such as squared returns, have been replaced with much more precise estimates, such as those based on ARCH models. This allows much more nuanced modeling, as, for example, in the chapter by Colacito and Engle, who measure the entire term structure of volatility. They construct a powerful new model of time-varying volatility that incorporates nonstationarity and hence changing distributions, nudging statistical volatility modeling closer to addressing uU. Similarly, Litzenberger and Modest develop a new model that allows for regime switching in the data, with different types of trading strategies exposed to different crisis regimes, and with regime transition probabilities varying *endogenously* and sharply with trading, hence allowing for "trade-driven crises."

In closing this subsection, we note that although better data and models may help transform u into K, the role of better data in dealing with U is necessarily much more speculative. To the extent that U represents a failure of imagination, however, the collection and analysis of data regarding near misses—disasters that were narrowly averted—may provide a window into the domain of U and alternative outcomes. The challenge is how to learn from near misses.

Better Theory. As we indicated earlier, the literature on the behavior of markets and institutions, and the decision making that drives them, is almost exclusively couched in K. Accordingly, risk prices can be set, investors can choose strategies that balance risk and reward, managers can operate to a known level of safety, regulators can determine a standard of safety, and so forth. Similarly, a variety of information providers, from rating agencies to hazard modeling companies, can assess risk for investors, if they want to verify or supplement their own efforts.

That literature not only relies on the potentially erroneous assumption of K, but also assumes that actors are sophisticated and rational. For example, the economic theory of individual decision making is based largely on expected utility maximization. A similar level of rationality is required in the sophisticated enterprise risk management models that are now available and increasingly in use.

Even in situations accurately described as K, however, the assumption of sophistication and rationality is questionable. As Granger emphasizes in his chapter, people's actual behavior often violates the seemingly innocuous axioms of expected utility, as many experiments have shown, and as an emergent behavioral economics emphasizes. If behavioral economics has had some success in the K world, one might suppose that it will become even more important in the uU world of scant knowledge. This point is addressed, for example, by Kunreuther and Pauly, who examine unknown but catastrophic losses, such as major acts of terrorism. They identify framing anomalies, such as an "it can't happen to me" mentality that forestalls action.[1]

Construction and application of such "better theories"—theories geared toward the worlds of u and U—appear throughout the volume. For example, Zeckhauser notes that investing in a K world may play into the hands of the math jocks, but not so when probabilities are unknown and the potential scenarios that can drive them unknowable, and he outlines some innovative strategies to cope in this world. The authors of other chapters ask whether, given that we can't anticipate the future, we can nevertheless arrange our affairs (write contracts, design organizational structures, formulate policies, etc.) such that

---

[1] However, it is somewhat difficult to entertain the usual alternatives to expected utility, such as prospect theory where the derivation of a weighting function for unknown probabilities seems an empty exercise.

we make good decisions in a wide range of possible futures. Scott, for example, stresses the importance of long-term incentives to focus the CEO on the long-term survival and value of the firm in an unknown future.

1.2.2. SHARE RISKS

The desirability of risk sharing is hardly novel. An emergent and novel theme, however, is the desirability—indeed, the necessity—of tailoring risk-sharing mechanisms to risk types.

Simple Insurance for **K.** Operations of financial institutions are greatly simplified in situations of **K**. Banks and insurance companies with known distributions of assets and liabilities can set appropriate risk-adjusted prices (interest rates and insurance premiums). The main challenge comes from the correlation structure of the assets and liabilities and from incentive problems, such as adverse selection and moral hazard.

Regulators' tasks are likewise simplified in **K**.[2] Regulators typically impose minimum capital requirements. They monitor institutions and may intervene in the event of distress, and their role is supplemented by rating agencies, which supply the market with information on default risk, thereby supporting the process of risk-adjusted pricing.

The general picture we see here is that, in the case of **K** risks, financial institutions can pool idiosyncratic risk and reserve against expected losses, such that the risks to bank depositors and insurance policyholders are small. The remaining systematic risk is controlled by setting economic/regulatory capital. Institutional defaults in this environment are not informational failures, but rather the result of inadequate provision of costly economic capital.

Mutual Insurance for **u.** For risks that are unknown, the potential events can be identified, but probabilities are difficult or impossible to assign. Moreover, one would like to broaden the definition to address correlation across different risks. One approach is to suggest that, for **u** risks, we know neither the probabilities nor the correlations. This definition is appropriate if we define events in terms of their consequences to individuals. Thus, different agents and institutions are each exposed to market risk, credit risk, operations risk, and so on. A second approach is to define events to include both individual and collective

---

[2] We hasten to add that the assertions of this subsection apply to situations diagnosed as **K** and *truly* **K**. Situations interpreted as **K**, but *not* truly **K**, can, of course, lead to tremendously divergent results, as emphasized by the recent financial crisis.

impacts, as, for example, with the following exhaustive and mutually exclusive events: (1) I suffer a 40% decline in portfolio value and you do not, (2) you suffer 40% decline and I do not, (3) neither of us suffers a 40% decline, and (4) both of us suffer a 40% decline.

Which approach is appropriate depends on context. However, the point is that some unknowns affect people differently, while others impact people collectively. Consider climate change. It can, by its nature, impact the entire world, and we are certainly unsure about the particular form and magnitude of many of its effects. Thus, it is in the realm of *u*, and the nature of the uncertainty surrounding global warming spans both the global and local impacts. The extent of any rise in sea level is unknown, but it will have a common impact on all coastal areas, exposing them all to increased flood and tidal surge risk. However, the impact of rising temperatures on drought risk may vary considerably across regions in ways that we do not fully understand and cannot predict. In the former case of rising sea level, the uncertainty is *correlated*, and in the latter case of drought risk, the uncertainty is of *lower correlation*. This distinction is important in determining how effectively *u* risk can be pooled in insurance-like structures.

In the case of uncorrelated unknowns, there is no real obstacle to the pooling of risk; for some locations, the probabilities (and, therefore, the randomly realized outcomes) turn out to be higher and for others, the probabilities turn out to be lower. This is simply a two-stage lottery; in stage 1, the distribution is randomly chosen and, in stage 2, the outcome is realized. Insurance mechanisms can cover both the stage 1 distribution risk and the stage 2 outcome risk as long as both are random and uncorrelated. Insurance on stage 1 is essentially hedging against future premium risk, and insurance in stage 2 is hedging future outcome risk.

For correlated unknowns, risk pooling is more challenging. The realization of stage 1 of the lottery will have a common impact on both the overall level of prices and on the level of economic capital required to undertake stage 2. Nevertheless, optimal risk-sharing arrangements are not too difficult to envision, in the tradition of those proposed by Borch (1962) for the case of known but correlated risks. A mutual-like structure can still achieve some degree of risk pooling for the idiosyncratic risk, and the systematic risk (whether from stage 1 or stage 2 of the lottery) can be shared across the population at risk by devices such as *ex post* dividends, assessments, or taxes.[3]

Kunreuther and Pauly present a case study of catastrophic risk insurance that blends aspects of simple insurance for *K* and mutual insurance for *u*, arguing

---

[3] Borch's theory closely parallels the capital asset pricing model, in which all people have scaled shares in the social wealth (i.e., the market portfolio).

that the same type of layered private–public program applies to both K risks and u risks (though presumably the details would differ). The idea is to provide potent incentives for mitigation of losses, while still using the risk-bearing capacity of the private insurance and capital markets to provide the greatest possible diversification benefit. The lowest layer would be self-insured. The second layer would be private insurance contracts with risk-based premiums. The third layer would be reinsured or otherwise spread through insurance-linked securities. The final layer would allocate the highest level of losses on an economy-wide basis, perhaps using multistate risk pools or federal government intervention as the reinsurer of last resort.

***Ex Post* Wealth Redistribution for *U*.** Borch's argument for mutualizing risk, which emphasizes that efficiency requires insuring idiosyncratic individual risk and sharing social risk, becomes even more persuasive as we move from u toward U. As we move into U it becomes impossible to specify, let alone price, risks that could be transferred by standard contractual devices, and it is correspondingly difficult to provide incentives to mitigate risks that cannot be identified. However, we do of course know that surprises, of an as-yet-unimaginable nature, can arise in the future and we can anticipate that we might want to react in predictable ways. For example, it is not uncommon for governments to redistribute wealth from taxpayers to victims *ex post*, when unknown or unknowable catastrophes occur, in attempts to equalize the impact across the population.

It is interesting to note that, in practice, there are large variations in *ex post* generosity, evidently associated with a political imperative to be especially generous when the scale of the disaster exceeds some threshold of saliency. Consider, for example, the two most notable U.S. terrorist events of recent years, the 9/11 attack and the earlier Oklahoma City bombing. The 9/11 victims' compensation allocated a total of $7 billion, which amounted to an average payment of $1.8 million per person, and compensation was paid to 93% of families. No such compensation was paid to victims of the smaller, though still major, Oklahoma City bombing.

Similarly, it appears that bailouts of failed financial institutions also must meet an implicit scale criterion, which, moreover, may be highly dependent on the perceived fragility of markets when the failure occurs. It is noteworthy, for example, that neither Northern Rock nor Bear Stearns, both of which were bailed out during a broader financial crisis, were counted among the large, complex financial institutions that the International Monetary Fund identified as critical to the functioning of the international financial system.

On the other hand, the incentives from such large-event bailouts can be perverse. Even for "exogenous" crises, such as natural disasters, knowledge of likely bailouts may make people less inclined to buy insurance and unwilling to invest in mitigation measures. Many crises, moreover, are at least partly "endogenous," or shaped by agents' actions—financial crises are an obvious example. This highlights a fundamental tension: *ex post* catastrophe bailouts may be socially desirable, but *ex ante* knowledge of the likelihood (or certainty) of such bailouts tends to raise the probability of catastrophe! Banks, for example, may be less inclined to practice financial discipline and their customers less inclined to monitor them. Addressing this moral hazard is central to designing effective financial regulation.

1.2.3. CREATE FLEXIBLE AND ADAPTIVE STRUCTURES

In a comment that spans both parts of our taxonomy, which grounds *KuU* in knowledge-as-measurement and knowledge-as-theory, Paul Kleindorfer notes that the balance between aleatory risk (dependent on an uncertain outcome) and epistemic risk (related to an imperfect understanding or perception) changes as we move from *K* though *u* to *U*. In particular, in a *K* setting, risk management will tend to focus on risk mitigation or transfer, but as we move toward *U*, risk management will stress adaptation and flexibility. Where risk is Known, it is likely that a market for trading that risk will emerge, as with commodity and financial derivatives and insurance contracts. Alternatively, if the process that generates the risk is understood, then risk can be mitigated *ex ante*. For example, as Kunreuther and Pauly point out, much exposure to known catastrophe risk can be mitigated by choosing location and by constructing wind- or earthquake-robust structures. *K* conditions imply that risk can be priced and that we will be able to make informed capital budgeting decisions.

Transfer and *ex ante* mitigation become more difficult in the case of *u* and *U*, in which risk management emphasis shifts to adaptation and flexibility, and to robustness and crisis response. These strategies are both *ex ante* and *ex post*. The knowledge that unknown and unknowable losses might strike suggests caution with regard to capital and investment decisions; for example, extra capital provides some buffer against the unknown, and required rates of return on investment might be more conservatively chosen in a *uU* environment.

Heightened awareness of the existence of *uU* risks is valuable, despite the fact that, by definition, such risks cannot be identified *ex ante*. We have mentioned the value of holding more capital as a buffer against such shocks, and we can think of this as simply a change in financial leverage (a change in the ratio of variable to fixed financing costs). Similarly, a change in operating leverage, the ratio of variable to fixed factor costs, can make any firm more robust to shocks, whether of the *K* or *u* or *U* variety. For example, Microsoft has operated with a high ratio of contract as opposed to payroll labor, which it can more easily reduce in unforeseen bad times.

Other examples of strategies that create organizational flexibility and adaptability are given by several contributors. For example, Scott notes that if the compensation of CEOs and other top managers is based on long-term wealth maximization, then it will motivate managers to manage crises in a way that protects shareholders. But this need not be purely after-the-fact improvisation. Indeed, properly structured compensation may motivate managers to anticipate how they should respond to crises and invest in crisis response capability. This may prove useful even if the anticipated crisis does not occur. For example, precautionary measures for dealing with Y2K, which proved uneventful, are nevertheless widely credited with enhancing the resilience of the financial system after the 9/11 terrorist attack on New York's financial center.

Kleindorfer also stresses crisis management, emphasizing the role of a crisis management team in creating response capability. Although crises may have unique and perhaps unanticipated causes (either u or U), the responses called for are often similar, and a well-prepared crisis management team can often limit the damage. For example, large shocks create uncertainty, and clearly articulated responses can reassure customers and investors, ensure that supply chains are secured, and so on. But well-designed responses can even snatch victory from the jaws of defeat. For example, after the cyanide scare with its Tylenol product, Johnson & Johnson withdrew and then redesigned its product and packaging, setting a standard that led its competition and secured competitive advantage.

Sound management of crises can not only mitigate their impact, but also generate new knowledge. Indeed, and perhaps ironically, crises are sometimes portals that take us from U and u toward K. For example, Hurricane Andrew in 1992, the Asian currency crisis in 1997, 9/11 in 2001, and the financial/economic crisis that began in 2007 all spurred new approaches to modeling extreme event risk. Hurricane Andrew led to an explosion of interest in catastrophe modeling and a consequent refining of modeling methodology. The Asian crisis led to a new interest in the properties of tail risk (fat tails and tail correlations), which have been incorporated in new generations of models. Finally, 9/11 led to the development of game theoretic catastrophe modeling techniques.

1.2.4. USE INCENTIVES TO PROMOTE DESIRED OUTCOMES

Risk management strategies must confront the issue of *incentives*, thwarting moral hazard by coaxing rational and purposeful economic agents to act desirably (whatever that might mean in a particular situation). We take a broad interpretation of "designing strategies," and here we discuss three: designing organizational/governance arrangements, designing contracts, and designing investment vehicles.

Organizations and Relationships: Principal/Agent Concerns in Corporate Governance. K risks can be identified and probabilities assigned to them. If knowledge is symmetric and actions are commonly observable by all parties, then simple contracts can be written in which actions are specified contingent on states of nature. In this simple world, there are no moral hazard and adverse selection problems. For example, insurance or loan contracts can be written, and banks and insurers would know the quality of each customer and price accordingly. Private wealth transfer caused by inefficient actions (the insured underinvesting in loss mitigation or borrowers taking on excessive risk) would be avoided because they were excluded by contractual conditions, and institutions would be able to monitor accordingly.

In principle, special purpose vehicles (SPV) work that way. They may be organized as trusts or limited liability companies and are set up for a specific, limited purpose, often to facilitate securitizations. In the securitization process, the SPV buys pools of assets and issues debt to be repaid by cash flows from that pool of assets in a carefully specified way. The SPV is tightly bound by a set of contractual obligations that ensure that its activities are perfectly transparent and essentially predetermined at its inception. SPVs tend to be thinly capitalized, lack independent management or employees, and have all administrative functions performed by a trustee who receives and distributes cash according to detailed contracts. SPVs are designed to be anchored firmly in the domain of K in order to fund assets more cheaply than they could be funded on the balance sheets of more opaque, actively managed institutions. The turmoil in the subprime market during the summer of 2007, however, revealed that the claims on some SPVs were much less transparent than assumed and that investors (and the ratings agencies they relied on) were, in fact, operating in a world of u rather than K. This led to a repricing of risk, and disruption of markets that spread well beyond the market for subprime-related securitizations.

Governance of most firms is not as straightforward as with SPVs. Partly the problem is one of complexity and division of labor. There are numerous potential states of nature facing firms, and contracts anticipating the appropriate response of managers to each possible state would be impossibly cumbersome. Moreover, envisioning shareholders (or their agents) writing such contracts presupposes that they already have the managerial skills they are seeking to employ. Indeed, the reason for employing managers is that they alone know the appropriate responses.

The division of labor issue can be cast as an information problem. Managers have much better knowledge than shareholders of how to deal with managerial opportunities and crises. In this light, the issue is not whether knowledge and skills can be acquired, but how they are distributed across stakeholders. Ken Scott digs much deeper into the informational aspects of corporate governance and explores how governance mechanisms may be designed when risks are unknown, *u*, to any party, or indeed unknowable, *U*.

Scott's particular focus is the risk management aspect of governance ("risk governance"), and he starts by contrasting the risk preferences of the major stakeholders. While diversified shareholders seek to maximize the value reflecting both the upside and downside of the distribution; relatively undiversified managers are probably more risk averse, and compensation is often designed to enhance their preference for risk. Government and regulators, presumably protecting the interests of consumers, also are more interested in downside risk, particularly the prospect of contagion, or systemic risk. Their attention is focused on how to avoid the prospect that firms will incur unsustainable losses.

For *K* risks, shareholder and societal interests are promoted by risk-neutral decision making and the governance problem is in large part one of furthering this objective through appropriate compensation design. But the fine tuning of compensation to provide risk-neutral incentives and correct reporting is not an easy task. Thus, Scott stresses the importance of establishing a "risk culture" within the firm. This can start with board members who demand that top managers articulate their risk management strategy, and it can flow down to division and project managers who conduct (marginal)[4] risk analysis. Coordination can be addressed by the appointment of a chief risk officer.

For *u*, part of the governance problem is mainly to encourage the acquisition of more information; that is, to convert *u* into *K* by investing in information. Another part of the issue is to design internal controls and board oversight of management actions. Scott makes the important point that these efforts might be more effective if management were unable to keep ill-gotten gains (resulting from manipulated earnings) in their bonuses.

The externalities caused by bank failure are classified as *u*. Control of this risk can be influenced by contract design, and Scott points to the perverse case that arises when derivative counterparties are given a favored position when banks go into receivership, which diminishes their incentives to monitor banks and price risk appropriately. For their part, regulators have addressed the bank failure risk in detail through the Basel I and II requirements, which are designed

---

[4] Marginal risk analysis ascertains the incremental contribution of each activity to the total risk of the firm.

to provide more information on risk and establish appropriate levels of regulatory capital. But more interesting is the shift in decision-making authority that occurs as a bank's capital declines. The "prompt corrective action" measures in U.S. law permit the downside risk preferences of regulators to trump the risk-neutral perspective of shareholders as the bank's capital declines.

For *U* risks, Scott proposes financial flexibility and managerial incentives linked to the long-term survival of the bank. Thus, as unknowns appear, managers will be rewarded for finding responses that protect the interests of the other stakeholders. The very nature of this risk implies that one cannot estimate with accuracy the additional capital needed to cushion against unforeseeable failures. Nevertheless, additional capital margins will reduce this prospect and an ordinal ranking of institutions is feasible.

The process by which knowledge is acquired (either facts or understanding) creates not only opportunities to use the new knowledge but also institutional stresses. Stresses occur because institutions are designed around increasingly outdated knowledge, with changing knowledge shared asymmetrically by the various stakeholders. In the past two decades or so, capital markets have undergone considerable changes. These include changes in our conceptual model of how markets work, as well as changes in the volume of data. The evolution in asset pricing, from the one-factor capital asset pricing model though to more recent multifactor models, as well as the revolution in derivative pricing together with advances in corporate financial theory, have changed the way investor and management decisions are made. These theoretical innovations have created a demand for new data to verify and calibrate the new models. This push for data has been spurred by phenomenal growth in computing power. Enhanced understanding of the underlying economic mechanisms and better data potentially allow all stakeholders to make decisions that better create value.

Accompanying the revolution in financial theory and explosion in data has been a market enhancement that Bravler and Borge label *capital market intensity*. More information and better understanding allow investors to monitor changes in a firm's fortune quickly and to act accordingly. Passive investors may simply buy or sell. But an increasing tendency to shareholder activism, especially in hedge funds, has led to investor involvement in corporate decision making. This is exercised by applying direct pressure to management, influencing board composition, removing management, and so on. In this way, investors can exert direct influence over management to seek preferred risk–reward profiles. At the same time, of course, the innovations bestow better tools on management to attend to investor needs. In particular, the sophisticated tools of financial engineering and the bewildering array of financial instruments permit almost unlimited flexibility to management to redesign its risk–reward profile.

In Bravler and Borge's view, increased capital market intensity challenges the traditional principal-agent-based model of corporate governance. The traditional model assumes that managers have a comparative advantage in both information and decision skills over investors, but investors induce managers to create value by means of incentive-compatible employment contracts. In the new world of capital intensity, the comparative advantage between (at least some) investors and managers is largely removed. Braver and Borge see a new model that is analogous to a two-sided market structure. The CFO acts as an intermediary between the management and investors: "The CFO is the agent of the company in the capital markets and the agent of capital market discipline inside the company." In fact, we would probably suggest that the CFO is still properly regarded as the agent of the company. However, this does not diminish the power of the Bralver-Borge observation that the CFO's role needs to be redefined to refocus corporate attention on value creation for investors and to use the potent strategies and instruments now available to achieve this end. If the CFO falls down on this task, increasingly activist investors may simply do it for themselves.

Contracts: Intentional Incompleteness and "Holdup." Things that are unknown now may become known as events unfold. 9/11 informed us of a different form and magnitude of terrorism. Recent financial crises, notably the Asian crisis and the subprime crisis, informed us of hitherto unsuspected correlations in tail risk that have now deepened our understanding of systemic risk. However, not only new events, but also new theory, can shift us from U toward K. For example, assets that might appear mispriced under a simple single-factor pricing model may appear well priced under a multifactor model. Unfortunately, retrogression also occurs. Statistical relationships that have proven stable over many years may suddenly break down. Institutional structures that were well understood may prove to have hidden flaws. Policies that seem reliable in normal times may fail to work in crises.

If we cannot anticipate events or do not understand their consequences, it becomes difficult to write effective contracts. For example, the insurance industry was recently surprised by several new classes of claims that it had not suspected and therefore had neither written them into coverage or explicitly excluded them. These included toxic mold damage to buildings and to the health of their residents, as well as the new forms of terrorism that blur the distinction between traditional terrorism and actual warfare. Other examples include innovative legal rulings that have substantially changed coverage from what seems to have been written into policies, including the (sometime) removal of the distinction between flood and wind coverage in post-Katrina claims and the earlier reinterpretations of coverage for "sudden and unexpected" liabilities to include "gradual and expected."

Insurance contracts are usually written for named perils, or written to include a broad class of perils insofar as they are not specifically excluded by contract language. Either way, the contract defines what is covered and what is not. If the covered perils are "known" in our terminology, a price can be set relative to the (known) expected loss and other distributional parameters that indicate the cost of capital. Even if events are unknown in the sense that they can be identified but cannot be assigned probabilities, contracts can still be written, although the setting of premiums becomes a challenge. But when events cannot even be specified, contracts cannot easily be imagined.

Doherty and Muermann ask whether risks that are indeed unknowable can be effectively transferred to insurers. Using incomplete contract theory, they argue that such risks can be, and are, allocated to insurers. When writing through independent agents and brokers, insurers vest the intermediary with considerable "holdup" power. Agents and brokers can move their books of business and may do so if they believe this serves the interests of their policyholders. Moreover, Doherty and Muermann argue that this holdup power is used to extend insurance coverage to include some nonspecified events. If a hitherto unknown event arises, the broker can decide whether it is one that can, and should, be insurable going forward (i.e., now that it has graduated from U to u or K). If so, the broker might use its leverage to bargain with the insurer for a settlement for its client. Indeed, such *ex post* bargaining may even be anticipated when contracts are written, and premiums adjusted upward accordingly. In this way, brokered markets can provide an orderly market in which unknown events can be insured despite the fact that the coverage is not formally specified in the contract.

Incomplete contracts may indeed be a common device for coping with the unknown. For example, employment contracts for CEOs and other top executives are incomplete insofar as they do not anticipate detailed scenarios and prescribe specific managerial responses. Instead, they rely on alignment of the interests of the CEO and shareholders through compensation design, and they allocate considerable discretion to the CEO to respond to events drawn from the whole *KuU* spectrum. In this way the CEO's skill is given considerable scope to respond quickly to new information.

Investment Vehicles: Riding "Sidecar" with Those Better Informed. Richard Zeckhauser examines investment in *uU* environments, where markets are thin and potentially enormous excess returns are available to those with resources and talents to venture into these little explored places. It helps to have billions to invest, steady nerves, complementary skills, and freedom from blame when things don't work out (as often happens). Warren Buffett and his ilk can prosper in this realm, but what about the rest of us? Can we also make sensible and profitable forays into this compelling and intimidating territory? Richard Zeckhauser raises this question in an unorthodox essay that draws both on his own experience (as a "sidecar investor") and on his deep insights in areas of economics not usually considered relevant to investors.

Consider the investor with money, steady nerve, and complementary skills. He or she may well be willing to make a speculative investment, accepting large risk for extraordinary expected returns. Can investors with lesser skills and resources attach themselves to this powerful motorbike and go along for the ride as a "sidecar"? It is certainly dangerous territory. The risks for the biker with the wherewithal to handle it can be enormous, and risks may be relatively greater for those riding sidecar. Moreover, dealing with those who are better informed exposes us to adverse selection risk, and this must be balanced against the absolute advantage from their superior resources and skills. Yet if we understand this trade-off, then there are opportunities for sidecar investments.[5] Using game theory and behavioral economics, Zeckhauser shows how to balance the adverse selection against the absolute advantage, and he gives instructive examples ranging from Russian oil investments to Warren Buffet's reinsurance ventures.

Disasters such as 9/11 and Katrina both diminish insurance capacity and usually enhance insurance demand, thus leading to excess demand, which is felt in a hardening of the insurance market. This hard market is felt most acutely in reinsurance, where postloss supply is especially scarce and prices soar. Often excess demand is fueled by a shift along the continuum from K to u to U; for example, 9/11 created major uncertainty about future terror risk, and Katrina fed our fears on the unknowns of global warming. The hardened reinsurance market, together with enhanced uncertainty of the future risk, creates just those conditions that Zeckhauser considers ripe for very high returns. Reinsurers possess the complementary skills (if, indeed, anyone does), but hedge funds have the funds and tolerance of ambiguity to partake. As a result, sidecar structures have bloomed, usually with hedge fund (and some other) investors taking investment shares on the same terms as reinsurance contracts. These differ from equity investment in the reinsurer in that they cover only specified risks and usually for a short time frame.

---

[5] Robert Edelstein notes that real estate syndicates are often structured that way. Investors have the money and the developer has the complementary skill and experience. In the end, however, the developer often has the money and the investors have the experience.

In reinsurance-based sidecars, absolute advantage probably trumps adverse selection. Although there may be some adverse selection in the original contractual relationship whereby the reinsurer "insures the primary insurer," there is unlikely to be much additional adverse selection in the derived relationship between the reinsurer and the sidecar investors. Thus, the value creation is driven by absolute advantage, and sidecar investors can share in this added value.

1.2.5. USE FINANCIAL POLICY TO LIMIT VULNERABILITY TO SHOCKS *EX ANTE* AND MITIGATE THE CONSEQUENCES *EX POST*

Financial policy becomes most relevant when a shock that was unknown or unknowable shifts the financial system from the domain of the known into the unknown. Financial policy makers are charged with limiting the vulnerability of the financial system to such shocks and mitigating the consequences of these shocks once they occur. Financial policy makers aim to promote monetary and financial stability. In practice, virtually every aspect of financial policy is subject to uncertainty. For example, how precisely should these objectives be defined? With regard to monetary policy, what amount of inflation is consistent with achieving stable, sustainable growth? What measure of inflation is appropriate? Is it feasible, both technically and politically, for the monetary authorities to prevent asset bubbles during periods of low and stable inflation?[6] With regard to prudential policy, the primary goal of financial stability must be to protect the functioning of the financial system in providing payments services and facilitating the efficient allocation of resources over time and across space. This may be threatened by a loss of confidence in key financial markets or institutions. But how safe should financial institutions be? Should all failures be prevented? Would the required restrictions on risk-taking by financial institutions reduce the efficiency of financial intermediation and reduce investment? Would this deprive the economy of the dynamic benefits of creative destruction? But if financial institutions should not be required to be perfectly safe, what degree of safety should the prudential authorities try to achieve?

What tools should be used to achieve these objectives? And what governance structure is most likely to motivate policy makers to act in the public interest? Public-sector compensation contracts are much more highly constrained than compensation contracts for senior executives in financial services firms. More

---

[6] Jacob Frenkel (Thornhill and Michaels, 2008, p. 4), former Governor of the Bank of Israel, has expressed doubt about whether the monetary authorities know enough to deflate bubbles before they become dangerous. He asserts that the real choice is "Which system do you want: one in which the [monetary authority] pricks three bubbles out of five or five out of three bubbles? Because we know for sure that it will not be able to solve four out of four."

fundamentally, when objectives are not crisply defined, it is difficult to establish and enforce accountability. Blame avoidance is, by default, a primary objective of most bureaucrats.

Although the prudential supervisory authorities have enormous, if ill-defined, responsibility, they have relatively little power to constrain risk-taking by profitable institutions that they believe to have excessive exposures to uncertain shocks. To guard against the arbitrary use of regulatory and supervisory power, most countries subject disciplinary decisions by officials to some sort of judicial or administrative review. To discipline a bank, a supervisor must not only know that a bank is taking excessive risk, but also be able to prove it to the satisfaction of the reviewing body—perhaps beyond a reasonable doubt. This leads to a natural tendency to delay disciplinary measures until much of the damage from excessive risk-taking has already been done.[7] It also leads officials to react mainly to what has already happened (and is, therefore, objectively verifiable) rather than to act on the basis of expectations about what may happen (which are inherently disputable). In Charles Goodhart's refinement of the *KuU* framework in which *K* is partitioned into actual past data and expected values, supervisors generally react to actual past losses rather than expected future losses, much less other aspects of the distribution of future losses, even when the governing probability distribution is believed to be known. Alan Greenspan (2008, p. 9), former Chairman of the Board of Governors of the Federal Reserve System, has expressed doubt about whether regulators know enough to act preemptively: "Regulators, to be effective, have to be forward-looking to anticipate the next financial malfunction. This has not proved feasible. Regulators confronting real-time uncertainty have rarely, if ever, been able to achieve the level of future clarity required to act preemptively."

Regulating with Imperfect Information. Information issues present a fundamental challenge to supervisory authorities who must oversee the solvency of regulated financial institutions. Neither past data nor expected future values can be relied on in times of crisis when difficult supervisory decisions must be made. Bank accounting has traditionally been a mix of historical cost accounting, accrual accounting, and mark-to-market accounting. This has sometimes undermined incentives for hedging risks by valuing a risky position and the offsetting hedge differently, thereby increasing the volatility of earnings, even though risk has been reduced. Many doubt that this mix of standards conveys

---

[7] As Kenneth Scott notes, the Prompt Corrective Action measures adopted in the United States are intended to constrain this tendency to forbear in the enforcement of capital regulations by removing a degree of supervisory discretion.

a true and fair account of the current position of a financial institution. New financial accounting standards require firms to classify assets in three different categories: (1) assets that can be marked to market based on quoted prices in active markets for identical instruments; (2) assets that are marked to matrix, based on observable market data; and (3) assets that are marked to model, based on judgment regarding how the market would price such assets if they were traded in active markets. This third category presents significant difficulties for regulators, who face a severe asymmetric information problem vis-à-vis the regulated institution. How can the regulatory authorities comfortably rely on the estimated values of category 3 assets? Opinions of auditors and ratings agencies may help the authorities avoid blame, but the key question, as Goodhart notes, is "Who has legal liability if the values are wrong?"

Part of the problem, as noted by Stewart Myers in a workshop that preceded this volume, is that financial theory offers only two kinds of tools for valuing assets that are not traded in active markets: (1) the present value of discounted cash flows, which works well in a world of K, where cash flows can be predicted and risks estimated; and (2) real option theory, which works well only if you can write a decision tree that captures most of the key uncertainties and decision points in the future. Fundamental values rest on relatively shaky foundations, and a shock may shift a price from the realm of K to that of u.

Even category 1 assets may present problems in a crisis. Setting aside the issue of asset price bubbles, market values can be relied on so long as assets are traded in broad, deep resilient markets. In such markets, however, assets tend to be priced on the basis of comparisons to their own past prices or to the prices of comparable assets. When a shock undermines confidence in these relative values and causes losses, traders tend to withdraw from markets until they regain confidence in their valuation models. Such shocks move prices from K to u. Concerns may arise about counterparties who may have had excessive exposures to the shock, and markets become thin. A flight to quality may occur and liquidity will be restored only when confidence in valuation models and counterparties is restored.

Crisis Prevention. Most policymakers would agree with Don Kohn that it is better to prevent crises than to try to manage and mitigate them once they have occurred. However, crisis prevention is an enormous burden, which falls mainly on the shoulders of the prudential authorities. Prudential regulation attempts to establish rules for the sound operation of financial institutions and critical elements of the financial infrastructure, such as clearing and settlement arrangements. Ideally, prudential policymakers should be looking beyond K to anticipate emerging sources of systemic vulnerability in order to calibrate appropriate prudential policies. In the dynamic world of modern finance this requires trying to understand how changing institutions, products, markets, and trading strategies create vulnerabilities to new kinds of shocks and new channels of contagion. But K cannot be neglected. Institutions still fail in familiar ways by taking, for example, excessive concentrations of credit risk, or by imprudently borrowing short and lending long.

Prudential supervisory authorities confront a number of trade-offs that must be made on uncertain terms. How safe should banks be? Goodhart notes that it is relatively easy to establish a set of penalties that would make the banking system perfectly safe, but largely irrelevant in intermediating between savers and investors. Scott argues that a central feature of corporate governance is aligning the risk-neutral preferences of well-diversified shareholders with risk-averse managers. This calculus is unlikely to take account of the systemic costs of an institution's failure and so the prudential authorities will presumably prefer a higher degree of safety, but how much higher?

How much competition is desirable? Competition is generally viewed as a positive feature of the financial system. It stimulates innovation and lowers the cost of financial services. But, it also reduces the charter values of incumbent banks and may lead to increased risk-taking. Goodhart notes that, over time, the official view regarding competition has swung from one extreme to another. During the Depression, the authorities tended to regard competition as a source of instability and implemented a number of reforms to constrain competition. More recently, the dominant trend has been liberalization of competition, although the current crisis in credit markets may cause a reversal.

Should financial innovation be encouraged? Securitization has facilitated diversification of risk, reduced costs, and liberated borrowers from dependence on particular lenders, but the subprime crisis has shown that it can also undermine credit standards and enable banks to achieve higher leverage by evading capital requirements. Derivatives have enabled financial institutions to partition and manage risks much more efficiently, but they can also be used to take enormous, highly leveraged risks. The growing sophistication of risk management techniques has enabled institutions to push out the boundaries of the known, but the very complexity of these techniques presents a challenge in the event of a crisis because it is very difficult for the authorities to comprehend the full range of positions and how they are managed. As Gomory (1995) warned in his essay on KuU, "[A]s the artifacts of science and engineering grow ever larger and more complex, they may themselves become unpredictable."

The supervisory authorities have a number of tools, which include licensing requirements, restrictions on certain kinds of activity believed to be excessively risky, liquidity requirements, capital requirements, and disclosure requirements. The authorities may also try to identify and encourage the widespread adoption of best practices in risk management, in effect urging the private sector to convert *u* into *K*.

By far, the most ambitious effort at prudential regulation has been the development of the Basel II standards for capital adequacy. Andrew Kuriztkes and Til Schuermann provide a framework for analyzing *KuU* in bank risk taking and show how the Basel II capital requirements correspond to this framework. They argue that a risk can be classified as *K* to the extent that it can be identified and quantified *ex ante*. They observe that the ability to estimate downside tail risks at a high level of confidence has enabled financial institutions to develop the concept of economic capital, the amount of capital needed to protect against earnings volatility at a prescribed level of confidence, usually set equal to the default rate associated with the financial institution's target debt rating. Economic capital has become the common denominator for measuring and aggregating risks in the financial services industry. Unfortunately, however, it is firmly rooted in the known and does not transplant readily to the unknown.

Kuritzkes and Schuermann classify a risk as *u* to the extent it can be identified *ex ante*, but not meaningfully quantified. A risk is classified as *U* if the existence of the risk is not predictable, much less quantifiable *ex ante*. Since these risks can't be quantified, they can't be managed. They can, however, sometimes be transferred. Kuritzkes and Schuermann employ this framework to analyze how *KuU* varies by risk type based on the richness and granularity of the data available to estimate each kind of risk. They conclude that *K* decreases and *u* and *U* increase moving along a spectrum from market risk, to credit risk, to asset/liability management risk, to operational risk, to business risk.

In addition, Kuritzkes and Schuermann analyze bank holding company data on earnings volatility to estimate the total amount of risk in the U.S. banking system and to allocate this total risk across risk types. They find that financial risks—market risk, credit risk, and asset–liability management risk—account for 70% of earnings volatility. Within financial risks, the breakdown is market risk 6%, credit risk 46%, and asset–liability management risk 18%. Nonfinancial risks—operational risk and business risk—account for the remaining 30% of earnings volatility. Within nonfinancial risks, the breakdown is operational risk 12% and business risk 18%.

Bank regulators began to take note of the evolving concept of economic capital when they expanded the original Basel Accord on Capital Adequacy to take account of market risk. The 1996 Market Risk Amendment provided an entirely new approach to setting capital requirements that relied on the way that leading banks were measuring and managing this risk. The original Accord set capital requirements roughly in line with expected losses. The concept of economic capital made clear that the role of capital should be to absorb unexpected losses, with reserves established to absorb expected losses. And so, instead of requiring banks to allocate their positions to crude risk buckets, or applying mechanical asset price haircuts to positions in an attempt to approximate risks, the regulatory authorities provided the opportunity for qualifying banks to rely on the supervised use of their internal models to determine their capital charges for exposure to market risk.

The internal models approach was expected to deliver several benefits. First, it would reduce or eliminate incentives for regulatory capital arbitrage because the capital charge would reflect the bank's own estimate of risk. Second, it would reward diversification to the extent that a bank's internal models captured correlations across risk positions. Third, it would deal more flexibly with financial innovations, incorporating them in the regulatory framework as soon as they were incorporated in the bank's own risk management models. Fourth, it would provide banks with an incentive to improve their risk management processes and procedures in order to qualify for the internal models approach. And fifth, compliance costs would be reduced to the extent that the business was regulated in the same way that it was managed. By and large, the internal models approach for market risk has proven to be highly successful, even when it was severely tested by the extreme market disruptions of 1997, 1998, and 2001, which is consistent with the view of Kuritzkes and Schuermann that market risk is largely K. This success, in combination with the progress made in modeling credit risk, led to calls from industry to revise the original Basel Accord to incorporate an internal models approach to capital regulation of credit risk.

Basel II attempts to extend this new approach to setting capital requirements to credit risk and operational risk. Although the supervisory authorities were convinced that credit scoring models had significantly expanded the amount of credit risk that could be regarded as falling in the domain of the known, they were skeptical that internal models of credit risk were as reliable and verifiable as models of market risk. While some kinds of credit risk, like retail lending, have rich and granular data sets comparable to market risk, other kinds of credit risk are less amenable to empirical analysis because data are sparse relative to past credit cycles and distinctly nongranular. In the end, the regulators rejected the supervised use of internal models, but permitted qualifying banks to use their internal model inputs—estimates of probability of default, loss given default, exposure at default, and duration of exposure—as inputs in the regulatory model that would determine capital requirements. These Pillar 1 capital requirements recognized the analytical and empirical advances banks had made in expanding the extent to which credit risk can be regarded as known.

Moving further to the right in the *KuU* spectrum, the decision to establish a Pillar 1 capital charge for operational risk has been much more controversial. In this instance the regulators were not simply adopting industry best practice as in the case of market risk and credit risk. They were attempting to advance best practice by requiring greater investment in measuring and managing operational risk. Moving operational risk into the domain of the known presents major challenges. Until quite recently, the industry lacked even a common definition of operational risk. Moreover, it is difficult to quantify and disaggregate, data are sparse, and theory is weak.

Because Basel II is an agreement negotiated among the members of the Basel Committee on Banking Supervision, it reflects a number of political compromises that undermine its aspirations for technical precision. This is most evident in the definition of regulatory capital, which is based on accounting values and includes a number of items that do not reflect an institution's capacity to bear unexpected loss. This undercuts the link to best practices in risk management.

Pillar 1 capital charges are intended to deal with known risks. Pillar 2, the supervisory review process, is intended to deal with unknown risks that can be identified, but are not sufficiently well quantified to establish Pillar 1 capital charges. Presumably, as theoretical and empirical advances succeed in moving some of these risks into the domain of the known, Pillar 1 capital charges will be established for them as well. In view of the analysis by Kuritzkes and Schuermann, it is surprising that asset–liability management risk is treated under Pillar 2, while operational risk is treated under Pillar 1. Although liquidity is inherently difficult to measure because it has at least three dimensions—price, time, and size—interest rate risk, another important aspect of asset–liability management risk, is much more easily quantified than operational risk and it has been a much more important source of volatility in bank earnings than operational risk. Kuritzkes and Schuermann thus raise the question of whether regulatory and industry resources might have been more usefully directed to standardizing the approach for characterizing and measuring asset–liability risk.

Benoit Mandelbrot and Nassim Taleb warn that many financial situations are often incorrectly diagnosed as *K*; that is, *u* and *U* are much more common than typically acknowledged. The past is never a perfect predictor of the future. New factors may become important and relationships estimated in times of normal market functioning tend to break down at times of market stress. What we thought was mild randomness often proves to be wild randomness, as financial markets are not governed by a Gaussian distributions. In Will Roger's phrase, a key risk is that what we think we know "just ain't so."

The principal tools of supervisory analysis in *u* are stress testing and scenario analysis. Stress testing requires economic judgment to formulate and calibrate

scenarios that expose potential vulnerabilities. It requires a careful consideration of which relationships will continue to hold and which relationships will
break down in time of stress. Mandelbrot and Taleb caution that traditional
stress testing, which relies on selecting a number of worst-case scenarios from
past data, may be seriously misleading because it implicitly assumes that a fluctuation of this magnitude would be the worst that should be expected. They
note that crashes happen without antecedents. Before the crash of 1987, for example, stress testing would not have included a 22% drop in share prices within
a single day. They note that just ten trading days account for 63% of the returns
on the stock market over the past 50 years. In their view, fractal methods should
be used to extrapolate multiple projected scenarios that would enable risk managers and prudential supervisors to evaluate the robustness of a portfolio over
an entire spectrum of extreme risks.

Goodhart emphasizes a different concern regarding stress testing and scenario analysis. What may matter most in crises are interactive effects that occur
when many institutions attempt to adjust their portfolios in the same way at the
same time. These are critical to understanding an institution's vulnerability in a
crisis, but are omitted from most scenarios.

Stress testing and the simulation of crises may be of value even if such crises
never occur. The data necessary to simulate a crisis may prove useful in monitoring vulnerability, and a careful consideration of the consequences of such a crisis
may lead to changes in strategy and/or risk management. Crises seldom unfold
according to the anticipated scenario, but strategies for responding to one kind
of shock may prove useful when a different kind of shock occurs. For example,
evacuation procedures that Morgan Stanley established after the bombing of the
World Trade Center in 1993 enabled the firm to safeguard all of their employees
in the much more severe terrorist attack on September 11, 2001.

The key element of regulatory discipline under Pillar 2, however, is the ability
of the prudential supervisor to impose an additional capital charge on an institution if they are uncomfortable with the results of its stress tests. This places
supervisors in the role of imposing discipline on an institution thought to be
vulnerable to a shock of unknown probability even though they are less well
paid and less well informed than bank managers. The history of bank supervision does not provide much basis for optimism that they will succeed.

Finally, how should prudential supervisors deal with U? As Scott notes, firms
can limit their leverage and maintain enough capital and liquidity to absorb
unknowable losses if they should occur. But how much slack is sufficient? That
itself is unknowable, but almost all of the things that banks could do to cope
with the unknowable are very costly, and competitive pressures may make it
very difficult to sustain such precautions. Should regulators therefore require

that banks hold capital substantially in excess of the regulatory minimum as a safeguard against unknown and unknowable shocks? Increasing capital charges for risks that cannot be identified becomes a deadweight cost and may lead to the circumvention of regulation, and hence riskier outcomes. It is inherently difficult for policy-makers to strike the proper balance between the efficiency losses associated with excessively onerous preventative policies and the cost effectiveness of responding *ex post* to adverse events. For regulators as well as firms, the appropriate amount of financial slack is an unknown.

Pillar 3 of the Basel II approach is intended to enhance market discipline by improving disclosure. The authorities may collect and publish data that helps market participants understand the current state of the economy and financial markets and the condition of regulated financial institutions. But growing reliance on dynamic trading strategies to manage risk has made it increasingly difficult to provide a meaningful picture of risk exposures. Positions may change so rapidly that information is out of date before it can be published. Moreover, the chief motive for market discipline—the fear of loss—is often undermined by the reluctance of the authorities to permit the creditors and counterparties of systemically important financial institutions to suffer loss.

The ambitious new Basel II approach attempts to incorporate in capital regulation what is known about risk management, but it may generate unintended consequences that could shift the financial system into the domain of the unknown. The attempt to force all major firms to adopt one version of "best practice," and especially the imposition of a regulatory model of credit risk, may increase the likelihood of herding, producing system-wide contagion in response to shocks. That is, Basel II fails to deal with systemic risk.

Crisis Mitigation. Because it is so difficult for prudential supervisors to fulfill their responsibilities *ex ante*, policy makers must often shift into crisis management mode to mitigate, *ex post*, the consequences of a shock. Kohn observes that in financial crises, u and U are more important than K. Policy-makers must deal with unknowns, such as the size of the disruption. How large will it be? How many firms will be involved? How long will it last? How likely is it to have serious spillover consequences for real economic activity?

Part of the problem is in anticipating the channels of contagion. Which firms have direct exposure to the shock? Which firms have indirect exposure because they are counterparties or creditors of the firms that sustain a direct impact or because they have similar exposures and could lose access to external financing? Which other firms might be placed in jeopardy because of the forced liquidation of assets in illiquid markets? Risk preferences and perceptions of risk are dynamic, and so a flight to quality often occurs. Market participants may sell assets whose prices are already declining and avoid any counterparty that might be impaired.

Another part of the problem is that policy makers must operate with incomplete knowledge about the current state of the economy and how their action (or inaction) may affect economic activity. Moreover, monetary policy operates with long and variable lags, and it is difficult to anticipate market responses to shocks. Yet the monetary authorities, Kohn argues, must immediately determine whether there is adequate liquidity in the financial system and whether monetary policy needs to be adjusted to counter the effects on the economy of a crisis-induced tightening of credit.

In a crisis, policy makers must try to push u toward K as quickly as possible. This requires close cooperation across regulatory authorities within a country, and increasingly, across borders. Inevitably, the primary source of information is major market participants. But conflicts of interest may corrupt flows of information. Information may be selectively communicated to serve the self-interest of market participants who might be the beneficiaries of crisis management policies. Does this argue for a direct role of the crisis manager in supervising systemically important institutions? The Fed insists that it does, but central banks lack such authority in many other countries (Herring and Carmassi 2008) and the new Treasury proposal for reforming the U.S. financial system removes supervisory authority from the Fed while increasing its responsibility for crisis management. How best to organize prudential supervision and crisis management remains a significant unknown.

Policy makers must also convey information in a crisis. Kohn raises the question of what is the appropriate response. They may urge firms to do what the policy makers believe they should do in their own self-interest, as happened in the LTCM crisis in 1998. But when is it appropriate to be reassuring? When might reassurance prove counterproductive?

Crisis management may inadvertently lead to larger future crises. If risk takers are protected from the full negative consequences of their decisions, they may be likely to take greater risks in the future. This presents a difficult dilemma for crisis management. The costs of inaction are immediate and obvious. It's easy to imagine damaging outcomes, and self-interested market participants will press for official support and can easily muster political support. Inaction in a crisis is likely to be subject to blame even when it is appropriate, which may contribute to an inherent tendency to oversupply public support. Once it has been provided, entrenched interests will lobby to keep it and new additional activity may depend on it. Moreover, moral hazard manifests itself slowly and may be difficult to relate to any one particular policy choice.

Kohn argues that moral hazard is less likely if policy is directed at the broad market rather than individual firms. From this perspective open market operations are a better means of adjusting aggregate liquidity to meet the demands that arise from a flight to safety. Although this kind of response may encourage risk-taking, it may also genuinely lower risk. Direct lending and bailouts are much more likely to distort incentives. Ultimately, efficient resolution policy may be the best safeguard against moral hazard. But in most countries policy makers lack the appropriate tools to resolve a large, complex financial institution without jeopardizing the rest of the financial system (Herring 2004).

1.3. ONWARD

The chapters that follow heighten our awareness of the existence of and distinctions among K, u and U risks, pushing in a variety of contexts toward improved risk measurement and management strategies. Because K risks are often amenable to statistical treatment, whereas uU risks are usually not (despite their potentially large consequences), substantial resources will continue to be deployed in academia, industry, and government to expand the domain of K when possible. Surely Gomory (1995) was correct in noting that "in time many things now unknown will become known," so it is appropriate for a significant part of this book to focus on K.

But as we also emphasize, there are sharp limits to expanding the domain of K, so it is also appropriate for a significant part—indeed, the larger part—of this book to focus on uU. The important issues in the world of uU are more economic (strategic) than statistical, and crucially linked to *incentives*: The central question is how to write contracts (design organizations, formulate fiscal or monetary policies, draft regulations, make investments, etc.) in ways that create incentives for best-practice proactive and reactive risk management for *all types* of risks, including (and especially) uU risks. As Gomory also notes, often "We *do not even know* if we are dealing . . . with the partly known, the mainly unknown or the unknowable" (our emphasis). We hope that this book pushes and speeds the evolution of financial risk management toward confronting K, u, and U equally.

REFERENCES

Andersen, T. G., T. Bollerslev, P. F. Christoffersen, and F. X. Diebold (2006). Practical volatility and correlation modeling for financial market risk management. In M. Carey and R. Stulz, eds., *Risks of Financial Institutions*. Chicago: University of Chicago Press for NBER, 513–48.

Borch, K. (1962). Equilibrium in a reinsurance market. *Econometrica* 30, 424–44.

Christoffersen, P.F. (2003). *Elements of Financial Risk Management.* San Diego: Academic Press.

Doherty, N.A. (2000). *Integrated Risk Management: Techniques and Strategies for Reducing Risk.* New York: McGraw-Hill.

Gomory, R. (1995). The known, the unknown and the unknowable. *Scientific American*, June.

Greenspan, A. (2008). The Fed is blameless on the property bubble. *Financial Times*, April 7, p. 9.

Herring, R.J. (2004). International financial conglomerates: Implications for national insolvency regimes. In G. Kaufman, ed., *Market Discipline and Banking: Theory and Evidence.* Amsterdam: Elsevier, 99–129.

Herring, R.J., and J. Carmassi (2008). The structure of cross-sector financial supervision. *Financial Markets, Institutions and Instruments* 17, 51–76.

Jorion, P. (1997). *Value at Risk: The New Benchmark for Managing Financial Risk,* (3rd ed., 2006). New York: McGraw-Hill.

Kelvin, W.T. (1891–1894). *Popular Lectures and Addresses.* Three volumes. London: MacMillan.

Knight, F.H. (1921). *Risk, Uncertainty and Profit.* Boston: Houghton Mifflin.

Rawls, J. (1971). *A Theory of Justice.* Cambridge, MA: Belnap.

Santayana, G. (1896). *The Sense of Beauty.* Dover Edition, 1955.

Thornhill, J., and A. Michaels (2008). Bear Stearns rescue a "turning point." *Financial Times*, April 7, p. 4.

2. Risk

A Decision Maker's Perspective

Sir Clive W. J. Granger

Risk is a pervasive but subtle concept, widely used and discussed but not well understood.[1] In the initial sections of this chapter I will attempt to discuss some of the sources of agreement between all groups and then mention the forms of disagreement and the implications.

It is convenient to start with a listing of the major groups in the economy who are concerned with risk:

a. *Uncertainty economists.* A group of economists who over a period of roughly half a century produced a powerful theory concerning behavior under uncertainty with many strong results that constrain the behavior of decision makers. This group includes workers such as Savage, von Neuman, Morgenstern, Samuelson, Arrow, Stiglitz, Rothschild, Allais, Machina, and Quiggin. This group already includes four Nobel laureates and others from it could well join them later.

b. *Financial economists and econometricians.* Theoretical and empirical economists who consider the economics of financial markets,

[1] I am very grateful for the many very helpful discussions with my friend and colleague Mark Machina, who allowed me to keep and develop my own views although they were quite different from his own. I would like to thank participants at seminars that I gave at the Wharton School, the University of Copenhagen , the University of Melbourne, the Queensland University of Technology, and the University of Canterbury, New Zealand.

including portfolio theory. Leading members are Sharpe, Merton, Scholes, Markowitz, Mundel, and Engle, all Nobel Prize winners.

c. *Insurance agents and economists.* It is clear why everyone in the insurance industry is interested in risk. A well-known economist in this area was Karl Borch.

d. *Financial agents and managers.* The practical, higher-level decision makers within the financial industry, such as trust managers and company treasurers.

e. *Professionals in other industries.* Structural engineers, medical practitioners, lawyers, meteorologists, and so forth.

f. *The public.* A large, diverse, and important group, often forgotten in discussions. This group includes most decision makers and particularly the consumers.

Quite recently Google recorded 510 million hits on the word "risk," many more than other popular words in economics such as "profit" or "tax," but less than "money." What needs to be asked is do all these people use the word "risk" in the same way, that is, do they use the same definition of risk? It will be seen that some parts of their beliefs are held in common but other components are quite different. Two ideas are held in common:

a. Risk is associated with uncertainty

b. Risk is associated with the tails of the distribution of returns

In the discussion above and in what follows a very standard situation is considered in which some "asset" is purchased, and over some future period the benefit or "utility" derived from the purchase is uncertain, and is thus best described in probability terms.[2] The first of the two statements above indicates that risk can only be found in situations that have to be described by probabilities, so that only if there is uncertainty can one get risk. However, according to some attitudes, it is possible to have uncertainty but no risk. Examples are given later. It should be emphasized that here words such as "risk" and "uncertainty" are not used in the classical Knightian sense where risk is concerned with known outcomes and probabilities, and uncertainty means known outcomes but unknown probabilities. These do not represent the use of these terms by standard economic decision makers in practice.

In all major dictionaries risk is associated with the occurrence of an unfortunate event. Examples are you buy a house but a fire or flood greatly reduces its value, you take a prescription drug but get a negative reaction, or you buy

---

[2] For simplicity of the discussion all of the probabilities involved will be considered to be subjective.

an asset and get an unacceptably low return. These would all be tail event risks; here all lower tail. These need not occur in the extreme tail, but just somewhere in the lower tail. A risk associated with the lower tail will be called *downside risk* and for convenience denoted d-risk.

An example of a dictionary definition is that from the *Oxford English Dictionary* (1993): "Risk, exposes to the chance of injury or loss. Danger. The probability of loss, injury or other adverse circumstances." Some economists, particularly those in the first two groups above, take the position that risks can occur in either tail, and these risks are called *two-tailed risks*. The fact that there are two definitions in use simultaneously can be confusing, particularly as some seminar speakers can use both in a single sentence without apparently realizing the confusion this can create. The two approaches lead to different measurements of risk and to approaches to risk management, which are interrelated and important topics and are discussed below.

The two definitions, involving one or two tails, are mutually exclusive. A person cannot claim to be logically using both definitions. It is a matter of personal opinion which definition one chooses, and so it would not be possible to prove that one is superior to the other. If one took a democratic vote the downside risk definition would win easily, as only the fairly small members of groups a and b generally use two-tailed risk; members of all the other groups use d-risk.

A simple example illustrates the different approaches just discussed. Consider a simple raffle in which you have won the first prize, which consists of two components: (a) win one million dollars, with probability ½; and (b) win two million dollars, with probability ½. The eventual amount won is decided by a coin toss by the organizer. The prize clearly involves an uncertain event, as probabilities are needed to describe it; the only question is whether it involves a risk? After all one has certainly won at least one million dollars, the only uncertainty is whether you get two or one million? You can find people arguing both sides. Would the positions change if the higher prize (b) became one million plus fifty dollars? You would not expect the answer to whether something is considered to be risk or not to depend on the amount of money involved. The type of risk considered in this example is clearly upper-tailed risk and therefore a component of two-tailed risk, but not of d-risk.

As a second example consider an owner of a group of assets, including some cash. These assets will provide a distribution of future returns over the next month, say. Now suppose that the owner takes $100 cash and buys lottery tickets. This will reduce the center of the distribution and increase probabilities in the extreme upper tail to some small extent. Thus, the downside risk is not changed but the upper-tail risk is increased. Presumably the asset's owner prefers the new distribution to the old one, which is why the tickets were bought.

This would be an example where someone prefers an increase in uncertainty and also, for some, an increase in a form of risk.

If one uses the two-tailed definition of risk, then risk is equated with uncertainty, as in "if there is uncertainty there must be risk." If one uses the downside risk definition then the statement becomes "if there is risk there must be uncertainty, but if there is uncertainty there need not be risk."[3] The two examples above provide illustrations. In the first case, once you have a million dollars the worse thing that can happen is that you do not get something extra. In the second example, once the tickets have been bought what you paid is a sunk cost and cannot be retrieved. The worst case now is that you win nothing; all other cases give some winnings, so there is clearly no downside risk.

Some individuals are claimed to be "risk-preferring," but to interpret this classification the type of risk involved needs to be specified. If one considers activities that involve downside risk, such as high-speed racing of various forms, bungee jumping, mountain climbing, or exploring flooded caves, for example, then this d-risk will need to be associated with large positive gains in pleasure from undertaking the activity. If the risk is upper tailed, such as gambling, then once the bet is placed there is no downside risk and the only uncertainty involves how much you will win. There can be a serious downside risk in gambling if you adapt a strategy to continue betting after making a loss.

2.1. MEASURES OF RISK

Most decisions concerning situations involving d-risk, including a wide variety of decision makers such as shoppers, employers, travelers, and investors, do not involve a specific measure or even definition of risk. These decision makers can compare pairs of distributions of returns, or utilities, possibly loosely constructed, and chose the one that is preferred. There are many such decisions made daily by the majority of individuals in the population. For example, I may buy an apple from a seller. My downside risk is that I will not enjoy its flavor and so the purchase has been a waste of time and money. The seller's downside risk is that I will not enjoy the apple enough to return on another day to buy fruit from him. In each case, we understand what type of risk is involved but we do not need a measure of it for a typical transaction to occur.

[3] This is an oversimplification since not everyone in a group will agree. For example, Grant and Quiggin (2004) do equate risk and uncertainty, but Rigotti and Shannon (2005) follow Knight (1921) in distinguishing between the two concepts when probability "can be measured precisely," which is not subjective.

Examples of situations in which a specific measure of risk becomes important are where one wants to trade in—that is, buy or sell—risk, or to trade one risk for another, or to formally manage risk. For two-tailed risk it is clear that the favorite measures are the variance and the mean absolute deviation. For a time series these are given by the following: for data y_t, $t = 1, \ldots, n$, the variance is

$$V_n - \frac{1}{n} \sum_{t=1}^{n} (y_t - \bar{y})^2$$

and the mean absolute deviation is given by

$$\mathrm{MAD}_N = \frac{1}{n} \sum_{t=1}^{n} |y_t - \bar{y}|$$

where $\bar{y} = \frac{1}{n} \sum_{t=1}^{n} y_t$ is the sample mean. If data are taken from the Gaussian distribution, the variance is the correct measure of spread, but in practice Gaussians rarely occur in financial series. If data are taken from a double-exponential distribution, then MAD is the relevant measure of dispersion. The variance is pragmatically the more useful but has poor statistical properties when data come from a distribution with long tails, as is often the case in finance. In the long-tail situation MAD is better, as seen by the fact that the square of a MAD term is like a variance component but the square of a variance term is fourth order, which is badly estimated with data from a long-tailed sample. The mean could be replaced by a truncated mean or by the median if the series contains many outliers, but such changes are rarely required. The variance is very widely used, often with little thought, and then identified with risk, so that for most students in business schools, for example, variance and risk are completely equated.

Turning to the measurement of downside risk, Nawrocki (1999) has provided a wide-ranging review of the topic and Fishburn (1977) presents some useful theory. They use the idea of a target value or return, denoted T, below which any achieved return would be considered disappointing.

A function $\rho(F)$ may be called a risk measure for the distribution F if

$$\rho(F) = \int_{-\infty}^{T} \varphi(T - x) dF(x)$$

where $\varphi(y)$ for $y > 0$ is a positive, nondecreasing function of y with $\varphi(o) = 0$. A particular case is the k lower partial moment:

$$\mathrm{LPM}(k) = \int_{-\infty}^{T} (T - x)^k dF(x), \quad x > 0$$

With $k = 2$ the LPM gives the below target semi-variance and if also $T = m$, the mean, one gets the below *mean* semi-variance. This last measure has a long history, as Markowitz mentions it in his 1959 book on portfolios. Even earlier, Borch (1990, chapter 2) states that in Tetans' work on insurance in 1786 he used the one-sided MAD form:

$$R = \frac{1}{2}\int_0^\infty |x - p| \, dF(x)$$

where "$F(x)$ is the probability that claim payments under the contract shall not exceed x" using the insurance premium p.

An obvious alternative measure of d-risk is to use lower-tailed quantile estimates, which is the basis for *value at risk*, or VaR, which interestingly was suggested by a group of bankers, who are people belonging to group d above rather than to group b. It is worth pointing out that the vast majority of decision makers, belonging to groups c, d, e, and particularly f, will be making their decisions about risky assets and objects without a precise measurement in mind and yet are able to make sound decisions. You often need only a ranking of relative riskiness to make the decision. However, the risks levels used in the decisions are the perceived d-risks rather than the actual ones. If one is going on a journey there may be several alternative methods of transport available, such as car, bus, train, and plane. The one selected will depend on cost, convenience, time involved, and the person's judgment about d-risk. In the United States buses and planes have low d-risk values and driving has clearly the highest level of actual risk. However, most drivers have an upward biased viewpoint about their driving ability and are likely chose the car for the journey. Personal opinions about d-risk do depend on whether or not you are in control. When one is in control d-risk is seriously underestimated, for example, when driving, swimming, or drinking. When one is not in control, d-risk can be greatly overestimated, such as the probability of being attacked by a shark when swimming in California or by a mountain lion while hiking in the mountains.[4]

Some of the most dramatic and memorable events involving downside risks are extremes, such as the greatest storm, the biggest tsunami, the largest explosion, the highest flood, and so forth. Strictly, to a statistician, an extreme is the minimum or the maximum of a set of data, so there are only two in a sample. You can consider a rolling sample and talk about the highest flood in the last five years, say, but this reduces the impact of the concept. In recent years a great

---

[4] Shark and lion attacks are very rare but get a great deal of publicity when they do occur; deaths on the roads are so common they are rarely reported.

deal of attention has been paid to modeling the extremes and the tail behavior of empirical distributions. The obvious feature is that there are very few data, however extremes are defined and if several markets are used. When data are rare the standard approach is to replace them with a theory. There are some very nice theories of the distributions of the extremes of independent series but how relevant these theories are for stock market returns is unclear, as they are certainly interdependent as the volatility results indicate. Statisticians are probably surprised that more attention is not paid to records rather than to extremes. A record is the largest (or smallest) in the sample *so far*, and thus will occur rather more often and have an interesting interpretation and a simple statistical theory that applies both to i.i.d. sequences and to some dependent series. It is easy to say that extremes and records are likely to be occurring with greater frequency than in the past, due to global warming, but it is difficult to be more precise.

2.2. UNCERTAINTY THEORISTS AND EXPECTED UTILITY

Uncertainty economists are a very important and influential group who have produced a powerful and attractive theory that essentially attempts to encompass this whole field. I will just touch on the highlights of the topics that are of greatest relevance for my general plan.

The theory starts with a set of apparently very plausible axioms about simple preferences, such as if I prefer A to B and I prefer B to C, then I should prefer A to C. There will be five or six such axioms, all quite simple and none appearing to be very controversial. From them first Savage and later von Neumann and Morgenstern proved that rational decision makers will not only have a distribution of utilities of returns to consider but to make a rational choice they should maximize the expected utility. Thus, if the consumer has a choice between three goods, say, each with an associated distribution of utilities, then the best choice is the one with the highest mean, or expectation.

For statisticians to be told that they can ignore all the other features of the distribution, (such as the contents of the tails, the width, or the skewness) and that they should only consider the mean clearly runs counter to their basic training; it is natural for them to be skeptical of it. The attacks on the theory concentrated on the logic of the axioms, which were found to be wanting under some sophisticated analysis. As a very simple and not necessarily acceptable example, consider the axiom given above but in a more realistic setting.

I am first asked to choose between an apple and an orange, and choose the apple, so Apple > Orange. I am now asked to choose between an orange and a banana, and choose the orange, so Orange > Banana. If I am now asked to choose between an apple and a banana the consistency axiom suggests that I should choose the apple, but, in fact, the conditions under which I am making the choice have changed, I now have an apple, and also an orange so I may well choose the banana unless I do not like that fruit. The axioms can easily be extended to get around this type of difficulty but they quickly lose their charm and simplicity. The final and decisive blow to the axioms were a series of "paradoxes" due to Ellsworth, Allais and Machina where participants in quite simple experimental games were found to behave in ways that were quite different from those predicted by the basic set of axioms.

Despite the breakdown in part of the basic theory, many of the definitions and consequences remain. Uncertainty economists equate risk with uncertainty, so that risk becomes two-tailed. The maximization of expected utility remains an important research concept for this group, although it is of more theoretical than practical relevance.

It is interesting to note that the uncertainty economists are users of two-tailed risk but do not approve of the use of variance as the measure of risk. They consider variance as insufficiently flexible or sophisticated to capture their beliefs and preferences. The uncertainty economists have some strong rules about commonly used terms, for example, "uncertainty" should be used only with cases where subjective probabilities are used. If one is considering the toss of a fair coin, where it can be agreed that the probability of a head is ½, then they would not describe the outcome as uncertain. It logically follows that there is no risk involved with a coin toss or the outcome of the spin of a roulette wheel as only objective probabilities are involved. However, such constraints are of little or no practical consequence in commerce or in finance, for example, and so will not be considered further.

2.3. *E-V* ANALYSIS

This section deals with consideration of mean–variance analysis of asset returns and some related topics. Whereas the previous section discusses some analysis that is very sophisticated theoretically but has little practical usefulness, this section has, in contrast, little deep theory but much that is pragmatically helpful.

Here, the distribution of returns is approximated by using just the mean (denoted E) and the variance (V). If the returns had a normal distribution, these are the sufficient statistics for it. However, it was certainly known by 1959, and probably earlier, that daily stock market returns are not Gaussian. *E-V* analysis was used by Markowitz (1952), when he first discussed "portfolio selection." It remains the predominant basic technique for portfolio analysis because it is well understood and its linear form makes it easy to use and to appreciate.

For a pair of E-V portfolios, for a given E one prefers the one with the smallest V and for a given V the preference is for the largest E. However, some pairs of portfolios cannot be ranked, as seen in the following example.

A simple but useful example (provided by Mark Machina) compares the following pair of random outcomes or prizes (here K = thousand):

    a. With prob. $\frac{1}{3}$ get \$20K and with prob. $\frac{2}{3}$ get \$5K

    b. With prob. $\frac{2}{3}$ get \$15K and with prob. $\frac{1}{3}$ get \$0

Each prize has E = 10K and V = 50K so that a standard (E, V) analysis cannot choose between them. However, surveys find that most people (although not everyone) prefer prize (b) to (a). It is worth noting that a portfolio with weights ½ in (a) and ½ in (b), taking the prizes to be independent, will give a mean of 10K and a variance of 25K, which in $(E$-$V)$ terms are superior to both individual prizes. However, I suspect that many people will still prefer (b) to this portfolio.

In the universe of investors there could be some who are believers in expected utility and some who use the E-V framework. Suppose that there are some investors who fall into both groups (which is possible), then it can be shown that their utility function $u(x)$, where x is the return on an asset, must take the form

$$u(x) = a + bx - cx^2$$

with x in the range from $x = 0$ to $x = b/2c$, and it is undefined outside this range. Anyone who claims to have some other utility function cannot belong to the special group being discussed.

Say an investor uses the lower partial moment measure of risk, discussed in section 2.1. Fishburn (1977) showed that if the expected utility approach was also in use, then the appropriate utility function is given as follows: for the risk function $\int_{-\infty}^{T} |T - x|^{\alpha} \, dF(x)$ the mean-risk model congruent with the expected utility model has utility

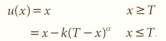

$$u(x) = x \qquad\qquad x \geq T$$
$$= x - k(T - x)^{\alpha} \quad x \leq T.$$

Some writers have disliked this result because it implies that the utility function is linear above T. This constraint can be removed by allowing investors to put constraints on the upper tails of the distribution, should they wish to do so.

An alternative to E-V, but one that simpler than considering the whole distribution, is to consider just three components: the lower tail, the middle, and the upper tail. The middle can probably be represented by the mean, which is quite uncontroversial although the median could be better, as it always exists. How far a tail extends is a personal decision, as is the question of whether or not to use the same measure for both tails. Using a downside risk measure puts all the weight on one tail, whereas using the variance puts equal weight on both tails and then adds them together. Both of these approaches are clearly over-simplifying what is seen in an actual distribution.

In the *E-V* world a simplified view of the performance of a portfolio is given by the Sharpe ratio, which is just the difference between the mean return of the portfolio and the current risk-free rate, all divided by the standard deviation of the returns. Similar quantities can be constructed using downside risk measures rather than the standard deviation. A class of such forms is called Kappa by Kaplan and Knowles (2004), given by

$$\text{Kappa}\,(k) = \frac{m - T}{\sqrt[k]{\text{LPM}(k)}}$$

where m is the portfolio mean, T is now the risk-free rate, and LPM is the lower partial moment defined in section 2.1.

K_1 is identical (after subtraction of one) to a previously introduced concept named Omega. Kaplan and Knowles estimate K_1, K_2, and K_3 for returns from eleven hedge fund indexes and several values of the truncation value. In general, there seems to quite large differences between K_1 and K_2 but only small difference between K_2 and K_3. It is unclear if it is worth investigating the practical usefulness of K for noninteger values of k.

Mention must be given to the common idea that *volatility* is usually closely related to risk, so that the higher the volatility the greater the risk. It is not clear that volatility is well defined in a statistical sense, even for a time series. It is most often used with stock returns and then applies to increases in activity in both tails of the distribution, so that the variance is the natural measure. In fact, dictionary definitions of volatility appear to equate this concept with variance. However, if we consider rainfall data for the southeastern United States, there will be a standard distribution. But for some years there will be an extra number of tropical storms, which can be thought of as producing increased volatility in the upper tail of the rainfall distribution, which is associated with a downside risk. Using mean-preserving spreads (as in Rothschild and Stiglitz 1970) it is possible to start with a standard-shaped distribution and then to move more mass into the lower tail, compensating with less mass in other parts of the below-mean area, creating a distribution with unchanged mean, greater downside risk, and increased variance, but no increased upside risk. Similarly, one can produce a distribution with the same mean and variance as the previous one and no extra downside risk, but with extra upper-tail risk. Thus, one can produce two distributions that are identical in (E, V) terms yet one is weighted downward and the other upward! Which one you select depends on your personal preferences.

There is an interesting insight, from Dick Herring, that upside volatility may be an indication, and perhaps the only one available, about the size of the d-risk. If an asset has been growing consistently upward, and to a surprising extent, that could suggest that a fall is about to occur, as the famous example of long-term capital management could show. Thus, in some situations u-risk needs to be considered even though one's ultimate concern is really with d-risk

2.4. MANAGEMENT OF RISK

Although measurement is an important topic, the question of how risk can be managed is far more important. Most risk management is concerned with downside risk; very little risk management is designed for upper-tail risk. For many forms of downside risk there are associated objects, called here *co-risks*, that are designed to alleviate this risk to some extent. Examples are home insurance to reduce the risks of fires and possibly floods and earthquakes; car insurance to reduce risks concerning auto crashes; air travel insurance and health travel insurance; buying a car with safe seat belts, air bags, and safe steering wheel construction; careful reading of instructions on medicine bottles; and keeping aware of changes in knowledge about health risks concerning common foods.

We can associate many d-risks with such co-risks, which are designed to lower the value of the risk. Some co-risks actually lower the risk, such as those concerning medicines or cars, but others, such as insurance, will just lower the financial cost associated with the risk. Well understood d-risks of long standing will usually have helpful co-risks but new d-risks may not have developed them yet. Measuring of a d-risk should be after the application of the appropriate co-risk when available. There will be no co-risk with upper-tailed risk as there is no desire to reduce or constrain it. There seems to be no market for shares in personal high gains such as finding a gold mine on your property or inheriting from a wealthy relative. I suppose that an eminent economist could sell shares in his or her future Nobel Prize for cash, should they win one, but I have not heard of this happening. It is possible that the existence of such a market could decrease the probability of the Prize being won.

In the standard insurance situation you pay a company a fairly small annual sum but should a low-probability event occur, in the downside tail, the company will pay you a large sum in partial compensation. The upper-tail equivalent would be for the company to pay you an annual small amount, but if you have a substantial windfall gain most of it will have to go to the company. Such "anti-insurance" arrangements are rare, but they may exist. An example could be an institution that employs inventors to think, with an agreement to receive part of the income derived from any resulting invention, and such institutions certainly exist.

For two-tailed risk an appropriate co-risk would be something that reduces the lower-tail risk and leaves the upper-tail risk unchanged. This is possible to accomplish by using various instruments, as discussed later, whereas standard linear portfolio methods, if they are designed to reduce the variance, will reduce the contents of both tails. Thus, the desirable reduction of downside risk is "paid for" by a corresponding reduction in the preferred upper tail of the return distribution.

Consideration of complicated investments involving derivatives, together with the taking of short and long positions, together with the idea of co-risks, insurance, and anti-insurance, could be a complicated discussion but a potentially interesting one. I leave that discussion for someone who is more qualified to undertake it.

The form and size of the co-risk, if it exists, will greatly depend on the form, novelty, and size of the risk, as will be discussed in section 2.5. The practical sides of risk management are well developed by the workers in groups (b) (financial economists), (c) (insurance), and (d) (financial agents and managers). As a non-expert, it is difficult to comment on the insurance industry, which to an outsider appears able to absorb sequences of substantial hits in a remarkable fashion. Participants in groups (b) and (d) deal with different types of questions and use different methods of managing risk, partly because they have different definitions of risk. Financial managers, in (d), will often list many of the risks that they are facing, and these are nearly always clearly downside. They use futures contracts, swaps, insurance, and loans of various terms to manage these risks. I understand that they also construct derivatives so that they can offload part of the d-risk. Much of this market is outside the scope of the typical small investor.

In group (b) the overwhelmingly favorite method of managing risks associated with portfolios of stocks, bonds, or similar financial assets is linear portfolio theory. The theory is convincing, easy to understand, but rather difficult to implement when many assets are involved, although this is no problem for modern mathematics and computing procedures. It also leads to interesting simplifications, such as the capital asset pricing model theory. However, as the measure of risk used in basic portfolio theory is the variance it thus corresponds to two-tailed risk. As stated before, if you chose a portfolio based on such a two-tail risk measure you do achieve one with less weight in the lower tail but you pay for it by reduced profitable opportunities in the upper tail. Alternatively, it is possible to form portfolios using minimization of a lower-tail risk measure, but computationally the procedure is much more difficult. However, a search of the web found several commercial companies claiming that they are able to form portfolios using d-risk measures. Another approach is to "sculpt" the asset return from its original shape to some preferred shape using mean-preserving spreads and the necessary derivatives. The procedure is by no means simple but it seems that it is becoming commonplace.

There is currently an active research literature on the mathematics of alternative approaches to risk. A useful survey can be found in McNeil et al. (2005), whose chapter 6 is concerned with aggregate risk, which is the risk of a portfolio. They consider a number of properties that mathematicians think a good measure of risk should have. A risk measure having these properties, expressed in terms of four axioms, is called *coherent*. The axioms may each appear to be sensible, although some can be debatable. For example, the second axiom of subadditivity "reflects the idea that risk can be reduced by diversification." It is found that risk measures based on quantiles, such as VaR (value at risk) are not coherent. This merely indicates that properties declared preferable by mathematicians are not the same as those required by financial decision makers.

2.5. KNOWN, UNKNOWN, AND UNKNOWABLE RISKS AND THEIR CO-RISKS

It is perhaps useful to categorize future risks into three main groups:

    a. *Known risks*, where the form of the risk and any related distribution can be specified quite fully. Here we are dealing with the numerous risks from everyday life concerning eating, travel, general health, standard interactions between people, aging, and making regular purchases. The corresponding co-risks will have usually have been established from prior experience and their usefulness will be understood and appreciated.

    b. *Unknown risks* are those where the form of the risk can be specified but as it has not been encountered by most, or all, of the population, its extent and full implications remain unclear. Possible examples are a virus that evolves into a new and unexpected form, a natural event of an unusually large magnitude in a location where it is not expected (such as a tsunami, earthquake, hurricane, or volcanic eruption), or a new virulent form of computer virus. Some terrorist attacks could belong to this category, but most are in the known classification. A further example is a risk that is known in one part of the world but suddenly occurs somewhere with no previous experience, such as a disease familiar in Africa being found in Argentina. Here the co-risk from the original country can possibly be imported to the new one.

It is difficult to have specific co-risks for risks of unknown form but successful generic co-risks exist and are widely applied. Here groups of people in need in one location are helped by similar groups in nearby locations or elsewhere. After a severe problem has occurred people will expect aid from neighbors, trade partners, and wealthier areas. This is more likely to happen if they have provided aid to others in their times of need. Clearly, the success of this type of operation depends on the magnitude of the problem and on its location. Nations should expect to provide this type of aid so that they can hope to receive similar aid when needed. I saw a description of the behavior of three very small island nations in the Pacific Ocean. They were self-supporting and were about forty miles apart. No regular trading took place between them, but boats from one island would occasionally raid another to capture some women, to keep the gene pool mixed, plus a few other special items. The island nations were essentially enemies. Every few years a very large storm would pass through this part of the Pacific and would often cross just one of the islands, causing devastation on it and leaving it completely vulnerable. The other two states would then compete to see which could be most helpful to the one that was hit. The reason is clear: it is a kind of insurance. If and when the storm hits them, they want their neighbors to come and help. This is a good example of generic co-risk.

It might be noted that this generic co-risk takes longer to organize on some scales and for some locations, as the experiences in Northern India and in Africa indicated in 2005.

    c. *Unknowable risks* includes all risks that cannot be identified in advance. No probabilities can be specified for some or all events and no realistic boundaries can be stated for the consequences. An example is a part of a comet striking the earth. It has been suggested that an actual example for the U.S. insurance industry has been the impact of various legal rulings about the health costs associated with asbestos in that country.

Turning to the question of the co-risk for unknowable risks, we can still expect the same generic form as above—that is, by getting help from others—but the scale of the disaster could be overwhelming! Unknowable risks of a small, containable size can be considered very much like most unknown risks, but very large unknowable risks belong in a separate category. In such a case the objective of the co-risk may change, from saving as many people as possible to ensuring that at least some vital components of the population, economy, and civilization survive. How one defines such an objective obviously needs further and careful discussion.[5]

     [5] An exhibition "SAFE: Design Takes on Risk," which shows "300 products meant to protect against perceived current dangers" went on display in late October 2005 and stayed until January 2, 2006 at the Museum of Modern Art, New York. A review appears in the *Economist* of October 29, 2005, page 82.

2.6. CONCLUSIONS

Risk clearly means different things to different people and various groups use and have alternative meanings for the word. All decision makers are familiar with situations involving risk and regularly make decisions without appearing to be too concerned about the precise definition or method of measurement used.

Most decision makers equate the idea of risk with something bad happening, here called downside risk. However, in some areas of finance and theoretical economics risk is equated with all parts of uncertainty and this leads to two-tailed risk, which is naturally measured by the variance of a distribution or sample. It is generally correct to say that the typical consumer, as well as financial managers, engineers, lawyers, and medics, use "risk" to mean downside, whereas many academics and financial investors use the word to mean two-tailed. This is only a problem in practice because speakers do not define which meaning they are using. The situation is made rather more complicated because everyone agrees that risk is associated with uncertainty, but the two groups disagree on the extent. The downsiders would say that you can have uncertainty without risk but the two-tailers state that in their theory uncertainty and risk are identical. Even if we believe that both groups agree on the definition of uncertainty, the implications are quite different. The big challenge for many investors now would seem to be deciding how to form portfolios, not necessarily linear, that reduce the lower tail without greatly reducing the upper tail of the asset return distribution.

REFERENCES

Borch, K. (1990). In K. Aase and A. Sandmo, eds., *The Economics of Insurance*. Amsterdam: North Holland.

Fishburn, P. C. (1977). Mean-risk analysis with risk associated with below target returns. *American Economic Review* 67, 116–26.

Grant, S., and J. Quiggin (2004). Increasing uncertainty: A definition. A Risk and Uncertainty Program Working Paper 4/R04, School of the Economics, University of Queensland.

Kaplan, P. D., and J.A. Knowles (2004). Kappa: A generalized downside risk-adjusted performance measure. Available on the web, at datalab.morningstar.com

Knight, F.H. (1921). *Risk, Uncertainty, and Profit*. Boston: Houghton Mifflin.

Markowitz, H. M. (1952). Portfolio selection. *Journal of Finance* 7, 77–91.

Markowitz, H.M. (1959). *Portfolio Selection*. New York: Wiley.

McNeil, A., R. Frey, and P. Embrechts (2005). *Quantitative Risk Management*. Princeton, NJ: Princeton University Press.

Nawroki, D. N. (1999). A brief history of downside risk measures. *Journal of Investing*, 8, 9–25.

Rigotti, L., and Shannon, C. (2005). Uncertainty and risk in financial markets. *Econometrica* 73, 203–43.

Rothschild, M., and J. Stiglitz (1970). Increasing risk, 1: A definition. *Journal of Economic Theory* 2, 223–43.

von Neumann, J., and O. Morgenstern (1947). *The Theory of Games and Economic Behavior*. Princeton, NJ: Princeton University Press.

3. Mild vs. Wild Randomness

Focusing on Those Risks That Matter

. . . .

Benoit B. Mandelbrot and Nassim Nicholas Taleb

Conventional studies of uncertainty, whether in statistics, economics, finance, or social science, have largely stayed close to the so-called bell curve, a symmetrical graph that represents a probability distribution. Used to great effect to describe errors in astronomical measurement by the 19th-century mathematician Carl Friedrich Gauss, the bell curve, or Gaussian model, has since pervaded our business and scientific culture, and terms like sigma, variance, standard deviation, correlation, R-square, and Sharpe ratio are all directly linked to it. Neoclassical finance and portfolio theory are completely grounded in it.

If you read a mutual fund prospectus, or a hedge fund's exposure, the odds are that information will incorporate some quantitative summary claiming to measure "risk." That measure will be based on one of the above buzzwords that derive from the bell curve and its kin. Such measures of future uncertainty satisfy our ingrained human desire to simplify by squeezing into one single number matters that are too rich to be described by it. In addition, they cater to psychological biases and our tendency to understate uncertainty in order to provide an illusion of understanding the world.

The bell curve has been presented as "normal" for almost two centuries, even though its flaws have always been obvious to any practitioner with empirical sense.[1] Granted, it has been tinkered with using such methods as complementary

---

[1] There is very little of the "normal" in the Gaussian: we seem to be conditioned to justify non-Gaussianity—yet, it is often Gaussianity that needs specific justification. To justify it in finance by a

"jumps," stress testing, regime switching, or the elaborate methods known as GARCH, but while they represent a good effort, they fail to remediate the bell curve's irremediable flaws. The problem is that measures of uncertainty using the bell curve disregard the possibility of sharp jumps or discontinuities. Therefore, they have no meaning or consequence. Using them is like focusing on the grass and missing out on the (gigantic) trees. In fact, while the occasional and unpredictable large deviations are rare, they cannot be dismissed as outliers because, cumulatively, their impact in the long term is dramatic. The good news, especially for practitioners, is that the fractal model is both intuitively and computationally simpler than the Gaussian. It too has been around since the 1960s, which makes us wonder why it was not implemented before.

The traditional Gaussian way of looking at the world begins by focusing on the ordinary, and only later deals with exceptions or so-called outliers as ancillaries.[2] But there is also a second way, which takes the so-called exceptional as a starting point and deals with the ordinary in a subordinate manner—simply because the ordinary is less consequential. These two models correspond to two mutually exclusive types of randomness: mild or Gaussian on the one hand, and wild, fractal, or *scalable power laws* on the other. Measurements that exhibit mild randomness are suitable for treatment by the bell curve or Gaussian models, whereas those that are susceptible to wild randomness can only be expressed accurately using a fractal scale.

Let us first turn to an illustration of mild randomness. Assume that you round up 1000 people at random among the general population and bring them into a stadium. Then, add the heaviest person you can think of to that sample. Even assuming he weighs 300 kg, more than three times the average, he will rarely represent more than a very small fraction of the entire population (say, 0.3%). Similarly, in the car insurance business, no single accident will put a dent on a company's annual income. These two examples both relate to the *law*

---

limit theorem necessitates assumptions that the evidence has been shown to be very restrictive, like independence or short-run memory, as well as other strictures that can rarely be verified. Likewise for the Poisson. Indeed, there are many processes that generate nonscalable randomness.

More technically, the idea that sums of i.i.d. finite variance random variables are Gaussian involves a *limit* or *asymptotic* behavior. Not only are i.i.d observations not the norm in natural life, something that was observed by Yule in 1925, but in the long-run we shall all be dead and science is mostly concerned with pre-asymptotic results, including the speed at which the limit is reached. It is far, far slower than can be deemed acceptable in practice—see the appendix that follows this chapter. All that the central limit theorem asserts is that the limit is Gaussian within a narrow central band, it does not prevent non-Gaussianity in the tails of the distribution.

[2] A key feature of the Pareto-Lévy-Mandelbrot fractal model is the presence of "jumps." Since then, to capture the outliers and conserve the results of neoclassical finance, many authors have "grafted" simplified jumps onto the Gaussian. This graft is used heavily in modern finance, but it is ultimately inadequate.

of large numbers, which implies that the average of a random sample is likely to be close to the mean of the whole population.

In a population that follows a mild type of randomness, one single observation, such as a very heavy person, may seem impressive by itself but will not disproportionately impact the aggregate or total. A randomness that disappears under averaging is trivial and harmless. You can diversify it away by having a large sample. There are specific measurements where the bell curve approach works very well, such as weight, height, calories consumed, death by heart attacks, or the performance of a gambler at a casino. An individual that is a few million miles tall is not biologically possible, but with a different sort of variable, an exception of equivalent scale cannot be ruled out with a different sort of variable, as we will see next.

3.1. WILD RANDOMNESS

What is wild randomness?[3] Simply put, it is an environment in which a single observation or a particular number can impact the total in a disproportionate way. The bell curve has "thin tails" in the sense that large events are considered possible but far too rare to be consequential. But many fundamental quantities follow distributions that have "fat tails"—namely, a higher probability of extreme values that can have a significant impact on the total. One can safely disregard the odds of running into someone several miles tall, or someone who weighs several million kilograms, but similar excessive observations can never be ruled out in other areas of life.

Having already considered the weight of 1000 people assembled for the previous experiment, let us instead consider their wealths. Add to the crowd of 1000 the wealthiest person to be found on the planet—Bill Gates, the founder of Microsoft. Assuming that his net worth is close to $80bn, how much would he represent of the total wealth? 99.9%? Indeed, all the others would represent no more than the variation of his personal portfolio over the past few seconds. For someone's weight to represent such a share, he would need to weigh 30m kg.

Try it again with, say, book sales. Line up a collection of 1000 authors. Then, add the most read person alive, J. K. Rowling, the author of the Harry Potter series. With sales of several hundred million books, she would dwarf the remaining 1000 authors who would collectively have only a few hundred thousand readers.

---

[3] The notions of mild to wild randomness were introduced in Mandelbrot (1997). Technically, they range from the purely mild to the totally wild.

So, while weight, height, and calorie consumption are Gaussian, wealth is not. Nor are income, market returns, size of hedge funds, returns in the financial markets, number of deaths in wars, or casualties in terrorist attacks. Almost all man-made variables are wild. Furthermore, physical science continues to discover more and more examples of wild uncertainty, such as the intensity of earthquakes, hurricanes, or tsunamis.

Economic life displays numerous examples of wild uncertainty. For example, during the 1920s, the German currency moved from three to a dollar to 4 trillion to the dollar in a few years. And veteran currency traders still remember when, as late as the 1990s, short-term interest rates jumped by several thousand percent.

We live in a world of extreme concentration where the winner takes all. Consider, for example, how Google grabs much of internet traffic, how Microsoft represents the bulk of PC software sales, how 1% of the U.S. population earns close to 90 times the bottom 20% or how half the capitalization of the market (at least 10,000 listed companies) is concentrated in less than 100 corporations.

Taken together, these facts should be enough to demonstrate that it is the "outlier" and not the regular that we need to model. For instance, a very small number of days accounts for the bulk of the stock market changes: just ten trading days represent 63% of the returns of the past 50 years.

Let us now return to the Gaussian for a closer look at its tails. The *sigma* is defined as a standard deviation away from the average, which could be around 0.7 to 1% in a stock market or 8 to 10 cm for height. The probabilities of exceeding multiples of sigma are obtained by a complex mathematical formula. Using this formula, one finds the following values.

Probability of exceeding
  0 sigmas: 1 in 2 times
  1 sigmas: 1 in 6.3 times
  2 sigmas: 1 in 44 times
  3 sigmas: 1 in 740 times
  4 sigmas: 1 in 32,000 times
  5 sigmas: 1 in 3,500,000 times
  6 sigmas: 1 in 1,000,000,000 times
  7 sigmas: 1 in 780,000,000,000 times
  8 sigmas: 1 in 1,600,000,000,000,000 times
  9 sigmas: 1 in 8,900,000,000,000,000,000 times
  10 sigmas: 1 in 130,000,000,000,000,000,000, 000 times
  and, skipping a bit,
  20 sigmas: 1 in 36,000,000,000,000,000,000,000,000,000,000,000,000,000,000,000,000,000,000,000,000,000,000,000,000,000,000, 000 times

Soon, after about 22 sigmas, one hits a googol, which is 1 with 100 zeroes after it.

With measurements such as height and weight, this probability seems reasonable, as it would require a deviation from the average of more than 2m. The same cannot be said of variables such as financial markets. For example, a level described as a 22 sigma has been exceeded with the stock market crashes of 1987 and the European interest rate moves of 1992, not counting the routine devaluations in emerging market currencies. The key here is to note how the frequencies in the preceding list drop very rapidly, in an accelerating way. The ratio is not invariant with respect to scale.

Let us now look more closely at a fractal, or scalable,[4] distribution using the example of wealth. We find that the odds of encountering a millionaire in Europe are as follows:

Richer than 1 million: 1 in 62.5
Richer than 2 million: 1 in 250
Richer than 4 million: 1 in 1000
Richer than 8 million: 1 in 4000
Richer than 16 million: 1 in 16,000
Richer than 32 million: 1 in 64,000
Richer than 320 million: 1 in 6,400,000

This is simply a fractal law with a tail exponent, or alpha, of 2, which means that when the number is doubled, the incidence goes down by the square of that number—in this case 4. If you look at the ratio of the moves, you will notice that this ratio is invariant with respect to scale. If the alpha were one, the incidence would decline by half when the number is doubled. This would produce a "flatter" distribution (fatter tails), whereby a greater contribution to the total comes from the low-probability events.

Richer than 1 million: 1 in 62.5
Richer than 2 million: 1 in 125

[4] Technically for us a fractal distribution defined as follows: $P_{>x} = Kx^{-\alpha}$, where $P_{>x}$ is the probability of exceeding a variable x and α is the asymptotic power law exponent for x large enough. This distribution is said to be scale free, in the sense that it does not have a characteristic scale: For x "large enough," the relative deviation of $(p > x)/(p > nx)$ does not depend on x, only on n. Other distributions are nonscalable. For example, in the density $p(x) = \exp[-ax]$, with tails falling off exponentially, the scale will be $1/a$. For the Gaussian, the scale is the standard deviation.

The effect that is not negligible is that finite moments exist only up to the exponent α. Indeed, for the function $x^n x^{\alpha-1}$ to have a finite integral from 1 (say) to infinity, one must have $n - \alpha < 0$, that is, $n < \alpha$. This does not allow the Taylor expansions required for Modern Portfolio Theory as, for scalable, higher terms are explosive. If $\alpha = 3$, as we tend to observe in stocks, the third and higher moments are infinite.

Richer than 4 million: 1 in 250
Richer than 8 million: 1 in 500
Richer than 16 million: 1 in 1000[5]

We have used the example of wealth here, but the same "fractal" scale can be used for stock market returns and many other variables—at least as a vague lower bound. In other words, this method provides an alternative qualitative method to the Gaussian. Indeed, this fractal approach can prove to be an extremely robust method to identify a portfolio's vulnerability to severe risks. Traditional stress testing is usually done by selecting an arbitrary number of worst-case scenarios from past data. It assumes that whenever one has seen in the past a large move of, say, 10%, one can conclude that a fluctuation of this magnitude would be the worst one can expect for the future. This method forgets that crashes happen without antecedents. Before the crash of 1987, stress testing would not have allowed for a 22% move. Using a fractal method, it is easy to extrapolate multiple projected scenarios. If your worst-case scenario from the past data was, say, a move of –5% and if you assume that it happens once every two years, then, with an alpha of two, you can consider that a –10% move happens every eight years and add such a possibility to your simulation.

Using this model, a –15% move would happen every 16 years, and so forth. This will give you a much clearer idea of your risks by expressing them as a series of possibilities. You can also change the alpha to generate additional scenarios—lowering it means increasing the probabilities of large deviations and increasing it means reducing the probabilities. What would such a method reveal? It would certainly do what sigma and its siblings cannot do, which is to show how some portfolios are more robust than others to an entire spectrum of extreme risks. It can also show how some portfolios can benefit inordinately from wild uncertainty.

Despite the shortcomings of the bell curve, reliance on it is accelerating, and widening the gap between reality and standard tools of measurement. The consensus seems to be that any number is better than no number—even if it is wrong. Finance academia is too entrenched in the mild, Gaussian paradigm to stop calling it "an acceptable approximation."

Let us repeat: the Gaussian (or Poisson) is *no* approximation. Any attempts to refine the tools of modern portfolio theory by relaxing the bell curve

---

[5] There is a problem of how large is "large." This scalability might stop somewhere, but we do not know where, so we might consider it infinite. The two statements, "very large but I don't know exactly how large" and "infinitely large" look different but are epistemologically substitutable (Taleb 2007b). There might be a point at which the distributions flip. This will show once we look at them graphically in the appendix.

assumptions, or by fudging and adding the occasional jumps will not be sufficient. We live in a world primarily driven by random jumps, and tools designed for random walks address the wrong problem. It would be like tinkering with models of gases in an attempt to characterize them as solids and call them "a good approximation." While scalable laws do not yet yield precise recipes, they have become an alternative way to view the world, and a methodology where large deviation and stressful events dominate the analysis instead of the other way around. We do not know of a more robust manner for decision-making in an uncertain world.

3.2. SOME OBSERVATIONS AND CONSEQUENCES OF GAUSSIAN AND FRACTAL MODES.

Here we observe some of the differences between Gaussian (nonscalable) and fractal (scalable) models. Table 3.1 provides additional color.

- By itself, no single number can characterize uncertainty and risk but, as we have seen, we can still have a handle on it so long as we can have a table, a chart, and an open mind.

- In the Gaussian world, standard tables show that 67% of the observations fall between −1 and +1 sigma. Outside of Gaussianity, sigma loses much or all of its significance. With a scalable distribution, you may have 80, 90, even 99.99% of observations falling between −1 and +1 sigmas. In fractals, the standard deviation is never a typical value and may even be infinite![6]

- When assessing the effectiveness of a given financial, economic, or social strategy, the observation window needs to be large enough to include substantial deviations, so one must base strategies on a long time frame. In some situations you will never see the properties.

- You are far less diversified than you assume. Because the market returns in the very long run will be dominated by a small number of investments, you need to mitigate the risk of missing these by investing as broadly as possible. Very broad passive indexing is far more effective than active selection.

---

[6] Even in "finite variance" cases where $\alpha > 2$, we just can no longer rely on variance as a sufficient measure of dispersion. See the appendix for an illustration of how a cubic exponent mimics stochastic volatility and can be easily mistaken for it.

TABLE 3.1
Comparison Between Nonscalable and Scalable Randomness

Nonscalable	Scalable
The most typical member is mediocre	The most "typical" is either giant or dwarf, i.e., there is no typical member
Winners get a small segment of the total pie	Winner-take-almost-all effects
Example: Audience of an opera singer before the gramophone	Today's audience for an artist
More likely to be found in our ancestral environment	More likely to be found in our modern environment
Subjected to gravity	There are no physical constraints on what a number can be
Corresponds (generally) to physical quantities, i.e., height	Corresponds to numbers, say wealth
Total is not determined by a single instance or observation	Total will be determined by a small number of extreme events
When you observe for a while you can get to know what's going on	It takes a long time to know what's going on
Tyranny of the collective	Tyranny of the accidental
Easy to predict from what you see to what you do not see	Hard to predict from past information
History crawls	History makes jumps

- Projections of deficits, performance, and interest rates are marred with extraordinarily large errors. In many budget calculations, U.S. interest rates were projected to be 5% for 2001 (not 1%); oil prices were projected to be close to $22 a barrel for 2006 (not $62). Like prices, forecast errors follow a fractal distribution.

- Option pricing models, such as Black-Scholes-Merton, are strongly grounded in the bell curve in their representation of risk. The Black-Scholes-Merton equation bases itself on the possibility of eliminating an option's risk through continuous dynamic hedging, a procedure incompatible with fractal discontinuities.[7]

- Some classes of investments with explosive upside, such as venture capital, need to be favored over those that do not have such potential. Technology investments get bad press; priced appropriately (in the initial

[7] Taleb (2007a) shows how Ito's lemma no longer applies and how we can no longer perform the operation of dynamic hedging to compress the risks.

stages) they can deliver huge potential profits, thanks to the small but significant possibility of a massive windfall.[8]

- Large moves beget large moves; markets keep in memory the volatility of past deviations. A subtle concept, fractal memory provides an intrinsic way of modeling both the clustering of large events and the phenomenon of regime switching, which refers to phases when markets move from low to high volatility.[9]

---

[8] The exact opposite applies to business we call "concave" to the large deviation, such as banking, catastrophe insurance, or hedge-fund arbitrage of the type practiced by Long Term Capital Management.

[9] This power-law decaying volatility differs markedly from the exponentially declining memory offered by ARCH methods.

Technical Appendix
Large but Finite Samples and Preasymptotics

• •

Ever since 1963, when power law densities first entered finance through the Pareto-Lévy-Mandelbrot model, the practical limitations of the limit theorems of probability theory have raised important issues. Let the tail follow the power-law distribution defined as follows: $P_{>x} = K\, x^{-\alpha}$, where $P_{>x}$ is the probability of exceeding a variable x, and α is the asymptotic power law exponent for x large enough. If so, a first partial result is that the largest of n such variables is given by an expression (Fréchet law) that does not depend on α. This maximum is known to behave like $n^{1/\alpha}$. A second partial result is that the sum of n variables is given by an expression that, to the contrary, does depend on the sign of $\alpha - 2$.

If $\alpha > 2$, the variance is finite—as one used to assume without thinking. But what does the central limit theorem really tell us? Assuming EX = 0, it includes the following classical result: EX infinite and there exists near EX a central bell region in which the sum is increasingly close to a Gaussian whose standard deviation behaves asymptotically like $n^{1/2}$. Subtracting nEX from the sum and combining the two partial results, one finds that the relative contribution of the largest addend behaves like $n^{1/\alpha-\frac{1}{2}}$. In the example of $\alpha = 3$, this becomes $n^{-1/6}$. Again asymptotically for $n \to \infty$, this ratio tends to 0—as expected—but the convergence is exquisitely slow. For comparison, examine for EX $\neq$ 0 the analogous very familiar ratio of the deviation from the mean—to the sum if the former behaves like the standard deviation times $n^{1/2}$. The latter—assuming EX $\neq$ 0—behaves like nEX. Therefore, the ratio of these two factors behaves like $n^{-1/2}$. To divide it by 10, one must multiply n by 100, which is often regarded as uncomfortably large. Now back to $n^{-1/6}$: to divide it by 10, one must multiply n by 1,000,000. In empirical studies, this factor is hardly ever worth thinking about.

Now consider the—widely feared—case $\alpha < 2$ for which the variance is infinite. The maximum's behavior is still $n^{1/\alpha}$, but the—subtracting nEX—sum's behavior changes from $n^{1/2}$ to the anomalous $n^{1/\alpha}$. Therefore, the relative contribution of the largest addend is of the order $n^{1/\alpha-1/\alpha} = n^0$. Adding all the bells and whistles, one finds that the largest addend remains a significant proportion of the sum, even as n tends to infinity.

Conclusion: In the asymptotic regime tackled by the theory, n^0 altogether differs from $n^{-1/6}$, but in the preasymptotic regime within which one works in practice—especially after sampling fluctuations are considered—those two expressions are hard to tell apart. In other words, the sharp discontinuity at $\alpha = 2$, which has created so much anguish in finance, is replaced in practice by a very gradual transition. Asymptotically, the Lévy stability of the Pareto-Lévy-Mandelbrot model remains restricted to $\alpha < 2$, but preasymptotically it continues to hold if α is not far above 2.

Figures 3.1 and 3.2 show the representation of the scalable section in the tails.

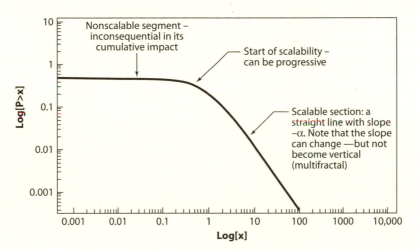

Figure 3.1. Looking at a distribution. Log $P > x = -\alpha \log X + C$ for a scalable distribution. When we do a log–log plot (i.e., plot $P > x$ and x on a logarithmic scale), as in figures 3.1 and 3.2, we should see a straight line in the asymptote.

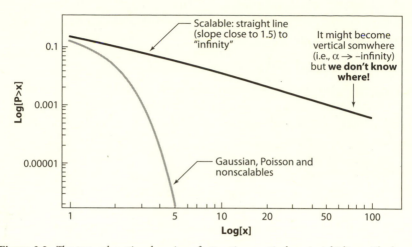

Figure 3.2. The two exhaustive domains of attraction: vertical or straight line with slopes either negative infinity or constant negative α. Note that since probabilities need to add up to 1, there cannot be other alternatives to the two basins, which is why we narrow it down to these two exclusively—as we said the two paradigms are mutually exclusive.

REFERENCES

Cont R., and P. Tankov (2003). *Financial Modelling with Jump Processes.* Chapman & Hall / CRC Press.

Mandelbrot, B. (1963). The variation of certain speculative prices, *Journal of Business* 36, 394–419; reprinted in P. H. Cootner, ed., *The Random Character of Stock Market Prices,* Cambridge, MA, 1964, 307–32.

Mandelbrot, B. (1967). Sur l'épistémologie du hasard dans les sciences sociales: invariance des lois et vérification des hypothèses, *Encyclopédie de la Pléiade* (Gallimard). *Logique et Connaissance Scientifique* (Dirigé par J. Piaget), 1097–113.

Mandelbrot, B. (1997). *Fractals and Scaling in Finance: Discontinuity, Concentration, Risk.* New York: Springer-Verlag. Reproduces earlier classic papers.

Mandelbrot, B. (2001). Stochastic volatility, power-laws and long memory. *Quantitative Finance* 1, 558–59.

Mandelbrot, B., R. L. Hudson (2004). *The (Mis)behavior of Markets: A Fractal View of Risk, Ruin, and Reward.* New York: Basic Books.

Taleb, N. N. (2007a). Scale Invariance in Practice, Working Paper.

Taleb, N. N. (2007b). *The Black Swan: The Impact of the Highly Improbable,* New York: Random House and London: Penguin.

4.   The Term Structure of Risk, the Role of Known and Unknown Risks, and Nonstationary Distributions

. . . .

Riccardo Colacito and Robert F. Engle

Long before the unprecedented collapse of the U.S. banking system that we have witnessed in the recent years, many people believed that there were grave risks facing our financial markets. These included the massive budget deficits, the balance payments deficits, the high cost of energy and many other raw materials, the uncertainty over Federal Reserve (FED) policy, war in Iraq that was going badly, global warming, and the extraordinary amount of U.S. debt that was and still is held by the Chinese government. In addition, there was a concern that the vast global derivatives market, the number of unregulated hedge funds, the merging of financial markets across national borders, and the explosive growth of private equity funds made the financial system more unstable and susceptible to meltdown. These concerns were not new; they had been serious topics of discussion for several years.

The extraordinary fact, however, was that the volatility of financial markets in the first years of the new century was about as low as it had ever been. This had been true for most of the years 2004–2006. This was the situation in the U.S. equity market but it was also true in global equity markets. The volatility had fallen to very low levels in most equity markets around the globe, as shown

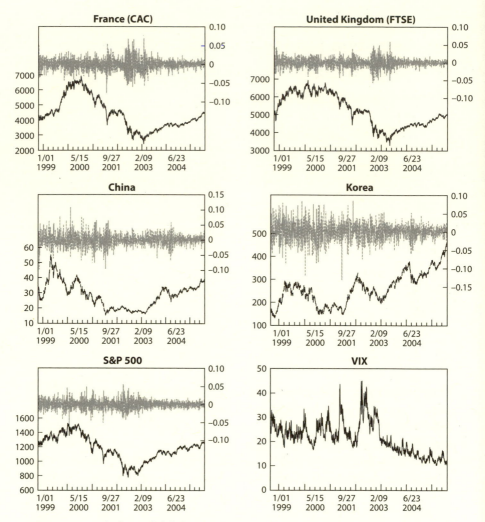

Figure 4.1. Volatilities of global equity markets. The first five plots report the returns (top line) and the levels (bottom line) of equity markets in France, United Kingdom, China, Korea, and United States. The sixth plot shows the volatility index in the United States.

in figure 4.1. It was also reflected in options prices, as can easily be seen by looking at a time-series plot of the volatility index, VIX.

These observations present a puzzle. Were financial markets ignoring these risks or were the risks not so serious? In this paper we present another resolution of the puzzle. Most of these risks are potential problems for the future. They are not risks in the short run, only in the long run. There may be a term

structure of risk that faces financial markets in general and individual investors in particular. This concept must be carefully defined and examined empiri-
cally. Finally, we must consider the implications for asset pricing and portfolio
construction.

4.1. MEASUREMENT

In this chapter we associate long-run risks with the probability and magnitude
of losses of a passive portfolio over a long horizon. Measuring this in nominal
terms is appropriate only if the changes in price level or purchasing power of
risk-free rates are minor adjustments. The analysis could be carried out in any
of these frameworks. We choose nominal returns to focus on the dynamics of
the financial markets rather than the nominal economy as a whole.

In contrast, Bansal and Yaron (2004) introduce long-run risks by postulating
a slowly varying factor in real consumption that induces variation in expected
returns. The long-run risk is thus the risk of a low consumption state, which
corresponds to a low return state. Without further elaboration, the prediction
of this risk in the distant future would not be changing over time as current
information would have little ability to predict these events. Conceptually, a
model more similar to ours would introduce the long-run risks into the variance of consumption, rather than its level.

To quantify these long-run risks, we follow Guidolin and Timmermann
(2006). We consider the long-run variance and long-run value-at-risk, LRVaR.
These measures are widely used in financial planning, but can be given a new
interpretation with long horizons. Unknown and unforecastable risks appear
in the historical data as surprising returns and are therefore a part of predicted
variance and VaR. Nonstationary risks can sometimes be corrected for and
therefore be used to improve risk assessment and decision making.

4.1.1. VOLATILITY FORECASTS AT VARIOUS HORIZONS

The task of forecasting volatility is one that can be accomplished only after a
model has been specified. But what is the reasonable set of assumptions that
one can make about the underlying economic model? It is common to assume
that returns follow a stationary process, with the understanding that this is a
statistical convenience and not an economic model. With stationary returns,
long-run risk is constant. This can be shown in a simple example that allows us
to introduce some of the notation that we will be using in the rest of the analysis. Let r_t be a mean zero random variable measuring the return on a financial
asset and assume that it follows a GARCH(1,1) process:

$$r_t = \sqrt{h_t}\, \varepsilon_t, \quad \varepsilon_t \sim N(0,1) \tag{4.1}$$
$$h_t = (1-\alpha-\beta)\omega + \beta h_{t-1} + \alpha r_{t-1}^2$$

Taking the unconditional expectation of squared returns, we obtain

$$E[r_t^2] = E[h_t] = \omega$$

which is our constant estimate of long-run risk. Long-run risk is the time average of short-run risk and the unconditional term structure of volatility risk is proportional to $\sqrt{T}$.

Nevertheless, long-run risk can change over time or at least there is no *a priori* reason to restrict our statistical model from this possibility. As a matter of fact, unknown and unknowable events can occur, and if *ex post* we say that there is a shift in the distribution, then *ex ante* we must assess the probabilities. The important question is whether the historical risks can be used to assess the future risks and this is a question of the stationarity of the distribution. If the distribution is stationary, then unknown and unknowable risks are already sensibly incorporated in the forecasts of future risk. But if the distribution is changing, then these changes must be modeled.

An example of a model that allows for time-varying, long-run risk is the spline GARCH of Engel and Rangel (2005), in which economic or exogenous variables, such as recessions, inflation, and macro volatility, increase the long-run variance. This is a multiplicative model in which the conditional variance is assumed to be the product of a long-run and a short-run component and where both terms can be time-varying. In particular, mean-zero returns follow the process

$$r_t = \sqrt{\tau_t g_t}\, \varepsilon_t, \quad \varepsilon_t \sim N(0,1) \tag{4.2}$$
$$g_t = (1-\alpha-\beta) + \alpha\left(\frac{r_{t-1}^2}{\tau_{t-1}}\right) + \beta g_{t-1}$$

where τ_t is a function of time and exogenous variables. By taking unconditional expectations of squared returns

$$E\left[r_t^2\right] = \tau_t E\left[g_t \varepsilon_t^2\right] = \tau_t E[g_t] = \tau_t$$

it is clear that τ_t can be interpreted as the long-run forecast of variance. We will also refer to this component as the low-frequency variance or sometimes the unconditional variance when it is a function of deterministic or exogenous variables. One possibility is that the long-run variance τ_t is an exponential quadratic spline of time:

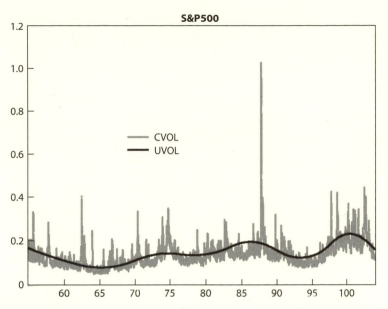

Figure 4.2. Long- vs. short-run volatility of the S&P 500. The spiked line is short-run volatility and the smooth line is long-run volatility.

$$\log(\tau_t) = \omega_0 + \omega_1 + \omega_2 + \sum_{k=1}^{K} \theta_k \left[\max(t - t_k, 0)\right]^2$$

Figure 4.2 reports the measure of short-run and long-run volatility for the S&P 500 forecasted by the spline GARCH model. The figure shows how there may be periods in which the short-run risk (thick line) is high, while the long-run risk is low and vice versa. The picture also shows how the volatility appeared to be at a record low level until 2006, while long-run volatility was higher. This was the case not only for the United States, but also for a large number of countries, as is documented in figure 4.3.

4.1.2. THE TERM STRUCTURE OF VALUE-AT-RISK

The value-at-risk T periods ahead from the current date is the α quantile of the conditional distribution of returns at time $t + T$. It is expressed mathematically as

$$Pr_t\left(r_{t+T} \le -VaR_{t+T}^{\alpha}\right) = \alpha$$

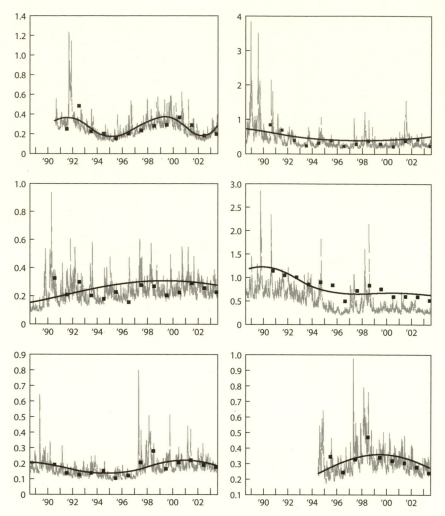

Figure 4.3. Measures of volatility. In each subplot, the spiked line represents the conditional volatility, the smooth line is the unconditional volatility, and the squares are the annualized realized volatility. Each panel is for a different country. From the top left to the bottom right: India, Argentina, Japan, Brazil, South Africa, and Poland.

As a benchmark we will consider the case of i.i.d. mean-zero returns: $r_t \sim N(0, h)$, $\forall t$. In this situation the value at risk is simply proportional to the square root of time:

$$VaR_{t+T}^{\alpha} = \sqrt{hT}\Phi^{-1}(\alpha) \qquad (4.3)$$

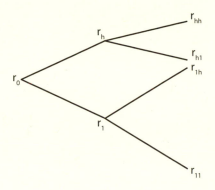

Figure 4.4. Asymmetric volatility: binomial tree. At each node returns have a symmetric distribution, but following periods of positive returns the volatility lowers, while after periods of negative returns the volatility increases. This implies an asymmetric distribution of multiperiod returns.

It is often convenient to standardize the measure reported in (4.3) by $\sqrt{T}$, in which case i.i.d. returns are equivalent to a constant term structure of risk.

When returns are not i.i.d., the term structure of VaR can slope upward or downward. An interesting case to consider is the one in which returns follow a TARCH(1,1) process:

$$h_t = \omega + \beta h_{t-1} + \alpha r_{t-1}^2 + \gamma r_{t-1}^2 \, I_{(r_{t-1} < 0)} \qquad (4.4)$$

$$r_t = \mu + \sqrt{h_t} \varepsilon_t$$

The law of motion of the conditional variance is such that following periods of negative returns there is an expectation for a relatively higher variance in the future. Although one-period returns are symmetrically distributed at each point in time, multiperiod returns are not as illustrated in figure 4.4. The probability that is attached to the extreme negative events that may occur many periods in the future has potentially important consequences that should be taken into account in the context of any asset allocation exercise.

Table 4.1 reports the estimate of the parameters of model (4.4) for a long dataset of daily observations on the S&P 500, ranging from 1950 to 2006. As

TABLE 4.1
TARCH(1,1): Estimation of Parameters

	ω	α	β	γ
Estimate	8.36×10^{-7}	0.035	0.918	0.074
Standard error	6.40×10^{-7}	0.003	0.003	0.002

Note. The sample period is 1950–2006.

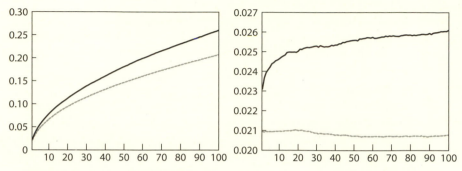

Figure 4.5. Value-at-risk of a TARCH Gaussian simulation. The left panel reports the VaR for T ranging from 0 to 100 of a TARCH(1,1) simulated from table 4.1 as a solid line, while the dotted line is the benchmark case of i.i.d. returns. The right panel reports $VaR\dfrac{a_{t+h}}{\sqrt{T}}$.

expected the asymmetric volatility parameter is positive and significant at a 95% level of confidence. Negative shocks have 3 times the effect of positive shocks in forecasting future variances.

Diebold et al. (1998) show that the common practice of converting 1-day volatilities to T-day estimates by scaling by $\sqrt{T}$ is inappropriate and produces overestimates of the variability of long-horizon volatility. Our work relates to theirs in that we quantify the impact of a TARCH(1,1) volatility process on the estimate of the VaR at a given future point. We address this task by simulating one million excess returns following process (4.4) and calibrating its parameters according to table 4.1. We then let T vary between 1 and 100 and construct the corresponding 1% value-at-risk. Figure 4.5 reports the results of this simulation. In comparing the VaR when returns follow an asymmetric process (thick line) with the VaR obtained under the assumption that returns are i.i.d. (dashed line) it is apparent that according to this risk measure, both long-run risk and short-run risk according to (4.4) exceed the risk for i.i.d. shocks. Particularly important, however, is the fact that this difference increases with horizon. That is, the term structure of risk can slope upward all the time.

4.2. IMPLICATIONS FOR ASSET ALLOCATION

It has recently emerged that volatility timing and traditional market timing are fundamentally related, as is well documented by Christoffersen and Diebold (2006). Fleming et al. (2001) and Fleming et al. (2003) study a 1-day horizon asset allocation problem and document the economic value of various conditional volatility estimators and realized volatilities. Engle and Colacito (2006) pointed out that correct volatility and correlation timing is typically worth

50–60 basis points when the investment horizon is one day. However, most portfolio managers have investment horizons longer than a day, even though they ultimately end up doing a static asset allocation exercise. It seems reasonable to think that an investor, aware that returns follow the TARCH process that we discussed in the earlier sections, would take the presence of a downside risk into account when choosing portfolio weights in this context. In this section we give a quantitative answer to the question of how much can an investor expect from optimally adjusting portfolio weights when the variance is asymmetric.

We shall focus on the simplest case in which the investor can only allocate her wealth among a risky and a riskless asset. We denote with w_{t+T} the share of the portfolio that is invested in the risky asset between times t and $t + T$ and with r_{t+T} the logarithm of the continuously compounded return on the risky asset in excess of the risk-free rate r^f between t and $t + T$. We assume that the agent wants to maximize terminal wealth according to an exponential utility function:

$$\max_{w_{t+T}} E_t - \exp\left\{-b\left(w_{t+T}r_{t+T}\right)\right\}\exp\left\{-br^f\right\} \tag{4.5}$$

where b is a preference parameter that reflects the absolute risk aversion. The risk-free rate is constant at a daily frequency. If log-returns are conditionally distributed as normals, an investor seeking to maximize her utility according to (4.5) could simply solve a mean-variance exercise:

$$\max_{w_{t+T}} E_t\left[w_{t+T}r_{t+T}\right] - \frac{b}{2}E_t\left[w_{t+T}^2 r_{t+T}^2\right] \tag{4.6}$$

However, if returns are not lognormally distributed, the equivalency of problems (4.5) and (4.6) does not hold anymore. We now develop an approximate procedure to choose portfolios according to (4.5) when the returns follow an asymmetric GARCH model. The first step is to approximate the utility function accounting for higher moments. The result, derived in the appendix, is

$$\max_{w_{t+T}} -\exp\left\{-bw_{t+T}\mu_{t+T}\right\}\left[1 + \frac{b^2}{2}w_{t+T}^2 h_{t+T} - \frac{b^3}{6}w_{t+T}^3 s_{t+T}\right] \tag{4.7}$$

where μ_{t+T}, h_{t+T} and s_{t+T} denote the conditional expectations of mean, variance, and third centered moment, respectively. This utility function formalizes the idea according to which investors like positive first and third moments and dislike second moments. Alternatively, agents are now concerned about the lower tail of the distribution that is depicted in figure 4.4. The solution can be calculated numerically based on the forecast first, second, and third moments. This optimization is simple, but does not produce a closed-form solution. In the experiment described below, the mean is constant. To forecast the third central moment we use a recursion developed in the appendix. Essentially, it computes

$E_t[(r_{t+1} + r_{t+2} + \cdots + r_{t+k})^3]$ in terms os $E_t[h_{t+k}^{3/2}]$. Then, approximating this by a Taylor series, the third moment can be forecast and used to optimize portfolios at each point in time. Clearly, the more negative the third moment, the less exposure to the risky asset will be chosen by this investor.

To quantify the benefit of knowing that returns follow an asymmetric volatility process, we simulate daily returns according to model (4.4) and then we compare two investors with the same objective function (4.5): one makes forecasts of the distribution of returns based on the TARCH(1,1) process reported in (4.4), while the other one believes that returns are distributed according to the GARCH(1,1) process in (4.1).[1] For the results to be comparable, we will assume that the two models agree on the unconditional forecasts of mean returns and variance.[2]

The metric that we adopt to quantify these benefits is based on the criterion function 4.5. For a given risk-free rate $\tilde{r}^f$, an agent who refrains from investing in the risky asset would obtain an average utility $U(\tilde{r}^f) = -\exp\{-b\tilde{r}^f\}$. By allocating a nonzero share of her portfolio in the risky asset at the actual risk-free rate r^f, she could instead expect a utility $U(r^f) = -E[\exp\{-b(w_{t+T}r_{t+T})\}\exp\{-br^f\}]$. The risk-free rate $\tilde{r}^f$ that would make her indifferent between the two strategies can be easily shown[3] to be equal to

$$\tilde{r}^f = r^f + \frac{-\log E \exp\{-bw_t r_t\}}{b} \tag{4.8}$$

Hence, our evaluation strategy that consists in obtaining sequences of optimal portfolio weights $\{w_{1,t}\}_{t=1}^T$ and $\{w_{2,t}\}_{t=1}^T$ based on forecasting from (4.4) and (4.1), respectively, and then comparing the "certainty equivalent" returns $\tilde{r}_1^f$ and $\tilde{r}_2^f$ based on the sample counterparts of the terms involving an expectation. It is natural to expect that $\tilde{r}_2^f$ will typically be greater than $\tilde{r}_1^f$: we want to quantify this benefit.

Figure 4.6 reports the percentage annualized gains when the investment horizons are 20 days (left panel) and 1 year (right panel). A number like 1 on the vertical axis means that an investor that is informed of the asymmetry in the volatility process and optimally adjusts portfolio weights would need 100 basis points in excess of what an investor that ignores the asymmetry would need in order to refrain from investing in the risky asset. We plot these gains for increasing values of the coefficient of absolute risk aversion, b. The average gain can be as high as 220 basis points and it is decreasing with b just because

---

[1] More precisely, we use these models to describe the process of returns in excess of their mean.

[2] The appendix also reports the details on how to compute multiperiod forecasts of third centered moments.

[3] We document this in the appendix.

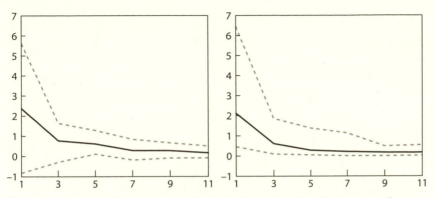

Figure 4.6. Annualized percentage gain from volatility timing when the investment horizon is 20 days (left panel) and 252 days (right panel). The vertical axis reports the extra return that an investor aware of the asymmetry of the volatility process could obtain. The horizontal axis reports the preference parameter *b*. The solid line is the average gain, while the dashed lines represent the 95% confidence interval.

the amount of wealth that is invested in the risky asset is decreasing with risk aversion. In moving from a 20-day to a year-long exercise, there is still a sizeable gain to be made. The decrease of the average benefit has presumably to be attributed to the difficulty of accurately forecasting the distribution of multiperiod returns as the horizon gets longer and longer.

Although this represents the outcome of the simplest example of portfolio allocation, the results reported in this section are suggestive of the fact that there is potentially a considerable gain that can be obtained by appropriately timing volatility over horizons that are longer than a day. Along these lines it is not hard to imagine that multivariate asset allocation experiments would yield even larger gains, which must be taken into account as the planning horizon increases.

4.4. CONCLUDING REMARKS

In this paper we have documented the presence of a term structure of risk and provided tools that can be used by academics and practitioners to actively manage portfolios in the presence of downward risk. The implications in the context of a simple asset allocation exercise are suggestive of the fact that taking into account time-varying asymmetries in the multiperiod distributions of asset returns can potentially result in significant financial gains. This provides a useful starting point for the exploration of the benefits that can be obtained in the context of large-scale systems.

Appendix

Approximation of the Utility Function

. . . .

Following the notation of section 4.3, the utility function is

$$U_t = E_t - \exp\{-bW_{t+T}\}$$

where $W_{t+T} = w_{t+T} r_{t+T}$. A third-order Taylor expansion around $w_{t+T} \mu$ delivers

$$U_t \approx -E_t \exp\{-bw_{t+T}\mu\}\left[1 - bw_{t+T}(r_{t+T} - \mu) + \frac{b^2}{2}w_{t+T}^2(r_{t+T} - \mu)^2 - \frac{b^3}{6}w_{t+T}^3(r_{t+T} - \mu)^3\right]$$

$$= -\exp\{-bw_{t+T}\mu\}\left[1 + \frac{b^2}{2}w_{t+T}^2 h_{t+T} - \frac{b^3}{6}w_{t+T}^3 s_{t+T}\right]$$

where s_{t+T} denotes the conditional third centered moment of the distribution of r_{t+T}. This is the analytical form we worked with in section 4.2.

MULTIPERIOD FORECASTS OF SECOND AND THIRD MOMENTS

Given the following process for the logarithm of excess returns,

$$r_t = \sqrt{h_t}\,\varepsilon_t$$

$$h_t = \omega + \alpha r_{t-1}^2 + \beta h_{t-1} + \gamma I_{r_{t-1}<0} r_{t-1}^2$$

the conditional forecast of the variance of multiperiod returns can be computed as

$$E_t\left[\left(\sum_{j=1}^{T} r_{t+j}\right)^2\right] = \sum_{j=1}^{T} E_t\left[r_{t+j}^2\right]$$

$$= \sum_{j=1}^{T} E_t h_{t+j}$$

$$= h_{t+1} + \sum_{j=1}^{T} \left[\omega \sum_{i=0}^{j-2} \left(\alpha + \beta + \frac{\gamma}{2} \right)^i + \left(\alpha + \beta + \frac{\gamma}{2} \right)^{j-1} h_{t+1} \right]$$

We shall denote the third centered conditional moment as

$$s_{t+j} = E_t \left[\left(\sum_{i=1}^{j} r_{t+i} \right)^3 \right]$$

The one period ahead third moment is equal to zero:

$$s_{t+1} = E_t \left[h_{t+1}^{3/2} \varepsilon_{t+1}^3 \right] = 0$$

The conditional third moment of two periods of continuously compounded returns is

$$s_{t+2} = E_t \left[\left(r_{t+1} + r_{t+2} \right)^3 \right]$$

$$= 3E_t \left[r_{t+1} r_{t+2}^2 \right]$$

$$= 3E_t \left[\sqrt{h_{t+1}} \varepsilon_{t+1} \left(\omega + \alpha h_{t+1} \varepsilon_{t+1}^2 + \beta h_{t+1} + \gamma I_{\varepsilon_{t+1} < 0} h_{t+1} \varepsilon_{t+1}^2 \right) \right]$$

$$= -\frac{12}{5} \gamma h_{t+1}^{3/2}$$

Similarly,

$$s_{t+3} = s_{t+2} + 3\sqrt{h_{t+1}} E_t \left[\varepsilon_{t+1} h_{t+3} \right] + 3E_t \left[\sqrt{h_{t+2}} \varepsilon_{t+2} h_{t+3} \right]$$

$$= s_{t+2} + 3\sqrt{h_{t+1}} E_t \left[\varepsilon_{t+1} \left(\omega + \alpha h_{t+2} + \beta h_{t+2} + \frac{\gamma}{2} h_{t+2} \right) \right] - \frac{12}{5} \gamma E_t \left[h_{t+2}^{3/2} \right]$$

$$= s_{t+2} + 3\left(\alpha + \beta + \frac{\gamma}{2} \right) \sqrt{h_{t+1}} E_t \left[\varepsilon_{t+1} h_{t+2} \right] - \frac{12}{5} \gamma E_t \left[h_{t+2}^{3/2} \right]$$

$$= s_{t+2} + 3\left(\alpha + \beta + \frac{\gamma}{2} \right) \left(s_{t+2} - s_{t+1} \right) - \frac{12}{5} \gamma E_t \left[h_{t+2}^{3/2} \right]$$

and

$$s_{t+j} = s_{t+j-1} + \left(\alpha + \beta + \frac{\gamma}{2} \right) \left(s_{t+j-1} - s_{t+j-2} \right) - \frac{12}{5} \gamma E_t \left[h_{t+j-1}^{3/2} \right], \quad \forall j \geq 4$$

where $E_t \left[h_{t+j}^{3/2} \right]$ can be approximated to a first order as

$$E_t\left[h_{t+j}^{3/2}\right] \approx \left(\overline{h}^{3/2} - \frac{3}{2}\overline{h}^{3/2}\right) + \frac{3}{2}\overline{h}^{1/2}E_t h_{t+j}$$
$$= k_0 + k_1 E_t h_{t+j}$$

COMPUTATION OF THE CERTAINTY EQUIVALENT RISK-FREE RATE

Given the utility function discussed in this paper, a sequence of portfolio weights $E_t\left[h_{t+j}^{3/2}\right]$ and the actual risk-free rate r^f deliver the following expected utility:

$$U(r^f) = -E\left[\exp\left\{-bw_t r_t\right\}\right]\exp\left\{-br^f\right\} \qquad (4.9)$$

An agent who allocates all of her wealth in the riskless asset at the rate $\tilde{r}^f$ obtains

$$U(\tilde{r}^f) = -\exp\left\{-b\tilde{r}^f\right\} \qquad (4.10)$$

The rate $\tilde{r}^f$ that makes the investor indifferent between (4.9) and (4.10) is computed as

$$U(r^f) = U(\tilde{r}^f)$$
$$-\log E\left[\exp\left\{-bw_t r_t\right\}\right]\exp\left\{-br^f\right\} = -\log\exp\left\{-b\tilde{r}^f\right\}$$
$$-\log E\left[\exp\left\{-bw_t r_t\right\}\right] + br^f = b\tilde{r}^f$$

from which it follows that

$$\tilde{r}^f = r^f + \frac{-\log E[\exp\{-bw_t r_t\}]}{b}$$

REFERENCES

Bansal, R., and A. Yaron (2004). Risks for the long run: A potential resolution of asset pricing puzzles. *Journal of Finance* 59, 1481–1509.

Christoffersen, P., and F.X. Diebold (2006). Financial asset returns, direction-of-change forecasting, and volatility dynamics. *Management Science* 52, 1273–1288.

Diebold, F.X., A. Hickman, A. Inoue, and T. Schuermann (1998). Scale models. *Risk Magazine* 11, 104–107.

Engle, R., and R. Colacito (2006). Testing and valuing dynamic correlation for asset allocation. *Journal of Business and Economic Statistics* 24 (2).

Engle, R., and G. Rangel (2005). The spline garch model for unconditional volatility and its global macroeconomic causes. Working paper.

Fleming, J., C. Kirby, and B. Ostdiek (2001). The economic value of volatility timing. *Journal of Finance* 56, 329–352.

Fleming, J., C. Kirby, and B. Ostdiek (2003). The economic value of volatility timing using realized volatility. *Journal of Financial Economics* 67, 473–509.

Timmermann, A., and M. Guidolin (2006). Term structure of risk under alternative econometric specifications. *Journal of Econometrics*, 131, 285–308.

5. Crisis and Noncrisis Risk in Financial Markets

A Unified Approach to Risk Management

Robert H. Litzenberger and David M. Modest

The litany of financial crises and economic losses caused by failed financial institutions during the last quarter-century has given a major impetus to the design, development, and implementation of robust enterprise-wide risk management systems[1]—the Hunt Brothers silver crisis of 1979/80; the U.S. savings and loan crisis in the 1980s; the Mexican Default and the Latin American Debt Crisis starting in 1982; the failure of Continental Illinois in 1984; the Bank of New York systems failure resulting in a $24 billion overnight overdraft at the Federal Reserve Bank of New York in 1985; the stock market crash of 1987; the equity market and property price collapse in Japan and the bankruptcy of Drexel Burnham in 1990; the Salomon Brothers treasury scandal in 1991; the Metallgesellschaft heating oil trading losses in 1993; the U.S. and European bond market crashes of 1994; the Orange County derivatives losses in 1994; the Mexican devaluation of the peso and the beginning of the tequila crisis in 1994; the Barings failure and Daiwa trading scandal in 1995; the Sumitomo copper metal trading scandal in 1996; the Asia crisis of 1997; the Russia and Long-Term Capital Management crises in 1998; the dramatic stock market

[1] The risk management framework discussed in the paper was developed during our time together at Azimuth Trust in 2003. We are grateful and indebted to all of our Azimuth Trust colleagues for their help in developing the model especially Alex Shapiro and Paul Toldalagi. We would like to thank Amy Litzenberger for editorial assistance, and René Stulz, Darrell Duffie, Philippe Jorion, and the NBER Working Group on the *Risks of Financial Institutions} for helpful comments.*

drop in the wake of 9/11; the Enron bankruptcy in 2001; the Allied Irish Bank trading losses in 2002; the Refco bankruptcy in 2005; the rapid demise of the hedge fund Amaranth in 2006; the subprime, credit, liquidity, and quantitative equity crises of 2007; the continuing contagion of the credit crisis throughout 2008 and into 2009 that resulted in severe declines in real estate values and stock and corporate bond prices, losses to relative value hedge funds and private equity funds, and the collapse, distressed sale and/or bailout of many large financial institutions including Bear Stearns, Lehman, Merrill Lynch, AIG, and Citigroup. However, an important aspect of such crises is often overlooked in enterprise-wide risk management systems: in a crisis period asset return distributions are determined by the interaction of traders liquidating their positions. Historical returns, variances, and covariances have little or no relevance to asset return distributions in crisis periods.[2]

Value-at-risk (VaR) is currently the most popular risk metric used by global financial institutions to report their firm-wide risk exposure.[3] VaR is an estimate of the loss threshold such that at a designated confidence interval, $1 - \alpha$, the probability of a loss greater than the threshold, over a specified horizon, is equal to α (e.g., 1 or 5%). Two main methods are used for computing VaR: a parametric approach and a nonparametric approach. The former is based on the estimated standard deviation of the current portfolio and a parametric assumption about the distribution generating future returns. The commonly used assumption of normality simplifies the analysis, since the sum of normally distributed random variables is normal, and hence the procedure works equally well with individual securities and portfolios. However, this approach does not reflect the empirical observation that returns have fat left tails. The nonparametric approach takes the current portfolio and generates a history of what the profit and loss for this portfolio would have been over a specified past period. To compute the appropriate VaR, one then reads off the relevant percentile from the constructed hypothetical historical P&L distribution. In general, the nonparametric approach is also unable to accurately reflect fat tails because of the relatively short data histories used. Due to these limitations, both approaches are often supplemented with stress tests and scenario analyses.

---

[2] In their classic book, Kindleberger and Aliber (2005) explore scores of global financial crises that have occurred over the last four centuries. Each has its own distinctive flavor, yet they share important traits. They are all marked by dramatic losses of financial wealth and many are accompanied by the ruin of major financial institutions. Despite their regular occurrence, they often appear decades apart and have affected a disparate collection of assets, including stocks, real estate, tulips, canals, commodities, bonds, railroads, precious metals, office buildings, foreign exchange, and golf courses.

[3] Jorion (2007) provides a comprehensive discussion of VaR.

VaR approaches are also deficient in that future price movements often depend on the context of the positions. For instance, consider two stocks involved in a merger arbitrage deal. The future price behavior of a position long the target and short the acquirer is likely to have little to do with how the isolated past return series behaved prior to the merger announcement. One additional shortcoming of the VaR framework is that it does not reflect the actual magnitude of the losses in the lower tail. Expected tail loss (ETL) is therefore a better measure of downside risk than VaR, since it accounts for the distribution of losses in the lower tail. It measures the expected loss conditional on the loss being greater than the specified α loss threshold.[4] The use of ETL coupled with the assumption of normally distributed returns merely applies a multiplier to the standard deviation to generate the risk metric. Hence, its value as a risk measure hinges on the nonnormality of returns and is especially beneficial in the presence of fat left-hand tails.

In response to large losses on proprietary European bond positions in 1994, Goldman Sachs developed an enterprise-wide internal risk management system that aggregated firm-wide trading positions and measured daily VaR based on historical variances and covariances between asset returns—a paramteric VaR approach.[5] In an attempt to capture gradual changes in variances and covariances, exponential declining weights were used in the estimation of the second moments. To account for fat tails, the 99.6 percentile of a mixed normal distribution was used to compute the loss threshold such that each year the daily loss would be expected to exceed the threshold not more than once.[6]

The simple intuitive lesson learned from the stock market crash of 1987 and the bond market crash of 1994 was that firm-wide directional exposure was particularly risky. Relative value trades, on the other hand, with their mean reverting properties and very low (or zero) historical correlations,[7] had very attractive expected return/risk characteristics under most backward-looking VaR paradigms. The result was a global proliferation of a wide range of rela-

[4] ETL also has the advantage of being a coherent measure of risk in the sense of Artzner et al. (1999), whereas VaR is not a coherent risk measure.

[5] While the aggregation of trading exposures across a wide range of trading instruments was a major accomplishment, the shortcomings of this system were exposed by the relative value hedge fund crisis in 1998.

[6] For the purposes of its annual report, Goldman Sachs reports the VaR at the 95% level for a one-day horizon based on a normal distribution. J.P. Morgan (JPM) began reporting VaR in its annual report in 1994. In contrast to Goldman, JPM reports its VaR based on the nonparametric approach using the current positions and a historical simulation of changes in market value over the past twelve months (J.P. Morgan Chase & Company 2005 annual report, p. 76.)

[7] To each other and to directional positions.

tive value trades—with VaR based risk limits implemented at the trader, desk, divisional, and firm-wide levels.

Relative value trading in fixed-income and equity markets was quite profitable over the ensuing few years and proprietary trading positions of investment banks and hedge funds grew rapidly. Long-Term Capital Management (LTCM), for instance, generated 28.15% gross returns for ten months in 1994 after their launch; 58.77% in 1995, and 57.47% in 1996. LTCM's spectacular performance and their notoriety spurred many imitators and capital flocked to these types of trades. Although different models were used to identify attractive trades, very similar positions were established across many different hedge funds and proprietary trading desks. Price aberrations in the cash markets that created relative value trading opportunities were quickly arbitraged away by the large pool of capital dedicated to relative value trades. This resulted in a substantial decline in the realized volatilities and the profitabilities associated with both individual relative value trades and portfolios of relative value trades.

LTCM's gross returns, for example, declined to 25.28% in 1997; and the monthly standard deviation of their returns declined to 1.64% in 1997 compared to 3.46% in 1994.[8] With the benefit of 20/20 hindsight, the reduction in volatilities that occurred in mean reverting trades was a sign of crowded trades, which indicated an *increase* rather than a decrease in catastrophic risk. At the end of 1997, LTCM returned $2.7 billion of capital to its investors—leaving it with an equity capital base of $4.67 billion.[9] At the time, LTCM's risk aggregator (a parametric form of a VaR model using input parameters that were in part based on historical data and in part based on expectations about future risk) forecasted its daily standard deviation of P&L at roughly $60 million.[10] Given the capital base of $4.67 billion, this was equivalent to an annual standard deviation of approximately 20%.[11] As of January 30, 1998, the realized daily volatility of percentage changes in the S&P 500 index during the previous 252 trading days was approximately 19%. Thus, LTCM's forecasted and realized

---

[8] The monthly standard deviation of returns was 1.80% in 1995 and 2.68% in 1996.

[9] Thirty-seven percent of its capital was returned in December 1997. The reduction in the volatility of the relative value trades, in part a reflection of the crowding of the trades, undoubtedly made LTCM more comfortable returning the capital than if volatility had increased.

[10] LTCM's risk aggregator assumed that positions at shorter horizons, such as a month, were more highly correlated than trades at longer horizons, such as over the course of the year. In December 1997, the aggregator predicted a daily standard of $81 million assuming the higher correlations and a daily standard deviation of $60 million at the lower correlations. Until the crisis in the fall, LTCM's risk aggregator consistently predicted higher risk than was actually realized. For instance, in January 1998, the realized daily standard deviation of P&L was $41 million. This information is taken from Modest (2001).

[11] And a realized annual standard deviation of approximately 14% based on the daily realized volatility of $41 million in January 1998.

daily volatilities were quite similar to that of the S&P 500. However, due to the complicated and multilegged structure of many of its trades, the distribution of future potential volatilities was much wider than the S&P 500.

In 1998, a series of events including the voluntary liquidation of the Salomon Brothers arbitrage unit at Citibank, the Russian devaluation of the ruble and default on its internal debt, and a large widening in credit spreads led to losses and increased volatilities of relative value trades.[12] The proliferation of risk management paradigms based on VaR measures, implemented with recent historical return data, had an impact on losses on relative value trades that was analogous to the impact of portfolio insurance on equity price declines in 1987. Initial losses on relative value trades and increases in volatility caused VaR risk limits to be violated and caused further liquidations of relative value trades. Seemingly unrelated trades, that were uncorrelated historically, became highly correlated simply because they were being liquidated simultaneously.[13] The markets for the various components of relative value trades became less liquid and some actually seized up for a period of time. Since firms (1) did not view themselves as price takers, (2) did not know the positions of other firms or their liquidation plans, and hence (3) did not want to *bang the market*, positions were slowly liquidated, which resulted in serial correlations and losses extending over multiple months. Trades that Goldman Sachs held in common with Long-Term Capital Management and likely with many other firms experienced two- and threefold increases in volatility, correlations between returns on these trades increased substantially, and these positions experienced large cumulative losses over a three-month period.

In the summer of 2007, losses in the subprime credit market, extreme movements in credit spreads, and the steep declines in prices of many buyout-related equities led to delevering by several large hedge funds and proprietary trading desks and ultimately to forced liquidations of positions held by many market-neutral quantitative equity strategies. This resulted in price movements far in excess of what could have been reasonably predicted based on past historical data. The extreme magnitudes of the relative price moves in early August are reflected, for example, in the net asset values for the publicly traded: Highbridge Statistical Market Neutral (HSKAX) mutual fund. This fund, between December 1, 2005 and the December 31, 2006, experienced a daily standard deviation of returns of 0.161%. During the seven days between August 2, 2007 and August 10,

---

[12] LTCM, for instance, for the first time lost money for consecutive months in May and June of 1998.

[13] The Brunnermeir and Pedersen (2007) model captures many aspects of this type of phenomenon. Chan et al. (2007) provide insights on how the serial correlation of hedge fund returns can be used to provide insights on the illiquidity of the underlying positons.

2007, the fund had returns equal to −0.25, −0.75, 0.81, −1.26, −2.30, −2.09, and +2.14%. These correspond to the following moves in units of historical standard deviation: −1.54, −4.62, −5.04, −7.82, −14.25, −12.97, and +13.25. Goldman Sach's CFO David Viniar, in commenting on the August 2007 experienced by the firm's flagship quantitative hedge fund, Global Alpha, stated that "We were seeing things that were 25-standard deviation moves, several days in a row."[14] The historical probability distributions in noncrisis periods, which serve as the basis of Viniar's comments and were estimated with many decades of daily historical data, have little or no relevance to this crisis period. The observed daily returns in August were generated by the simultaneous liquidations of similar trading positions by many levered quantitative equity funds and proprietary trading desks. A wide range of seemingly unrelated quantitative equity strategies became correlated because they were being liquidated at the same time. Liquidations increased in intensity from August 2 through August 9 as some highly levered hedge funds were desperate to de-lever and some proprietary trading desks were ordered to liquidate positions to reduce the firms' franchise risks. The post-liquidation recovery only partially mitigated the losses of funds and desks that dramatically reduced their positions at market lows.

Hence, an important lesson from the 1998 and 2007 relative value crises is that variances, covariances, and serial correlations estimated from recent historical return data are misleading indicators of potential losses in *trade-driven* financial crises. Losses can be endogenously caused by crowded trades and the reaction of traders to initial trading losses and increases in market volatility. In retrospect, this should also have been a lesson learned from the 1987 stock market crash (where portfolio insurance was a crowded trade) and the 1994 bond market crash (where the long bond carry trade was a crowded trade). The response of Goldman Sachs and other firms to their experience in 1998 was to place greater reliance on stress tests and scenario analysis over longer time horizons in managing trading risks. For example, a credit spread widening scenario over a three-month horizon was used to set risk limits for Goldman Sachs' credit-sensitive fixed-income positions. The process of establishing trading limits based on stress testing credit spreads established a risk culture at Goldman Sachs that controlled its exposure to the subprime mortgage crisis in 2007 and the resulting contagion effects through early 2009. Unfortunately, such elementary risk controls were apparently not in place at Merrill Lynch, which was sold to Bank of America (who required government support to be induced not to cancel the sale after more information about their portfolio was revealed, and AIG and Citigroup, which only are able to survive based on huge

---

[14] Goldman pays the price of being big," *Financial Times*, August 13, 2007.

government loans. Nevertheless, firms continue to use VaR implemented with historical variances and covariances because of the analytical tractability of this model in aggregating risk across different types of trades; and its mechanistic appeal to regulators.

The present chapter builds on these lessons to develop an analytically tractable risk management metric that more accurately measures potential exposures to financial crises and also captures volatility during noncrisis times. We develop a multiple-regime stress-loss risk framework that assumes markets are characterized by quiescent (noncrisis) periods most of the time; interspersed with infrequent crisis periods where 4–5 sigma events can occur with nonnegligible probabilities. The framework is flexible and can incorporate an arbitrary number of crises. One of the primary lessons of 1998 and 2007 is that returns can be correlated due to the capital underlying a collection of trades (or strategies), regardless of any underlying economic rationale.[15] This is an important feature of our model. We include crises that are directional in nature and capture severe directional moves such as those that occurred in 1994 and 1987, and we incorporate crises that capture strategy-based (or trade-based) crises such as occurred in 1998 and 2007.[16] We also include the possibility of relative value and directional crises occurring together such as in 2008 and early 2009.

A crisis is associated with a negative strategy return and a dramatic increase in volatility where the magnitude of the negative shock depends on many factors, including the liquidity of the instruments underlying the strategy, the aggregate size of the positions pursuing the strategy, the crowdedness of the trades in the strategy, and the trade complexity. When a crisis occurs, all investments with exposure to an affected strategy are impacted causing correlations of returns to tend toward one during crisis periods—an empirical feature that any realistic risk model must capture. Our model also has the desired features: (1) it can accurately predict portfolio volatility during normal, noncrisis times, (2) it captures in a realistic fashion stress moves during crisis periods, (3) it is consistent with the empirical observation that returns in many financial markets are characterized by distributions with fat left tails, and (4) it provides a unified framework for comparing trades whose risk may be composed of different proportions of typical day-to-day noncrisis volatility and crisis risk.

The remainder of the chapter is organized as follows. Section 5.2 presents our model. In section 5.1.1, we characterize financial markets as consisting of

[15] Another lesson, as argued by Soros (2008), is that the price effects in turn affect the fundamentals.
[16] It could be argued that the stock market crash of 1987 was also trade-based, due to the the crowding of the portfolio insurance *trade*, and not based on any change in underlying fundamentals. The bond market crash of 1994 came on the heels of six straight increases in short-term interest rates by the Federal Reserve, but was exacerbated by the proliferation of the long bond carry trade.

quiescent or noncrisis volatility periods and periods of severe market stress, and define the set of feasible states. In section 5.1.2, we discuss the computation of expected tail loss and show that it can be expressed as the probability-weighted average of state contingent put options. Section 5.2 shows how the model can be used to decompose the risk of a portfolio between crisis and noncrisis risk, and how to decompose the strategy (or individual asset) contributions to the two types of risk. The model is also used, in a Black–Litterman spirit, to examine the expected returns that are consistent with a given portfolio allocation and how expected returns would have to change to justify a portfolio tilt away from an initial allocation. In section 5.3, we discuss the practical implementation of the model in the context of a fund of hedge funds manager. Section 5.4 concludes the discussion.

5.1. THE MODEL

5.1.1. CRISIS RISK AND THE STATE SPACE

In this paper, we assume that financial markets are characterized by quiescent, noncrisis periods, infrequently interspersed by crisis periods of severe market stress. Let us assume there are C types of financial crises. For $C > 2$, the number of states, S, is equal to

$$S = C + 2 + \sum_{k=2}^{C-1} \frac{C!}{k!(C-k)!} \tag{5.1}$$

For example, if there are three types of crises, there are eight possible states: one noncrisis state (the quiescent period that occurs most of the time), three single-crisis states, one three-crisis state, and three two-crisis states.[17] In each state, returns are assumed to be generated by a state-dependent normal distribution where the state-dependent moments can vary over time. The state probabilities for a given period, π_s, can be chosen to be consistent with either independently distributed crises or crises that are correlated. These probabilities can also vary over time, although in our implementation we assume they are constant.

Assets impacted by a given type of crisis have their state-dependent standard deviations increase by a crisis multiplier, and suffer a crisis-dependent downward mean shift equal to a Z-value times their state-dependent standard deviation. This downward mean shift is equivalent to a perfectly correlated component of returns. This will cause the correlation of all *assets* impacted by

---

[17] For $C = 1$, $S = 2$: one noncrisis state and one crisis state. For $C = 2$, $S = 4$; one noncrisis state, one two-crisis state, and two single-crisis states.

a particular crisis to tend toward one during the crisis, although they will not be perfectly correlated. In implementing the model, it is natural to think of an *asset* at the primitive level, such as an individual equity or specific bond. However, one of the important lessons of 1998 and 2007 is that forced liquidations can cause *trades* to be correlated and, in fact, send individual *assets* in directions counter to that which would be predicted by the economics driving the security's cash flows.

Take the case of Royal Dutch and Shell Transport in 1998. The Royal Dutch–Shell Transport group of companies was created in February 1907 when the Royal Dutch Petroleum Company of the Netherlands and the Shell Transport and Trading Company Ltd of the United Kingdom merged their operations. The terms of the merger gave 60% of the new company to the Dutch shareholders and 40% to the British holders. Until July 20, 2005, the group was a dual-listed company. Royal Dutch was a member of the S&P 500 and traded primarily in New York and the Netherlands. Shell Transport traded primarily in London although ADRs did trade in New York. Royal Dutch tended to trade at a premium to Shell Transport (relative to the 60/40 split of earnings) in part because of its inclusion in the S&P 500. LTCM had a $2.1 billion dollar arbitrage position: long Shell Transport and short Royal Dutch. In 1997, the average discount between the two sets of shares was less than 8.83%.[18] During LTCM's difficulties in the August–October 1998 period, the discount expanded to a peak of 18.53%—as the market became concerned LTCM would be forced to liquidate its position rapidly.[19] Thus, the 1998 crisis resulted in two nearly identical assets moving in opposite directions. This phenomenon displayed itself again with great force in August 2007 when equities typically held long by market-neutral equity hedge funds plummeted and equities typically held short by the same funds rose dramatically—with overall market levels relatively unaffected. This suggests the need for a risk system to be focused not only on individual assets, but also on *trades*.

For the purposes of illustrating our model, in section 5.4, we assume that the probability of a given state occurring, π_s, is constant over time. A period in our model must thus be no shorter than the typical length of a crisis event—to insure that the probability of being in a crisis at date $t + 1$ is independent of whether a crisis occurred at date t. We choose a period to equal a quarter. A quarter horizon seems sufficient to allow for the prolonged impact of a crisis on illiquid trades and also reflects the importance of the investment banks'

---

[18] The percentage spread is defined as the market value of Royal Dutch in USD less 1.5 times the market value of Shell Transport in USD divided by 1.5 times the market value of Shell Transport in USD. The calculation is done using closing ADR prices from New York.

[19] The peak spread was reached on October 8, 1998.

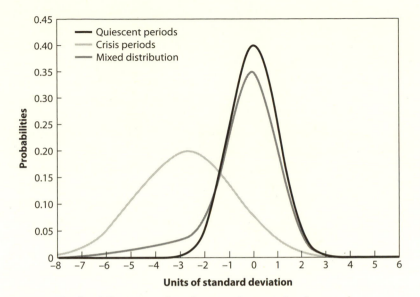

Figure 5.1. Graphical illustration of simple two-regime stress loss framework.

quarterly reporting cycles. Figure 5.1 graphically illustrates the conditional state-dependent and unconditional returns distributions in a simple two-state stress-loss framework.

The lighter-colored dashed distribution is the standardized distribution *conditional* on noncrisis; the darker dotted distribution is the standardized distribution *conditional* on a crisis. The *conditional* crisis distribution reflects (1) a downward mean shift to reflect the downward *perfectly correlated component* of a crisis, and (2) an increase in volatility relative to the nonncrisis state. The distribution drawn in solid black is the unconditional distribution that is the probability-weighted distribution over the noncrisis (quiescent) and crisis states.

5.1.2. CRISIS RISK AND EXPECTED TAIL LOSS

A natural measure of crisis risk in our model, as discussed above, is the expected tail loss (ETL) at a prespecified percentile level, $(1 - \alpha)$, and over a designated horizon, τ.[20] The ETL at the 95% percentile level is depicted in Figure 5.2.

---

[20] For instance, as noted in their annual reports, Goldman Sachs focuses on VaR at a $1 - \alpha$ percentile level of 95% and a daily horizon; J.P. Morgan Chase reports its VaR at a $1 - \alpha$ percentile level of 99% and the same daily horizon.

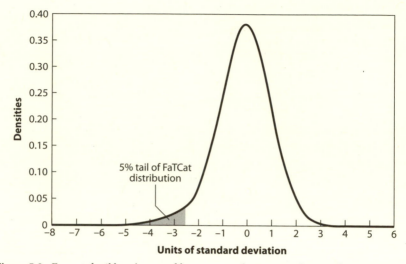

Figure 5.2. Expected tail loss (expected losses are on the Y axis and units of standard deviation on the X axis).

Our framework allows for the aggregation of ETL across assets and the measurement of the contribution of individual assets (or strategies) to portfolio ETLs. Under the assumption of normality within each state, the solution for the state-contingent ETL is similar to the well-known formulation for the value of a put option when asset returns are normally distributed. The overall expected tail loss is expressed as the probability-weighted average of state contingent put options. The assumptions of state-dependent normal distributions combined with a finite number of crisis classifications result in a well-defined fat tail distribution as the number of asset increases. This contrasts with the use of mixed normal distributions with independent mixing probabilities across assets, where the limiting distribution is normal as the number of assets increases.

More formally, the ETL, on portfolio (or asset) p may be expressed as

$$\text{ETL} \equiv \mathbf{E}\left[\tilde{R}_p \mid \tilde{R}_p \le A\right] = \sum_s^S \pi_s \mathbf{E}\left[\tilde{R}_p \mid \tilde{R}_p \le A, s\right] \qquad (5.2)$$

where

S is the number of states
π_s is the probability of state s occurring
R^p is the portfolio rate of return in excess of the risk-free rate
$\mu_{p,s}$ is the portfolio mean rate of return in state s

$\sigma_{p,s}$ is standard deviation of the portfolio's return in state s

A is a return threshold that depends on the percentile choice, α[21]

Substituting for the expected value operator, ETL can be rewritten:

$$\text{ETL} = \sum_{s}^{S} \pi_s \int_{-\infty}^{A} xf\left(x, \mu_{p,s}, \sigma_{p,s}\right) dx / \alpha \qquad (5.3)$$

where $f(\cdot)$ denotes the standard *state-dependent* normal probability density function of the normalized portfolio returns.

Analytically integrating the right-hand side of equation 5.3 gives the closed-form solution for the expected tail loss—*conditional* on A, the α percentile return threshold for the mixed normal distribution:

$$\text{ETL} = \sum_{s}^{S} \pi_s \left[\mu_{p,s} F\left(\frac{A - \mu_{p,s}}{\sigma_{p,s}}\right) - \sigma_{p,s} f\left(\frac{A - \mu_{p,s}}{\sigma_{p,s}}\right) \right] / \alpha \qquad (5.4)$$

where $F(\cdot)$ denotes the standard *state-dependent* normal cumulative distribution functions of the normalized portfolio returns.[22]

The threshold A can be estimated numerically using

$$\sum_{s}^{S} \pi_s F\left(A, \mu_{p,s}, \sigma_{p,s}\right) = \alpha \qquad (5.5)$$

The 1980s and 1990s were very turbulent times in global financial markets. Especially for those participants active in the markets, it seemed that hundred-year floods were occurring at least every five years. At Goldman Sachs, there was considerable discussion about the frequency of recurrence of such events for the purpose of determining the adequacy of the noncrisis profitability levels of different trading businesses. One quarter in five years (20 quarters) was subjectively determined as the basis for determining which trading activities were sufficiently profitable to continue. In this paper, we make the same assumption and assume a 5% probability of a given crisis in any quarter, $\alpha = 0.05$, in implementing the model.

---

[21] Although A should more formally be written $A(\alpha)$, for simplicity of notation we write it as A. A is also an implicit function of the state-dependent means and standard deviation as shown in relation 5.4. A also corresponds to what is called the $(1 - \alpha)$ percentile VaR.

[22] This derivation is similar to Brennan's (1979) derivation of the value of a call option under normally distributed returns and exponential utility. Under risk neutrality, the product of alpha and the ETL formula is the forward value of a put option that exercises when the price is below A, but does not require the payment of A.

5.2. CONTRIBUTIONS OF INDIVIDUAL ASSETS TO PORTFOLIO RISK

5.2.1. MARGINAL CONTRIBUTION TO EXPECTED TAIL LOSS

Consider portfolio $p^\dagger$ that has a portfolio weight of w_i in the ith asset and $(1-w_i)$ in portfolio p. The state-dependent mean, $\mu_{p\dagger,s}$, and standard deviation, $\sigma_{p\dagger,s}$, of this new portfolio are

$$\mu_{p\dagger,s} = w_i \mu_{i,s} + (1-w_i)\mu_{p,s} \tag{5.6}$$

and

$$\sigma_{p\dagger,s} = \left[w_i^2 \sigma_{i,s}^2 + (1-w_i)^2 \sigma_{p,s}^2 + 2w_i(1-w_i)\sigma_{ip,s} \right]^{1/2} \tag{5.7}$$

where $\sigma_{ip,s}$ denotes the state-dependent covariance between the returns on asset i and the returns on portfolio p.

To evaluate the marginal impact of the ith asset on the ETL of the portfolio, equation 5.4 is differentiated with respect to w_i subject to the constraint given by 5.5 and evaluated at $w_i = 0$. The following expression defines the sensitivity of the portfolio's expected tail losses to changes in the portfolio weights:

$$\left. \frac{d\text{ETL}}{dw_i} \right|_{w_{i=0}} = \frac{1}{\alpha} \sum_s^S \pi_s \left\{ \left(\frac{d\mu_{p\dagger,s}}{dw_i} \right) F(\cdot) + \mu_{p\dagger,s} \left(\frac{dF(\cdot)}{dw_i} \right) \right.$$
$$\left. \left. - \left(\frac{d\sigma_{p\dagger,s}}{dw_i} \right) f(\cdot) - \sigma_{p\dagger,s} \left(\frac{df(\cdot)}{dw_i} \right) \right\} \right|_{w_{i=0}} \tag{5.8}$$

where the derivatives with respect to the portfolio weights are evaluated at $w_i = 0$. The differentiation of equation 5.4 with respect to w_i is a closed-form solution holding A constant. While A must be solved for numerically based on constraint 5.5, the implicit differentiation of A based on 5.5 can be done analytically, as shown in the appendix.

The fractional contribution of the ith asset to the ETL of portfolio $p^\dagger$ is equal to the product of its portfolio weight, w_{ip}, and its *expected tail loss* beta with respect to portfolio $p^\dagger$, which is given by

$$\beta_{i,p\dagger}^{\text{ETL}} = 1 + \frac{\left. \frac{d\text{ETL}}{dw_i} \right|_{w_{i=0}}}{\text{ETL}} \tag{5.9}$$

The calculation of fractional contributions to portfolio ETL is analogous to the calculation of the marginal contribution of the ith asset to the variance of a portfolio as the product of its portfolio weight, w_{ip}, and its volatility beta, $\beta_{i,p\dagger}$ (σ^2), where

$$\beta^{\sigma}_{i,pt} = 1 + \frac{\left.\dfrac{d\sigma_{pt}}{dw_i}\right|_{w_i=0}}{\sigma_{pt}} \tag{5.10}$$

However, unlike the more familiar volatility beta, the ETL beta cannot be estimated as a slope coefficient of a least-squares regression.

5.2.2. The Optimal Portfolio and Implied Risk Premia

Consider the optimization problem of an investor whose utility function trades off expected excess return and expected tail loss, and poses her investment decision as a series of one-period problems.[23] Since a portfolio's risk premium (R_p) and ETL per dollar of equity are proportional to leverage, the *unlevered* portfolio with the highest ratio of risk premium to ETL when combined with borrowing or lending is optimal. This is depicted in figure 5.3, where the tangency portfolio is denoted by p^*.

The contributions of individual assets to the portfolio's ETL are used to derive the necessary and sufficient conditions for maximizing this reward-to-risk ratio. The first-order conditions for an optimal portfolio are

$$\frac{E_i(p^*)}{\beta_i^{ETL}} = \frac{E_j(p^*)}{\beta_j^{ETL}} = E_{p^*} \qquad \forall i,j \tag{5.11}$$

where p^* is the optimal tangency portfolio and the *crisis* betas reflect marginal contributions of the individual assets contribution to the portfolio's ETL, and $E_i(p^*)$ is the expected return on asset i that is consistent with portfolio p^* being the optimal portfolio.

An unconstrained mean-variance optimizer is highly sensitive to small differences in expected returns in that relatively these differences can produce portfolios with extreme weights.[24] Hence, solving for optimal portfolio weights is not a well-posed problem in that the results are highly unstable. Black and Litterman (1990) proposed an alternative approach that determines the necessary return forecast to justify a portfolio tilt. The approach of the current chapter is in the spirit of their paper. Let p represent a base or reference portfolio. Given the choice of portfolio p, the first-order conditions for the optimal

---

[23] In practice, some asset owners may care about both expected tail loss and portfolio volatility during normal times. Investment banks, for instance, typically care about expected tail loss—as it can threaten the viability of the firm's future. They also care about expected quarter-to-quarter volatility of trading profits and losses, since equity analysts use this as a gauge of management's risk management prowess. In this chapter, for simplicity, we assume that ETL is the sole relevant measure of portfolio risk.

[24] See, for instance, Best and Grauer (1991).

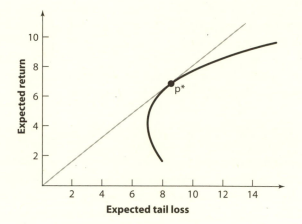

Figure 5.3. Expected return (Y axis)/expected tail loss frontier (X axis).

portfolio weights in equation 5.11 imply the risk premia for each asset that are necessary for the portfolio weights to be optimal.

Possible choices for the base portfolio p include the market portfolio of all assets (including hedge funds and other alternative assets), a hedge fund market portfolio such as the Morgan Stanley Capital International (MSCI) asset-weighted hedge fund index, or a fund of hedge fund's existing portfolio. The first choice is appropriate for analyzing the portfolio of a high net worth investor and the first-order conditions may be interpreted as market equilibrium conditions under the assumption of identical beliefs across investors. This gives a CAPM in expected return–ETL space. The second choice is appropriate for an enhanced index fund of hedge funds that views its mandate as determining hedge fund strategy tilts from the MSCI strategy weights that would increase the portfolio's risk premium per unit of ETL, $E_p/$ETL, analogous to the Sharpe ratio in mean–standard deviation space.[25] The final choice is appropriate for a fund of hedge funds manager desiring to increase the $E_p/$ETL ratio through reallocating either hedge fund strategy weights or hedge fund manager weights.

Consider a candidate portfolio p^* that a manager is considering as an alternative to the base portfolio p. For p^* to be a portfolio optimum, $E_i(p^*)$ has to equal the Bayesian posterior estimator of the risk premium for asset i. Thus, the portfolio equilibrium conditions on risk premia at the new equilibrium are the implicit posterior Bayesian estimator. This estimator has to also be the minimum variance convex combination of the Bayesian prior, $E_i(p)$ (which is equal

---

[25] The risk premium refers to the expected return over the relevant risk-free rate.

to the original risk premium implied by the original base portfolio being an equilibrium portfolio), and the forecasted risk premium, $E_i(f)$ (sample estimator). Assuming that the forecast error of the prior and the sample estimators are independent, the Bayesian posterior estimators may be expressed as

$$E_i(p^*) = \frac{E_i(p) + k^2 E_i(f)}{1+k^2} \qquad \forall i \qquad (5.12)$$

where k is the confidence in the forecasted risk premium (sample estimator) relative to the base equilibrium risk premium (prior estimator), which is measured as their relative standard error of forecasts.[26] When $k = 0$ and there is zero confidence in the forecasted risk premium, the posterior estimate is simply the base equilibrium/prior risk premium. For $k = 1$ equal confidence is placed in the forecasted risk premium and the prior equilibrium risk premium and they are equally weighted. Similarly, as $k \to \infty$ and the confidence in the prior equilibrium risk premium, $1/k$ approaches zero, the posterior estimate converges to the forecasted (sample) risk premium.

Since the implied equilibrium risk premia for both the base portfolio and the reallocated portfolio are known from the first-order conditions and the base portfolio's risk premium/ETL ratio, the equation may be solved for the implied forecasted risk premia necessary for the forecast to be consistent with the new portfolio being an equilibrium portfolio:

$$E_i(f) = E_i(p^*) + \frac{1}{k^2}\left[E_i(p^*) - E_i(p)\right] \qquad \forall i \qquad (5.13)$$

5.3. FUND OF HEDGE FUNDS IMPLEMENTATION

This multiple-state stress-loss model was developed in 2003 during our time together at Azimuth Trust, a hedge fund of funds. The need for a model like this is apparent from a cursory examination of the fat left tails associated with hedge fund strategy returns. Consider, for instance, the historical volatility of returns for the fixed income arbitrage strategy. During the period from 1990 to 2006, this strategy had annual volatility of returns equal to 4.15%.[27] Coupled with the assumption of normally distributed returns, this implies a maximum predicted three-month loss of −4.30% during any given five-year period. This compares with the −13.96% that was experienced in the fall of 1998. The returns

---

[26] Let $\sigma_i(f)$ denote the standard error of the sample/manager forecast and $\sigma_i(p)$ denote the standard error of prior forecast. k is then given by $(1/\sigma_i(f))/(1/\sigma_i(p)) = \sigma_i(p)/\sigma_i(f)$.

[27] The data are taken from *Hedge Fund Research* for the January 1990–May 2006 period. The annual volatility of the returns presumes the monthly returns are serially correlated over time.

for credit and distressed security hedge fund strategies show a similar pattern: annual volatility of –5.94%, a predicted maximum three-month loss of –6.14% based on normally distributed returns, and a realized worst three-month loss of –12.82%.

While the model presented above is sufficiently general to handle an arbitrary number of types of crises, in practice the implementation of the model is more straightforward with a small number of crises. For example, Azimuth Trust implemented the model with three types of crises: (1) a relative value hedge fund crisis, (2) an equity market collapse, and (3) a macroeconomic hedge fund crisis. Our approach at Azimuth Trust was to use this framework to determine strategy allocations to the different hedge fund strategies. Once strategy allocations were determined, we attempted to find the best collection of funds that would give us the desired strategy exposures.

Each hedge fund that is affected by a given type of crisis has its standard deviation go up by a fund-specific crisis multiplier.[28] The standard deviations of non-affected funds are unchanged.[29] The portfolio of hedge funds' state-dependent standard deviation is calculated using the hedge funds' state-dependent standard deviations and an unchanged correlation matrix. The *perfectly correlated* component of a crisis is modeled as a downward mean shift for each affected fund that is equal to 1.645 times its state-dependent crisis standard deviation. The portfolio mean is calculated by weighting the noncrisis means of unaffected funds and the crisis means for funds affected by the crisis. The crisis multiplier for an individual hedge fund is subjectively determined based on many factors, including (1) the liquidity of the underlying instruments, (2) the size of its positions, (3) the crowdedness of the trades, (4) the complexity of its trades, (5) the amount of leverage used by the funds, and (6) the funds' risk management policy.

One of the important lessons from 1998 and 2007 is that hedges, which from an underlying fundamental perspective should be expected to reduce risk, can in crises serve to exacerbate trading losses. Consider the case of convertible bond arbitrage in 1998. One sensible way to hedge a long convertible bond position is to use swaps to hedge the interest rate exposure, the underlying stock

---

[28] Hedge funds may be impacted by more than one crisis. Consider a long/short equity hedge fund that operates with a net long exposure of 35%. This fund can be expected to be impacted by both a relative value hedge fund crisis, which will affect the hedged part of its portfolio, and an equity market collapse, which will severely affect is net long exposure.

[29] It is sensible to think of an individual hedge fund's standard deviation as consisting of a systematic part that is a result of exposure to one or more strategies, and a fund-specific idiosyncratic part. The idiosyncratic part should reflect both idiosyncratic market risk factors (e.g., risk concentration), and operational and credit risk exposures.

to hedge the net delta, index options to hedge exposure to aggregate changes in the level of volatility, and a credit instrument to hedge the credit risk. In the fall of 1998, one would have been better off not hedging the aggregate vega exposure of convertible positions as the implied volatility of convertibles dramatically contracted while at the same time the implied volatilities of index options dramatically increased.[30] This is an example of why more complex trades can be expected to behave worse in a crisis and why they require a higher crisis multiplier. In a similar spirit, more crowded trades, trades that are larger in absolute size, and trades in more illiquid securities can also be expected to be subject to higher crisis losses and hence warrant a higher crisis multiplier—as forced liquidation for liquidity or risk reasons are more likely to lead to distressed selling.

One of the nice features of our multiple-regime stress-loss framework is that it allows a decomposition of the risk of the portfolio by both contribution to ETL and contribution to noncrisis portfolio volatility in a consistent unified framework. This decomposition analysis is presented in table 5.1. Overall, the portfolio has an expected volatility of returns of 4.5% per annum and an expected tail loss of −5.6%.[31] The table contains information on the hedge fund strategy weights for the portfolio,[32] the strategy expected volatilities, which are a subjective input to the model,[33] the expected maximum three-month stress loss,[34] the contribution of each strategy to the portfolio's ETL and volatility, the strategy ETL and volatility betas, and the set of expected excess returns (over Libor) that are consistent with this portfolio being optimally constructed.

It is interesting to contrast the risk contributions of the global macro and fixed-income arbitrage strategies to the portfolio's overall risk. In this example, 21.00% of the fund's assets are invested in global macro strategies. Although

[30] This reflected LTCM's significant long position in convertibles and its short position in index volatility, especially at the longer end of the volatility term structure.

[31] Given a volatility of 4.5% and the assumption of normally distributed returns, the expected tail loss would be −4.6%. As noted above, the ETL measures the actual magnitude of the expected tail loss, whereas the traditional VaR measure only provides a loss threshold. Based on the multiple-state stress-loss model, the traditional 95% one-quarter VaR is −4.4%. Given an assumption of normality, the 95% one-quarter VaR would be −3.7%.

[32] These weights roughly corresponded to the asset-weighted weights in the MSCI hedge fund index as of January 2007. We have reallocated funds from their multiprocess category into other hedge fund strategies. We assume that the global macro strategy is affected by its own macroeconomic crisis; long/short equity and event-driven strategies are affected by an equity market crisis; and the remaining strategies are impacted by a relative value hedge fund crisis.

[33] As discussed by Chan et al. (2007), the monthly returns of many hedge fund strategies exhibit significant serial correlation. Our subjective expected volatilities are a weighted combination of the standard volatility estimator and a synchronicity-adjusted volatility estimator.

[34] This is also an input to the model and depends on our subjective estimate of the strategy crisis multiplier. The factors that are important in determining the appropriate multiplier were discussed above.

TABLE 5.1

Hedge Fund Strategies Asset Allocation Example

Strategy	$ Allocation	Strategy expected volatility	Strategy ETL	Contribution to portfolio ETL	βETL	Contribution to portfolio volatility	βσ	Implied expected excess return
Global macro	21.00%	6.00%	–8.00%	16.12%	0.77	23.99%	1.14	4.90%
Long/short equity	41.02%	5.50%	–7.00%	39.80%	0.97	48.05%	1.17	6.20%
Credit and distressed securities	17.68%	4.50%	–9.00%	24.40%	1.38	15.96%	0.90	8.90%
Fixed income arbitrage	5.75%	2.50%	–8.00%	6.57%	1.14	1.35%	0.24	7.40%
Convertible and volatility arbitrage	5.27%	4.50%	–7.00%	4.83%	0.92	2.88%	0.55	5.90%
Statistical arbitrage	3.59%	2.50%	–4.00%	1.83%	0.51	0.87%	0.24	3.30%
Event-driven and merger arbitrage	5.70%	6.00%	–8.00%	6.45%	1.13	6.89%	1.21	7.30%

global macro strategies tend to have relatively high volatility, they tend to perform well in stress periods when asset prices tend to move in a sustained manner. Thus, global macro accounts for 16.12% of the portfolio's expected tail loss compared to 23.99% of the portfolio's volatility during noncrisis periods. Fixed income arbitrage behaves in a very different manner. As table 5.1 illustrates, 5.75% of the fund's assets are invested in fixed-income arbitrage strategies. This investment accounts for 6.57% of the portfolio's expected tail loss, but only 1.35% of the portfolio's volatility during noncrisis periods. The largest category of hedge funds in the MSCI index is long/short equity hedge funds, which include funds with a significant long bias, market-neutral funds, and funds with a persistent short bias.[35] Those type of funds account for 41.02% of the dollar portfolio allocation. Their contribution to ETL and portfolio volatility are 39.80 and 48.05%, respectively.

The strategy ETL and volatility betas, as defined in equations 5.9 and 5.10 and also presented in table 5.1, are a different way of representing strategy's contributions to the portfolio's ETL and standard deviation. The strategies with the two lowest ETL betas are statistical arbitrage (0.51) and global macro (0.77). Given its low $ allocation, a marginal increase in the allocation to this strategy has very little impact on the portfolio's overall ETL. A marginal increase in the allocation to global macro has relatively little impact on the ETL because it is impacted by its own macroeconomic crisis and provides diversification against relative value hedge fund and equity crises. The two strategies with the highest ETL betas are credit and distressed securities (1.38) and fixed-income arbitrage (1.14). This reflects the size of their losses during relative value crises and the importance of relative value hedge fund crises in determining the portfolio's overall ETL. While fixed-income arbitrage has one of the largest ETL betas, no strategy has a lower volatility beta (0.24)—reflecting its modest portfolio weight and its volatility during noncrisis periods. The big contributors to the portfolio's volatility are event-driven and merger arbitrage with a volatility beta of 1.21 and long/short equity with a volatility beta of 1.17. Global macro's volatility beta is also above average at 1.14—reflecting a relatively high $ allocation and high volatility during noncrisis periods.

Given a set of assumptions about the noncrisis standard deviations, the correlations of strategy returns, the crisis multipliers, and a choice of base portfolio p, our framework can be used, as discussed above, to generate the set of implied expected returns that are consistent with the given portfolio weights being optimal. The results of this exercise are also presented in table 5.1. The last column of numbers in table 5.1 provides the implied expected excess returns that are

---

[35] On average, funds in this category have a beta that is roughly 1/3 of the S&P 500.

TABLE 5.2
Portfolio Tilts and Required Excess Returns: Equal Confidence in Forecast and Prior

Strategy	−50% Portfolio weight	−25% Portfolio weight	Base implied excess return	+25% Portfolio weight	+50% Portfolio weight
Global macro	0.8%	3.4%	4.9%	6.3%	7.5%
Long/short equity	3.3%	5.1%	6.2%	7.7%	8.6%
Credit and distressed securities	6.0%	7.6%	8.9%	9.9%	10.7%
Fixed-income arbitrage	6.4%	6.9%	7.4%	7.8%	8.3%
Convertible and volatility arbitrage	5.5%	5.7%	5.9%	6.1%	6.2%
Statistical arbitrage	3.2%	3.25%	3.3%	3.35%	3.4%
Event-driven and merger arbitrage	6.9%	7.1%	7.3%	7.5%	7.6%

consistent with the given strategy portfolio weights being optimal—given that the overall expected return on the portfolio is 6.4%. Fixed-income arbitrage accounts for 5.75% of the dollar investment in this portfolio and 6.57% of the portfolio's expected tail loss. The table indicates that the implied expected excess return for fixed-income arbitrage is 7.4% over the riskless rate (Libor). This expected return makes the 5.75% portfolio weight optimal, in the context of the other holdings, and assuming the manager makes her investment decision solely on the basis of expected excess return and ETL. If, instead, the investor made her investment decision solely on the basis of expected excess return and volatility, the implied expected excess return for fixed-income arbitrage would be less than 100 basis points over Libor. Global macro is a strategy that provides good diversification during relative value hedge fund crises although it contributes significantly to the normal month-to-month volatility of portfolio returns (23.99%). For this portfolio construction to be optimal, this strategy must yield an expected excess return of 4.9%—which reflects its low contribution to the portfolio's ETL.

As discussed section 5.2.2, this framework can be used to guide a fund of hedge funds manager who takes the MSCI hedge fund index as a benchmark and attempts to add value through strategy tilts and asset allocation. Table 5.1 presents, in the context of our risk model, the implied risk premia that are consistent with the MSCI hedge fund strategy weights being optimal. For portfolio p^* to be an optimal improvement over the benchmark, the implied risk premia for each strategy in the new portfolio ($E_i(p^*)$) has to equal the Bayesian posterior estimator of the risk premium for asset i given by equation 5.12. Tables 5.2 and 5.3 present the implied risk premia required to tilt away from the MSCI

TABLE 5.3

Portfolio Tilts and Required Excess Returns: Confidence in Forecast Is One-half of Prior

Strategy	−50% Portfolio weight	−25% Portfolio weight	Base implied excess return	+25% Portfolio weight	+50% Portfolio weight
Global macro	−3.2%	1.0%	4.9%	8.5%	11.4%
Long/short equity	−4.7%	1.4%	6.2%	9.8%	12.2%
Credit and distressed securities	1.8%	5.7%	8.9%	11.4%	13.4%
Fixed-income arbitrage	4.9%	6.2%	7.4%	8.5%	9.6%
Convertible and volatility arbitrage	5.0%	5.5%	5.9%	6.3%	6.7%
Statistical srbitrage	3.1%	3.2%	3.3%	3.4%	3.5%
Event-driven and merger arbitrage	6.3%	6.8%	7.3%	7.7%	8.2%

strategy weights under two different assumptions: (1) equal confidence in the forecasted risk premia (sample estimator) relative to the base equilibrium risk premia (prior estimator), i.e., $k = 1$, (table 5.2); and (2) where the confidence in the forecast is one-half the prior, i.e., $k = \frac{1}{2}$ (table 5.3).[36]

The first rows of tables 5.2 and 5.3 present the implied risk premia required for tilting away from the MSCI strategy allocation of 21% to global macro. An investor requires a higher expected return to justify a greater allocation to global macro and a lower expected return to justify a smaller allocation. As table 5.2 indicates, increasing the strategy weight for global macro from 21 to 26.25% (a 25% increase in portfolio weight) is justified if an investor expects the excess return on the strategy to be 6.3% rather than 4.9%—assuming equal confidence in the forecast and in the prior. If the investor has less confidence in her forecast, the required expected risk premia must be higher. This is illustrated in comparing the corresponding risk premia in tables 5.2 and 5.3. In table 5.3, where $k = \frac{1}{2}$, the risk premia required to justify a 25% increase in strategy weight is 8.5%—220 basis points larger than the corresponding risk premium in table 5.2.

The risk premia in table 5.2 show that there is an important and intuitive relation between the changes in risk premia required to justify various portfolio tilts and (1) the size of the base strategy allocation and (2) the nature of its crisis exposure. In general, strategies with small portfolio allocations (and hence

---

[36] When the portfolio weight is shifted away from a strategy, we assume it is proportionally reallocated to the other strategies.

small impacts on the overall portfolio ETL) require relatively small changes in risk premia to justify tilts compared to strategies with larger allocations. For example, the strategy with the smallest base allocation is statistical arbitrage (3.2%). It takes only a 5-basis-point risk premium change to justify either a 25% increase or decrease in its strategy allocation. Contrast this with the strategy with the largest allocation that is also affected by relative value hedge fund crises: credit and distressed securities arbitrage. Table 5.2 shows that it would require a 100-basis-point increase in risk premia (from 8.9 to 9.9%) to justify a 25% increase in the allocation to the credit strategy and a 130-basis-point decrease in risk premia (from 8.9 to 7.6%) to justify a 25% decrease. The largest MSCI strategy allocation is to the long/short equity category, 41.02%. A 25% increase in the allocation to this strategy requires a relatively large 150-basis-point increase in risk premia (from 6.2 to 7.7%) and a corresponding decrease in allocation would require a 110-basis-point decrease (from 6.2 to 5.1%) in risk premia to justify the tilt.

The increases and decreases in risk premia required to justify the portfolio tilts in table 5.3, when there is less confidence in the forecast relative to the prior, are significantly more pronounced than the corresonding changes in premia reported in table 5.2. In fact, negative risk premia are required to justify 50% decreases in strategy allocations to global macro and long/short equity. Similar intuition drives both of these results. Global macro is the only strategy affected by a macroeconomic crisis in this implementation of the model. Since the probabilities of a given crisis occurring are assumed to be independent, global macro provides a very important diversification function for hedge fund investors. Hence, to diminish its portfolio allocation by 50% (from 21 to 10.5%), one would have to expect the strategy to earn 320 basis points *less* than the riskless rate—otherwise, it would be optimal to have greater exposure. Long/short equity has the largest allocation in the MSCI asset-weighted index, with an allocation of 41%. A decrease of 50% in this allocation and the concomitant reallocation to the other strategies would dramatically increase the portfolio's exposure to both relative value hedge fund crises and macroeconomic crises. Hence, an investor would have to expect a risk premium 470 basis point less than Libor to justify a portfolio tilt reducing exposure to long/short equity by 50%. The other numbers in table 5.3 also show more dramatic swings than those in table 5.2, but are less noteworthy.

Although it is beyond the scope of this chapter, the same framework could be used to analyze the contribution of individual hedge funds to the portfolio's ETL and portfolio's volatility, and to the strategy's ETL and the strategy's volatility. In applying the framework to individual hedge funds, it is natural to think of some portion of an individual hedge fund's returns coming from a systematic component, the strategy returns, and some portion coming from an idiosyncratic component. This suggests, as mentioned above, that the funds' expected volatilities will depend on both the forecasted strategy and idiosyncratic volatilities. These idiosyncratic volatilities will presumably reflect fund-specific market, operational, and credit risk factors.[37]

5.4. CONCLUDING REMARKS

In this chapter, we have developed a multiple-regime stress-loss risk framework that incorporates the idea that financial markets are characterized by quiescent periods most of the time, interspersed by occasional periods of crisis. The framework allows an arbitrary number of crises and permits crises that are both directional in nature and crises that may be associated with trades— building on one of the central lessons of past financial crises: that positions may be correlated not only because of the underlying economic fundamentals but because the capital across trades is correlated. The crisis periods are characterized by a sharp decline in returns and periods of increased volatility. The returns distributions, conditional on a given crisis, are assumed to be normally distributed. The unconditional distribution of returns, which is a mixture of normal distributions, has fat left tails that characterize unconditional empirical returns distributions. The risk framework is able to capture, in a *unified* setting, noncrisis period volatility during typical periods and stress losses during crisis periods. This stands in sharp contrast to most practitioner risk management frameworks, which use VaR to measure potential losses during normal periods and then supplement it with ad hoc stress-loss scenarios.

Our risk management framework requires calibration based on subjective *ex ante* assessments of crisis probabilities and stress losses during crises. The rareness of crisis events makes it virtually impossible to estimate these probabilities exclusively based on past data. In addition, the changing nature of financial crises—in large part due to the rapid pace of innovation in financial markets— makes it extremely difficult to model losses during crisis periods solely on the basis of past data and without regard to the structure of current *trades*.[38] For an

---

[37] In practice, idiosyncratic risk can be quite important given many of the notable hedge fund failures of the two decades such as: the Granite Fund (1994), Long-term Capital Management (1998), Manhattan Fund (2000), Maricopa Funds (2000), Lipper & Company (2002), Beacon Hill Asset Management (2002), Eifuku Master Fund (2002), Lancer Offshore Fund (2003), Millenium Partners (2003), Bailey Coates Cromwell Fund (2005), Aman Capital (2005), MotherRock (2006), and Amaranth (2006).

[38] The philosophy underlying our risk management framework thus contrasts sharply with the extreme value theory literature, which seeks to improve estimation of extreme tail probabilities solely based on historical asset returns.

investor in hedge funds, the potential losses are likely to depend on many factors, including the liquidity of the financial assets underlying the strategies, the aggregate position sizes pursuing the strategy, the crowdedness of the trades, and the complexity of the trades.

One natural measure of risk in our framework is expected tail loss ETL. We show that for an investor who trades off expected excess returns and ETL, the first-order portfolio optimality conditions require the ratio of expected excess return to ETL beta to be equal for each asset in the portfolio. In a world of identical investors, an ETL CAPM would hold rather than the usual Sharpe-Lintner-Mossin CAPM. We apply the framework to the portfolio problem of a fund of hedge funds investor, and show how the framework can be used to decompose the risk of the portfolio and derive the implied expected excess returns for each hedge fund strategy that is consistent with a set of portfolio weights being optimal. We also analyze how an investor can combine subjective return forecasts with prior beliefs implied by a benchmark portfolio to tilt strategy allocations in an optimal and internally consistent manner.

In this implementation, we assume that a period is a quarter, the occurrence of different types of crises are independent, the probability of a crisis is time and state invariant, the state-dependent moments of the distribution are constant over time, and there are three types of crises. However, the framework is flexible: it allows for multiple crises, and the probabilities of the states of the world and the moments of the returns distributions can be made to be time varying. We also presumed that the manager of the fund, in constructing her optimal portfolio, poses her investment problem as a series of one-period decisions in which she trades off expected excess return and expected tail loss. In practice, the manager might also care about the volatility of her portfolio—since the month-to-month volatility is likely to impact her ability to attract capital.[39] In this case, the framework could be extended to allow the investor to trade off expected excess return and a weighted average of ETL and noncrisis volatility. Another interesting extension would be to consider the problem faced by a pension fund manager who seeks to construct an optimal allocation to hedge funds and other alternative assets to complement her exposure to traditional stocks and bonds. We leave this for further work.

---

[39] This would be similar to the situation faced by the top management of an investment bank. Although losses during crises periods could threaten the firm's future viability, quarter-to-quarter volatility is tracked by stock analysts as an indicator of management's risk control prowess. Hence, top management is likely to want to monitor and control both noncrisis period volatility and stress losses during crisis events.

Appendix

In this appendix we provide the analytical derivatives needed to compute the *expected tail loss* beta of asset i with respect to portfolio $p^\dagger$. As in the text of the paper,

S is the number of states
π_s is the probability of state s occurring
A is a return threshold that depends on the percentile choice

In addition, define the normalized return threshold in state s, a_s, as

$$a_s = \frac{A - \mu_{pt,s}}{\sigma_{pt,s}}$$

Consider portfolio $p^\dagger$ that has a portfolio weight of w_i in the ith asset and $(1 - w_i)$ in portfolio p. The expected tail loss, ETL, may be expressed as

$$\text{ETL} = \sum_s^S \pi_s \left[\mu_{pt,s} F(a_s) - \sigma_{pt,s} f(a_s) \right] / \alpha \qquad (5.14)$$

where $F(\cdot)$ denotes the standard *state-dependent* normal cumulative distribution function of the normalized portfolio returns, $f(\cdot)$ denotes the corresponding standard *state-dependent* normal probability density function, and equation 5.14 is subject to the constraint

$$\sum_s^S \pi_s F(a_s) = \alpha \qquad (5.15)$$

The ETL in each state depends on the state-dependent mean, $\mu_{pt,s}$, and standard deviation, $\sigma_{pt,s}$ of the portfolio, which are given by

$$\mu_{pt,s} = w_i \mu_{i,s} + (1 - w_i) \mu_{p,s} \tag{5.16}$$

and

$$\sigma_{pt,s} = \left[w_i^2 \sigma_{i,s}^2 + (1 - w_i)^2 \sigma_{p,s}^2 + 2w_i(1 - w_i)\sigma_{ip,s} \right]^{\frac{1}{2}} \tag{5.17}$$

where $\sigma_{ip,s}$ denotes the state-dependent covariance between the returns on asset i and the returns on portfolio p.

The derivative of the ETL with respect to w_i is

$$\left. \frac{d\text{ETL}}{dw_i} \right|_{w_{i=0}} = \frac{1}{\alpha} \sum_s^S \pi_s \left\{ \left(\frac{d\mu_{pt,s}}{dw_i} \right) F(a_s) + \mu_{pt,s} \left(\frac{dF(a_s)}{dw_i} \right) \right.$$
$$\left. \left. - \left(\frac{d\sigma_{pt,s}}{dw_i} \right) f(a_s) - \sigma_{pt,s} \left(\frac{df(a_s)}{dw_i} \right) \right\} \right|_{w_{i=0}} \tag{5.18}$$

where the derivatives with respect to the portfolio weights are evaluated at $w_i = 0$ and where equation 5.18 is subject to the constraint

$$\left. \sum_s^S \pi_s \frac{dF(a_s)}{dw_i} \right|_{w_{i=0}} = 0 \tag{5.19}$$

The analytical derivative given by equation 5.18 is the key component needed for the expected tail loss beta of asset i with respect to portfolio p^t.

We now provide the analytic derivatives for the components of equation 5.18. The derivatives of the state-dependent mean and standard deviation with respect to w_i are

$$\left. \frac{d\mu_{pt,s}}{dw_i} \right|_{w_{i=0}} = \mu_{i,s} - \mu_{p,s} \tag{5.20}$$

$$\left. \frac{d\sigma_{pt,s}}{dw_i} \right|_{w_{i=0}} = \rho_{i,p,s} \sigma_{i,s} - \sigma_{pt,s} \tag{5.21}$$

where $\rho_{i,p,s}$ is the correlation between the returns of the ith asset and portfolio p in state s.

Using the chain rule, we can write the derivatives of the cumulative distribution and density functions of the normalized portfolio returns with respect to the portfolio weights as

$$\left. \frac{dF(a_s)}{dw_i} \right|_{w_{i=0}} = \left(\frac{da_s}{dw_i} \right) \left(\frac{dF(a_s)}{da_s} \right) \right|_{w_{i=0}} \tag{5.22}$$

$$\left. \frac{df(a_s)}{dw_i} \right|_{w_{i=0}} = \left(\frac{da_s}{dw_i} \right) \left(\frac{df(a_s)}{da_s} \right) \right|_{w_{i=0}} \tag{5.23}$$

The component derivatives are

$$\left. \frac{da_s}{dw_i} \right|_{w_{i=0}} = \frac{1}{\sigma_{pt,s}} \left\{ \left. \frac{dA}{dw_i} \right|_{w_{i=0}} - \left(\mu_{i,s} - \mu_{p,s} \right) - a_s \left(\rho_{i,p,s} \sigma_{i,s} - \sigma_{p,s} \right) \right\} \tag{5.24}$$

$$\frac{dF(a_s)}{da_s} = f(a_s) \tag{5.25}$$

$$\frac{df(a_s)}{da_s} = -a_s f(a_s) \tag{5.26}$$

Substituting the right-hand-side of equation 5.24 for $\left. \frac{da_s}{dw_i} \right|_{w_{i=0}}$ in relations 5.22 and 5.23 and using (5.25) and (5.26) gives

$$\left. \frac{dF(a_s)}{dw_i} \right|_{w_{i=0}} = \frac{f(a_s)}{\sigma_{pt,s}} \left\{ \left. \frac{dA}{dw_i} \right|_{w_{i=0}} - \left(\mu_{i,s} - \mu_{p,s} \right) - a_s \left(\rho_{i,p,s} \sigma_{i,s} - \sigma_{p,s} \right) \right\} \tag{5.27}$$

$$\left. \frac{df(a_s)}{dw_i} \right|_{w_{i=0}} = -a_s \left. \frac{dF(a_s)}{dw_i} \right|_{w_{i=0}} \tag{5.28}$$

Substituting the right-hand-side of equation 5.22 into (5.19) and solving for the derivative of the $\alpha\%$ tail upper bound with respect to the portfolio weights (i.e., $\left. \frac{dA}{dw_i} \right|_{w_{i=0}}$) gives

$$\left. \frac{dA}{dw_i} \right|_{w_{i=0}} = \sum_s^S \pi_s \frac{f(a_s)}{\sigma_{p,s}} \left[\left(\mu_{i,s} - \mu_{p,s} \right) + a_s \left(\rho_{i,p,s} \sigma_{i,s} - \sigma_{p,s} \right) \right] \div \left(\sum_s^S \pi_s \frac{f(a_s)}{\sigma_{p,s}} \right)$$

$$\tag{5.29}$$

Note that A is the $(1 - \alpha)$ percentile VaR for the state-dependent normal distribution. Hence, this last derivative may be interpreted as the sensitivity of the VaR to changes in the weight of asset i in the portfolio.

This completes the analytical expression for $\left. \frac{dETL}{dw_i} \right|_{w_{i=0}}$.

REFERENCES

Artzner, P., F. Delbaen, J-M Eber, and D. Heath (1999). *Coherent Measures of Risk, Mathematical Finance* 9, pp. 203–228.

Best, M. J., and R. R. Grauer (1991). On the sensitivity of mean-variance-efficient porfolios to changes in asset means: Some analytical and computational results. *Review of Financial Studies* 4, 315–342.

Black, F., and R. Litterman (1990). Asset allocation: Combining investor views with market equilibrium. Goldman Sachs & Company Fixed Income Research, September 1990.

Brennan, M. J. (1979). The pricing of contingent claims in discrete time models, *Journal of Finance* 34, 53–68.

Brunnermeier, M. K., and L. H. Pedersen (2007). Market liquidity and funding liquidity. Working paper, February 2007.

Chan, N., M. Getmansky, S. M. Haas, and A. W. Lo (2007). In M. Carey and R. Stulz, eds. *Systemic Risk and Hedge Funds in Risks of Financial Institutions.* Chicago: University of Chicago.

Jorion, P. (2007). *Value at Risk: The New Benchmark for Managing Financial Risk*, 3rd ed. New York: McGraw-Hill.

J.P. Morgan Chase & Company Annual Report, 2005.

Kindleberger, C. P., and R. Aliber (2005). *Manias, Panics and Crashes*, 5th ed. Hoboken, NJ: Wiley.

Modest, D. M. (2001). Long-term capital management: An internal perspective. Presentation at Yale School of Management, April 10, 2001.

Soros, G. (2008). *The New Paradigm for Financial Markets: The Credit Crisis of 2008 and What It Means.* New York: Public Affairs.

6. What We Know, Don't Know, and Can't Know about Bank Risk

A View from the Trenches

Andrew Kuritzkes and Til Schuermann

This chapter addresses how the known (K), the unknown (u), and the unknowable (U) vary by risk type within banking.[1] We propose that knowledge of risk differs systematically by risk type—for example, with more being known about market risk than credit risk, and less being known about nonfinancial risks than financial risks. Understanding the nature of the differences across risk types and their relative contribution to total earnings volatility can shed light on the portion of the risk space within banking that is known and knowable—and hence manageable—versus unknown and unmanageable.

Our primary concern is to describe what practitioners—including risk managers and policy makers—know, don't know, and can't know about bank risk. Our focus is on a current snapshot of the banking industry, recognizing that the boundaries of K, u, and U shift over time. In particular, we look to evidence of contemporary industry practice to help position risks within our framework.

[1] We would like to thank Arturo Estrella, Dick Herring, Beverly Hirtle, David Jones, Jose Lopez, James Morgan, Sid Sankaran, Kevin Stiroh, Stefan Walter, and participants of the *KuU* conferences at the Wharton School, January 2005, and in Boston, January 2006, for helpful comments and suggestions, as well as Matthew Botsch and Kristin Wilson for excellent research assistance. Any remaining errors are, of course, our responsibility. Any views expressed represent those of the authors only and not necessarily those of the Federal Reserve Bank of New York or the Federal Reserve System.

An important indicator of current practice is the New Basel Capital Accord, or Basel II—the major international regulatory initiative to develop more risk-sensitive capital requirements for banks—which reflects a concerted attempt by regulators to codify "best practice" in banking as it relates to risk and capital measurement (BCBS 2001a, §99).

We start from the premise that risk is the potential for deviation from expected results, and that practitioners are particularly concerned with adverse deviation. Within this context, we define the known, the unknown, and the unknowable in terms that are closely related to the distinction made by Knight (1921, chapter 7) between risk and uncertainty.[2]

- A risk is *known* (*K*) if it can be identified and quantified *ex ante*. For a practitioner, risk quantification has developed a specific meaning: the ability to estimate downside tail risks or extreme loss events at high confidence levels associated with a bank's solvency standard. This concept is what underlies economic capital, the common denominator for risk measurement that has emerged within the banking industry. An economic capital approach to risk quantification is the basis on which capital requirements for credit, market, and operational risks are set under Basel II.

- A risk is *unknown* (*u*) if it belongs to a set of risks that can be identified but not meaningfully quantified at present. An example of an unknown risk might be the impact of reputation risk following the criminal indictment of a bank's CEO for fraud. While the general class of reputation risks can be identified, the consequences are likely to be too diffuse and fact-specific to be meaningfully quantified *ex ante*. Over time, it may be possible for reputation risks to be linked to causal factors and estimated discretely, in which case reputation risks will become more "known," but that is not the case given prevailing information and technology. For this reason, Basel II specifically excludes reputation risks from the category of "operational risks" for which banks must hold capital (BCBS 2005, §644).

- A risk is *unknowable* (*U*) if the existence of the risk or set of risks is not predictable, let alone quantifiable, *ex ante*. An example of a risk that was probably unknowable prior to 9/11 was the threat to businesses located in the World Trade Center that terrorists would fly aircraft into the Twin Towers, causing the buildings to collapse. Arguably, despite the 1993 bombing at the World Trade Center, this form of attack was not something that a bank risk manager could have anticipated (let alone quantified), even if the risk should have been foreseeable to some within the national security community. The discontinuity in the

---

[2] For further and more in-depth discussions of the definitions of the known, unknown and unknowable, see chapter 2 by Granger in this volume.

market for terrorism insurance pre- and post-9/11 suggests that the insurance sector, at least, had not predicted the possibility of such an attack before 9/11.

Based on these concepts, the first part of this paper proposes a framework for positioning different sources of bank risk in the K, u, U space. Consistent with how risk is defined by practitioners, we define bank "risk" as deviation from expected earnings—or, equivalently, earnings volatility—and disaggregate risk into five main categories. The first three categories include market risk from trading activities, credit risk, and structural interest rate risk from asset/liability management, which together constitute the main sources of financial risk. The remaining two categories refer to sources of nonfinancial risk, and include operational risk and "business risk"—this last category being a catchall for residual nonfinancial earnings volatility.

Given the available evidence, we rank order these risks based on two main characteristics: *quantification*, which reflects their ability to be measured, and *granularity*, which reflects their ability to be disaggregated. According to our ordering, market risk is the easiest risk to quantify and disaggregate, followed by credit risk, asset/liability risk, operational risk, and business risk. We argue that K increases as both the ability to measure and disaggregate risk increases; and conversely, that u and U increase as the ability to measure and disaggregate risk decreases. It follows that practitioners and policymakers "know" the most about market risk and the least about business risk. The boundary between what they know and don't know determines the portion of bank risk that currently is (or at least can be) managed. The portion of risk that is unknown is unmanaged, and the portion that is unknowable is largely unmanageable.[3]

The second part of the chapter attempts to size the known versus unknown portions of risk through empirical research on bank earnings volatility. First, we ask how much bank risk is there in total? Our analysis precedes the credit crisis and financial market turmoil that began in mid-2007. Nevertheless, it establishes, for the 300+ U.S. bank holding companies that had total assets of at least $1bn (2005Q1 dollars) from 1986Q2 to 2005Q1, what the total level of earnings volatility (as reflected by quarterly deviation in returns on Basel I risk-weighted assets) is at varying quantiles. The analysis includes tail observations out to the 99.9% level corresponding to a 0.1% one-year default probability, the level to which the Basel II risk weights are calibrated. Significantly, we conclude that the current minimum Basel I required regulatory capital level of 8% for banks protects quarterly earnings volatility at roughly the 99.98%

---

[3] This is not to say that risk that is unknown or unknowable cannot be transferred—to depositors, bondholders, the FDIC, or insurers. It is to say, rather, that you can't actively, or consciously, manage what you don't know.

level—consistent with the quarterly default probability of an A- rated bond. If we consider a minimum of 6%, corresponding to a Tier 1 capital threshold, the commensurate quarterly earning volatility protection is 99.94%. We compare the quarterly analysis with annual data available back to 1981 and find that this 8% (6%) capital cushion corresponds to an annual default probability of 0.28% (0.49%), or a confidence level of 99.72% (99.51%), which is equivalent to the annual default rate of a BBB (BBB–) rated bond. For the largest banks, that is, those with at least $10bn in assets (2005Q1 dollars), the 8% (6%) regulatory capital cushion is consistent with an annual default probability of 0.12% (0.37%), or a 99.88% (99.63%) confidence level, which maps to an A– (BBB) credit rating, though the large bank results are based on a much smaller sample.[4] To our knowledge, this is the first study to estimate the total amount of bank risk from a large pool of earnings volatility data.

Next, we estimate the relative contribution to bank earnings volatility from each of the five sources of risk identified in our taxonomy. We find that although the most is "known" about market risk, it contributes the least to bank earnings volatility—only 5% of total risk at the 99.9% level. Not surprisingly, credit risk is the major risk facing banks, accounting for about half of total earnings volatility at the 99.9% level. But more surprisingly, by our measure asset/liability risk accounts for 18% and nonfinancial risks account for 30% of total risk, respectively, at the same confidence level. Based on the results of other studies, we split the 30% estimate of nonfinancial risk into 12% for operational risk and 18% for business risk—the category about which, according to our framework, the least is known. All of these risk proportions are robust to choice of tail quantile from 99 to 99.95%.

Finally, we find that the diversification benefit, meaning the difference between the whole and the sum of the parts, is about one-third.

The last section of the chapter draws some tentative implications of the empirical findings for both practitioners and policy makers. First, our analysis allows the minimum regulatory capital requirements of the Basel II framework to be calibrated based on an empirical solvency standard. Basel II's requirement that banks hold minimum total (Tier I plus Tier II) capital of 8% of RWA translates into an annual solvency standard of 99.72%—roughly the equivalent of a BBB credit rating. A BBB rating is not a high solvency standard for a bank: It is the second lowest rung on the investment grade ladder, and this may explain why most banks hold excess capital relative to regulatory minimums (Berger et al. 2008). The low solvency standard associated with the regulatory minimums raises the question of whether the Basel II capital levels are sufficient to protect the banking system. Whatever the policy judgment, the point is that calibration

---

[4] The quarterly results do not differ by size.

of regulatory capital requirements should be based on a sound empirical understanding of the implied solvency standard.

Second, for practitioners, our risk decomposition suggests that the historical focus on market and credit risk management—while not unimportant—only covers about half of total bank earnings volatility. Significant returns to risk management can be expected from progress in the other three categories of risk that are less well understood.

Finally, from a policy perspective, Basel II's three-pillar framework has the flexibility to accommodate differences in how much we know, don't know, and can't know about the distinct risk types. Pillar 1, which adopts a rules-based approach to setting minimum capital requirements, should focus on the more known risks, such as market and credit risk, whereas Pillar 2, which relies on judgment-based supervisory reviews of a bank's overall risk profile, is better able to address the less well understood risk types. (Pillar 3, which stresses market discipline through improved disclosure, is meant to reinforce the first two pillars.) In this context, it is perhaps surprising that Basel II imposes a new Pillar 1 capital charge for operational risk, a relatively small source of earnings volatility about which we know comparatively little, while leaving asset/liability risk as a matter for supervisory discretion under Pillar 2 and ignoring business risk altogether—even though asset/liability risk and business risk account for over one-third of total earnings volatility. For both practitioners and policy makers, the message may be to stop looking for keys under the lamppost. The search for improvements in risk management should focus on the sources of risk that are the least "known" and have the greatest impact on earnings volatility.

A few important caveats should be borne in mind when interpreting these findings. First, our analysis precedes the credit crisis that began in 2007 and subsequent market turmoil. The ordering of risks in the K, u, U space is also reflective of market practices that prevailed before the crisis. In hindsight, the ten or so years through 2005 (the cutoff for our analysis) may turn out to be a high-water mark for confidence in risk management based on an unusually benign period of bank risk. Nevertheless, our K, u, U framework and empirical findings are instructive, even if the results would be revised with more recent data.

Indeed, while the full sample used here, consisting of 300+ banks and extending back to 1981, has statistical advantages, it obscures important structural changes over sample subperiods. Some observers point to the introduction of the Federal Deposit Insurance Corporation Improve Act (FDICIA) in 1991 and the increasing use of risk transfer in the later 1990s as evidence of a "regime shift" toward lower risk within our sample period.

Robustness checks confirm that splitting the sample in 1993 reveals a significant difference between the first and second periods, both in terms of total risk and risk allocation. For instance, 99.9% VaR levels are more than double in the first period than in the second using quarterly data, and more than triple using annual data. The difference in risk levels between the two periods suggests that earnings volatility depends heavily on the state of the world, and that higher capital levels are required to achieve the same solvency standard during "bad" periods than "good" ones. The change in total risk is also accompanied by a change in allocation. The more recent period shows a noticeable shift away from credit risk and toward market, structural interest rate, and nonfinancial risk as sources of earnings volatility.

Similarly, our total sample fails to reflect differences in risk profile between large and small banks. A separate robustness check splits the sample based on bank size. Over the full sample period, large banks—defined as banks with assets greater than $10bn in 2005 dollars—experience fewer extreme adverse outcomes than smaller banks.

Finally, just as a bank's risk profile is, to a degree, endogenously determined by the state of our knowledge of risk, so too does it depend on the influence of government policies. The existence of a safety net, such as deposit insurance or a lender of last resort, may cause bank managers to take on more risk—or hold less capital—than is socially optimal; see Santos (2001) for a survey of this rich literature. Thus our empirical findings are conditioned on the presence of such a safety net in the U.S. banking system. For example, the FDIC assumes a major portion of the tail risk of banks' loss distribution. The shape of that distribution is governed by the risk taking behavior and capital levels of banks. Kuritzkes et al. (2005), using a bottom-up Merton-based approach, compute the implied solvency level of the bank insurance fund at the FDIC at the end of 2000, and find that it ranges from 99.85% (about a BBB+ rating) to 98.83% (about a BB rating), depending on the model and choice of parameters. Any policy conclusions drawn from our study need to recognize that bank capital levels and earnings volatility are not exogenously determined, but reflect the institutional features of the banking system.

6.1. POSITIONING BANK RISKS ALONG THE *K, u, U* SPECTRUM

6.1.1. RISK MEASUREMENT, EARNINGS VOLATILITY, AND ECONOMIC CAPITAL

Among practitioners, risk in banking is typically defined in terms of earnings volatility (Rajan 2005). Earnings volatility creates the potential for loss. Losses, in turn, need to be funded, and it is the potential for loss that imposes a need for banks to hold capital. Capital provides the balance sheet cushion that absorbs (downside) earnings volatility and prevents a firm from becoming insolvent (Berger et al. 1995).

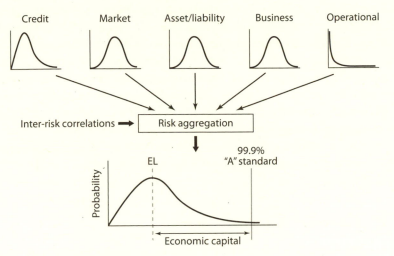

Figure 6.1. Standalone (marginal) and total (joint) risk distributions and economic capital for five principal risk types in banking.

The link between earnings volatility and capital is central to the way risk is measured in banking. Increasingly, risk is measured in terms of value-at-risk (VaR) or, equivalently, economic capital—the amount of capital needed to protect against earnings volatility at a prescribed confidence interval.[5] The reason for measuring risk at a stated confidence interval is that volatility, by itself, is insufficient to describe the whole distribution of earnings. Two distributions with dramatically different shapes and differing amounts of downside risk can have the same volatility. VaR scales the volatility to a specified confidence interval so as to create a common currency for risk that allows different risk factors to be directly compared. This is illustrated in figure 6.1, where the stylized earnings (or loss) distributions for different bank risks are shown to have very different shapes, but, assuming a common time horizon, can each be measured in equivalent terms at the same confidence interval. Moreover, the stand-alone amounts for these risks can be aggregated (although, because of diversification effects, not by simple addition) to create a single loss distribution for the bank overall (Kuritzkes et al. 2003; Rosenberg and Schuermann 2006).

The confidence interval for economic capital is usually set equivalent to the default rate associated with a bank's target debt rating or solvency standard.

---

[5] We will use VaR and economic capital somewhat interchangeably. Strictly speaking this is appropriate only if the risks are scaled to a common horizon, typically one year. See, for instance, the discussion in Jorion (2001, ch. 16).

Assume, for example, that a bank's target debt rating is A–, and that the annual default rate for A– rated bonds is 0.1% or 10 basis points (bp).[6] In this case, the bank would set the ruler for economic capital to be the amount of annual earnings volatility at the 99.9% confidence level, on the theory that this would determine the amount of capital the bank needs to remain solvent in all but 10 bp of possible loss scenarios—equivalent to the default risk of an A– rated bond.

While there is an internal logic for measuring risk at the same confidence interval as the bank's solvency standard, doing so implies an ability to quantify extreme events far out in the tail. To the extent that knowledge means being able to measure risks in terms of economic capital, then the threshold for K is set very high.

6.1.2. TAXONOMY OF BANK RISKS

As risk management techniques have progressed, economic capital models have been extended to new classes of risk, providing greater resolution on the composition of total earnings volatility (Allen et al. 2004). These developments are reflected in the evolution of bank capital regulation under the Basel framework. In 1988, when the original Basel Capital Accord (Basel I) was adopted, bank risk management was overwhelmingly focused on credit risk (BCBS 1988).[7] Basel I based regulatory capital requirements solely on the size of a bank's credit assets, with varying risk weights intended to reflect (crude) differences in the levels of credit risk. In 1996, the Market Risk Amendment to Basel I (BCBS 1996) subjected the price risk of trading positions to an explicit capital charge, and helped institutionalize value-at-risk measures for market risk within trading books. More recently, Basel II has singled out "operational risk"—defined to include losses from internal failures and external events—as a specific category of nonfinancial risk and is imposing a new capital charge to cover losses associated with operational risk.

Current practice among leading financial institutions is to break down earnings volatility into five main sources of risk. This breakdown, illustrated in figure 6.2, includes

---

[6] For no reason other than expediency, we shall be using S&P nomenclature. For a discussion of estimating default rates by credit rating see section 6.2.1.

[7] At the time the Basel I Accord was adopted, the risk management structure of a typical large bank could be described as consisting of a credit department that made loan approval decisions, reporting to a chief credit officer, who was responsible for the bank's credit risk performance. Risk disclosure was limited to information about nonperforming loans and charge-offs, with no information disclosed about trading risks, asset/liability risks, and nonfinancial risks. With a few notable exceptions (such as Bankers Trust), banks had yet to build up broader risk management infrastructures or appoint chief risk officers or disclose information about noncredit risks (Holton 2003, chapter 1).

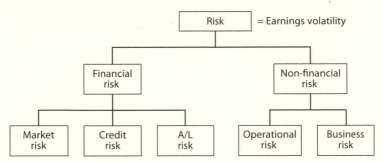

Figure 6.2. Taxonomy of bank risks.

1. *Market risk*, or the earnings impact associated with adverse price movements in the bank's principal trading positions
2. *Credit risk*, or the potential for losses due to the failure to pay of credit counterparties;
3. *Structural asset/liability risk*, or the earnings impact resulting from funding mismatches in assets and liabilities and the exposure to shifts in interest rates
4. *Operational risk*, or (BCBS 2005, §644) "the risk of loss resulting from inadequate or failed internal processes, people, and systems, or from external events"
5. *Business risk*, or the potential for losses from residual sources of nonfinancial earnings volatility.

The first three categories are sources of financial risk that are a direct result of a bank's role as financial intermediary or investor. Since the assumption and transfer of financial risk are, in many respects, the defining features of a financial institution, these risks can be expected to predominate in banking. The latter two categories refer to risks that are nonfinancial in nature and common to all firms. Business risk, in particular, is a broad catchall that includes all sources of nonfinancial risk not directly attributable to internal failures or external events. This category covers a host of sins, ranging from a drop in demand, a cost spike, technological obsolescence, regulatory change, price wars, and failed strategies, and can be expected to be the dominant risk faced by nonfinancial firms.[8]

---

[8] To be sure, some business risks can be measured somewhat granularly, albeit with low precision. For example, bank branch managers may have detailed knowledge of local business and customer flow.

6.1.3 Framework for *K*, *u*, and *U*

Given the taxonomy of bank risk, we can describe the known, the unknown, and the unknowable from the perspective of a practitioner. We posit that *K*, *u*, and *U* vary according to two main factors. The first is *quantification*: *K* increases, and *u* and *U* decrease, as the ability to quantify risk increases. This relationship is axiomatic—it follows directly from our definition of *K*, *u*, and *U*—but it is important to recognize that the ability to quantify risk differs systematically by risk class.

The second factor is *granularity*: *K* increases, and *u* and *U* decrease, as the ability to measure risk at lower levels of aggregation increases. The granularity dimension reflects systematic differences in the ability to measure and manage risks at multiple levels in the organization. The more granular the understanding of risk, the better one is able to identify it, measure it, and control it. In market risk, for example, the marginal impact of individual trades on a bank's overall market position can be measured, possibly even in real time, with a fairly high degree of accuracy. Risk managers can therefore manage the risks of individual trades, as well as the cumulative risk in a bank's trading businesses, through dynamic VaR limits. In business risk, by contrast, some risks, such as reputation risks, may manifest themselves only at the firm-wide level, and may not be capable of being disaggregated to lower levels. The inability to disaggregate such risks makes them more difficult to control at the source.

Based on these factors, we propose a framework for positioning the sources of risk in banking within the *K*, *u*, and *U* space. As illustrated in figure 6.3, the five main sources of bank risks can be ordered in terms of their ability to be quantified and disaggregated. We rank the risks in this framework, from the most quantifiable and granular, and hence most "known," to the least. Our framework also has a time dimension to it: the current ordering of risks, and contours of the *K*, *u*, and *U* curves, reflect the existing state of contemporary practice. Over time, the boundaries of the known are generally pushed out, as risks become more finely classified, additional data is collected, and new models are developed. At the same time, "regime shift" can cause the known space to contract, as relationships that were previously thought to be stable are disrupted by sudden changes in underlying behavior, market dynamics, or exogenous factors.

The rationale for the current positioning of bank risks within the framework is as follows.

Market Risk. Market risk is the most readily quantifiable and granular of the major classes of bank risk. Market risk models date back to the late 1980s, when VaR was first defined as a concept for measuring the risks of trading positions

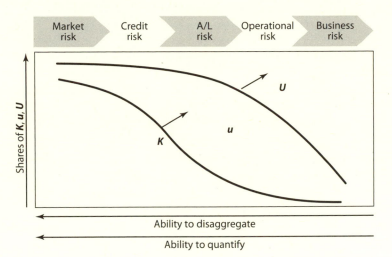

Figure 6.3. Framework for *K*, *u*, and *U* for bank risks. *K*, *u*, and *U* shares are represented vertically. Over time the shares for each bank risk type will likely move outward, as illustrated by the arrows.

(Holton 2003, chapter 1). By the mid-1990s, when the Market Risk Amendment to the Basel Accord was enacted, VaR models had become widely commercially available. The adoption of VaR models for market risk is now nearly universal among banks active in market making and proprietary trading, with VaR calculated at least daily on virtually all trading positions. And while there are differences in calculation approach—for example, parametric VaR versus historical simulation—the underlying methodologies are highly standardized across the industry (Jorion 2001; Allen et al. 2004).

The early development of VaR models reflects the rich data environment for market risk—at least, in liquid markets. Market risk factors are typically observed at high frequency, usually daily, and for the major currencies, interest rates, and equity indices, ultra-high-frequency observations (many trades per minute) are available (Andersen et al. 2003).

In terms of granularity, market risk VaR can be determined at successive levels of aggregation, from the consolidated firm-wide trading book to individual trader positions, to the risk impact (positive or negative) of a marginal trade on the portfolio. Indeed, trading room systems technology allows individual traders to see the VaR impact of individual trades in real time.

Not surprisingly, given the state of market risk measurement, the regulatory capital treatment for market risk is more advanced than for other risk types.

TABLE 6.1
Basel Regulatory Capital Treatment of Bank Risk Sources

	Basel I capital charge	Basis for Basel I capital	Basel II capital charge	Basis for Basel II capital
Market risk	Yes	Internal VaR models	Yes	Internal VaR models
Credit risk	Yes	Crude regulatory weights	Yes	Internal ratings models
A/L risk	No	—	No	Pillar II EVE test
Operational risk	No	—	Yes	Internal loss models
Business risk	No	—	No	—

Table 6.1 summarizes the regulatory capital treatment under current Basel I rules and proposed Basel II rules for market risk and the other main risk categories. Market risk is the only risk type under existing Basel I rules for which firms are allowed to use their own internal VaR models (with a regulatory-defined scalar) to calculate the level of regulatory capital. Since market risk is modeled daily and measurable at even higher frequency, it is possible to backtest market risk VaR calculations and conduct forecast evaluations against actual results in a statistically meaningful fashion (Diebold et al. 1998a; Lopez and Walter 2001).

Although we consider market risk to be the most "known" of the bank risks, our knowledge is far from perfect. Illiquid instruments, which "trade by appointment," may have daily VaRs calculated for them, but the underlying volatilities may not be very meaningful. Once illiquid, assets made more liquid via securitization can revert quite suddenly to their former less liquid state, making their inclusion in standard VaR machinery questionable. More liquid instruments, such as currencies with managed exchange rates, are subject to regime change, as evidenced by the breakup of the European Exchange Rate Mechanism in September 1992. Even the best models sometimes fail to capture complex correlations—witness the collapse of LTCM in the fall of 1998 (Jorion 2000). For this reason, we regard a portion of the space in market risk as unknown and unknowable.

Abstracting from such structural changes, there are limits to the accuracy of market risk models. Marshall and Siegel (1996) conducted a narrow experiment focusing on commercial VaR models. They supplied the same portfolio to eleven different vendors and found 95% one-day ahead VaR estimates to vary across vendors between 1% for simple FX forwards up to 28% for more complex interest rate options. Pritsker (1997) looked at variation in accuracy and computational time across six different VaR approaches for nonlinear instruments (in his case, FX options) and found a wide range in computational time (unsurprising) and accuracy (surprising). If such a broad range of outcomes is seen with relatively easy to measure market risk, that range is likely to be much wider for the other risk types.

Credit Risk. Credit risk measurement has progressed at a rapid pace since Basel I was adopted in 1988, although there is still a significant drop in the ability to quantify credit risk relative to market risk. At the transaction level, the use of credit rating models is now widespread for measuring expected loss, based on estimates of the probability of default (PD), loss given default (LGD), and exposure at default (EAD) of individual exposures. At the portfolio level, credit portfolio models such as KMV's Portfolio Manager calculate unexpected loss and economic capital, based on structural models of credit risk correlations. The broad framework for measuring credit risk at both the transaction and portfolio levels is standardized across the industry, albeit the internal models and parameters used by individual banks are highly customized (Crouhy et al. 2001).

The transaction-level attributes of credit risk indicate that credit risk measurement is highly granular, in principle down to the level of individual loans. This is the level at which credit risk is priced and managed, and a wide range of quantitative applications—including pricing tools, RAROC (risk-adjusted return on capital) measures, and hedging models—support decision-making at this level.

Significantly, Basel II adopts many of the latest credit risk measurement methodologies for setting capital requirements for credit risk. Under the internal ratings-based (IRB) approach, banks will be allowed to use internal rating models to determine the transaction level risk attributes of credit exposures (BCBS 2001b). However, because there is a broad range in the correlation assumptions of credit portfolio models used by the industry (BCBS 1999), Basel II requires the mapping of transaction-level risk measures to capital to be based on a regulatory formula employing a universal correlation assumption (BCBS 2005, §272).[9] The regulatory mapping limits the ability to isolate

---

[9] Basel II has five supervisory portfolios, each with its own somewhat different risk weight function, which differ, primarily, in their correlations.

marginal risks of individual loans so as to differentiate economic capital levels based on varying degrees of portfolio diversification.

As with market risk, the state of knowledge within credit risk varies by asset class. More is known about relatively liquid credit classes, including (in the United States) corporate bonds, mortgages, credit cards, other consumer receivables, and loans to publicly rated, large corporates, and less is known about illiquid credit classes, such as loans to small businesses, commercial real estate, and middle-market companies (Treacy and Carey 2000).

Even in the more liquid asset classes, credit risk quantification can only go so far. Default is a rare event, and sparse data sets—unlike the ultra-high-frequency observations in market risk—limit the accuracy of measurement at both the transaction (PD, LGD, EAD) and portfolio (UL, economic capital) levels. Moreover, since credit default rates vary over the business cycle, the calibration and validation of credit risk measures pose unique challenges. This is evident in the 2004 Quantitative Impact Study (QIS 4) undertaken by regulators in the United States of anticipated changes in capital levels under Basel II. Both the level and dispersion of the QIS 4 results across banks somewhat surprised the regulators, and is one of the factors that led them to postpone (yet again) the implementation date for Basel II from 2008 to 2011.[10]

At the transaction level, Carey and Hrycay (2001) find bias in credit scoring and mapping models used for determining PD. They also find bias due to ratings instability, as well as evidence of regime shifts and cyclical instability. PD estimates also exhibit a wide range. For example, using 25th and 75th percentile estimates for a given PD rating, they compute a range of implied Basel II style capital estimates for a typical portfolio. Going from the 25th to 75th percentile in PD estimates translates to a more than doubling the level of implied capital.

At the portfolio level, Koyluoglu et al. (2000) compare three commercial models, CreditMetrics, CreditRisk+, and KMV's Portfolio Manager, and find that, similar to the market risk studies (e.g., Hendricks 1996), the choice of tail probability or VaR level matters. Differences across models were modest at the 99% VaR level (max to min difference about 40%), but were almost two to one at the 99.9% VaR level.

With the spread of securitization technology, the line between market and credit risk is blurring. Indeed, most banks treated ABS (asset backed securities) largely like most other market traded securities by incorporating them into their (market risk) VaR machinery. The sudden broad shifts in market liquidity

---

[10] See remarks by Governor Susan Schmidt Bies before the Institute of International Bankers, Washington, DC, September 26, 2005; available at www.federalreserve.gov/boarddocs/speeches/2005/20050926/default.htm.

seen in 2007 and 2008 have arguably recrystallized some of those blurred lines and thereby questioned the appropriateness of treating ABS with the standard market risk VaR approach, which is geared toward highly liquid instruments. In the absence of market prices for the securities issued by ABS vehicles, market participants have reverted to more traditional credit risk approaches in assessing the risk of the always-illiquid collateral backing up the ABS—as a way of risk managing those ABS. Moreover, the credit risk in ABS and other new forms of credit derivatives, such as CDS and related counterparty risks, are inherently less known than the risk for traditional credit instruments as the market learned during the recent financial crisis. Overall, the two-to-one range in results reported by Carey and Hrycay at the transaction level and by Koylouglu et al. at the portfolio level, are consistent with the view that credit risk is less easily quantified than market risk.

. The research in credit risk measurement also suggests that credit risk is subject to more unknowns than market risk. Structural shifts in default risk, recovery levels, utilization rates, and credit correlations can all have a major impact on credit quantification. Credit risk is also subject to unknowable regime change—such as a change in bankruptcy laws in the United States. For example, Gross and Souleles (2002), in looking at the impact of bankruptcy regulation on consumer debt in the United States, find that as bankruptcy costs decline, default likelihoods increase, often substantially. See also Domowitz and Sartain (1999).

Structural Asset/Liability Risk. Structural asset/liability risk is related to market risk, although the measurement problem is far more challenging. While the dominant risk factor in asset/liability risk is movements in interest rates—and there is a long tradition among both financial economists and practitioners in modeling interest rate paths—this is not where the principal difficulty lies. The challenge comes from the need to characterize indeterminate cash flows on both the asset and liability side; from the valuation of embedded options and hedges in a bank's investment portfolio; from the long holding period assumed for a bank's structural balance sheet; and, perhaps most importantly, from the lack of convergence on a measurement standard (Bessis 1998, Saunders 2000). And once asset and liability cash flows are characterized according to their effective interest rate duration, there is the further challenge of incorporating funding effects due to changes in a bank's own credit spreads. In periods of market illiquidity the funding effects can be significant and can lead to funding costs exceeding asset yields for certain classes of short-term liabilities.

With regard to cash flow characterization, a bank's sensitivity to changes in interest rates is dependent on the cash flow mismatches across all assets and liabilities. Determining the cash flow mismatches, in turn, requires estimating the duration of indeterminate maturity liabilities—such as "core" demand deposits or cash management accounts—whose effective maturities may be much longer than stated contractual maturities. In addition, fixed assets, tax obligations, and leases all have cash flow characteristics that are not certain, and assumptions need to be made about their maturity characteristics. The approaches to estimating duration for indeterminate maturity cash flows blend art and science, with many banks still reverting to rules of thumb (Mays 1996).[11]

Investment in securities with interest rate optionality—especially mortgage-backed securities with prepayment and extension risks—also complicates risk measurement. The valuation of these embedded options and related hedges is far from an exact science—as reflected in the 2004 accounting restatements of both Freddie Mac and Fannie Mae.

At the same time, unlike with trading positions, the holding period for a bank's structural asset/liability position is assumed to be a long time horizon, typically one year. Short-term volatility in interest rates, however, can lead to dramatic changes in a bank's asset/liability risk. The long holding period makes the impact of dynamic management policies, such as stop-loss limits, more difficult to anticipate.

Nevertheless, at least since the U.S. S&L crisis, structural asset/liability risk has been actively monitored in most major banks. Yet unlike market or credit risk, there is no standardized approach for asset/liability risk measurement. In fact, practitioners do not even agree on whether the appropriate measure is an earnings approach based on net interest revenue volatility, or a value approach based on changes in the economic value of equity (EVE) (defined as the present value of assets minus liabilities [Koch and MacDonald 2000, chapter 9; FRBSL 2004]). The measurement debate is partly driven by the arcane accounting treatment of interest earnings from a bank's investment portfolio, with some assets (but not necessarily corresponding liabilities) receiving mark-to-market treatment, while other assets (those deemed to be "available for sale" or "held to maturity") are recognized on an accruals basis.[12] Lack of consensus on how to

---

[11] The impact of changes in duration assumptions can be significant: for a $100bn bank funded 25% with core deposits, changing the effective maturity assumption on core deposits from 3 years to 5 years would have a duration impact of 0.5 years on the bank's overall gap position. This implies a $500 MM increase in the bank's economic value of equity under a 100-bp interest rate shock.

[12] Under U.S. GAAP, the mark-to-market changes in investment portfolio assets that are "available for sale" or "held to maturity" do not hit a bank's reported net income, but are disclosed in a footnote to the financial statements. At the same time, the MTM changes in the available-for-sale portfolio reduce a bank's tangible common equity ratio, but the MTM changes in the held-to-maturity portfolio do not. The hodgepodge of accounting treatment has created genuine confusion over what the relevant unit of "risk" is in Treasury portfolios and how it should be measured.

measure asset/liability risk was reported to be a major reason why interest rate risk outside the trading book was not subjected to an explicit (Pillar 1) capital charge under Basel II but is covered under Pillar 2 instead (BCBS 2005, §762).

Given the lack of standardization, it is not surprising that there is a wide range of sophistication in asset/liability risk measurement. Simplistic approaches include calculating the impact of fixed rate shocks—such as a 100- or 200-bp parallel shift in yield curves—on the bank's EVE and net interest revenues. Basel II suggests such a simple 200-bp parallel shift test as a means of identifying banks that are outliers in terms of asset/liability risk. More sophisticated approaches subject the balance sheet to full simulation of interest rate movements, and calibrate outcomes based on probabilistically weighted scenarios (including tail-risk scenarios) (Bessis 1998).

In terms of granularity, funds transfer pricing, common in most banks, allows the value of assets and liabilities to be disaggregated (based on behavioral assumptions) to pools of deposits and transactions. In principle, though, A/L risk is a high-level risk that is usually measured and managed at the level of the consolidated balance sheet.

Operational Risk. Operational risk is the newest risk class to emerge as a discrete category. Prior to the early consultative papers for Basel II, there was no agreement on what the definition of operational risk was, let alone how to measure it. Basel II established a standardized definition and classification scheme for operational risk—subdividing internal and external events into seven recognized categories, limiting operational risks to the "direct" consequences of operational losses, and excluding indirect consequences, such as reputation effects, from the definition. Going forward, Basel II requires that banks seeking to adopt the advanced measurement approach for operational risk (the only option available for U.S. banks) develop internal economic capital models to estimate a bank's exposure to operational losses at the 99.9% level over a one-year horizon (BCBS 2005, §655–659). Prior to the Basel II pronouncements, operational risk was often included together with other nonfinancial risks as "operating risk," and measured in economic capital frameworks, if at all, through analogs and benchmarks such as revenue and expense ratios (Uyemura and van Deventer 1992; Netter and Poulson 2003).

Basel II has catalyzed a major industry effort to model and measure operational risks. The challenge in operational risk measurement, however, is that operational losses appear to be extremely fat-tailed (De Fontnouvelle et al. 2006a; Rosenberg and Schuermann 2006). The losses that are most relevant for measuring economic capital are, by definition, low-frequency, high-severity events that are difficult to observe within any one firm. For this reason, Basel

II requires that banks incorporate information from external data and extreme loss scenarios in their operational loss models. Banks have experimented with a number of different quantitative techniques to fit the tails of operational loss distributions, including techniques from extreme value theory, EVT (Netter and Poulson 2003; Allen et al. 2004).

Despite the recent progress, it is fair to say that operational risk measurement is still at a relatively early stage of development. A standard approach for quantifying operational risk has yet to emerge. And small changes in parameter estimation can have a dramatic impact on results at the 99.9% level. For example, De Fontnouvelle et al. (2006b) apply EVT techniques to estimate the operational risk loss distributions for six banks, based on internally reported data. The resulting estimates are not very precise. In a comment on the De Fontnouvelle et al. (2006b) paper, Kuritzkes (2006) shows that differences in the shape parameter of the generalized Pareto distributions estimated for the six banks were consistent with a ten to one range in resulting economic capital.

Equally, because of the focus on extreme tail events, operational risks are difficult to break down to lower levels of aggregation. The risks that can be observed within individual business units tend to be high-frequency, low-severity risks—not the low-frequency, high-severity risks that are relevant for economic capital. Tail risks—for example, legal liability risk for accounting misstatements or securities class action lawsuits—often need to be imputed from external data sources and may only be meaningful at the level of the firm.

Consistent with the immature state of operational risk measurement, the world of the unknown in operational risk is commensurately larger than for market, credit, or A/L risks. Arguably, operational risk contains risks that are recognized today that were previously unknowable. An example referred to above was the World Trade Center attack on September 11, 2001, the direct consequences of which are an "external event" included within the Basel II definition of operational loss. Kuritzkes and Scott (2005) note the general category of legal risk as being subject to *ex post* judicial and regulatory interpretations, some of which may not be foreseeable *ex ante*. Examples of such risks could include the vulnerability of Swiss banks to holocaust claims in the mid-1990s, four or five decades after the accounts of holocaust victims were mishandled, as well as more recent rulings and regulatory decisions in the aftermath of the Enron and WorldCom scandals holding banks to be vicariously liable for customer fraud. Brown et al. (2005) show how this type of *ex ante* legal risk influences management behavior and earnings forecasts.

Business Risk. Business risk is the last frontier of risk classification and measurement. As with operational risk before Basel II, there is no standard definition of business risk, which is sometimes also referred to as "strategic" risk (Slywotzky and Drzik 2005). Within the taxonomy above, business risk is best understood by reference to what it is not: it is residual earnings volatility that is *not* caused by any of the other defined categories, including market, credit, A/L, or operational risks.

Given the catchall nature of business risk, it is difficult to isolate the independent drivers of residual earnings volatility. Conceptually, business risk reflects the fact that a firm's revenues may be volatile while its costs are somewhat rigid, even after the effects of market, credit, asset/liability, and operational risks have been stripped out. The resulting profit margin reflects the degree to which a firm is able to manage costs relative to revenues and avoid an operating loss— the basic risk that all firms face and which explains why nonfinancial firms cannot operate on infinite leverage.

Nevertheless, many banks do not include an explicit measure of business risk within their economic capital frameworks. For those banks that do, business risk is measured through one of a few alternative approaches: the simplest approach is to infer business risk capital requirements from the capitalization levels of nonfinancial firms that are engaged in similar activities (e.g., processing, consulting, IT services). Another approach is to strip out financial and operational risks from publicly reported data on bank earnings and construct a proxy measure of business risk volatility for a sample of peer banks. A third approach is to develop an explicit model of residual revenue volatility and cost rigidity at the business line level. None of the approaches are based on causal factors of business risk, and little progress has been made in systematically identifying the individual sources of business risk volatility (Slywotzky and Drzik 2005).

In terms of granularity, business risk is easiest to observe at the bank-wide level. Of all the risk types, it is the one we are the least able to break down to lower levels of aggregation. This is not to say that business risk is not "managed," but simply that it is hard to manage in a granular fashion. Banks, like the Basel II regulators, have tended to ignore the impact of business risk, or seem to think of it as indistinguishable from "strategy."

6.1.4. PUTTING THE PIECES TOGETHER

Referring again to figure 6.3, our positioning of bank risks in the K, u, U space can be summarized in a few propositions:

1. Our knowledge of bank risk increases as our ability to quantify risk increases.
2. Our knowledge of bank risk increases as our ability to disaggregate risk to more granular levels increases.

3. Our knowledge of bank risks shifts over time, as new risks become discretely classified and subject to measurement with increasing granularity (or historical relationships break down and become unstable in periods of market turmoil).

Based on these propositions, the evidence from market practice suggests that
4. Our current knowledge of market risk > credit risk > structural asset/liability risk > operational risk > business risk.

Although we know more about the ordering of risks than the contours of the K, u, and U curves within the risk space, we reason that
5. The known curve falls off steeply between financial and nonfinancial risks, as market, credit, and structural asset/liability risks are much easier to quantify and disaggregate than operational or business risk.
6. The U curve also rises steeply for operational and business risk, given the diffuse nature of these risks and the lack of historical focus on their underlying causes.

6.2. EMPIRICAL ANALYSIS

In this section we analyze the earnings volatility of a large sample of U.S. bank holding companies (banks) using publicly available regulatory reporting data to answer two questions: (1) how much bank risk is there in total (in the United States, at least)? (2) What is the relative contribution to overall risk from each of the five sources of risk identified in our taxonomy? By quantifying earnings volatility systematically, we hope to shed light on the dimensions of K, u and U in the bank risk space.

Our sample range is 1986Q2 though 2005Q1 for quarterly analysis and 1986 to 2004 for annual analysis using Y-9C regulatory reports. The sample period begins in 1986Q2 because prior to that, trading income, needed to parse out market risk, was not reported separately. All banks with at least $1bn in total assets at the beginning of each year are included for a total sample of 22,770 bank-quarters.[13] While our sample period contains only two recessions, and mild ones at that, it does include a period of significantly higher than average bank failures, 1988–1991, but not the severe stress encountered in the Great

---

[13] Total assets, reported in nominal dollars, were deflated using the GDP deflator to 2005Q1 dollars. This would err toward including more rather than fewer banks. Note that we did not account for mergers and acquisitions.

Depression of the 1930s or the more recent stresses experienced since 2007.[14] We also extend the annual analysis for overall risk back to 1981 as a robustness check. The extended annual sample includes the more pronounced 1982 recession.

6.2.1. How Much Total Risk?

Given that practitioners and others define risk in terms of earnings volatility (Rajan 2005), we look to actual variations in a bank's reported net income to determine how much bank risk is there in aggregate. To allow direct comparison across banks, earnings need to be converted into a return-based measure. An obvious approach for doing this would be to divide (pretax) net income by total assets to yield a return on assets (ROA) measure. This method, however, treats all asset types the same: a treasury bond would be the same as a loan to a small, new firm. Regulatory reports provide risk-weighted assets (RWA) based on the Basel I risk weights. Although crude, and certainly much cruder than under a Basel II style risk weighting, RWA is nevertheless preferable to unweighted (total) assets as it makes at least some adjustment for the risk of the underlying asset. Unfortunately, Basel I RWA has only been available since 1996. In an attempt to adjust total assets from the beginning of our sample period we take a simple approach and examine the ratio of RWA to total assets for the available sample period for the industry as a whole and backfit to the beginning of the sample.

The resulting ratio of net income to RWA, which we call return on risk-weighted assets (RORWA), determines our measure of earnings.[15] The average quarterly RORWA in our sample is 0.34%, or 1.35% on an annualized basis. As risk, and hence capital, is concerned with deviations from expected returns, for what follows we compute deviations in RORWA by subtracting, from each period's observation, the average RORWA over the sample period for each bank— neutralizing for bank holding company (or bank) effects. To be precise, let $Y_{i,t}$ be the net income for bank i in period t, and let $RWA_{i,t}$ be the corresponding level of risk-weighted assets. We then define RORWA for the ith bank in period t as

[14] Carey (2002) using a resampling-based approach does try to mimic this "Great Depression" scenario.

[15] Although Basel I style risk-weighted assets do capture some off-balance sheet exposure, the picture is not complete. But however incomplete, so long as the proportion captured has stayed relatively constant, our backcasting method would capture a similar proportion of off-balance sheet exposures. Earnings from those exposures, whether positive or negative, are captured in the numerator of our RORWA metric.

$$r_{i,t} = \frac{Y_{i,t}}{RWA_{i,t}}$$

(6. 1)

and mean-adjusted RORWA as

$$\tilde{r}_{i,t} = \frac{Y_{i,t}}{RWA_{i,t}} - \frac{1}{T_i}\sum_{t=1}^{T_i} r_{i,t}$$

(6.2)

where bank i is observed for T_i periods. For simplicity in what follows we shall refer to equation 6.2 as RORWA (i.e., always the mean-adjusted return). The quarterly standard deviation or volatility across 22,770 (quarterly) RORWAs is 0.40%, or 0.80% on an annualized basis.[16]

Under the Basel framework (both Basel I and Basel II), regulatory capital requirements are also expressed in terms of RWA, with banks being required to hold sufficient capital C such that

$$\frac{C_{i,t}}{RWA_{i,t}} \geq C_{\min} > 0,$$

(6.3)

for some threshold $C_{\min}$. Typically $C_{\min} = 0.08$.[17] Given that annualized volatility of RORWA is 0.80%, regulatory capital levels, it turns out, are sufficient to enable banks to withstand a 10σ annual event in RORWA. If we assume that the RORWA returns are normally distributed, the likelihood of such an event is infinitesimally small: less than once in 1000 trillion years. Should we feel safe?

The answer is not nearly as safe as assumptions of normality would lead one to believe. Figure 6.4 shows the distributions of RORWA calculated over quarterly and annual frequencies. It is apparent that each of these distributions is very fat-tailed, with a kurtosis of 123 for the quarterly and 40 for the annual data; it is 3 for a normal distribution. Under temporal aggregation we would expect the lower-frequency data to be closer to normality, as is indeed the case

---

[16] A potential disadvantage with this approach of subtracting the bank mean return is that a bank with, say, an average return of 20% that has a "bad" return for one period of 5% would have a deviation of –15%. This would be observationally equivalent for a bank with a mean of 5% and a bad one-period return of –10%. Naturally, we would care differently about the latter than the former case. To check we repeated the entire analysis without deviation in means and found that the tails of the return distribution to be somewhat more extreme even though the mean, of course, was higher (positive instead of zero), suggesting that the former example is indeed pathological and the latter typical.

[17] The actual capital requirements are, of course, somewhat more complex as they involve differentiated types of capital (Tier 1 vs. Tier 2). We use the 8% threshold for convenience and to allow for easier comparison to other studies in the literature where a simple 8% cutoff is typical. At times we also make reference to a 6% Tier 1 threshold. Of course, it is straightforward to use different thresholds.

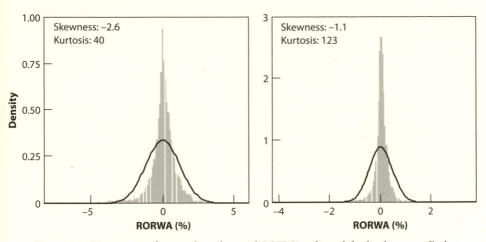

Figure 6.4. Histograms of quarterly and annual RORWA, adjusted for bank means. Each chart has superimposed the normal density with the same mean (0) and standard deviation as the data.

here. Each distribution is also somewhat negatively skewed, with a coefficient of skewness of –1.1 for the quarterly and –2.6 for the annual returns.

There are enough data to allow for nonparametric analysis of the tails, meaning we can estimate tail quantiles directly from the empirical distribution, though for small quantiles in the far tails the estimates are likely to be noisy. Because bank earnings are subject to common effects, other approaches, such as EVT, may not be suitable, as they require the data to be independently distributed (Diebold et al. 1998b).

Zeroing in on the tail, table 6.2 reports empirical percentiles for the left tail of the quarterly RORWA distribution. For example, the 0.1st percentile (or 99.9% tail) in the data is a quarterly RORWA of –4.85%, and there are 23 observations that are "worse" (i.e., more negative). All of those tail observations occurred between 1986 and 1992, mostly incurred by Texas and New England banks. Based on the empirical record, if banks hold at least 8% capital, they would be unable to withstand an adverse RORWA event in about two quarters out of every 10,000. These events happen considerably more often than the 1 in 1000 trillion implied by a normal distribution. Indeed, a –8% quarterly RORWA is around the 0.02nd percentile, or the 99.98% tail; using a 6% threshold, the percentile is the 0.06th, or the 99.94% tail.

The probability of a loss exceeding 8% can be interpreted through the lens of economic capital as the implied solvency standard of the Basel capital requirements. To translate the solvency standard into familiar terms, we map the bank

TABLE 6.2
Left Tail of Earnings Distribution/VaR (%)

	0.01 99.99	0.03 99.97	0.05 99.95	0.1 99.9	0.5 99.5	1 99
RORWA (%)	−9.69	−7.69	−7.14	−4.85	−2.67	−1.75
Number of observations beyond percentile	3	7	12	23	114	228

Note. Left tail percentiles for quarterly return on risk-weighted assets (RORWA). 22,770 bank-quarters, 1986Q2–2005Q1. All returns are deviations from bank mean. Data source: Y-9C regulatory reports.

loss probabilities to empirical default frequencies of rated corporate bonds. Although different approaches have been applied for estimating the PDs for corporate bond ratings, the most common approach—and the one used by the rating agencies themselves—is the frequentist or cohort approach, which divides the number of defaults from a given rating over the number of rated firms in the quarter (year).[18] We apply the cohort approach to estimate annual default probabilities for S&P ratings based on rating histories from 1981 to 2004. The PDs turn out to have roughly a log-linear relation across credit ratings, meaning that PDs increase exponentially as one descends the rating spectrum; see figure 6.5. If we assume that this log-linear relationship holds across the entire spectrum, we can impute a PD value for the investment grades, where default observations are scarce. The resulting annual and implied quarterly PDs by rating are presented in table 6.3, shown in basis points.

With these default probabilities, it is straightforward to map the left tail percentiles in table 6.2 to an implied credit rating. Recall that a bank with 8% (6%) capital would be able to withstand an adverse quarterly RORWA with 99.98% (99.94%) confidence—or a default probability of 2 bp (6 bp) per quarter. This solvency standard corresponds to a low investment grade credit rating of around A− (BBB+); see table 6.3.

---

[18] In the cohort approach, ratings migrations within the quarter (year) are ignored. An alternative duration-based approach (Lando and Skødeberg 2002) is able to account for these movements by estimating migration, and hence default, intensities, resulting in a nonzero PD estimate for a rating even if no default from that rating has been observed, as is the case for the AAA rating, for instance. This method requires the rather strict assumption that ratings follow a Markov process, and several studies have documented non-Markovian behavior in credit ratings (Altman and Kao 1992; Nickell et al. 2000). Hanson and Schuermann (2006) show that neither method produces precise PD estimates, and that observed default rates are indeed inconsistent with a Markov model.

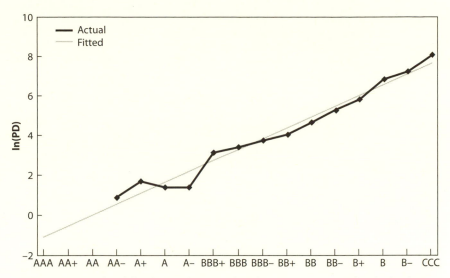

Figure 6.5. Actual and fitted annual PDs, in logs (i.e., PDs are assumed to be log-linear across the rating spectrum). Actual PDs are estimated using the cohort approach with S&P rating histories for all corporates from 1981 to 2004. No actual defaults for ratings AA and higher were observed in this sample period.

The typical horizon to which economic capital is set is one year, so we proceed to check the quarterly results against annual earnings using year-end data from 1986 to 2004, resulting in 5841 bank-years. Quarterly data allows us to better explore the far tails, but we may still compare the two frequencies so long as the calibration is to a common standard, namely a default likelihood or an implied credit rating, albeit frequency consistent.

In table 6.4 we present RORWA, in percent, of total earnings measured at quarterly and annual frequencies at varying quantiles (the quarterly returns are from table 6.2).[19] The results can be thought of as a value at risk: for example, looking at the 0.1st percentile, quarterly returns worse than −4.85% and annual returns worse than −9.81% have been seen for 0.1% of bank-quarters/years. These percentiles (VaRs) can also be mapped to their corresponding quarterly and annual default rates using table 6.3. For example, what rating corresponds to an annual (quarterly) default rate of 10 bp (i.e., a 99.9% VaR)? The implied annual rating closest to 10 bp is A−, and the implied quarterly rating closest to 10 bp is BBB−. Therefore, a bank with 4.85% capital (relative to RWA) would be

[19] There are not enough data to allow us to explore the annual results beyond the 5-bp tail.

TABLE 6.3

Smoothed Annual and Quarterly PDs by Rating Using S&P Rating
Histories for All Corporates from 1981 to 2004, in basis points

Rating	Annual PD (smoothed)	Implied quarterly PD[a]
AAA	0.3	0.075
AA+	0.6	0.15
AA	1.0	0.25
AA–	1.7	0.425
A+	3.0	0.75
A	5.0	1.25
A–	9.0	2.25
BBB+	23	5.75
BBB	30	7.50
BBB–	42	10.50
BB+	57	14.25
BB	105	26.25
BB–	197	49.25
B+	337	84.25
B	943	235.75
B–	1,385	346.25
CCC	3,254	813.50

Note. The dashed line separates investment grades (above) from speculative grades (below).

[a] In the presence of non-Markov behavior, quarterly PDs are not simply equal to ¼ of annual
PDs. However, the differences are quite minor, and we use these estimates as guidelines for mapping our empirical analysis into implied credit ratings.

protected against quarterly earnings volatility at the BBB– level. Note that the
same amount of capital would only protect the bank against annual earnings
volatility at roughly the 1st percentile, equivalent to a BB rating.

More relevant from a regulatory capital perspective is the solvency standard associated with an 8% (6%) capital cushion. Using the longer sample, a
–8% (–6%) annual RORWA event is associated with a tail probability of 0.28%
(0.49%), which corresponds to a BBB (BBB–) rating—or two (one) rating
notches lower than the implied A– quarterly rating reported above. It is interesting to note that the implied annual solvency standard is somewhat less
conservative than the 99.9% annual confidence interval used in Basel II for
measuring credit, market, and operational risks. Given estimation and model
errors, however, the two confidence intervals (99.9 vs. 99.72%) could be interpreted as being reasonably close.

These results are consistent with Carey (2002) who uses resampling techniques on a representative corporate loan portfolio to assess the amount of

TABLE 6.4
Left Tail of Earnings Distribution/VaR (%)

	0.05/99.95	0.1/99.9	0.5/99.5	1/99
Implied rating: quarterly, annual	BBB+, A	BBB-, A-	BB-, BB+	B+/B, BB
Quarterly (1986Q2–2005Q1)	–7.14	–4.85	–2.67	–1.75
Annual (1986–2004)	–10.27	–9.81	–5.95	–4.12
Annual (1981–2004)	–14.74	–10.81	–6.00	–4.38

Note. Implied credit rating for left tail percentiles for quarterly and annual return on risk weighted assets (RORWA), in percent. Implied credit ratings are presented in table 6.3. Quarterly data are 1986Q2–2005Q1 for a total of 22,770 bank-quarters, first annual data is 1986–2004 for a total of 5841 bank-years, chosen to match the quarterly sample period, and second annual data are 1981–2004 for a total of 7396 bank-years. All returns are deviations from bank mean. *Data source*: Y-9C regulatory reports.

economic capital needed under various economic conditions. In particular, based on the experience of 1989–91, a moderate stress scenario, Carey finds that the loss rate over a two-year horizon at the 99.5% (99.9%), is 7.63% (8.80%), respectively (Carey 2002, table 3), versus our one-year loss estimates of 6.00% (10.81%) (Carey 2002, table 2). Our results are also consistent with those of Lucas et al. (2001), who report one-year likelihoods of exceeding 8% capital ranging from 1bp to 100bp (i.e., 99.99 to 99% VaR), depending on assumptions about average credit quality of the portfolio and the distribution of the underlying risk factor. Note, however, that both of these studies examine credit risk only, while our results attempt to encompass all risk types. Indeed, we show in the next section that credit risk makes up just under half of the total risk pie.[20]

6.2.2. RELATIVE RISK CONTRIBUTIONS

Having answered the first question—how much risk is there in total?—we are ready to address the second: what is the relative contribution from each of the five major risk types of the risk taxonomy outlined in section 6.2.2? Since, by definition, the different sources of risk in our taxonomy manifest themselves as

---

[20] Note also that we cannot, however, simply divide our total risk numbers by two as there is interrisk diversification to contend with. We show in section 6.2.2 that the difference between the whole and the sum of the parts is about one-third.

earnings volatility, we seek to isolate the impact of each of the individual risk sources on RORWA. Using disaggregate data from the Y-9C regulatory reports, we outline a simple approach to measuring how each risk type affects bank reported net income—the numerator of RORWA. This approach will allow us to understand the relative size of the components of RORWA volatility, and will also highlight the difference between the whole and the sum of the parts. That difference can be thought of as the diversification benefit across the different risk types.

We start from the identity that bank pretax net income (i.e., earnings) can be expressed as follows:

Pretax net income   = Net interest income (interest income less interest
                              expenses)
                           + net gains (losses) from securities
                           + income (loss) from trading
                           − provisions
                           + other income (service charges, fiduciary, fees,
                              and other income)
                           − noninterest expenses
                           + net extraordinary items.

We may then think about mapping these income statement items to risk types as illustrated in figure 6.6. We see that these line items can be grouped into financial and nonfinancial sources of net income, and then mapped to individual risk categories. The parsing of total nonfinancial risk into its two components, operational and business risk, is taken up below.

The mapping of income items to risk types is better for some of the risk categories than for others, but overall the scheme seems to provide a reasonable basis for decomposing earnings volatility into risk sources. The cleanest alignment is between market risk and trading income. Market risk is synonymous with volatility in the trading profit and loss (P&L), while trading income reflects the P&L results of a bank's market making and proprietary position taking activities.[21] For credit risk, we take provisions as the relevant measure (as

---

[21] While all banks are subject to minimum capital standards due to credit risk, only banks with a *significant* market risk exposure are required to calculate a risk-based capital ratio that takes into account market risk in addition to credit risk. U.S. regulators deem market risk exposure to be significant if the gross sum of trading assets and liabilities on the bank's balance sheet exceeds 10% of total assets or $1 billion (USGAO 1998, page 121). As reported in Hirtle (2003, table 1), at the end of 2001 there were only 19 bank holding companies (BHCs) that were subject to market risk capital standards. Nonetheless, many of the larger banks still engage in some trading-related activity, and, indeed, almost half of the banks in our sample reported nonzero trading income.

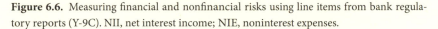

Figure 6.6. Measuring financial and nonfinancial risks using line items from bank regulatory reports (Y-9C). NII, net interest income; NIE, noninterest expenses.

opposed to net charge-offs) because provisions are what enter the calculation of net income. Put another way, variation in provision levels is what causes volatility in reported earnings and hence RORWA. Provisions, nonetheless, are an imperfect measure of credit risk. Two main disadvantages of using provisions as a proxy for credit risk are timing and loss smoothing. Typically, provisions are made in anticipation of accounting losses and are concurrent with or even lag economic losses. This forecasting element may allow banks to smooth earnings (although this is severely frowned on by the Financial Accounting Standards Board (FASB) regulation and the Securities and Exchange Commission) and so could lead us to underestimate the contribution of credit risk to overall risk. A separate robustness check using net charge-offs instead of provisions shows that the two results are quite close, and the choice between provision and charge-offs appears to make little difference to our analysis.

Structural asset/liability risk is, in a sense, residual financial earnings volatility once trading gains (losses) and provisions have been stripped out. This is measured by net interest income (NII) plus gains (losses) on securities. Variations in NII (excluding credit provisions) are due either to volume effects (which are captured by scaling NII by risk weighted assets) or to changes in the term structure and spread levels of interest rates (including a bank's own credit spreads on liabilities)—the basic definition of asset/liability risk. Further, principal gains/losses on securities held in the bank's investment portfolio (as opposed to the trading book, which is considered market risk) are also caused by changes in rates or spread levels, and so should be included as an additional source of asset/liability related earnings volatility.

Finally, total nonfinancial risk represents residual earnings volatility not attributable to market risk, credit risk, or structural asset/liability risk. This is given by the remaining income items: all other income (services charges, fiduciary fees, and other income), less noninterest expenses (NIE), plus net extraordinary income. Note that inclusion of all operating expenses in this category is consistent with the notion that business risk captures variations in margins due to fixed (or rigid) expenses. While total nonfinancial risk includes both operational risk and business risk, the line items in bank income reporting do not allow the impact of these two risks to be segregated. Instead, we turn to other empirical research on operational risk (imperfect as it is) to fix the proportion of nonfinancial risk that appears to be due to operational losses.

As noted above, these mappings are hardly perfect. For instance, interest income volatility could increase by lending to riskier borrowers, thus mixing credit risk with our measure of structural interest rate risk. Similarly, fees on loan commitments mix credit risk with nonfinancial risk. Nonetheless, we believe that these counterexamples are relatively atypical and that our simple approach provides a reasonable approximation to risk type attribution.

In each case the dollar values are divided by our estimated risk-weighted assets, RWA, to arrive at a risk-specific "return." As in the RORWA analysis, we look at deviations in the return measures from bank-specific averages. While the overall focus is on large negative outcomes, for credit risk we look at the right tail, namely unusually large provisions, as being adverse.

Table 6.5 shows empirical results for our earnings volatility measures (following equation 6.2 expressed as a percentage of RWA) for each of the risk categories at different tail quantiles. The numbers in parentheses correspond to the percentage contribution to total risk, measured as the sum of the parts across the risk sources at each quantile. The last row shows the percentage difference between the sum of the parts and overall net earnings volatility from table 6.2, which can be interpreted as the interrisk diversification benefit. To take one quantile, such as the 0.1% tail, the single largest source of earnings volatility is credit risk, worth 3.57% of RWA corresponding to 47% of the total, and the smallest risk is market risk, worth -0.43% of RWA corresponding to just 6% of the total. (Note that for credit risk, proxied by provisions, a larger (positive) value corresponds to a worse outcome.) The sum of the individual risks at the 0.1% tail (99.9% VaR) is -7.67%, and this far exceeds the 0.1% tail of total RORWA, which is -4.85% from table 6.2. The difference arises from diversification across risks. In other words, if all of the risk types were perfectly correlated in the tails, then a 0.1% event in one risk type would correspond perfectly to the 0.1% event in all other risks. Clearly, this is not the case, and the degree of diversification at this quantile is 37%.

Several things are striking about the results. First, the relative contribution is remarkably stable across quantiles, so that our conclusions about which risks

TABLE 6.5
Left Tail of Earnings Distribution/VaR (%)

Risk Type	0.01 99.99	0.03 99.97	0.05 99.95	0.1 99.9	0.5 99.5	1 99
Market (trading)	−0.93 (5)	−0.71 (5)	−0.57 (5)	−0.43 (6)	−0.16 (4)	−0.11 (4)
Structural A/L	−4.62 (25)	−2.41 (17)	−2.01 (19)	-1.36 (18)	−0.80 (20)	−0.61 (22)
Credit[a]	8.06 (44)	6.79 (48)	4.74 (46)	3.57 (47)	1.89 (47)	1.21 (44)
Total nonfinancial[b]	−4.71 (26)	−4.17 (30)	−3.00 (29)	−2.30 (30)	−1.17 (29)	−0.83 (30)
Operational	(11)	(12)	(12)	(12)	(12)	(12)
Business	(15)	(18)	(17)	(18)	(17)	(18)
Sum of risks	−18.32	−14.07	−10.32	−7.67	-4.03	−2.77
Total risk	−9.69	−7.69	−7.14	−4.85	-2.67	−1.75
Diversification benefit	47	45	31	37	34	37

Note. Allocation by risk type for the left tail of the earnings distribution, measured in return on risk-weighted assets (RORWA). Note that for credit risk, proxied by provisions, that a larger (positive) value corresponds to a worse outcome. Diversification benefit is the difference between the sum of the risks (tail components) and the total (reported in table 6.2). All values in percent, 22,770 bank-quarters, 1986Q2–2005Q1, net of bank mean.

[a] Note that large positive provisions correspond to large credit risk realizations.

[b] We split total nonfinancial risk into operational and business risk using a 60%/40% allocation following Kuritzkes (2002).

matter the most are not sensitive to the choice of tail quantile or confidence interval. For instance, credit risk, the dominant risk type, makes up just under half the total: between 44 and 48%, across the tail quantiles from 1.0 to 0.01%. Market risk in the trading book is by far the smallest source of risk, from 4 to 6% of the total. These results are consistent with industry benchmarks as reported in Kuritzkes et al. (2003) and other studies, such as Hirtle (2003) and Rosenberg and Schuermann (2006), though they are arrived at using rather different methods.

Second, risk types that have, to date, not been subject to a regulatory capital charge, namely structural asset/liability risk and nonfinancial risk, make up about half of the total risk. As noted above, nonfinancial risk contains operational risk, which will be subject to a capital charge under Basel II, and business risk, which will not be. While there is limited evidence for the appropriate weighting between these two risk types (reflecting the primitive state of quantification of nonfinancial risks), Kuritzkes (2002) argues for slightly more than half to business and somewhat less for operational, which would imply that the latter contributes around 12–14% of the total. A 12% allocation to operational risk is also broadly in line with Basel II's suggested calibration for operational risk, as well as with Allen and Bali (2007), and De Fontnouvelle et al. (2006a).

On this basis, we adopt 12% as a measure of operational risk contribution, and classify residual nonfinancial risk as business risk.

Structural asset/liability risk, which under Basel II is subject to regulatory capital under Pillar 2 (but is not part of the minimum capital requirement under Pillar 1), makes up about one-fifth of total risk. This, too, is consistent with industry benchmarks reported in Kuritzkes et al. (2003).

Finally, the difference between total risk and the sum of the parts is between 31 and 47%, very much in line with results obtained by Rosenberg and Schuermann (2006), who report a diversification benefit of 45% across market (trading only), credit, and operational risk, using a completely different approach based on copulas, although somewhat higher than results reported by Dimakos and Aas (2004), who report a 20% benefit for the same three risk types.

Risk diversification is obtained if the components that make up the sum are imperfectly correlated. While we would expect events that drive large market losses, such as unfavorable movements in interest rates or equity prices, also to influence A/L risk and perhaps even credit risk, we would not expect those losses to march in lockstep. Estimates of this kind of dependence can be captured through the correlation of the quantiles or rank correlations, and in table 6.6 we present the median Spearman's rank correlations between the earnings components and of the components with total (pretax) earnings across 888 banks. For each bank we computed the set of rank correlations across time, and the table entries represent the median across those banks, the idea being that this is the correlation profile of a typical bank in our sample.

It is apparent that many of the correlations are small and several are negative. Going down the first column, the correlation of total pretax earnings with the components, net interest income plus net gains on securities, our proxy for asset/liability risk, is correlated a modest 0.500 with total earnings; trading income, the market risk proxy, is only weakly correlated at 0.023; while the correlation with provisions, the credit risk proxy, is of the same size as asset/liability risk at –0.386 and has the expected sign—earnings decline when provisions increase. Similarly, earnings increase when other income, the proxy for total nonfinancial risk, increases (correlation is 0.389). The correlations between the earnings components, which may be thought of as proxies for interrisk correlations, show the source of some interrisk diversification. For instance, other income (nonfinancial risk) appears to act as a hedge against asset/liability risk: their correlation is –0.481.

There is no guarantee that the correlations reported in table 6.6, which are estimated over the entire sample, are necessarily reflective of the tails. Tail dependence is notoriously difficult to estimate with any accuracy (Poon et al.

TABLE 6.6

Median Spearman's Rank Correlations of Total (Pretax) Earnings
and the Four Major Components across 888 Banks

	Total pretax earnings	NII + net sec	Trading income	Provisions	Other income
Total pretax earnings	1.000				
NII + net sec	0.500	1.000			
Trading income	0.023	0.027	1.000		
Provisions	−0.386	0.123	0.049	1.000	
Other income	0.389	−0.481	−0.082	−0.143	1.000

Note. Based on quarterly return on risk-weighted assets (RORWA). 22,770 bank quarters, 1986Q2–2005Q1. All returns are deviations from bank mean. NII + net sec is net interest income plus net gains on securities, a proxy for ALM risk; trading income is a proxy for market risk; provisions is a proxy for credit risk; other income is all other income plus net extraordinary items less noninterest expenses and is a proxy for total nonfinancial risk.

2004). Prudential risk management suggests that implied hedges across different categories of income may not hold during times of market turmoil.[22]

6.2.3. ROBUSTNESS CHECKS

In this section we conduct a series of robustness checks along two important dimensions: bank size and sample period. First, it is possible that the tails of the RORWA distribution may be dominated by small banks, and thus drawing inferences from the full sample about large banks may not be appropriate. Moreover, large banks may have a different business mix than smaller banks, implying a different risk type allocation. We check for large bank effects by repeating our analysis only for banks with more than $10bn in assets (2005Q1 dollars). Since this reduces the sample by more than 75%, we restrict the large bank analysis to quarterly data.

Second, our full sample period extends from 1981 through 2004 (1986Q1 through 2005Q2 for the quarterly analysis), but the latter half of the period was much more benign for banks than the first half. The early period was marked by two recessions, serious emerging market debt and real estate lending problems, and the New England and Texas banking crises, culminating in the highest

---

[22] See, for instance, Longin and Solnik (2001), who find that correlations increase in bear but not in bull markets.

TABLE 6.7
Left Tail of Earnings Distribution/VaR (%): Robustness Check

	Number of obs.	0.05/99.95	0.1/99.9	0.5/99.5	1/99
	Implied rating:	BBB+, A	BBB–, A–	BB–, BB+	B+/B, BB
Quarterly (1986Q2–2005Q1)	22,770	–7.14	–4.85	–2.67	–1.75
Quarterly, big banks (1986Q2–2005Q1)	5,153	–5.95	–3.92	–2.42	–1.72
Quarterly (1986Q2–1992Q4)	7,963	–9.43	–7.59	–3.59	–2.79
Quarterly (1993Q1–2005Q1)	14,807	–3.25	–2.98	–1.36	–0.92
Annual (1981–2004)	7,396	–14.74	–10.81	–6.00	–4.38
Annual (1981–1992)	3,680	–16.80	–14.74	–7.89	–5.34
Annual (1993–2004)	3,716	–8.32	–4.58	–3.20	–2.31

Note. Implied credit rating for left tail percentiles for quarterly and annual return on risk-weighted assets (RORWA), in percent, for different sample periods. Big banks are defined as banks with more than $10bn in assets (2005Q1 dollars). Implied credit ratings are presented in table 6.3.

rate of U.S. bank failures since the Great Depression in 1991. In the second period, bank failure rates dropped significantly, due in part to the improved macroeconomic environment. We check for differences in both aggregate risk and risk contribution across the two periods by splitting our sample. Given that new regulation in the form of FDICIA was enacted at the end of 1991 and the full implementation of the first Basel Accord took effect in 1991–92, we think it is reasonable to extend the first period through the end of 1992, and start the second period at the beginning of 1993. Since the sample size is reduced, we confine our analysis just to the 99.9% (or 10 bp) tail.

The results are presented in table 6.7, where the full-sample results are repeated from table 6.4, for easier comparison. The first comparison is size: large banks appear to experience fewer extremely adverse RORWA outcomes then do smaller banks. For instance, the 99.9% VaR is –3.92% (quarterly) for large banks but –4.85% for all banks.

The differences are more dramatic across time periods. For instance, 99.9% VaR levels are more than double (–7.59 vs. –2.98%) in the first period than in the

TABLE 6.8
Left Tail of Earnings Distribution/VaR (%): Robustness Check

Risk Type	0.05 99.95	0.1 99.9	0.5 99.5	1 99
A given cell (using first cell)	1986Q2–2005Q1: all banks (5), large banks (7) All banks: 1986Q2–1992Q4 (3), 1993Q1 – 2005Q1 (10)			
Market (trading)	5, 7	6, 8	4, 7	4, 7
	3, 10	3, 9	3, 6	2, 6
Structural A/L	19, 29	18, 20	20, 20	22, 20
	16, 28	12, 24	13, 31	13, 31
Credit	46, 41	47, 46	47, 43	44, 44
	54, 24	58, 22	56, 21	60, 22
Total nonfinancial	29, 22	30, 26	29, 29	30, 29
	27, 37	27, 42	28, 44	25, 42
Diversification benefit	31, 55	37, 48	34, 42	37, 38
	33, 51	32, 42	27, 46	23, 49

Note. Allocation by risk type for the left tail of the earnings distribution, measured in return on risk weighted assets (RORWA). All values in percent. The first entry in a given cell uses the total sample and is taken from table 6.5. The second entry is for large banks, and the next two are for the first and second subperiod (1986Q2–1992Q4, 1993Q1–2005Q1) respectively. Diversification benefit is the difference between the sum of the tail components and the total (reported in table 6.2).

more recent period using quarterly data, and triple using annual data (−14.74 vs. −4.58%). While the probability of a −8% RORWA occurring is 0.28% over the whole sample period, it is 0.49% in the first sample period, corresponding to about a BBB– rating, and only 0.05% in the second (A). An implication is that calibration of capital standards depends on the state of the world, and that higher capital levels are required to achieve the same solvency standard during "bad" periods than "good" ones.

Next we investigate whether the risk allocation is sensitive to bank size and sample period using the quarterly data. The results are summarized in table 6.8, where the first entry in a given cell uses the total sample and is taken from table 6.5 for easy comparison. The second entry is for large banks, and the next two are for the first and second subperiods (1986Q2–1992Q4, 1993Q1–2005Q1), respectively. Size seems to have a rather small impact on the risk allocation. Large banks seem to have somewhat more market (trading) risk at 7–8% of the total rather than 4–6% for all banks. Their level of asset/liability risk is a little higher, and they seem to have a little less credit risk and a bit more nonfinancial risk. That modest difference in business mix, however,

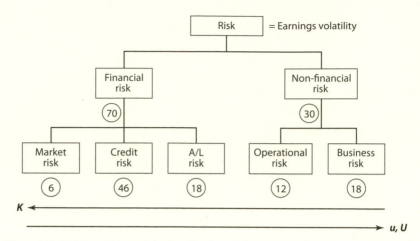

Figure 6.7. Risk taxonomy revisited, with risk contribution. Numbers in circles are percent risk allocation.

results in a larger diversification benefit ranging from 38 to 55% in contrast to 31 to 37% for all banks.

The choice of sample period has a more pronounced effect on risk allocation. When looking at all banks in our sample, the contribution to total earnings volatility seems to have shifted away from credit risk and toward market, structural A/L, and nonfinancial risk in the recent period. In fact, based on the experience since 1993, credit risk accounts for only about 22% of total earnings volatility—an improbably low calibration relative to Basel II and industry norms.[23] We caution against extrapolating solely from the second period.

6.2.4. IMPLICATIONS FOR K, u, AND U

If we accept the rank ordering of risks in terms of the K, u, U framework in section 6.2.3, we are now in a position to say something about how much we know and don't know about the different sources of bank risk. Figure 6.7 reproduces our risk taxonomy, with the percentage contributions from each source, as reported in table 6.5 using the whole sample period and all banks. It turns out that we know the most about the least significant source of risk, market risk.

---

[23] As credit instruments have become more tradable, and credit assets have shifted from the banking to the trading book, credit risk too has shifted. In this way our reported credit risk is likely biased downward.

We know the least about business risk, which accounts for 18% of total earnings volatility and is thus three times bigger than market risk. More generally, the two risks that practitioners have spent the most time quantifying—market and credit risk—account for only about half of total earnings volatility. The three risks—structural asset/liability risk, operational risk, and business risks—whose measurement approaches are nonstandardized and underdeveloped—account for the other half. The two nonfinancial risks with the largest amount of unknowns and unknowables account for nearly a third of total risk. And splitting nonfinancial risk based on prior research and the Basel II calibration suggests that operational risk (12%) is actually a less significant source of earnings volatility than business risk (18%)—the last frontier of risk quantification.

6.3. IMPLICATION FOR POLICY: PRIVATE AND PUBLIC

Our findings on the magnitudes of bank risk and their positioning in the K, u, and U space have implications for policy, both public (supervision and regulation) and private (business strategy). First, the sizing of the overall bank risk pie allows regulatory capital levels, such as those specified in the Basel II framework, to be calibrated based on an empirical solvency standard. Using earnings volatility data from before the 2007 credit crisis, Basel II's requirement that banks hold minimum total (Tier I plus Tier II) capital of 8% of RWA translates into an annual solvency standard of 99.72%—roughly the equivalent of a BBB credit rating. A BBB rating is not a high-solvency standard for a financial institution: It is just one step above the minimum threshold for investment grade. This may explain why banks historically have held excess capital well above regulatory minimums. At the same time, the split sample analysis shows that much more capital may be required to achieve the same solvency standard during "bad" periods than good ones. Looking ahead, efforts to recalibrate regulatory capital standards should be based on a sound empirical understanding of the implied solvency standard, incorporating more recent data. At the same time, the bigger the source of risk, the more attention it should command from risk managers and regulators. And the more "known" a risk is, the greater our ability to manage it.

The relative contribution of the different sources of bank risk, as reflected in figure 6.8, can be seen to justify the attention risk managers and regulators have historically paid to credit risk. Credit risk is the largest source of bank earnings volatility. Although our knowledge of credit risk falls short of market (trading) risk, whose rich data environment enables the most robust economic capital modeling, we have an increasingly strong understanding of credit risk fundamentals, at least for traditional forms of credit risk. This view is reflected in the proposals to allow (and, for the largest U.S. banks, require) highly granular, transaction-level quantification of credit risk under Basel II. Taken together, the relatively advanced state of knowledge of credit and market risk covers half of the total risk pie.

Looking forward, however, significant returns to risk management can be expected from progress in the three categories of risk that are less well understood. From a policy perspective, Basel II imposes a new Pillar 1 capital charge for operational risk, a relative small source of earnings volatility, while ignoring both asset/liability and business risk, which together account for over one-third of total earnings volatility.[24]

It is perhaps surprising that the regulators chose to tackle operational risk—which, according to our risk positioning is relatively hard to measure and subject to many unknowns—rather than seek to standardize the approach for characterizing and measuring asset/liability risk. Subjecting asset/liability risk to an explicit capital charge would have completed the regulatory capital framework for all of a bank's financial risk taking. Instead, an important source of financial risk is left out of the picture. One need not look too far back to understand the significance of risks inherent in structural asset/liability positions—they were, of course, the defining feature of the U.S. savings and loan debacle. More recently, the acute funding risks embedded in large off-balance sheet vehicles like structured investment vehicles (SIVs) were a direct result of poorly managed maturity mismatch. Simply put, if the regulators feel comfortable placing operational risk under Pillar 1, they should feel at least as comfortable doing so with asset/liability risk.

At the same time, the focus on operational risk management sparked by the inclusion of operational risks within the Basel II framework should not lead to a false sense of comfort. Operational risk, as defined in Basel II, appears to account for only about 12% of total earnings volatility and less than half of nonfinancial risk. The more important source of nonfinancial earnings volatility is business risk, which is still largely unexplored (see figure 6.3). It is far from clear, however, whether regulators should seek to impose a mandatory capital charge for this risk source.

The existing risk profile of banks may in part be explained by the state of K, u, and U. Bank managers may have felt more comfortable taking market and credit risk because they thought they understood it and could manage it. Or, equally, they may have used their knowledge of credit and market risk to carefully control this portion of risk taking so as to keep total earnings volatility within acceptable bounds. As more is learned about the harder to measure risk types, new products will likely evolve to help manage these risks better. This, in turn, may make banks more willing to assume other risks. In this way, there is

---

[24] To be sure, interest rate risk is covered under Pillar 2.

likely to be an endogenous link between the level of risk knowledge, on the one hand, and banks' business activities and risk profile, on the other.

We have already seen a transformation in bank risk taking as financial innovation, especially in the area of derivatives, has spread. For instance, the development and subsequent spread of credit derivatives and securitizations, such as credit default swaps and CDOs, has allowed banks to shed significant amounts of traditional credit risk. But the reduction in traditional credit risk has come with a concomitant increase in counterparty risk and also new forms of nonfinancial risk—such as operational (legal/fiduciary) risks and reputation effects associated with breakdowns in the securitization process.

For both practitioners and policy makers, the message may be to stop looking for keys under the lamppost. The search for improvements in risk management should focus on the sources of risk that are the least "known" and have the greatest impact on earnings volatility.

REFERENCES

Allen, L., and T. Bali (2007). Cyclicality in catastrophic and operational risk measurement. *Journal of Banking & Finance* 31, 1191–235.

Allen, L., J. Boudoukh, and A. Saunders (2004). *Understanding Market, Credit and Operational Risk*, Malden, MA: Blackwell.

Altman, E. I., and D.L. Kao (1992). Rating drift of high yield bonds. *Journal of Fixed Income*, March, 15–20.

Andersen, T., T. Bollerslev, F.X. Diebold, and P. Labys (2003). Modeling and forecasting realized volatility. *Econometrica* 71, 529–626.

Bangia, A., F. X. Diebold, A. Kronimus, C. Schagen, and T. Schuermann (2002). Ratings migration and the business cycle, with applications to credit portfolio stress testing. *Journal of Banking & Finance*, 26, 235–64.

Basel Committee on Banking Supervision (BCBS) (1988). Internal convergence of capital measurement and capital standards. www.bis.org/publ/bcbs04A.pdf, July.

Basel Committee on Banking Supervision (BCBS) (1996). Amendment to the Capital Accord to incorporate market risks (No. 24). www.bis.org/publ/bcbs24a.htm, January.

Basel Committee on Banking Supervision (BCBS) (1999). Credit risk modelling: Current practices and applications. www.bis.org/publ/bcbs49.htm, April.

Basel Committee on Banking Supervision (BCBS) (2001a). Overview of the new Basel Accord. www.bis.org/publ/bcbsca02.pdf, January.

Basel Committee on Banking Supervision (BCBS) (2001b). The internal ratings based approach. www.bis.org/publ/bcbsca.htm, May.

Basel Committee on Banking Supervision (BCBS) (2005). International convergence of capital measurement and capital standards: A revised framework. www.bis.org/publ/bcbs118.htm, November.

Berger, A. N., R. J. Herring, and G. P. Szegö (1995). The role of capital in financial institutions. *Journal of Banking & Finance* 19, 393–430.

Berger, A. N., R. De Young, M. J. Flannery, D. Lee, and O. Oztekin (2008). How do large banking organizations manage their capital ratios? *Journal of Financial Services Research* 34, 123–49.

Bessis, J. (1998). *Risk Management in Banking*, New York: Wiley.

Brown, S., S. A. Hillegeist, and K. Lo (2005). Management forecasts and litigation risk. Working paper, available at ssrn.com/abstract=709161.

Carey, M. (2002). A guide to choosing absolute bank capital requirements. *Journal of Banking & Finance*, 26, 929–51.

Carey, M., and M. Hrycay (2001). Parameterizing credit risk models with ratings data. *Journal of Banking & Finance* 25, 197–270.

Crouhy, M., D. Galai, and R. Mark (2001). *Risk Management*. New York: McGraw Hill.

De Fontnouvelle, P., V. DeJesus-Rueff, J. Jordan, and E. Rosengren (2006a). Capital and risk: New evidence on implications of large operational losses. *Journal of Money, Credit and Banking* 38, 1819–46.

De Fontnouvelle, P., J. Jordan, and E. Rosengren (2006b). Implications of alternative operational risk modeling techniques. In M. Carey and R. Stulz, eds., *Risks of Financial Institutions*. Chicago: University of Chicago Press, chapter 10.

Diebold, F. X., T. A. Gunther, and A. S. Tay (1998a). Evaluating density forecasts with applications to financial risk management. *International Economic Review* 39, 863–83.

Diebold, F. X., T. Schuermann, and J. D. Stroughair (1998b). Pitfalls and opportunities in the use of extreme value theory in risk management. In A.-P.N. Refenes, A. N. Burgess, and J. D. Moody, eds., *Advances in Computational Finance*. Amsterdam: Kluwer Academic, chapter 1. Reprinted in *The Journal of Risk Finance*, Winter 2000, (1: 2), 30–36.

Dimakos, X.K., and K. Aas (2004). Integrated risk modelling. *Statistical Modelling* 4, 265–77.

Domowitz, I., and R. L. Sartain (1999). Determinants of the consumer bankruptcy decision. *Journal of Finance* 54, 403–20.

Federal Reserve Bank of St. Louis (2004). Bank director's training: Asset & Liability Committee, available at www.stlouisfed.org/col/director/alco/reviewreports_financial modeling.htm.

Gordy, M. (2000). A comparative anatomy of credit risk models. *Journal of Banking & Finance* 24, 119–49.

Gordy, M. B. (2003). A risk-factor model foundation for ratings-based bank capital rules. *Journal of Financial Intermediation* 12, 199–232.

Gross, D. B., and N. S. Souleles (2002). An empirical analysis of personal bankruptcy and delinquency. *Review of Financial Studies* 15, 319–47.

Hanson, S., and T. Schuermann (2006). Confidence intervals for probabilities of default. *Journal of Banking & Finance* 30, 2281–301.

Hendricks, D. (1996). Evaluation of value-at-risk models using historical data. *Federal Reserve Bank of New York Economic Policy Review* 2 (1), 39–69.

Herring, R., and T. Schuermann (2005). Capital regulation for position risk in banks, securities firms and insurance companies. In H. Scott, ed., *Capital Adequacy Beyond Basel: Banking, Securities, and Insurance*, Oxford, UK: Oxford University Press, chapter 1.

Hirtle, B. (2003). What market risk capital reporting tells us about bank risk. *Federal Reserve Bank of New York Economic Policy Review* 9, 37–54.

Holton, G. A. (2003). *Value-at-Risk: Theory and Practice*. San Diego, CA: Academic Press.

Jorion, P. (2000). Risk management lessons from long-term capital management. *European Financial Management* 6, 277–300.

Jorion, P. (2001). *Value at Risk*, 2nd ed. New York: McGraw-Hill.

Knight, F. H. (1921). *Risk, Uncertainty, and Profit*, Boston, MA: Hart, Schaffner & Marx; Houghton Mifflin.

Koch, T. W., and S. S. MacDonald (2000). *Bank Management*, 4th ed. Orlando, FL: Harcourt.

Koyluoglu, H. U., A. Bangia, and T. Garside (2000). Devil in the parameters. In Credit Risk Special Report, *Risk* 13:3, S26–S30.

Kuritzkes, A. (2002). Operational risk capital: A problem of definition. *Journal of Risk Finance*, Fall, 1–10.

Kuritzkes, A. (2006). Comment on De Fontnouvelle, Jordan, and Rosengren. In M. Carey and R. Stulz, eds., *Risks of Financial Institutions*, Chicago, IL: University of Chicago Press.

Kuritzkes, A., and H. Scott (2005). Sizing operational risk and the effect of insurance: Implications for the Basel II Capital Accord. In H. Scott, ed., *Capital Adequacy: Law, Regulation, and Implementation*, Oxford, UK: Oxford University Press, chapter 7.

Kuritzkes, A., T. Schuermann, and S. M. Weiner (2003). Risk measurement, risk management and capital adequacy of financial conglomerates. In R. Herring and R. Litan, eds., *Brookings-Wharton Papers in Financial Services*, 141–94.

Kuritzkes, A., T. Schuermann and S. M. Weiner (2005). Deposit insurance and risk management of the U.S. banking system: What is the loss distribution faced by the FDIC? *Journal of Financial Services Research* 27, 217–243.

Lando, D., and T. Skødeberg (2002). Analyzing ratings transitions and rating drift with continuous observations. *Journal of Banking & Finance* 26, 423–44.

Longin, F., and B. Solnik (2001). Extreme correlation in international equity markets. *Journal of Finance* 56, 649–76.

Lopez, J.A., and C.A. Walter (2001). Evaluating covariance matrix forecasts in a value-at-risk framework. *Journal of Risk* 3, 69–98.

Lucas, A., P. Klaassen, P. Spreij, and S. Straetmans (2001). An analytic approach to credit risk of large corporate bond and loan portfolios. *Journal of Banking & Finance* 25, 1635–64.

Marrison, C. (2002). *The Fundamentals of Risk Measurement*. New York: McGraw Hill.

Marshall, C., and M. Siegel (1996). Value at risk: Implementing a risk measurement standard. *Journal of Derivatives* 4, 91–111.

Mays, E. (1996). Interest-rate models used by depository institutions. In F. J. Fabozzi and A. Konishi, eds., *The Handbook of Asset/Liability Management: State of the Art*

Investment Strategies, Risk Controls and Regulatory Requirements, Chicago: Irwin Professional Publishers, chapter 7.

Netter, J. M., and A. Poulsen (2003). Operational risk in financial service providers and the proposed Basel Capital Accord: An overview. *Advances in Financial Economics* 8, 147–71.

Nickell, P., W. Perraudin, and S. Varotto (2000). Stability of rating transitions. *Journal of Banking & Finance* 24, 203–27.

Poon, S.-H., M. Rockinger, and J. Tawn. (2004). Extreme value dependence in financial markets: diagnostics, models and financial implications. *Review of Financial Studies* 17, 581–610.

Pritsker, M. (1997). Evaluating value-at-risk methodologies: Accuracy versus compuational time. *Journal of Financial Services Research* 12, 201–42.

Rajan, R. G. (2005). Has financial development made the world riskier? Presented at the 2005 Economic Symposium at Jackson Hole, WY, sponsored by the Federal Reserve Bank of Kansas City.

Rosenberg, J. V., and T. Schuermann (2006). A general approach to integrated risk management with skewed, fat-tailed distributions. *Journal of Financial Economics* 79, 569–614.

Santos, J.A.C. (2001). Bank capital regulation in contemporary banking theory: A review of the literature. *Financial Markets, Institutions & Instruments* 10, 41–84.

Saunders, A., and L. Allen (2002). *Credit Risk Measurement—New Approaches to Value at Risk and Other Paradigms*, 2nd ed. New York: Wiley.

Slywotzky, A. J. and J. Drzik (2005). Countering the biggest risk of all. *Harvard Business Review* 83, 78–88.

Stiroh, K. (2004). Diversification in banking: is noninterest income the answer? *Journal of Money, Credit and Banking* 36, 83–88.

Treacy, W. F., and M. Carey (2000). Credit risk rating systems at large U.S. banks. *Journal of Banking & Finance* 24, 167–201.

United States General Accounting Office (USGAO) (1998). *Risk-based Capital: Regulatory and Industry Approaches to Capital and Risk*. Report to the Chairman, Committee on Banking, Housing, and Urban Affairs, U.S. Senate and the Chairman, Committee on Banking and Financial Services, House of Representatives, GAO/GGD-98-153.

Uyemura, D., and D. van Deventer (1992). *Financial Risk Management in Banking: The Theory and Application of Asset and Liability Management*. Chicago, IL: Dearborn Financial Publishing.

7. Real Estate through the Ages

The Known, the Unknown, and the Unknowable

· ·

Ashok Bardhan and Robert H. Edelstein

> What can we reason, but from what we know?
> Of Man what see we, but his station here,
> From which to reason, or to which refer?
> —**Alexander Pope**, *An Essay on Man*

Real estate and land are among the oldest asset markets with which humans have had extensive experience.[1] The significance of agricultural, residential, and commercial real estate assets in human history can scarcely be exaggerated. Social structure, marriage institutions, interstate relations, and, more broadly, socio-economic organization have been affected by and simultaneously have influenced the nature and functioning of real estate markets. The complex interaction of real estate markets with social, political, cultural, and economic institutions through the ages, combined with the impact of technological changes, makes the task of assessing what is or was known, unknown, and unknowable in real estate economics and real estate investment particularly daunting. Indeed, the current subprime mortgage-generated financial crisis further underscores the complex and uncertain nature of real estate markets and their linkages to other sectors of the economy. As a directing principle of our analysis, we shall follow the taxonomy of the known (K), the unknown (u),

[1] The authors would like to thank Samir Dutt, Richard Herring, Cynthia Kroll, and Desmond Tsang for comments and suggestions.

and the unknowable (*U*), or *KuU*, defined in terms of knowledge as a measurement issue and knowledge as a theoretical construct.[2]

Both empirical and theoretical elements underscore the distinctive *KuU* nature of real estate. For example, real estate is lumpy, though perhaps less so in the last decade with developments in securitization. Housing is a mixed consumption–investment good, and the socio-political nature of housing, as it straddles family, community, and society through economic and financial ties, creates a distinctive asset class.

In the case of commercial real estate, its linkages to production and distribution aspects of the economy result in its attributes being a function of derived demand. These real estate characteristics make its risk profile, the dynamics of uncertainty surrounding it, and the composition of *K*, *u*, and *U* unique across the spectrum of asset classes. Among other distinguishing characteristics of real estate is the extent to which the interplay between real and nominal variables is reflected in prices, although some interplay is indicative for the pricing of many other assets as well; for instance, demographics and financial institutional arrangements have joint, interactive effects in the determination of real estate prices and outputs. The issue of what is known, unknown, and unknowable is, of course, significantly different for demographics vis-à-vis financial variables, whether in the context of knowledge as a measurement or a theoretical issue. After all, demographics play a key role in virtually all real estate markets, and are considered to be one of the relatively "known" variables of our times.

Figure 7.1 provides a schematic overview of our application of the *KuU* framework to real estate. It suggests that a number of economic and noneconomic factors are intertwined in the determination of real estate outcomes. The uncertainty, risk profile, and "knowability" of the latter interact with and are dependent on the uncertainty of this mix of factors.

The reasoning applied to financial markets and the conclusions derived therein, using the *KuU* approach elsewhere in this volume, are also largely applicable to the finance and investment aspects of real estate. We shall therefore analyze real estate markets, including real estate finance and investment, primarily through the historical prism of the shifting boundaries between what is known, what is unknown, and what is unknowable, with a particular focus on

---

[2] The notion of a measured or measurable probability distribution is critical in this framework. *K* signifies that the distribution is specified, *u* that probabilities cannot be assigned to all events, and *U* that the events themselves are unknown in advance. The "theory" approach stresses the underlying conceptual model. Put slightly differently, *K* is when there is common knowledge about the underlying model, *u* occurs when there is no accepted paradigm, but there are competing models/concepts, and U where there is an overall absence of a conceptual underpinning or model (see Diebold, Doherty, and Herring, this volume).

Figure 7.1. Framework for analyzing *KuU* and real estate.

what distinguishes real estate markets and real estate investing from the broader world of finance. The motivation for utilizing this framework is to examine both the epistemology of uncertain and risky elements associated with real estate, as well as to analyze the evolution of our understanding of real estate "risk."

7.1. HISTORICAL BACKGROUND, OR THE EVOLUTION OF THE *KuU* REAL ESTATE FRONTIER

> The process of discovery is very simple. An unwearied and systematic application
> of known laws to nature causes the unknown to reveal themselves.
> —**Henry David Thoreau** (1849). A week on the Concord and Merrimack rivers.
> In *The Writings of Henry David Thoreau*, vol. 1, 387–88.

Development of real estate markets, practices, and institutions over time and space has impacted the evolution of the *KuU* path; from what was once thought to be unknowable, through the simply unknown, and into the realm of the known. Demand and supply factors have affected the relative composition of the three elements of *KuU*. Our historical approach sheds highlights how several noneconomic sources of uncertainty have interacted with real estate markets through the ages.

Over time societal and civilizational advances outside the immediate ambit of real estate have significantly impacted the latter. For instance, the development of property rights for land created the first "defensible property" and marks a seminal moment in real estate markets, in terms of engaging a primary historical element of a fundamental uncertainty involving the trinity of usage, the benefits accruing from usage, and their appropriation. Bowles and Choi (2002) give us the general historical–economic context in which this break-through transpires: "individual property rights provided a better system of co-ordination among members of groups only after the ambiguity of possession endemic to the hunter gatherer economy was attenuated with the domestica-tion of crops and livestock. Thus, it was by clarifying possession that the advent of agriculture may have permitted what we call the first property rights revo-lution." It may be the first event in history that clearly enunciates the balance between costs and benefits, and the linkages to risk-taking at the basic level of food and habitat. In the words of Baker (2003), "Economists . . . reason that land ownership emerges when the benefits to owning are greater than the costs of defense . . . the benefits to ownership occur because land use externalities are internalized when land is owned, and the costs of defense are understood as exclusion costs."[3]

For many centuries, a major historical uncertainty revolved around the sup-ply of real estate; to wit, the extent of habitable land available in the world. Indeed, we did not fully comprehend the extent of our ignorance of the world-wide supply/availability of land until perhaps the late Middle Ages. In terms of our framework, the unknowable was the completely unanticipated "discovery" of the additional "new world" land supply. Major land masses were being dis-covered, surprising as it may seem today, until just a few hundred years ago. In addition to this basic unknown/unknowable, as in, for example, the existence of the Americas, there were a few simple unknowns, such as the amount of habitable land in, say, Siberia. Over time, our understanding of the total supply of land has progressed from U to u to K.[4]

Geographic discoveries, war, and social revolutions, as well as major socio-cultural developments, have impacted the universe of what was known and what was uncertain about real estate related issues. An illustration of how larger social and economic changes affected real estate markets in the Middle Ages and the composition of uncertainty surrounding them is provided by Fernand Braudel in a memorable passage about the early stages of urbanization in Europe in the as yet pre-industrial 16th century: "landed estates ended up on the market. . . . In Europe as a whole, there are some very revealing price series on land sales

---

[3] The existence of commons and fuzzy rights to land at various points in time in different coun-tries further illustrates the importance and the impact of societal norms for real estate related issues.

[4] However, as we discuss later, future environmental changes may affect the supply side in un-expected ways.

and many references to the regular rise in prices. In Spain in 1558 for instance, according to a Venetian ambassador . . . properties (i.e., land) which used to be sold at 8 to 10%, that is, 12.5 or 10 times their revenue, are now selling at 25 to 20 times their revenue . . . they have doubled with the abundance of money. . . . This movement was of course everywhere linked to the economic and social transformation which was dispossessing the old landowners, whether lord or peasant, for the benefit of the new rich from the towns."[5] At the time, future social upheavals, including the impending massive rural–urban migration, the changing feudal structure, and industrial capitalism were unforeseeable, as was their impact on land and other markets, since the social structure and issues surrounding land ownership were so intricately intertwined.

At a micro-socio level, the evolution of the structure of the family and the household has been another source of unexpected changes on the demand for real estate, particularly in the sphere of housing. Living arrangements have changed dramatically over the centuries, albeit not always along a straightforward and foreseeable path, from a setup involving joint families and households to independent, nuclear families and households, with a concomitant impact on the number of housing units demanded as well as the space allocation per unit. Living space requirements have also been altered by the changing institutions of domestic servitude, which in turn are a function of social changes, migration-related factors, economic and social inequality, urban structure, and the availability of job opportunities.[6]

The creation of specialized real estate was another development that impacted real estate markets in a nonforeseeable way. Separation of commercial and residential real estate was brought about by the rise of professionalization as well as by organizational imperatives. A craftsman's or an artisan's office/workshop and home were often the same, indeed as were the offices of a family business. The changing structure of work, brought about by task specialization and technology, and the reorganization of the workplace engendered the need to operate cooperatively in a neutral space and provided the impetus for the genesis of warehouse, retail, and, later, manufacturing as well as office real estate. The appearance of business organizations, such as partnerships and corporations, the

---

[5] Braudel (1982b, page 51).

[6] See Ray and Qayum (2009) on domestic servitude. As another example of social practices impacting living arrangements, and hence urban design, Chandler (1987) notes that in earlier days "Chinese cities . . . (had) . . . an especially low density because of the Chinese refusal to sleep below anyone, so their houses were . . . nearly all of just 1 story. Hence, inland Chinese cities had a density of only about 75 per hectare, and even in seaports or the imperial capital the density hardly exceeded 100."

growth of capitalism generally, and the subsequent mushrooming of a white-collar workforce gave the first fillip to demand for office space.

Conquests, discoveries, and changing patterns of international trade have transformed the organization of real estate through the location, emergence, and development of cities. As George Modelski claims, most of the major cities of the ancient world (between 3500 BC and 1200 BC) have disappeared into the mists of time. None of the cities of the earliest civilizations of Mesopotamia, Egypt, and the Indus River Valley have retained their importance; indeed, most do not exist today. Most ancient and medieval empires were primarily land-based, whether in the case of the territorial campaigns of Alexander of Macedonia or of Chingiz Khan. Most of the major cities of the time were in the hinterland, controlling access to strategic land assets and straddling critical trading routes. On the other hand, for the seafaring enterprise of relatively modern colonialism, and of modern global economic integration, the logic of trade and development required cities on the coast. The geographical distribution of major cities in precolonial and colonial/postcolonial India serves as a vivid illustration of how wrenching economic and political changes can affect the urban landscape. Thus appeared the relatively recent Bombays, Calcuttas, and Shanghais, replacing the Agras (Agra, where the Taj Mahal is located, was a major city under the Moghul empire) and the Xians (the ancient Imperial Chinese capital). Of course, not all ancient cities have withered away under the churning and dislocating impact of global capitalism. That path dependence is of crucial importance is borne out by examples such as Delhi and Beijing, both historic hinterland cities, yet still retaining their importance.

Apart from social, economic, and political changes, technological advances have also modified the uncertainty frontier. The invention of new materials and development of advanced engineering techniques have allowed the construction of skyscrapers, breaking the bondage of building scale to plot size, and leading to intensive land usage. Similarly, developments in the field of finance, such as the creation of fiat money, banking deposits, and promissory notes, have severed the constraints of time and space, and connected those who save to those who invest, leading to the emergence of modern finance, including real estate finance.

A historical approach that embraces broader socio-economic trends is necessary for understanding real estate, which is an integral part of the "structures of daily life." Such an approach helps us understand that events and circumstances that seemed unknowable or inconceivable, and not merely unknown, at various times in history were so largely because they were not part of the "system," but dwelled in the realm of other aspects/branches of society, and were in turn impacted by a myriad other unidentified factors.

7.2. THE PRESENT STATE OF KNOWLEDGE

This section deals with the present state of our knowledge of the known, unknown, and unknowable in real estate, and the concomitant taxonomy of risk. In the general hierarchy of the risk–return dichotomy, it is widely acknowledged that real estate is either lower or on par with the risk–return profile of common stocks and higher risk–reward than T-bills, municipal bonds, mortgage-backed securities, and investment-grade corporate bonds, in that order. A number of risk attributes are common to real estate investments and financial assets. Some categories of risk that affect real estate are similar to risks for other classes of investment assets, whether it be in common stocks or government securities, and some are specific to real estate.[7] We summarize these elements of uncertainty in terms of the KuU framework.

7.2.1. ENVIRONMENTAL RISK

While some environmental factors may be unknown a priori, over time some other environmental parameters may become "apparent" with the advance of medical or geological sciences. The dangers of asbestos, radon, other toxic materials, and seismic fault lines have become better understood over time. The long-term risks posed by global warming to coastal communities are yet another category of risks that seem to have migrated from an "unknowable," in the sense of the absence of any prior epistemological framework, to a mere "unknown" (both in terms of measurement and theory), or a somewhat accepted distribution of probabilities based on simulations, data, and related scientific work. However, there may still exist in the realm of the unknowable the future genesis of new diseases and catastrophes that we cannot even imagine today, and that, in turn, may cause further alterations in migration patterns, living arrangements, and urban spaces.

7.2.2. LOCATION RISK

The "location, location, location" mantra can also be read as "risk, risk, risk." The lumpy, sunk-cost nature of real estate, tied to a particular location, is a defining attribute of real estate, and as such exposes investors to unique multifaceted risks. Changing demographics, tastes, commuting patterns, and idiosyncratic economic shocks can all transform location from desired to shunned, and vice versa. Of course, the desirability of some real estate locations does not

[7] See Brueggeman and Fisher (2001) for a list of commonly accepted real estate-related risks.

necessarily need to change; there is also some constancy when it comes to a few neighborhoods, which seem to have remained fashionable for decades, if not centuries. While a number of these location drivers may be foreseeable to a certain extent, the overall interplay of myriad mini-uncertainties would suggest that location might be placed in the *u* category.

7.2.3. LIQUIDITY AND LUMPINESS RISK

Real estate, being a lumpy asset, at least in its nonsecuritized form, is subject to more liquidity risk than most asset classes. Particularly in periods of feeble demand, real estate location and product specificity exacerbate the liquidity risk and the expeditious coming together of buyers and sellers. The liquidity risk of residential and commercial real estate can be quite pronounced. For example, residential real estate in the growing California market has had episodes in the early 1980s and early 1990s where its value declined to the order of 20–30%. The most striking feature of these declines was both the reduced availability of traditional financing and significant downturn in sales volume. Much of the liquidity problem relates to the inability (e.g., the savings and loan crisis) and/or the unwillingness of financial institutions to lend. The financial crisis of 2007–09 has thrown the liquidity issue into sharp relief. Sales volumes have fallen drastically, but the market for securities backed by real estate, both residential and commercial, has also frozen up due to uncertainty surrounding their intrinsic value, and the value and composition of underlying real assets. Hence, the structure of real estate financial transactions can sometimes engender a move in our understanding, from the realm of the known to the unknown, and even the unknowable.

7.2.4. REGULATORY AND LEGISLATIVE RISK

Zoning regulations, property tax laws, eminent domain, rent control, and other "interventions" by government and local authorities are always in a position to affect real estate operations and profitability. Examples abound of how changes in governmental regulations and policy or, indeed, the lack thereof as can be seen from the genesis of the present crisis, can affect the bottom line of real estate owners, lenders, and investors. At the Federal level, in 1982, a set of new income tax laws were introduced to stimulate the economy. One of the by-products of these laws was a significant increase in depreciation allowances for real estate investments. In the office and apartment sectors, a tight market combined with these new, more generous tax laws created a surge in production of office and apartment buildings, and the establishment of "tax-efficient syndication vehicles." This boom came to an abrupt halt, in part, because of Federal tax laws passed in 1986, which reduced depreciation allowances and created barriers to tax sheltering through syndications. Ultimately, there was a major and prolonged downturn in the commercial real estate markets.

Other examples of governmental intervention having an impact on real estate markets include local rent control regulations in such cities as San Francisco, Santa Monica, and New York City. On the other hand, the absence or laxity of government regulation can play havoc in complex, interconnected financial markets with potentially severe market failures, such as information asymmetry, coordination issues, and collusion and collision of vested interests. To the extent that "inscrutable are the ways of government, particularly local ones," it is anyone's guess whether this category of risks fits under the rubric of an unknown or an unknowable!

7.2.5. FINANCIAL RISKS

Real estate equity and debt investors confront termination risks caused by complex debt-related options for prepayment and default. Investors in mortgages and mortgage-backed securities are subject to an almost unique form of uncertainty and risk, involving prepayment by mortgage borrowers that may alter significantly the future expected revenue stream. The importance of a correct assessment of the prepayment speed is underscored by the fact that unanticipated prepayment changes and incorrect pricing of the prepayment risk can lead to increased investor cash flow volatility and uncertainty in mortgage security markets. Highly sophisticated models, both theoretical and empirical, have evolved to improve the evaluation of the prepayment risk, including callable bond models, compound options, hazard models, and so forth.[8]

Perhaps the most interesting dilemma for prepayment analysis is the apparent periodic breakdown of sophisticated statistical prepayment models. This, in part, is the result of the changing nature of the real estate financial system, that is, a general easing of the availability of credit for commercial real estate investing as well as for residential ownership. As the financial market changes, the "old" prepayment models, predicated on statistical behavioral relationships of the past, will tend to have major breakdowns. Dynamically, *KuU* in this context is a renewal process by which you move from uncertainties to a better understanding of prepayment behavior, only to have your knowledge shattered by a world in flux driving you back to previous levels of knowledge about prepayment risk. However, a number of research advances in the field of prepayment

---

[8] For some examples, see Chinloy (1989) and Hall and Lundstedt (2005).

modeling have generated a critical mass of insights for understanding the risk associated with prepayment.

On the other hand, system-wide defaults in the case of an economy-wide crisis are either "unknown" or "unknowable" because of the myriad factors involved. For large financial institutions, such as Fannie Mae or Freddie Mac, with significant portfolio positions, a "bust" in the housing market can expose them to significant credit risk. In commercial real estate, yield maintenance for mortgages and/or defeasance clauses mitigate prepayment risks for the lender or debt investor. However, large-scale, single-property real estate debt instruments create significant credit risk, as in the CMBS (commercial mortgage-backed security) market, and the more recent commercial real estate collateralized debt obligation and credit default swap market. These types of securitized debt instruments have been utilized with increasing frequency in large transactions for privatizing public REITs. Thus, the nature of credit risk is changing substantially in unanticipated ways, requiring constant dynamic updating for investors, as they attempt to readjust knowledge about credit risk into the known category.

7.2.6. BUSINESS RISK

Commercial real estate demand is derived demand, ultimately emanating from the state of health of the user–business sectors. Unanticipated shocks to businesses, industries, sectors, occupations, and regions may adversely affect rents and values, and hence real estate investor returns. The overall business risk of a real estate entity is a combination of economic market risk and financial risk. Put somewhat differently, if you were to construct an office building in a particular city or location, the economic markets that create derived demand for office space will determine the economic performance of your building. The heterogeneous nature of real estate and the complex linkages to different kinds of business activity, as well as the plethora of variables that enter in forecasting business activity, squarely place the science of gauging this particular risk in the category of an unknown, since many of the "probabilities" are unknown and there is no universally accepted risk model.

7.2.7. MACRO RISK

The nexus between the larger macroeconomy and the real estate sector is magnified by the size of the latter, and complicated by its role in both the investment- and consumption-related segments of the national accounts. The latter mitigates the risk element to the extent that even if the investment returns are under threat, the consumption benefits are vulnerable only in cases of catastrophic events (which are dealt with elsewhere in this volume). One of the most significant channels through which the macroeconomy affects real estate is via credit markets and through the medium of interest rates. Obviously, interest rates being an integral "cost element" of the economy tend to affect all economic activity; however, real estate is typically highly leveraged and is especially sensitive to interest rate changes. In other words, standard financial risk in the form of debt financing is a common, substantial component of the risk structure of real estate investments. Unexpected inflation risk can adversely impact returns if the revenue streams do not compensate sufficiently to counter the negative effect of changing inflation expectations on interest rates, and required yields. While inflation is also a common risk shared with other kinds of investment, real estate lease indexation may allow operating income to adjust for unexpected changes in inflation. Like most other sectors, real estate is also vulnerable to unforeseeable, unanticipated, adverse supply shocks, whether originating in environmental/resource markets in the normal course or as a result of natural or manmade disasters.

The recently fizzled boom in housing markets in many countries and in certain regional markets in the United States raised concerns about the unknown risks from a potential housing bubble. A clear consensus on the criteria for designating whether this was a bubble emerged only post facto; earlier there was frequent reference to sound fundamentals, such as the backlog of an affluent home buying age cohort from the tech boom of the 1990s, the regulatory constraints on supply, the easy availability of credit, and the historically low mortgage rates. The inherently uncertain nature of social psychology and mass "psychosis" linked to fleeting interactions and possible arbitrary changes in household decisions make any "boom" a decidedly "unknown" category and perhaps an unknowable, *ex ante*, even though historic price–rent ratios have tended to be a good indicator. The potential size of the economic and financial disruption of a housing catastrophe is an extreme example of an event with low probability but with extremely heavy social losses—and our inability to calculate properly the mathematical expectation of this rare combination.

Again, history has several interesting examples of financial bubbles, including in real estate markets. Seventeenth-century Holland was perhaps the richest country in the world because of the lucrative trade between Europe and the spice and textile centers of Asia. The influx of goods, the spread of affluence, the development of financial markets, and the feverish speculative atmosphere led to an upward price spiral for real estate. The devastating impact of the plague and the sobering effect of the tulip mania combined to burst that bubble. Piet Eichholtz says that this historical episode—in which unpredictable disasters combined unpredictably—has relevance for today. "In the wake of these twin calamities, house prices dropped 36 percent. . . . It's true that economic and social conditions were different back then. But major crises do happen, and we can't necessarily predict them. Will bird flu be a major disaster? Will there be more hurricanes? I don't know. Nobody knows." (Shorto 2006).

• • • • • • •

While the interaction of "real" and "nominal" variables insinuates itself into risk analysis for many kinds of investment, it is a distinguishing hallmark of real estate markets. Part of the dichotomy of nominal and real variables is the asymmetry between the rapid response (i.e., the almost instantaneous adjusting financial markets) and the slow or sluggishly adjusting markets (e.g., in real estate), particularly during declines. Observed transactions for housing prices, for example, do not decline as rapidly as they rise, with much of the downside risk being borne by occupants who choose to ride it out.

7.2.8. GLOBALIZATION AND REAL ESTATE

The two major forces driving the new global economy are (1) increasing global economic and financial integration, seen in the huge upsurge of international trade and investment, and (2) the rapid development and dissemination of new technologies, particularly advances in information technology. Both have tended to influence real estate in unexpected ways, increasing the uncertainty about the potential impact on real estate in the future.

Economic research is beginning to take cognizance of the effect of global economic and financial integration on real estate markets. While nontradable, localized real estate might seem immune to the forces of globalization, increasing integration of financial and economic activities has altered significantly both real estate investments and real estate markets. Global transactions have now extended their influence to the real estate sector, resulting in cross-border investments in real estate, international development projects, and multinational real estate ventures, as well as internationally funded housing developments. The role of global imbalances, global financial flows, and their impact on interest rates and mortgage rates in the United States has added another layer of risk and uncertainty to the existing mix.

Bardhan et al. (2004) show that openness has a positive impact on urban rents because of the relative supply inelasticity of real estate, emanating from its unimportable/nontradable nature, and Bardhan et al. (2008) provide evidence that excess returns (i.e., the risk premium) of publicly traded real estate firms decrease with openness, after adjusting for effects of global capital markets, domestic macroeconomic, and firm-specific variables, as well as international currency arbitrage. The finding is consistent with increasing global financial integration and cross-border capital flows. Yet another evolving branch of literature analyzes the impact of global sourcing of industrial supply chains on industrial clusters and agglomerations, and the consequent impact on urban space and real estate demand.

Globalization and technological changes have substantially reduced transportation and communications costs, and have led to increased labor mobility/migration connected to more efficient markets as well as greater integration of national real estate markets. Another indirect path by which global developments and integrated markets affect the evolution of urban space and real estate is through the impact of the secular and cyclical changes in energy prices, caused in part by the secular and cyclical gyrations in demand arising from the growth dynamics of the economies of Asia.

7.2.9. TECHNOLOGY AND REAL ESTATE

The Internet and its related technological developments are now being used by the real estate industry for purposes of marketing, as a communication medium, and as a platform for collaborative activity resulting in new firms creating new forms of value. The interaction and interplay of the Internet and the real estate industry has the potential to alter market composition, economic variables, and organizational structure in ways that are not entirely foreseeable. Much of our assessment is therefore of a speculative nature because of the "unknown" and perhaps even "unknowable" nature of the interaction of the many factors involved, as well as the paucity of available data, the relative novelty of the topic, and the unpredictable ways in which any new, general-purpose technology can develop and impact the economy.

The lowering of transactions and search costs, the easier, instantaneous access to information, could possibly lead to a shortening of the transaction cycle and may perhaps even lead to a lower, "natural" vacancy rate, due to the lowering of the frictional component in matching buyers and sellers. The disintermediating effect of the Internet has led the brokerage community to restructure their operations, and there is tentative evidence that growth in e-commerce has led to a shift in demand from retail to warehousing space for certain goods and commodities. The greater geographic reach induced by the usage of the Internet in real estate transactions can lead to enhanced tradability and increased turnover, promote market deepening and geographic mobility, and perhaps mitigate differences in returns across regions. On the other hand, the informational and geographic disconnect brought about by technology, globalization,

Exhibit 7.1

Selective, Subjective Summary of *KuU* in Real Estate

- Demographics (**K**)
- New materials and engineering advances can radically alter notions of space, affecting both supply and demand in a known, sometimes unknown, and perhaps unknowable manner (**K**, **u**, **U**)
- New kinds of financing—e.g., reverse mortgages—may affect legacy behavior in unknown ways (this is probably both **u** and **U**)
- Globalization and tradability of real estate—it is still location, location, location but just not local, local, local any more! (**u**, **U**)
- Prepayment related issues (**K**, **u**)
- Environmental shocks and catastrophic issues (some **u** some **U**)
- Social trends and psychology (**u**, **U**)
- Systemic risk factors (**u**, **U**)

and complex securitization means that the ultimate owner–investors and lenders have little knowledge of the underlying characteristics of the originated loan and, in case of crisis, little possibility of cooperative restructuring.

Exhibit 7.1 summarizes the list of variables impacting real estate and classifies them in the *KuU* framework. Demographics are at one end of the spectrum as a factor that is known (**K**) in terms of its future evolution and possible impact on real estate; and environmental and catastrophic shocks, the possibility of major global economic and technological developments and socio-cultural trends occupy the other end of the spectrum.

Many aspects of uncertainty, as well as the specific risks enumerated earlier, fit into a standard litany of real estate related risks. Demographics, for example, are a vital determinant of real estate demand, and are believed to be relatively deterministic. The magnitude of the home-buying age cohort in the general population 20 years from now is known with reasonable certitude, and, hence, its impact on real estate demand is "known." Hedonic index models for real estate prices as functions of real attributes, such as the number of rooms and floor area, generate "known" price distributions. Benchmarking models are another attempt at applying what is known for developed countries as a whole, say regarding the proportion of outstanding mortgage volumes or home-ownership rates as a function of demographic, economic, financial, and real estate variables, to countries with embryonic real estate markets. Once a reliable, well-behaved empirical relationship for the mortgage markets in developed countries is created, one can estimate mortgage market potential for developing countries with fledgling real estate markets. The implicit assumption of such analysis is that the structural relationships between the variables for emerging economies should be as in the developed countries. The intuition is that there are "universal" proportions or ratios, and that there is a stable relationship that implies a cross-country "known" phenomenon.[9]

This summary might be subjective and debatable; variables that we designated as U might be disputed by many economists as belonging to u. The idea that "there are few potential events that we cannot ascribe some heuristic level of probability to" seems to be the refrain among many of our colleagues. Also, as pointed out by scientists in other non-social science disciplines, many events are in U space because of the "real-time computing" constraints, such as in investment decisions, weather forecasting, and so forth.

7.3. CONCLUDING REMARKS AND LOOKING FORWARD: DEALING WITH THE UNKNOWN AND THE UNKNOWABLE

> There is a chasm between knowledge and ignorance
> which the arches of science can never span.
> —**Henry David Thoreau** (1817–1862), U.S. philosopher, author, naturalist

As Barrow (1999) observes, the sign of maturity in science has been the recognition of ultimate barriers, the attempt to find limits to its own usefulness, and for its formulas to "predict that there are things which they cannot predict, observations which cannot be made, statements whose truth they can neither affirm nor deny." The path-breaking works of Godel, Heisenberg, and Turing have given us a series of theoretical insights and technical results dealing with impossibility, uncertainty, undecidability, and intractability (see Merry 1995). But as Traub (1996) suggests, these results concern formal systems and it is not clear what the implications are for the social sciences, in general, and economics and finance, in particular—"Typically students learn what is *known* in science while scientists study the *unknown*. An area that is starting to be explored is what is *unknowable* in principle." It does not necessarily follow that these circumscribing theorems limit our search for knowledge in any way. Perhaps, as in music, where it is only after one knows the constraints that one can be aesthetically creative, perhaps it is only after the unknowable is delineated in

---

[9] See Jaffee and Levonian (2001).

science that one can effectively probe the mere "unknown" in the universe, and, dare one say it, even in matters pertaining to the social sciences.[10]

In the context of the present research agenda it is imperative to delineate the factors that will guide us in this journey into the unknown, and to create solutions for modeling unknowable and unknown supply shocks and demand uncertainties in real estate markets in the future, as well as formulate long-term policies and strategies to deal with them. A number of issues arise when the future of real estate investing and management is explored through the *KuU* prism: How does one design and promote appropriate governance structures, new institutional arrangements, provision of insurance, and a social safety net to better manage risk in real estate? The possibility of catastrophic economic–financial, environmental, and geological events, as well as the emergence and spread of contagions of unknown origin brings to the fore the role of the state or government structures in preparing for, managing, containing, and rolling back their adverse impact on life and property. The rapid global dissemination and impact of local events and their negative fallout suggests that flexibility, dynamism, and expeditious responsiveness by private and public authorities will be essential. Without question, there is a major role for government institutions, as well as joint public–private partnerships, in regulation and in risk mitigation, particularly in preparation for major unforeseen occurrences. The high proportion of wealth held in real estate, as well as its wide and relatively more egalitarian ownership globally, compared to financial and other assets, may lead to calls for some modicum of social insurance for mitigating adverse effects of unpredictable events.

Many of the new approaches to and techniques for risk mitigation and management that are being considered in an increasingly interconnected and hence more uncertain world are common to the universe of real estate, as well as to the world of finance. New kinds of contractual arrangements may arise in the face of the unknown and unknowable, as well as in response to new developments in risk sharing, global diversification, securitization, opening up of new markets, and so forth. Contractual incompleteness, while usually arising from transactions costs, and which can dwarf the benefits of contracting for each and every contingency, is also caused by the uncertain states of the world. As Scott (2006) argues, "in reality, contracting parties confront a vexing problem: The future is unknown and unknowable. As a result, when the level of uncertainty is high, it simply costs too much for contracting parties to foresee and then describe appropriately the contractual outcomes for all (or even most) of the possible states of the world that might materialize." Economists and legal experts

---

[10] The musical parallel is attributed to Isaac Stern, the violinist.

have made considerable contributions to the theory and practice of optimal contracting under the complex and uncertain conditions confronting businesses and investors today, whether it is in analyzing the pros and cons of soft and flexible contractual terms or issues of enforcement. Further developments in this field can provide methods for dealing with these contractual issues in an efficient and equitable manner, reconciling different incentive structures, ownership schemes, range of contingencies, and the specifics of the real estate and real estate finance business.

Innovations arise in the realms of both technology and society. In the latter case, the wellspring of innovation could reside in preferences, social arrangements, the polity, or the panoply of social, political, and economic rules that govern human societies. Interactions of mere unknowns can give rise to unknowables. The long-term impact of the one-child policy in China, which may lead to a unique situation in human history with future generations devoid of siblings, cousins, uncles, and aunts, is unclear. New combinations of uncertainties may be precipitated by evolving financing arrangements, such as reverse annuity mortgages; these instruments are impacted by socio-cultural intergenerational developments, legacy issues, and broader social security-related matters. These factors in turn might provide scope for co-operative behavior (e.g., loss sharing or contingent financing) both for individuals and institutions in order to adjust to the unknown, and as potential arrangements that are seen as mutually beneficial.

Rapid economic growth in emerging economies and the entry of India and China into the global economic system have had an impact on everything from prices for natural resources to global interest rates; rising energy prices might yet hold interesting implications for location, density, and sprawl in the industrialized world. As an aside, it may be mentioned that the field of study of emerging economies, particularly regarding economic and financial issues, is skewed in favor of the "known," primarily because of the benchmarking method mentioned earlier. The understanding is that many of the features and structural attributes of developed economies will be adopted by emerging economies, including trends, such as decreasing household size, and variables, such as the proportion and weight of services sectors, the home-ownership rate, and so on.

There are, of course, some aspects in the search for the unknowable that might be classified as trivial: for example, the intrinsic unknowability of the future or the irreversibility of time. The question acquires an intriguing dimension only when we approach the boundary between the unknown and the unknowable, and can demarcate the two. Risk management by and large tries to shift risks that are considered unknown into the category of known risks, and tries to mitigate the costs associated with things that remain unknown; one might add that the expanded taxonomy including the unknowable promotes the further mitigation of search costs and proper allocation of intellectual and financial resources. The complicated interplay of social, cultural, technological, and other factors impacting real estate, a recurring theme of this paper, seems to complement Zeckhauser's chapter in this book regarding the complementary skills determining who will be the winners among investors of the future. Generalist skills that can connect many fields and exercise judgment on "out of the system" probabilities in the sphere of society and polity may be prized more in the future, raising questions about how to inculcate such skills through training and education programs.

Apart from systematic scientific inquiry, as suggested by the Thoreau quotation earlier, it is not clear what kind of causal mechanism lies behind the progression from U to u and thence to K. If one accepts that there are two kinds of unknowables—U that are unknowable either in the trivial sense mentioned before, or as a matter of accepted scientific principles and reasoning, and U that are a result of the "barriers of age and technology"—then while the movement from the merely unknown to the known is relatively systematic, the movement out of U would seem to be more a result of broad social evolution: the cross-pollination of ideas and activities in often unrelated human endeavors. In other words, it is very often the "law of unintended knowledge spillovers" that seems to mitigate the unknowable space. A broad-fronted social and ecological evolution can throw up surprises, such as the possibility of regression from K back to the unknown. For example, it is ironic that the knowledge of the total supply of land, mentioned at the beginning of this paper as having evolved from U to u to K, may have now partially reverted to that previous uncertain state. Although heavily debated, the possibility that global warming may negatively impact habitable coastal land availability cannot be completely discounted.

Part of the problem in applying the *KuU* framework to social sciences is that the subject matter itself is affected by the process of our studying it through the agency of rational interacting actors. As Gomory (1995) says, "We are likely to build an increasingly artificial, and hence increasingly knowable, world." On the other hand, technological developments and globalization of real estate and financial markets will lead to increased participation and interactions of large networks, rendering many processes less governable and the issue of understanding outcomes more complex and unpredictable. The present financial and economic crisis will hopefully add to our knowledge and understanding of the nature of linkages between and among housing, the broader real estate sector, the financial system, and the economy at large.

REFERENCES

Baker, M. J. (2003). An equilibrium conflict model of land tenure in hunter–gatherer societies. *Journal of Political Economy* 111 (1).

Bardhan, A. D., D. M. Jaffee, and C. A. Kroll. The Internet, e-commerce and the real estate industry. At repositories.cdlib.org/iber/fcreue/reports/6100/.

Bardhan, A. D., R. Edelstein, and C. Y. Leung (2004). A note on globalization and urban residential rents. *Journal of Urban Economics* 56 (3).

Bardhan, A. D., R. Edelstein, and D. Tsang (2008). Global financial integration and real estate security returns. *Real Estate Economics* 36 (2).

Barrow, J. D. (1999). *Impossibility: The Limits of Science and the Science of Limits.* Oxford University Press.

Bowles, S., and J.K. Choi (2002). The first property rights revolution. Santa Fe Institute Working Paper No. 02-11-061.

Braudel, F. (1982a). *Civilization and Capitalism, 15th–18th Century,* Vol. I: *The Structures of Everyday Life.* Harper & Row.

Braudel, F. (1982b). *Civilization and Capitalism, 15th–18th Century,* Vol. II: *The Wheels of Commerce.* Harper & Row.

Brueggeman, W. B., and J. Fisher (2001). *Real Estate Finance and Investments,* McGraw-Hill/Irwin.

Chandler, T. (1987). *Four Thousand Years of Urban Growth: An Historical Census,* Lewiston.

Chinloy, P. (1989). The probability of prepayment. *The Journal of Real Estate Finance and Economics* 2 (4), 267–83.

Eichholtz, P. M. A. (1997). A long run house price index: the Herengracht index, 1628–1973. *Real Estate Economics* 25.

Gomory, R. (1995). The Known, the Unknown and the Unknowable, *Scientific American,* June.

Hall, A., and K. G. Lundstedt (2005). The competing risks framework for mortgages: Modeling the interaction of prepayment and default," *Risk Management Association Journal,* September.

Jaffee, D. M., and M. Levonian (2001). The structure of banking systems in developed and transition economies. *European Financial Management* 7 (2).

McEvedy, C. (1986). *Penguin Atlas of Ancient History.* Penguin.

Merry, U. (1995). *Coping with Uncertainty: Insights from the New Sciences of Chaos, Self-organization, and Complexity.* Praeger.

Modelski, G. Cities of the Ancient World: An Inventory (–3500 to –1200). faculty.washington.edu/modelski/WCITI2.html.

Ray, R., and Qayum, S. (2009). *Cultures of Servitude.* Palo Alto, CA: Stanford University Press.

Scott, R. E. (2006). The law and economics of incomplete contracts. *Annual Review of Law and Social Science* 2, 279–97.

Shorto, R. (2006). Amsterdam House: This very, very old house. *NYTimes,* March 5.

Traub, J. F. (1996). The unknown and the unknowable. Santa Fe Institute Working Paper No. 96-10-07.

8. Reflections on Decision-making under Uncertainty

- -

Paul R. Kleindorfer

> Chance favors the prepared Mind!
> —**Louis Pasteur** *(1822–1895)*

8.1. INTRODUCTION TO KNIGHTIAN UNCERTAINTY AND *KuU* PROBLEMS

Frank Knight (1885–1972) completed his doctoral thesis at Cornell in 1916, at a time when great geopolitical uncertainties were unfolding in horrific ways in World War I.[1] A minor revision of his thesis later became the essence of his celebrated book (Knight 1921), which remained the centerpiece of his economic contributions at the University of Chicago, where Knight joined other great economists in creating the intellectual fabric of risk, uncertainty, and profit that has become the foundation of modern finance and business strategy.

The essence of Knight's contribution was arguably his recognition that the modern firm was not just a means of solving the contracting problems that Ronald Coase eventually put to rest, but was also a mutualization institution that absorbed shocks and allowed capital recovery for investments, and that implemented and rewarded entrepreneurial initiative. In the process, Knight also made the key distinctions between management and decision making under conditions of certainty, risk and uncertainty, which is the focus of this volume.

[1] I am grateful for discussions on the ideas of this paper with George B. Kleindorfer, Howard Kunreuther, and Jerry Wind, who continue to inspire my journey into *KuU* territory. Comments on a previous draft by Enrico Diecidue and Paul Schoemaker are gratefully acknowledge.

For Knight, the essential distinction between risk and uncertainty was that *risk* was characterized by known probability distributions with observable outcomes, and such outcomes could therefore be completely contracted on in the market (e.g., in insurance contracts for negative outcomes). *Uncertainty*, on the other hand, was characterized by a decision-making context in which probability distributions on outcomes were not or could not be known with assurance at the time of choice. Knight argued that it was precisely a willingness to take action under uncertainty that allowed entrepreneurs and firms to make profits, even under perfect competition. Refinements in these concepts have taken place since Knight's original treatise, and we will revisit a few of these refinements below. However, I continue to appreciate the essential groundwork that was initially laid by Knight for understanding decision making as taking place along a continuum of the known, unknown, and unknowable (the *KuU* metaphor of this volume), representing an increasing lack of codified and accepted knowledge underlying the outcomes associated with choice.

Interestingly, World War I also saw another of the 20th century's great economists, John Maynard Keynes (1883–1946), begin his voyage of discovery in the area of *KuU* choice. Keynes was among the economic experts supporting the British delegation at the deliberations leading to the Treaty of Versailles in 1919. As he considered the likely economic consequences of punitive actions against Germany, he also continued work on his treatise on subjective probability theory, inspired no doubt by the imponderables that were all too evident to him in the negotiations among the Versailles parties. His life and interests as an economist were affected permanently by these deliberations, and his work on macroeconomics and monetary policy were imbued, as a result, with a sense of the limits of control of governments and central bankers and the consequent need for flexibility in response to the often unpredicted and unknowable consequences of economic activity.[2] *The Treatise on Probability* (Keynes 1920) argued that probabilities, or degrees of belief, as he called them, were an important element of everyday life and the conduct of choice, and that these could not be isolated from the evidence underlying statements of likelihood, which involved mental models of causation and prediction and other cognitive activities that were by their very nature personal or subjective to the decision maker.

---

[2] The overview in the present volume by Donald Kohn of the contemporary guise of these problems in the Federal Reserve System would, I think, find a resonant nod of appreciation by Lord Keynes. Certainly, the unfolding events of the financial crisis of 2007–2009 further underscore the consequences of complexity and uncertainty for decision making and control by central bankers.

The important role of subjectivism emphasized by Keynes is one central element of the *KuU* metaphor.[3] Echoing the editors' introduction to this volume, the other central element is the set of models or theories used by individuals and groups to interpret and connect observable data to outcomes. While mental models and causal reasoning in economics were largely ignored in the early formalizations of finance and economics, these issues are now clearly center stage in both econometrics (e.g., the work of Granger noted in this volume), decision sciences (e.g., Kleindorfer et al. 1993), and business strategy (e.g., Wind and Crook 2005). Suffice it to say that, since the Carnegie School of decision making and behavioral choice was launched by Herbert Simon and Allen Newell in the 1950s, economics and decision sciences have been grounded in the foundational notion that to the extent that human action is purposeful it is based on predictions of consequences of competing choices, using mental models to predict these consequences. Whether these models are well-formed theories, based on science, merely heuristic rules of thumb, or perhaps even wildly erroneous notions of how the world functions, mental models are the basis of purposeful action and choice. We note below some of the implications of our model-dependent reasoning in the recent discussions for *KuU* problems relating to "model uncertainty," "epistemic risk," and other concepts that are currently used to capture the intersection of *KuU* with the choice of supporting models and theories.

---

[3] Of course, subjectivism had long been an active area of inquiry in philosophy, beginning with Plato and Aristotle, with its possibilities and limitations examined in Immanuel Kant's celebrated *Critique of Pure Reason* (1781). The particular reason for the rebirth of subjectivism in the 20th century is due in good measure to what might be called the "brilliant failure" of logical positivism, which attempted to resuscitate empiricism and objectivism in science through a solid grounding of it in mathematical logic. Positivism achieved great visibility and vigor through the work of Bertrand Russell and Alfred North Whitehead in their pioneering work on the foundations of mathematics and logic, the *Principia Mathematica* (1913) and the ensuing contributions of Russell's student Ludwig Wittgenstein in his use of this theory as the foundation for his research on what would now be called mathematical linguistics. The positivist's program of finding a unique correspondence between logical propositions and "facts in the world" was dealt two heavy blows by the Heisenberg uncertainty principle in physics (published in 1927) and Kurt Gödel's celebrated incompleteness theorems (published in 1931). Together these results showed mathematically that it would it be possible neither to establish the asserted correspondence nor, even it were established, to propose a parsing algorithm that would determine the truth or falsity of well-formed propositions based on these "facts." Some things, in the end, are simply unknowable and others cannot be communicated in purely logical and objective terms from one party to another! In this sense, the rebirth of subjectivism and *KuU* theory were an essential part of the philosophy of the 20th century, as well as an important accompaniment to the development of modern economics and finance. For an interesting account of the history and contributions of positivism, and the debate on subjectivism, see Weinberg (1960).

The issue of subjectivity of beliefs, as formulated by Keynes, was taken up further in the pioneering work of Frank Ramsey (1903–1930). Ramsey, who died all too young at 26, made seminal contributions to the theory of taxation and public finance. He was also a gifted mathematician and logician. While he appreciated the subjectivity of probability and its anchoring in the human experience that Keynes had introduced, he pointed out several unsatisfactory features of the Keynes treatment, including, in particular, his treatment of induction (the idea of drawing general conclusions from limited samples). Going beyond his critique of Keynes, Ramsey (1926) developed the fundamental insight that was eventually to result in the first fully satisfactory treatment of choice under uncertainty in the brilliant treatise of Leonard Savage (1917–1971). The Savage work, *The Foundations of Statistics,* was published in 1954, a decade after the Von Neumann–Morgenstern (1944) resolution of choice under Knightian risk.[4] The Ramsey insight underlying the Savage approach was that, in decision making, beliefs (e.g., about likelihoods of events) and values (e.g., about the consequences of decisions) cannot easily be disentangled. He therefore proposed a revealed preference theory that integrated the interaction in choice of beliefs and values.[5] The Savage theory and its precursors in Keynes, Ramsey, and von Neumann–Morgenstern provided a parsimonious and usable theoretical construct, subjective expected utility theory (SEUT), which presented a model of rational choice that encompassed differences in beliefs and values among individuals. Elaborations of this framework in a general equilibrium context of SEUT-rational actors trading in a market economy was soon to follow, inspired

[4] The Keynes-Ramsey debate on subjective probability theory was further explored by several prominent authors in the quarter of a century that elapsed between the publication of Ramsey's work in 1931 and the eventual publication of Savage's solution to the problem in 1954. In this regard, one should note the work of de Finetti (1931, 1937) on probability theory, the philosophical work of Ludwig Wittgenstein, Rudolf Carnap, and the Vienna school (see Carnap 1950), and the work of John von Neumann and Oskar Morgenstern on game theory and the foundations of choice under risk, published in 1944. These precursors, together with the growing sense of the importance of having a formal theory of decision making under uncertainty in economics, were important in the huge leap forward made in the early 1950s in formalizing the micro foundations of finance and economics. Given the contributions involved in these precursors, the "Savage framework" could well be called the "Ramsey-Von Neumann-Morgenstern-Savage framework."

[5] The paradigmatic version of the Ramsey-de Finetti insight is this: Suppose a person is given a choice between two gambles, X and Y, which have monetary outcomes x and 0, and y and 0 respectively, in which $x > y$. Suppose the outcome x in X is predicated on the truth of proposition P and the outcome y in Y is predicated on the truth of proposition Q. Then if the person chooses Y over X, it must be the case that the probability of Q (being true) is judged by the person to be greater than the probability of P (being true). This sort of "rational" integration of beliefs, values, and choice became an essential foundation for the Savage axioms of subjective expected utility theory.

by the work of Arrow and Debreu.[6] Therewith, SEUT provided the platform on which portfolio theory, financial trading, rational expectations, and so much else of the superstructure of modern finance could be constructed.

To complete the circle of early *KuU* heroes in economics, it is important to note the contributions of Friedrich Hayek (1899–1992) and Ludwig von Mises (1885–1973) and the Austrian school.[7] For the Austrian school, subjectivity and associated uncertainty were crucial elements of economics. For one thing, its lucid elaboration by von Mises vitiated whatever intellectual life was left in Marxism as an economic theory by noting the superiority of subjective value theory for emerging market-based theories of economics relative to the clumsiness of the Marxian ("objective") labor theory of value. For another, the emphasis on personal responsibility and entrepreneurial purpose was crucial in explaining the motive force behind economic development and profit, and the process through which human action led to market outcomes. The Austrian school held that uncertainty and subjectivism were not just of philosophical interest, but they are quintessential to the functioning of the economy and to the nature of innovation and entrepreneurship. In this sense, they echoed and reinforced the *KuU* metaphor of Frank Knight and his successors in the Anglo-American school of subjectivity in economics.

The above precursors of our knowledge about management and finance in *KuU* environments argue for the necessity of uncertainty in human affairs, and the fact that the nature of this uncertainty is inherently subjective. However, these precursors do not suggest any prescriptive or normative approaches to management under conditions of unknown probabilities (the *u* world) or unknowable probabilities and outcomes (the *U* world), other than, perhaps, "life is an uncertain affair; do the best you can." Indeed, my personal observation after watching students and executives wrestle with their respective worlds for over 40 years is that the human species seems to be addicted to certainty, denying both the *u* and the *U* of the *KuU* metaphor and adhering tenaciously to the notion that only Knightian risk is worthy of discussion or contemplation. For various reasons, many of them reflected in the papers in this book, this view is changing.

---

[6] Now commonly referred to as Arrow-Debreu-McKenzie equilibrium theory, following the work of Lionel McKenzie in the 1980s. See Debreu (1959) and Arrow and Hahn (1971) for the two major monographs on the foundations of general equilibrium theory; see the survey paper McKenzie (1999) for McKenzie's contributions..

[7] A survey of von Mises contributions to *KuU* theory is von Mises (1973), which is a translation of his work from the early 1930s. The book has an excellent introduction by Guido Hulsmann on the Austrian school. Chapter 5 of this book contains von Mises' summary of the fundamental problems and approaches of the "subjective theory of value."

In the sections that follow, I review some of the tools, concepts, and approaches that have emerged to cope with the far side of *KuU* thinking, and some of the research challenges that still await us. For ease of exposition, I will consider the differentiating features of *KuU* choice, separately, for individual decision-making (which has been the focus of most research on the subject of *KuU*) and for the organizational or management level. As the world of risk (the *K* world) is well understood, I will focus on the *uU* worlds of *KuU* theory, using the world of known conditions (Knightian certainty or risk) only as a contrasting baseline.

8.2. INDIVIDUAL DECISION-MAKING UNDER KNIGHTIAN UNCERTAINTY

For a single decision maker, capturing the essential ingredients of uncertainty and ignorance in the *KuU* metaphor requires expanding the standard framework of decision sciences to encompass explicit formation of belief intensity and the models or theories used to predict choices with consequences. In doing so, I will follow the decision sciences literature in using the term "ambiguity" to refer to a decision situation between Knightian risk and uncertainty, whereby something may be known about the probabilities of unknown states or parameters affecting the decision context, but perhaps not with the complete precision associated with Knightian risk.

Figure 8.1 shows the ingredients of choice under ambiguity or uncertainty, following Kleindorfer et al. (1993). A few points should be noted. First, in contrast to the choice under risk, ambiguity and uncertainty require attention be paid to the belief formation process, including the choice of appropriate models/theories that can be used as guides to action. Little attention has been given in economics and finance to the belief and mental modeling process, focusing rather on certainty and Knightian risk.[8] Exceptions include research on the rules of evidence (Shafer 1976), on various forms of "belief calculus" on how to combine beliefs from multiple sources in consistent ways (Schocken and Kleindorfer 1989), and the study of modeling errors (the fact that different models may provide different results for the same data; Dempster 1968). The standard modeling error problem can be stated simply enough: One model or source of data yields one choice as being optimal (relative to that model), while

[8] On this point, see Taleb (2001) for a detailed assessment of all the shortcuts financial decision makers use to avoid confronting uncertainty. A recent paper making the point that decision theorists and economists have paid little attention to the belief formation process is Gilboa et al. (2008), who also review the formal literature on the subject. Kleindorfer et al. (1993) review calibration and other literatures related to biases in belief formation processes, for which there is an extensive literature in psychology.

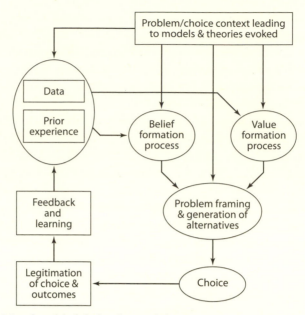

Figure 8.1. Mental models, beliefs, values, and choice.

other models and potential data yield other choices as optimal. In this situation, the choice problem requires not just that one choose optimally in the face of an accepted causal model, but one must also weigh the plausibility of alternative models/data in some manner. Intuitively, concepts of adaptive control, robustness, and worst-case error analysis arise naturally in this setting. I will not review the extensive statistical and econometric literature on these subjects here. The central point is that the key problem for choice in repetitive situations with good data is computational, whereas the key problem in the uU world shifts to the evaluation of multiple competing models and data sources.

The standard approach to multiple competing models of reality has been robustness or sensitivity analysis (to the extent that the competing models can be characterized by parametric variations of some meta-model). The original theory (e.g., Dempster 1968) for addressing this problem as a choice problem was "second-order probability theory" in which (in the spirit of Savage) each possible model was viewed as a competing state of the world. By assigning subjective likelihoods that each of these models was the true model, one could generate a two-stage problem, with the first stage reflecting the probability of each model being the true model and the second stage reflecting the consequences of various choices given each particular model. The resulting generalized choice problem would then be a trade-off between the decision maker's knowledge about the validity of various models and the consequences (both upside and downside) of choices under various models.

Later writings on model-based uncertainty analysis recognize two basic types of risk associated with **KuU** worlds: epistemic and aleatory risk. Epistemic risk (from the Greek word *episteme* meaning "knowledge") arises from our lack of knowledge about the appropriate model or theory that might be valid or relevant for a particular phenomena, and aleatory risk (from the Latin root *aleator* for dice player) arises from randomness inherent in a phenomenon (though this randomness itself may be defined or qualified by the underlying epistemic assumptions made).[9] While there is a gray area in defining epistemic and aleatory risk, the key difference is that epistemic risk can be reduced through exploration and knowledge acquisition, whereas aleatory risk cannot be reduced by such informational activities. This fundamental difference has given rise to a number of related approaches to decision making under uncertainty, based on the value of information (e.g., the work of Raiffa [1968] on decision analysis and the more recent research on information gap theory by Ben-Haim [2006]). These differences are also essential elements of modern treatments of operational risk in banking and insurance in extreme value theory (e.g., Cummins et al. 2006).

Perhaps the most general model advanced to frame the problem of integrating epistemic and aleatory risk (the problem of prediction and explanation under **KuU** conditions) is that of the British philosopher Stephen Toulmin (1958). His "theory of argument" is a general framework, firmly grounded in subjectivism, which encompasses the data underlying belief formation, specific and general models supporting beliefs, and rebuttal models that qualify beliefs. The overall process can be thought of as weighing pros and cons among competing models in deriving a *plausibility* or degree of confidence in a given belief. With an eye on figure 8.1, Toulmin's theory of argument is grounded on prior experience and available data, specific to the person, to the problem context, and possibly to broader fields of science in support of theories that might be used for predictive purposes in a particular problem context.[10]

[9] For example, as described by Kunreuther and Pauly in chapter 10 in this volume, in predicting the consequences of, say, earthquakes, recurrence rates for seismic activity, for propagation of seismic energy and for geological conditions, and the contents and fragility of buildings all represent epistemic assumptions that are necessary for modeling insurance losses from seismic activity in a particular region. In addition to these sources of epistemic uncertainty, there is a natural randomness associated with the effects of such earthquakes. Such randomness would remain unresolved even if one knew for a fact when and where earthquakes would occur, the complete geology of a particular region, and all relevant details of affected buildings.

[10] Using the Toulmin framework in support of decisions under uncertainty is elaborated in Kleindorfer et al. (1993), chapter 3. As an example of its general structure for prediction theory,

A further important element of figure 8.1 is legitimation.[11] This refers to the process by which choices are explained *ex post*, making sense of these both to the decision maker as well as to other stakeholders. The anticipation of an open legitimation process *ex post* can be expected to have a significant effect on choice itself, as well as on the espoused theories used for belief and value formation. Often it is legitimation that leads us to use "accepted models" or particular data that are in common use. In that way, if a negative outcome occurs, one can take shelter in the company of fellow travelers. I revisit this issue below, but it should be clear that in the uncharted terrain of *uU* worlds, legitimation is of a different character than for established problems with well-defined and accepted public data and models/approaches that have been validated by both research and practice.

Let us now consider formal theories and experimental evidence on *KuU* theory at the level of individual choice. I begin with Savage and his intellectual heirs. I then consider a few of the experimental and empirical results raised by *KuU* theory.

8.2.1. FORMAL THEORIES OF CHOICE UNDER UNCERTAINTY

Imagine a single decision maker facing a choice over various alternatives *f*, *g*, and *h*, as represented in table 8.1 (which follows Savage (1954)). In this table, the (mutually exclusive and collectively exhaustive) states of the world are labeled $S = \{s_1, \ldots, s_n\}$ and the entries $U_i(x)$ represent the utility that the decision maker derives from choosing $x = f, g, h$. Following Anscombe and Aumann (1963), these utilities themselves may derive from random variables,

---

consider the following. If a wheel is set free at the top of a hill, an observer might make a plausible prediction with considerable confidence that the wheel will roll down the hill. In the Toulmin theory of argument, the observer would "back up" the plausibility of this prediction with both personal experiences as well as Newtonian theory (if that were known to the observer) and all the interlocking corroborative data of that more general theory. Rebuttals to the prediction would be in the form of making sure that there were no unseen impediments or barriers to the wheel beginning its anticipated descent. The power of this theory becomes apparent in more general problem settings, where analyses of underlying data, theories of specific warrant, general theories of further support, and rebuttal conditions and theories are integrated under Toulmin's prescription of attaining a balance among all of these elements in the process of prediction and belief formation.

[11] The most famous modern writer on the subject of legitimation is the German philosopher Jürgen Habermas. A summary of the legitimation theory of Habermas in the context of decision theory under *KuU* conditions is chapter 5 of Kleindorfer et al. (1993). A very short summary of this theory could be stated as follows: a credible anticipation of being held accountable not just for outcomes but for the logic that led to them will have predictable effects on the nature of the choice process itself. The current financial crisis is an interesting case in point for legitimation theory in the sense that if complexity and regulatory shortcomings mask underlying actions, this will also have predictable consequences.

TABLE 8.1
Illustrating Subjective Uncertainty

	s_1	s_2	$\cdots$	s_n
f	$U_1(f)$	$U_2(f)$	$\cdots$	$U_n(f)$
g	$U_1(g)$	$U_2(g)$	$\cdots$	$U_n(g)$
h	$U_1(h)$	$U_2(h)$	$\cdots$	$U_n(h)$

but of the traditional risk sort, so that (we assume here) there is no difficulty computing the decision maker's choice once both the alternative (f, g, or h) and the state of the world are known ($s_1, s_2, \ldots, s_n$). As explained by Wakker (2006), the states of the world may be best thought of in a world of Knightian uncertainty as corresponding to certain observable events (e.g., market or political events) ($E_1, \ldots, E_n$), where state of the world s_i is said to occur if event E_i occurs.

The Savage theory assumes that the decision maker has sufficient knowledge to assign subjective relative likelihoods $p_1, \ldots, p_n$ to the states of the world $s_1, \ldots, s_n$ (or equivalently to the events $E_1, \ldots, E_n$) in a consistent fashion (i.e., the p_i's are to be thought of as the subjective probability that state s_i will occur, so that they are nonnegative and sum to one). The Savage axioms assure that the decision maker's preferences among alternatives such as f, g, h can be computed using the standard expectation operator across the states of the world, with the final utility of alternative x computed as

$$V(x) = \sum_{i=1}^{n} p_i U_i(x), \quad x = f, g, h \tag{8.1}$$

and where the choice among the alternatives f, g, h would then be the alternative with the greatest expected utility: $V(f)$, $V(g)$, or $V(h)$.

Consider a simple example, where an investor faces mutually exclusive opportunities f, g, and h (one of them being a default investment) and where the payoffs from these opportunities depend on the state of the economy and perhaps other unknown factors that will influence returns. These unknown states are represented by $S = \{s_1, \ldots, s_n\}$, where $U_i(x)$ represents expected returns from alternative x if the state of the world is s_i. Savage's theory provides an axiomatic foundation for concluding that that the investor would use the rule summarized in (8.1), choosing the opportunity f, g, or h by trading off the subjective likelihood that the economy will find itself in each of the respective states of the world against the profitability of each investment in these states.

Suppose, however, that all that can be reasonably assured for our investor is that some states of the world are "highly unlikely" for the relevant future, and, indeed, that only two states of the world, say s_1 and s_2 are assumed to be relevant, but even for these two states of the world, the probabilities p_1 and p_2 are not known with confidence. Two questions immediately arise: (1) what does the term "highly unlikely" mean? and (2) how should one deal with the now ambiguous state of knowledge of the probabilities of s_1 and s_2 in this new problem? Various approaches to these two problems have been proposed in the axiomatic choice literature, perhaps the best known due to Gilboa and Schmeidler (1989) and Schmeidler (1989).[12]

The first of these provides an axiomatic approach that yields as an outcome a choice rule that associates the least-favorable conditions with any elements of a choice situation that are not known with certainty (this is the famous MaxMin rule due originally to Abraham Wald (1950) for the case where several prior distributions could reasonably be advanced in a particular decision context). One might think of this as a "safety-first" rule that assumes a malevolent nature choosing the worst possible state of the world for any choice one is about to make. Knowing this, the decision maker would choose that alternative which maximized his expected utility over alternatives, given a least-favorable outcome in terms of states of the world that would occur after the choice is made. Note that in this case, the decision maker might have evidence to suggest that only certain belief structures/probabilities could be reasonably associated with states of the world. This might suggest constraints of the form, for example, $p_1 \leq p_2, p_3 \geq p_4 + p_5, p_1 = 0.1, p_5 = 0.4$, and $p_1 = 2p_4$ (the last meaning that s_1 is twice as likely as s_4). Taken together, these beliefs would spell out some likelihoods precisely, while others would remain imprecise. If the resulting set of feasible state probability vectors is specified as Δ, then the rule implied by the Gilboa-Schmeidler theory is the Wald MaxMin rule, namely, choose the alternative x that maximizes:

$$V(x) = Min\left\{ \sum_{i=1}^{n} p_i U_i(x) \Big| \ p \in \Delta \right\} \qquad (8.2)$$

The second approach, due to Schmeidler, provides a rather general solution to the question of incompleteness of likelihood specifications over the state space. It is based on the idea of nonadditive measures of likelihood to capture ambiguity, and follows earlier work by Dempster (1968) and Shafer (1976) on this same theme. To illustrate this very powerful idea in its simplest form, consider the

---

[12] A summary of recent theoretical advances is provided in Klibanoff et al. (2005) and Nau (2006), both of which extend the Gilboa and Schmeidler work to articulate differences in preferences and beliefs in situations that involve both ambiguous and nonambiguous probabilities (the latter being the standard Knightian risk context).

above investment example, and assign a further measure to the completeness of the decision maker's information, say some number $c \leq 1$ (where $c < 1$ is taken to mean that the decision maker has less than complete confidence in her assessment of the underlying state probabilities). Assume that the investor begins with a standard probability distribution $p_1, \ldots, p_n$ on some relevant states of the world (so that, in particular, $p_1 + \cdots + p_n = 1$). Define a new probability distribution $\mu(p, c)$ as follows. For any subset of states $A \subseteq S$, define the likelihood of A as

$$\mu(A) = \sum_{i \in A} c p_i, \ A \neq S; \quad \mu(S) = 1 \tag{8.3}$$

The reason that $\mu(p, c)$ is referred to as a nonadditive measure of likelihood is that for any $A \subseteq S, A \neq S$, (8.3) implies that $\mu(A) + \mu(S \setminus A) = c$, so that if $c < 1$, the sum of the likelihoods of a set A and its complement $S\setminus A$ do not sum to one.[13] One can think of the parameter c as connoting the surety that the states s_1 and s_2 do, indeed, provide a complete description of the states of the world that could occur. In this particular case, the Schmeidler theory results in the following valuation of a given alternative x:

$$V(x) = c\left(\sum_{i=1}^{n} p_i U_i(x)\right) + (1-c)\left(Min\{U_i(x) | i = 1, \ldots, n\}\right) \tag{8.4}$$

which is a weighted sum of the usual Savage measure of expected utility (8.1) and the worst-case outcome (for alternative x), with the weight specified by the incompleteness parameter, $1 - c$. Of course, this is only one simple example of the Schmeidler theory, which encompasses considerable flexibility to reflect ambiguity in belief structures and its interaction with normal (expected utility) value structures. One aspect of this generality to be noted is the nonlinearity of the mathematical process integrating values (in this case, the $U_i(x)$ terms) with beliefs (in the above example, the p vector and the completeness parameter c). This nonlinearity has made it difficult to generalize the standard problems of finance (e.g., portfolio theory, investment theory, and valuation of financial contracts/instruments) to the more complex world of incomplete belief structures.[14]

[13] For example, if $S = \{1, 2\}$ and $p_1 = 0.4$, $p_2 = 0.6$, and $c = 0.9$, then the measure $\mu(p, c)$ would be given by $\mu(\emptyset) = 0$, $\mu(s_1) = 0.36 = 0.9 * 0.4$; $\mu(s_2) = 0.54 = 0.9 * 0.6$, $\mu(s_1 \text{ or } s_2) = \mu(S) = 1$. Note that this is a nonadditive measure since $\mu(s_1) + \mu(s_2) < 1 = \mu(s_1 \text{ or } s_2)$.

[14] See the paper of Dow and Werlang (1992) for the simplest example of incorporating nonadditive likelihood measures in the portfolio context. See also the advances and applications of the Schmeidler theory surveyed in Gilboa (2004). Several problems must be overcome to apply this theory in practice. First is the elicitation problem of quantifying both beliefs and values, including uncertainty elements, in a form usable by the theory. Second is the computational problem used to apply the theory to a particular decision setting; this is less of a problem these days, but it can still be important if the set of options is large. Third is the deeper analysis of optimal choices

8.2.2. Experimental Evidence on Individual Choice under Uncertainty

Let me now note some experimental results related to **KuU** theory. The first paper in economics to clearly substantiate the fact that human decision makers act differently under conditions of unknown states (the **u** world) than under Knightian risk was a paper by Daniel Ellsberg (1961). In his famous challenge to SEUT theory, now known as the Ellsberg paradox, the following choice situation was presented to subjects in an experiment.[15]

An urn contains 30 red balls and 60 black balls or yellow balls (with the proportion of these last two colors unknown). Subjects are told that the number of black or yellow balls was determined by a random process prior to the experiment, but the details are not revealed. Subjects are asked to choose between choices A and B in situation I and C and D in situation II.

Situation I
    Choice A   Win $100 if a red ball is pulled
                     Win $0 if a black or yellow ball is pulled
    Choice B   Win $100 if a black ball is pulled
                     Win $0 if a red or yellow ball is pulled

Situation II
    Choice C   Win $100 if a red or yellow ball is pulled
                     Win $0 if a black ball is pulled
    Choice D   Win $100 if a black or yellow ball is pulled
                     Win $0 if a red ball is pulled

---

as a function of the elicited beliefs and values. This is difficult in most applications. Contrast, for example, the Markowitz-Sharpe-Lindner portfolio problem using market data to characterize returns and to compute the efficient frontier, and Sharpe ratios to explore the investor's risk appetite. The results of this process are relatively intuitive and can be executed within a time frame that could support decision making. Not so with any of the uncertainty formulations that have been advanced thus far. There are evidently a lot more degrees of freedom in expressing what one knows and doesn't know than there are in determining optimal choices under the standard belief/ probability structure, which assumes, in essence, that probabilities are fixed for a given problem context. Research continues, of course, but whenever subjectivity and personally weighted evidence enter the problem, the key barrier is no longer computation but rather elicitation from the decision maker of his/her beliefs and values. Finding shortcuts around this elicitation problem while faithfully capturing key elements of the decision maker's actual beliefs remains an unachieved goal of research to date.

[15] This experiment has remained a gold standard for research on **KuU** problems. A recent experimental analysis and revisiting of the Ellsberg results is provided by Halevy (2007).

By a wide margin, the most popular choice for subjects was to prefer A to B in situation I and D to C in situation II. Yet a little reflection shows that these preferences are inconsistent with the Savage SEUT theory (or any theory linear in probabilities). Letting p_1 = probability of a red ball, p_2 = probability of a black ball, and p_3 = probability of a yellow ball, and using (8.1) we would find according to SEUT theory that "A preferred to B" and "D preferred to C" imply the following two inequalities:

$$p_1U(100) + (p_2 + p_3)U(0) > p_2U(100) + (p_1 + p_2)U(0) \qquad (8.5)$$

$$(p_2 + p_3)U(100) + p_1U(0) > (p_1 + p_3)U(100) + p_2U(0) \qquad (8.6)$$

It is easy to see (canceling $p_2U(0)$ in (8.5) and $p_3U(100)$ in (8.6)) that these two inequalities are contradictory. What this means is that there can be no viable SEUT set of beliefs and preferences (the former represented by p_1, p_2, p_3 and the latter by the utility function U) that could possibly represent the modal preferences of subjects in this experiment. Quite apparently, the modal choices of A and D over B and C reflect a preference for nonambiguous lotteries. This preference was further underlined in accompanying verbal protocols for the experiment. Subjects were clearly averse to the ambiguity about the probabilities in this very simple setting.

The Ellsberg experiments remained a paradox for received theory for some time. The nonadditive theory of Schmeidler or the multiple priors (MaxMin) theory of Gilboa and Schmeidler finally provided a consistent theory for the modal choices here. The reason is that these theories have the power to capture what is, in effect, the ambiguity aversion evident in the subjects' choices in Ellsberg's experiments (e.g., in the Gilboa-Schmeidler theory, ambiguous probabilities or outcomes are evaluated in worst-case terms, leading to ambiguity aversion). The Schmeidler theory received additional support as a vehicle for explaining choice in uncertain environments through the work of Tversky and Kahneman (1992). In their path-breaking work on cumulative prospect theory (extending their earlier work on prospect theory), they advanced a theory of descriptive choice that, as it turns out, has the same formal representation as the Schmeidler normative theory introduced above.[16] In so doing, they provided

---

[16] I pass over here the important fact that the Tversky-Kahneman theory has an additional piece of apparatus, the reference point or status quo, which is quite important to explaining a host of experimental findings about differences in choice behavior in the domain of gains versus losses. The point I am making about formal equivalence here concerns the role of the weighting function, first introduced by Quiggin (1982) in his rank dependent expected utility theory. The interested reader can follow the outlines of this fascinating interplay between descriptive theory and normative theory development in Tversky and Wakker (1995) and in the survey by Wakker (2006).

a key link between normative theory and the important work they and others had done in the course of the 1980s on behavioral anomalies of choice under uncertainty. I will not review the details of the connection between these two theories (both formal representations of choice, but one normative and the other based on experimental evidence). Suffice it to say that the story did not end with noting the (near) formal equivalence of these two theories.

Two other matters are of interest in the experimental history of *KuU* choice. The first of these is termed the "source of the uncertainty" and the second falls under the heading of legitimation. On the first point, Tversky and Fox (1995) noted important and systematic differences in the nature of choice when the source of uncertainty underlying the outcomes was held to be "objective" and "mechanistic" (think of this as chance determined by a roulette wheel) versus chance outcomes determined subjectively (think of this as determined by the outcome of an event, like a sporting or market event, the likelihood of which requires judgment to estimate). Thus, in describing the preferences and beliefs of a decision maker under Tversky and Kahneman's cumulative prospect theory (and variants thereof), the nature of the nonadditive belief function underlying these choices depends not just on the decision maker but on the source of randomness itself. This is not very encouraging for those looking for a simple unifying theory of choice that they could use to underpin, say, portfolio theory. What this says is that alternative data sets may give rise not just to alternative beliefs, but also to alternative weightings of these beliefs in decision making, at least if the current nonadditive models of choice are to be used as the foundation for choice.

A second interesting set of experimental results has to do with legitimation. This matter was first examined by Curley et al. (1986). They used the Ellsberg paradox setting described above, but they added the following wrinkle. Subjects assigned monetary values to the various choices in the Ellsberg paradox setup (where a higher monetary value for one choice versus another was interpreted as preferring that choice). After they made a number of such monetary value assignments, some of these were selected at random and "played," where "played" meant that they were given their declared monetary value, and the subjects actually played the corresponding Ellsberg lottery and were rewarded according to the outcome. They would therefore see the results of their choice in situations I and II of Ellsberg for some of the lotteries they chose. In addition, for some experimental treatments, subjects were told that they would be shown (after their choice was made) the actual number of black and yellow balls (the ambiguous state of the world in the Ellsberg setup). In other cases they would not know the number, but would just be shown the actual outcome of drawing a ball from the urn. Finally, in some instances the actual draw of the urn (and their choice of

TABLE 8.2
Curley et al. (1986): Legitimation

	Observability to Group	
Ex post ambiguity	Outcome observable to group	Outcome not observable to group
High	(H, O) Known to subject, played in front of the group	(H, N) Known to subject, played after group has left
Low	(L, O) Not known to subject, played in front of the group	(L, N) Known to no one, played after group has left

bets) would be done in front of their group of fellow subjects, while in others the outcomes would only be done with each individual privately. The group was never informed of the actual number of black and yellow balls, even when the individual was. The experimental setup is shown in table 8.2.

Curley et al. (1986) recorded the differences that subjects were prepared to pay to avoid ambiguity (this "ambiguity premium" was just the difference between what they were prepared to pay for the nonambiguous choices under the Ellsberg setup relative to the ambiguous choices). The results of the experiment were that there was no significant difference between the high and low individual knowledge states (i.e., no significant differences if the subject were informed of the number of black and yellow balls after choices had been made). However, there were significant differences in the ambiguity premium between the conditions of group observability. When the group could observe the playing of the ambiguous lottery, and this was known in advance, subjects were prepared to pay significantly more to avoid the ambiguous outcome. One explanation for this, based on legitimation theory, is that when subjects anticipate the need to be able to explain (or even expose) to others the amount of money they had been willing to pay for these lotteries, ambiguity becomes even more undesirable than it is in isolated personal choice settings.

In a related paper, Heath and Tversky (1991) examined differences in choice between risks that were based on "objective probabilities" and those based on subjective events, such as the outcome of sporting events or elections. What they found is that those who thought of themselves as experts in a field preferred to bet on their judgments rather than on equivalent chance events (i.e., chance events that had the same probability of a positive outcome as what the expert predicted for the judgment event in question), while the opposite was true of those subjects who viewed themselves as lacking expertise in a particular area. One explanation for this phenomenon is that those who thought of themselves as "experts" understood that they would be able to justify their choices better, both when the outcomes of these choices were positive as well as negative. The point of these and other experiments is that the nature of anticipated legitimation, even in experimental settings, can have significant effects on the outcomes of choice under uncertainty.

The psychological and behavioral decision-making literature on choices under ambiguity and uncertainty has considered several other important issues that I note briefly here.[17] First, individuals tend generally to be overconfident and myopic (the General Custer effect, "I haven't lost a battle yet!") and, as the Heath and Tversky study above suggests, this is, if anything, exacerbated when expertise and judgment are required. Second, there is considerable inertia in mental models (one explanation for which being the cognitive energy it takes to reintegrate a new mental model with existing beliefs). The result is that, rather than adopting a posture of balancing supporting and rebuttal evidence on the validity of their current model, there is rather a search for confirmatory evidence that one's current model is the right way to go. As Mandelbrot and Taleb point out in chapter 3 in the current volume, this results in far too many hundred-year events occurring every 5 years, giving rise to cries of "oops" and "duh," but rarely to an adjustment of our mental models (in their case the model of Gaussian theory). Third, there are herd dynamics and contagion effects evident in the use of models. Some of these are understandable in terms of minimizing coordination costs of social coordination (a point underscored by Schelling (1978) and Beck (1992)). Others are the result of complex network interactions, such as those argued to underlie some of the liquidity problems in the current financial crisis (Allen and Babus 2009). Finally, there appears to be a mix of the rational and irrational when it comes to dealing with the unknown. Part of this arises undoubtedly from our biological heritage in seeking meaning and order in life so that we can continue to function without undue neurosis. And, certainly, the mere thought of making choices of consequence under conditions of ambiguity and ignorance calls out for company.[18]

In general, the golden ideal embodied in figure 8.1 of rational analysis in the face of uncertainty and ignorance seems not to be the first impulse of human

---

[17] The literature on these matters is discussed in detail in Kleindorfer et al. (1993) and Schoemaker (2002).

[18] The increased need for traveling companions in uncertain times may be understood as the result of the existential need for reinforcement and endorsement of our worth as individuals, where this comes primarily through our interaction with others, per the trenchant writings of Soren Kierkegaard and Martin Buber.

decision makers. Rather, our impulse seems to be to use models and data that have worked passably well in the past, and that seem to be supported by many fellow travelers. If the models we use for navigating *KuU* worlds have been crowned with some formal dignity by academic or professional credentials or practices, so much the better. The dangers of this approach may be evident to the reader, and the cure (namely, unrelenting skepticism and continued challenging of our knowledge base) obvious. However, like healthy eating and daily exercise, I suspect the costs of this very rational approach are also obvious.

8.3. ORGANIZATIONAL DECISION-MAKING AND STRATEGY FOR *KuU* ENVIRONMENTS

Let us now turn to organizational decision-making in *KuU* environments.[19] My point of departure is that globalization, together with its technological underpinnings in new communication technologies, has fundamentally changed the level of interdependency of financial and market activities, with many more actors involved in these activities directly or indirectly, and in real time. The increased interdependency and speed of responses means that organizational decision-making and action confront a considerably expanded set of states of the world conditioning outcomes. The resulting increase in complexity currently exceeds organizational abilities to incorporate these increased states into decisions at the time they are made. The result implies something like the intuitive import of the *KuU* spectrum underlying our discussion. What can be done about this from a management perspective is suggested by the anthropomorphic metaphor of an explorer entering uncharted terrain. That individual would do well to prepare mentally for surprises, to be agile and unencumbered by heavy baggage, to have increased acuity and perhaps communication capabilities to home base, and in general to have developed the ability to react to unforeseen and unforeseeable exigencies as they arise. This anthropomorphic metaphor of the prepared, agile explorer is helpful in describing some of the research on these questions and the initiatives being implemented in various organizational contexts to cope with the far side of the *KuU* world that is unfolding before us.

The last two decades have seen immense changes in the forces and institutions that govern economic activity. They encompass the ongoing changes

---

[19] The ideas of this section are explored in much greater detail in Kleindorfer and Wind (2009). the ideas here on network-based strategies and competencies form the core of a cooperative research project between the Wharton's SEI Center for Advanced Studies in Management and the INSEAD Social Innovation Centre.

associated with the European Union, and the changes in liberalization and governance initiated by the World Trade Organization.[20] New markets and new forms of contracting are supporting outsourcing, unbundling, contract manufacturing, and a variety of other forms of extended value constellations. The Internet has empowered consumers and given rise to peer-to-peer networks. In the process, it has transformed whole industries—the impact of Skype on the telecommunications industry, search engines (Google) and e-retailing, and the growth of eBay, to mention a few of the more evident signs of change. In tandem, revolutionary developments in transportation and logistics (the rise of FedEx, UPS, and DHL) are providing new global fulfillment architectures for B2B and B2C. These mega-trends are summarized in figure 8.2.

Consider the area of logistics as an example of the interdependent trends exhibited in figure 8.2. A mere twenty years ago, logistics (maritime, air, and land-based) was considered a mature industry, operated by "real men," which meant lots of inefficiencies and empty backhauls, huge cycles of overcapacity and undercapacity, and head-butting competition. The communications and information revolution gradually gave way to improved routing and scheduling, and eventually to improved utilization through regional coordination of capacity. But it was clearly the mega-trends of figure 8.2 that took logistics to an entirely new level, driven by outsourcing and huge increases in intraregional and international trade. Expansion of physical capabilities at air hubs and ports began in the 1990s and has continued unabated, with Hong Kong and Dubai the most evident examples, but with increases in capacity in nearly every established port and air hub. This was accompanied by increased sophistication and intermediation activities of brokers and forwarders, followed by the development of financial overlays and trading instruments for air cargo and shipping capacity.[21] The logistics industry is an interesting example of how physical markets have dovetailed with financial and information markets in supporting and profiting from globalization and outsourcing as shown in figure 8.2.

Similar changes are occurring in a host of markets from energy to insurance and banking. In every case, we see the power of the market being used to provide better information and better coordination, with the instruments of finance, hedging, and arbitrage playing essential roles in promoting improved discovery of scarcity values and prices. Arguably these mega-trends represent a critical element of the present economic environment for management to

---

[20] For a readable account of these changes and their implications for management and governance, see Friedman (2005).

[21] Kavussanos and Visvikis (2006) describe the growth in options trading on shipping capacity. Kaminski (2004) describes related hedging options on aviation fuel and bunker oil.

Continuing Growth in Global Trade
Total Exports (Manufacturing & Services) 2001 = $7.7 Trillion
Total Exports (Manufacturing & Services) 2007 = $17.2 Trillion

Globalization
• Increasing cross-border trade flows
• Increasing demand for cross-border logistic & other services
• Outsourcing

Technology drivers
• Communications
• Internet
• Science

Markets, risk & volatility
• Increasing deregulation and liberalization/WTO
• Expansion of e-markets and available hedging instruments

Customer empowerment
• Integrated service offerings
• e-commerce
• e-empowerment via global markets

Growth of supporting infrastructure for logistics and contracting

Figure 8.2. Key trends driving profitability and uncertainty for management.

respond to unknown and unknowable environments. By relying on the aggregation and discovery power of markets, and the valuation signals available through financial instruments overlaying the goods and services provided in these markets, a great deal of otherwise opaque uncertainty can be understood, mitigated, and managed.[22]

However, the changes described above have also introduced new and poorly understood risks. Just to focus on financial services, Buehler and Pritsch (2003) trace the tide of bankruptcies and other forms of financial distress that continue to plague the financial services industry, noting that in the period of 1998–2002 for their sample of 90 financial institutions, some 150 instances of financial distress took place (see their paper for the definition of financial distress). Even given the volatility of the period in question, this rather astonishing level of 1.67 instances of financial distress per institution over a five-year period suggests something is amiss. What was amiss, according to Buehler and Pritsch, was a lack of appreciation of the magnitude of the changes that had occurred in global markets and the level of new risk and uncertainties these represented,

[22] See Kleindorfer and Wu (2003) for a description of new contracting and hedging strategies being followed in manufacturing industries as a result of these changes. See Kunreuther and Pauly, chapter 10 in the present volume, for a discussion of similar changes in the global (re-)insurance industry.

coupled with a lack of appropriate management systems for understanding enterprise vulnerabilities and correlations across different lines of business, and for responding to discontinuities in the environment before they became full-blown crises. In addition, as the current financial crisis has made clear, increased complexity and resulting lack of transparency resulted in counter-party and liquidity risks of many financial instruments designed to promote increased market intermediation in risk bearing and transfer. Research in the area of interdependency and risk has picked up on these ideas and pointed to contagion and other network effects as central to the new uncertainties of the financial services industry.[23]

The risk in financial institutions noted above is also evident in manufactur-ing. On the positive side, technologies such as Web-based tools have helped improve coordination and remove information distortions. A classic example is the collaboration between Wal-Mart and P&G leading to the now widespread practice of vendor-managed inventory. The basic vision driving supply chain design and plant management in manufacturing has clearly been the anthropo-morphic metaphor of "leanness." However, while the resulting "leaner" supply chains reduce inventory costs, companies have started to experience some of the negative consequences of leanness in uncertain environments.[24] In addition to the risks of mismatch in supply and demand, disruption has now become a major source of risk in global supply chains. Disruption risks include op-erational risks (equipment malfunctions, unforeseen discontinuities in supply, human-centered issues from strikes to fraud) and risks arising from natural hazards, terrorism, and political instability. Disruption risk has increased sig-nificantly because of the longer and more complex global supply chains now enabled through globalization.[25] The Taiwan earthquake of September 1999, which sent shock waves through the global semiconductor market, the terrorist attack on the World Trade Center on September 11, 2001, and the August 14, 2003 blackout in the northeastern United States are but a few reminders of the potential for significant disruptions to supply chains. Given these events, and the increasing reliance on cross-country supply chains, it is not surprising that

---

[23] Allen and Gale (2000) provide the foundation for this analysis. For a recent discussion of the theory of networks in finance, see Allen and Babus (2009).

[24] See Sheffi (2005) for a call to retreat from mere "leanness" to "resilient supply chains", with clear echoes of our explorer heading into uncharted terrain.

[25] Hendricks and Singhal (2005) analyze announced shipping delays and other supply chain dis-ruptions reported in the *Wall Street Journal* during the 1990s and show, based on matched-sample comparisons, that companies experiencing such disruptions underperform their peers significantly in stock performance as well as in operating performance as reflected in costs, sales, and profits.

enterprise risk management has become a high-priority topic for senior management and shareholders in manufacturing.

Beyond the traditional notion of risk, involving capital reserves and response capabilities for unforeseen contingencies, a fundamental driver of the need for a new vision of coping with the evident move to the far side of the *KuU* metaphor derives from the increased complexity of the systemic interactions that are the core of network-based models of firms and their interactions with their customers, trading partners, and the markets in which they operate. In particular, complexity theory and systems theoretic notions deriving from general networks and artificial intelligence are beginning to provide new insights on risk and resilience of firms in the new economy. Some well-known examples may serve to illustrate:

- Power laws and scale-free networks dramatically increase risks. There may be significantly increased long-tail impacts on net-centric businesses resulting from the fact that there will be both the usual high-frequency local disturbances (with controllable and lower losses) as well as very low-frequency but potentially catastrophic events for interconnected subnetworks of the overall value constellation.[26] The anthropomorphic desiderata of adaptation, resilience, and process/organizational time to maturity become more important than optimization under conditions of high uncertainty and complexity.

- Peer-to-peer interactions also conform to scale-free networks and the "empowered customers" may be dramatically shaped in their behavior by network interactions even though they often do not know it. "Fractal marketing" and "fractal finance" will play a key role in the future in understanding and predicting behavior in markets for both goods and capital.[27]

These challenges suggest that increased complexity and network-based interdependence arising from globalization are the roots of the increased emphasis on management in *KuU* environments. Recent work in organization science and business strategy on this problem can only be sketched here, but it follows the basic anthropomorphic metaphor of our explorer going into uncharted territory. Some of the key areas can be briefly noted.

---

[26] See the Mandelbrot and Taleb, chapter 3 in this volume, for a discussion. For network effects, see Allen and Babus (2009). For the evolving work on artificial intelligence, see the GECCO website and publications (Genetic and Evolutionary Computation Conference): www.sigevo.org/gecco-2008/.

[27] See Mandelbrot and Hudson (2004) on financial implications of these changes and Wind and Mahajan (2001) on the marketing implications.

8.3.1. ESTABLISHING PURPOSE THROUGH STRATEGY AND LEADERSHIP

Russell Ackoff is perhaps the best-known proponent of the view that a company navigating rough terrain must have a well-charted course that reflects its purpose and strategic intent, that is, it needs to design its own future. Ackoff proposes the "idealized design approach" (Ackoff et al. 2006) as a disciplined way of crafting such a design. Amit and Zott (2001) argue similarly that crafting new business models to accommodate the dictates of the network economy requires a strong commitment and a decisive direction for company strategy. Michael Useem (1998) and many others have emphasized the importance of leadership in times of great uncertainty. As Paul Schoemaker (2002) has suggested, a key question is how much strategy and predetermined direction can there be if uncertainty is truly high? Under highly uncertain conditions, exploration, learning, and flexible response become central rather than traditional planning and strategy.

8.3.2. CREATING AN ORGANIZATION WITH REDEPLOYABLE COMPETENCIES

Core competency theory (Hamel and Prahalad 1994) has focused on making a company unassailable through the development of competencies, both technology-based and organizational, which serve to define the value proposition for the products and services produced by the company and are not easily imitable by competitors. The resulting confluence of the core competency movement with the paradigm of process management augured many of the changes that have occurred in the past decade, including unbundling of value chains and outsourcing (while maintaining core competencies firmly in control of the "mother company"), and the contracting and supply-chain innovations that have occurred in parallel with these. Size and core capabilities are a reasonable defense against many uncertainties. Indeed, as Zott and Amit (2009) argue, the rise of the resource-based view of strategy reflects a response to increases in environmental uncertainty, as the RBV approach entails less focus on product/market planning and more on flexible redeployment of resources.

8.3.3. CREATING A RESILIENT AND RESPONSIVE ORGANIZATION

Jay Galbraith (1977) was a pioneer in studying the appropriate fit between an organization and its environment. He noted that successful organizations tended to decentralize when facing more turbulent environments, and also engaged in other organization innovations to increase the information processing capabilities of the organization when faced with environmental complexity.

These thoughts were elaborated in a slightly different tone by Williamson in his analysis of the boundaries of the firm (e.g., Williamson (1996) and, more recently, by Santos and Eisenhardt (2005)) in studying organizational design in the internet age. Beyond these general contributions to organization design, the topics of crisis management and business continuity assurance have surfaced as essential elements of responsive and resilient organizations (e.g., Sheffi 2005), following the World Trade Center attacks on September 11, 2001, and the growing awareness of the costs of supply chain and operational disruptions experienced in the past decade.

8.3.4. Creating Leanness, Opportunism, and Flexible Response

The "lean organization" paradigm has been recognized in two ways in responding *KuU* conditions. First is the time-based leaning of supply chains noted in the discussion above and exemplified by the Dell Computer story (see, e.g., Sheffi 2005). Second, is the outsourcing and divesting of noncore processes epitomized by the Lou Gerstner years at IBM, in which huge chunks of the business were divested in order to get back to a capital base and competencies that represented a lean organization with all the necessary core assets to control its destiny. Flexibility and opportunism have been emphasized in the "real options" approach to corporate strategy and project execution. As explained by Bowman and Moskowitz (2001) and Loch et al. (2006), the essential idea is to approach strategy and multistage projects, be they new technologies, new facilities, or new markets, as part of a portfolio of prepared options, with selective execution of individual projects as opportunities present themselves (i.e., if and only if these projects turn out to be "in the money").

8.3.5. Improving Organizational Acuity and Long-term Vision

Beginning with Royal Dutch Shell's use in the late 1960s, scenario planning has become a key approach to environmental uncertainty. As explained cogently by Paul Schoemaker (2002), scenario planning helps to map the environment 10 to 15 years out (beyond the limits for which normal market and pricing signals would be useful), and identify key stakeholders and uncertainties that could be sources of profit or vulnerability for a company in the future. If trends and uncertainties are anticipated, a company can prepare a "playbook" of contingent response strategies that allow it to switch among strategies with some degree of grace and, perhaps, ahead of its competitors. Scenario planning and related scanning mechanisms (see Day and Schoemaker 2006) have seen a surge in recent use because of perceived increases in long-term uncertainties, such as the course of climate change and political reactions to it, ideological conflicts, and the speed and success of key technological innovations (such as the hydrogen-powered automobile).

8.3.6. LEGITIMATION IS DIFFERENT UNDER *KuU*

The problems of legitimation and governance at the organizational level are compounded with those we already saw at the individual level. The tendencies noted above toward lean organizations and decentralization must face controls on levels of financial commitment and risk to which an organization can be exposed based on actions of individual employees. The lessons of Barings Bank and Enron, and now the global financial crisis, have shown the limits of un-checked action, whether on the trading floor or in the boardroom. Many inno-vations and regulatory changes have occurred recently in an attempt to provide some discipline to the problems associated with playing with the house money, from Basel II in banking to Sarbanes-Oxley in general governance. The search continues for workable solutions to responsible controls that do not extinguish entrepreneurship and innovation.

8.3.7. HEDGING AND DIVERSIFICATION

The long-hallowed strategy, and the core of the international reinsurance mar-ket, is diversification. By taking thin slices of risks in separate markets, corre-lated risks can be shared among a larger number of competing capital providers. Similarly, hedging strategies have become the centerpiece of protecting against undue volatility in individual company cash flows, whether these are caused by commodity price fluctuations or the weather. The pioneering work of Karl Borch (1919–1986) and advances since then in the science of risk-bearing and diversification are summarized in Doherty (2000). Interesting new work in this area is focusing on understanding and hedging correlated risk patterns due to network and contagion effects, as noted in Allen and Babus (2009).

The above admittedly selective list of current initiatives and research activi-ties shows, I think, that the effects of increased complexity and uncertainty in today's business environment have led to a recognition that the economy has moved to the far side of *KuU* territory. In short, the above list highlights the creation of new management systems for enterprise risk management and crisis management, new strategic initiatives in scenario planning and scanning, and a general deepening of diversification and hedging strategies. These themes underscore the anthropomorphic metaphor of an explorer in *KuU* territory that I have used to structure my discussion. In one sense, these organizational innovations reflect a Darwinian evolution of survival benefits for companies that have adopted the right niche strategies relative to the new environment. At another level, in the spirit of Lamarckian evolution, this is evolution that can be influenced by the foresight of the well-prepared explorer, who brings the right options along on the voyage, who is able to move quickly to exploit these when opportunities present themselves, and who has improved his long-range vision so as to see these opportunities in time to respond.

8.4. CONCLUDING COMMENT

The reader will hopefully take from these reflections a sense of the incompleteness of research on *KuU* problems, but at the same time the very necessity of this incompleteness. Since the dawn of intellectual history, the subject of epistemology (how much we can really know about our external environment) has been a fundamental field in philosophy. In philosophy, we have seen wave after wave of objectivism and subjectivism, with the current upper hand being in the hand of the subjectivists. Given the unsettled state of this long debate, it is not surprising that the keen force of logic alone has not settled the issue of how best to navigate the maze of belief, value, and choice under *KuU* conditions of interest in this volume. To be sure, examination of this question by psychologists, economists, and decision scientists in the last 100 years has brought some progress in mapping the territory through axiomatic theory and experimental testing. But, arguably, these approaches, while dressed up in formal attire, leave one not a whole lot better off than we were 100 years ago when it comes to coping with the far side of *KuU* problems.[28] Certainly, we have increased computer power to explore the "unknown" and to undertake robustness studies, scenario planning, and other activities that improve our ability to avoid cliffs and to preplan contingent responses to exigencies so as to be better prepared to react to them. Moreover, chastened by evidence of increased complexity of the global economic and financial environment and the visible and painful failures of a number of companies in the present financial crisis, many organizations are improving their ability to detect and respond to environmental uncertainties. However, we remain very much a product of our own very human limited abilities. This will continue to make the journey into the far side of *KuU* territory both more perilous and more interesting.

---

[28] On this point, it is worth recalling the tone of Taleb (2001) in his discussion of *KuU* problems, who suggests that the approach to *KuU* problems should not be principally driven by the premature codification of our enduring state of incomplete knowledge, but rather by a continuing cultivation of humility and skepticism in addressing the (in-)adequacy of our theories and data in the light of human needs.

REFERENCES

Ackoff, R. L., J. Magidson, and H. Addison (2006). *Idealized Design*. Philadelphia: Wharton School.

Allen, F., and A. Babus (2009). Networks in finance. Forthcoming in P. R. Kleindorfer and Y. Wind, eds., *The Network Challenge: Strategy, Profit and Risk in an Interlinked World*. Upper Saddle River, NJ: Wharton.

Allen, F., and D. Gale (2000). Financial contagion. *Journal of Political Economy* 108, 1–33.

Amit, R., and C. Zott (2001). Value creation in e-business. *Strategic Management Journal* 22, 493–520.

Anscombe, F. J., and R. J. Aumann (1963). A definition of subjective probability. *Annals of Mathematical Statistics* 34, 199–205.

Arrow, K. J., and F. H. Hahn (1971). *General Competitive Analysis*. San Francisco: Holden-Day.

Beck, U. (1992). *Risk Society*. London: Sage.

Ben-Haim, Y. (2006). *Info-Gap Decision Theory: Decisions Under Severe Uncertainty*. New York: Academic Press.

Borch, K. H. (1968). *The Economics of Uncertainty*. Princeton, NJ: Princeton University Press.

Bowman, E. H., and G. T. Moskowitz (2001). Real options analysis and strategic decision making. *Organization Science* 12, 772–77.

Buehler, K. S., and G. Pritsch (2003). Running with risk. *McKinsey Quarterly*, December, 40–50.

Carnap, R. (1950). *The Logical Foundations of Probability Theory*, 1962 ed. Chicago: University of Chicago Press.

Cummins, J. D., C. M. Lewis, and R. Wei (2006). The market value impact of operational risk events for U.S. banks and insurers. *Journal of Banking and Finance* 30, 2605–34.

Curley, S., F. Yates, and R. A. Abrams (1986). Psychological sources of ambiguity avoidance. *Organizational Behavior and Human Decision Processes* 38, 230–56.

Day, G., and P.J.H. Schoemaker (2006). *Peripheral Vision: Detecting the Weak Signals That Will Make or Break Your Company*. Boston: Harvard Business School Publ.

Debreu, G. (1959). *Theory of Value*. New York: Wiley.

de Finetti, B. (1931). Sul significato soggettivo della probabilità. *Fundamenta Mathematicae* 17, 298–329. Probabilism: A critical essay on the theory of probability and on the value of science (translation of 1931 article) in *Erkenntnis* 31, September 1989.

de Finetti, B. (1937). Foresight: Its logical laws, its subjective sources (translation of the 1937 article in French) in H. E. Kyburg and H. E. Smokler, eds. (1964). *Studies in Subjective Probability*. New York: Wiley.

Dempster, A. P. (1968). A generalization of Bayesian inference. *Journal of the Royal Statistical Society, Series B* 30, 205–47.

Doherty, N. A. (2000). *Integrated Risk Management*. New York: McGraw-Hill.

Dow, J., and S. Werlang (1992). Uncertainty aversion, risk aversion, and the optimal choice of portfolio. *Econometrica* 60, 197–204.

Ellsberg, D. (1961). Risk, ambiguity and the savage axioms. *Quarterly Journal of Economics* 75, 643–69.

Friedman, T. L. (2005). *The World Is Flat*. New York: Farrar, Strauss & Giroux.

Galbraith, J. R. (1977). *Organization Design*. Reading, MA: Addison-Wesley.

Gilboa, I., ed. (2004). *Uncertainty in Economic Theory: Essays in Honor of David Schmeidler's 65th Birthday*. London: Routledge.

Gilboa, I., and D. Schmeidler (1989). Maxmin expected utility with a non-unique prior. *Journal of Mathematical Economics* 18:141–53.

Gilboa, I., A. Postlewaite, and D. Schmeidler (2008). Probability and uncertainty in economic modeling. *Journal of Economic Perspectives* 22, 173–88.

Halevy, Y. (2007). Ellsberg revisited: An experimental study. *Econometrica* 75, 503–36.

Hamel, G., and C. K. Prahalad (1994). *Competing for the Future: Breakthrough Strategies for Seizing Control of Your Industry and Creating the Markets of Tomorrow*. Boston: Harvard Business School Press.

Heath, C., and A. Tversky (1991). Preference and belief: Ambiguity and competence in choice. *Journal of Risk and Uncertainty* 4, 5–28.

Hendricks, K., and V. Singhal (2005). Supply chain disruptions and corporate performance. *Production and Operations Management* 14, 35–52.

Kaminski, V. ed. (2004). *Managing Energy Price Risk*. London: Risk Press.

Kavussanos, M. G., and Visvikis, I. D. (2006). *Derivatives and Risk Management in Shipping*. London: Witherby.

Keynes, J. M. (1920). *A Treatise on Probability*. London: Macmillan.

Kim, W. C., and R. Mauborgne (2005). *Blue Ocean Strategy*. Boston: Harvard Business School Press.

Kleindorfer, P. R., H. Kunreuther, and P.J.H Schoemaker (1993). *Decision Sciences: An Integrative Perspective*. Cambridge, UK: Cambridge University Press.

Kleindorfer, P. R., and J. Wind, eds. (2009). *The Network Challenge: Strategy, Profit and Risk in an Interlinked World*. Upper Saddle River, NJ: Wharton.

Kleindorfer, P. R., and D. J. Wu (2003). Integrating long-term and short-term contracting via business-to-business exchanges for capital-intensive industries. *Management Science* 49, 1597–1615.

Klibanoff, P., M. Marinacci, and S. Mukerji (2005). A smooth model of decision making under ambiguity. *Econometrica* 73, 1849–92.

Knight, F. H. (1921). *Risk, Uncertainty and Profit*. Boston: Houghton Mifflin.

Loch, C. H., A. DeMeyer, and M. T. Pich (2006). *Managing the Unknown*. Hoboken, NJ: Wiley.

Mandelbrot, B., and R. L. Hudson (2004). *The (Mis)Behavior of Markets*. New York: Basic Books.

McKenzie, L. W. (1999). Equilibrium, trade, and capital accumulation. *Japanese Economic Review* 50, 371–97.

Nau, R. F. (2006). Uncertainty aversion with second-order utilities and probabilities. *Management Sciences* 52, 136–45.

Quiggin, J. (1982). A theory of anticipated utility. *Journal of Economic Behavior and Organization* 3, 324–43.

Raiffa, H. (1968). *Decision Analysis*. Reading, MA: Addison-Wesley.

Ramsey, F. P. (1926). Truth and probability. In F. P. Ramsey (1931), R. B. Braithwaite, ed., *The Foundations of Mathematics and Other Logical Essays*. London: Kegan, Paul, Trench, Trubner; New York: Harcourt, Brace, 156–98.

Santos, F. M., and K. M. Eisenhardt (2005). Organizational boundaries and theories of organization. *Organization Science* 16, 491–508.

Savage, L. J. (1954). *The Foundations of Statistics*, 1972 ed. New York: Dover.

Schelling, T. C. (1978). *Micromotives and Macrobehavior*. New York: Norton.

Schmeidler, D. (1989). Subjective probability and expected utility without additivity. *Econometrica* 57, 571–87.

Schocken, S., and P. R. Kleindorfer (1989). Artificial intelligence dialects of the Bayesian belief revision language. *IEEE Transactions on Systems, Man, and Cybernetics* 19, 1106–21.

Schoemaker, P.J.H. (2002). *Profiting from Uncertainty*. New York: Free Press.

Shafer, G. (1976). *A Mathematical Theory of Evidence*. Princeton, NJ: Princeton University Press.

Sheffi, Y. (2005). *The Resilient Enterprise*. Cambridge, MA: MIT Press.

Taleb, N. N. (2001). *Fooled by Randomness: The Hidden Role of Chance in Life and in the Markets*. London: Texere.

Toulmin, S. E. (1958). *The Uses of Argument*. Cambridge, UK: Cambridge University Press.

Tversky, A., and C. R. Fox (1995). Weighing risk and uncertainty. *Psychological Review* 102, 269–83.

Tversky, A., and D. Kahneman (1992). Advances in prospect theory: Cumulative representation of uncertainty. *Journal of Risk and Uncertainty* 5, 297–323.

Tversky, A., and P. P. Wakker (1995). Risk attitudes and decision weights. *Econometrica* 63, 1255–80.

Useem, M. (1998). *The Leadership Moment*. New York: Three Rivers Press.

von Mises, L. (1973). *Epistemological Problems of Economics*, 3rd ed., 2003. Auburn, AL: Ludwig von Mises Institute.

von Neumann, J., and O. Morgenstern (1944). *Theory of Games and Economic Behavior*, 1953 ed. Princeton, NJ: Princeton University Press.

Wakker, P. P. (2006). Uncertainty. In L. Blume and S. N. Durlauf, eds., *The New Palgrave: A Dictionary of Economics*. Forthcoming, London: Macmillan.

Wald, A. (1950). *Statistical Decision Functions*. New York: Wiley.

Weinberg, J. R. (1960). *An Examination of Logical Positivism*. Littlefield: Adams.

Williamson, O. E. (1996). *The Mechanisms of Governance*. New York: Oxford University Press.

Wind, Y., and C. Crook, with R. Gunther (2005). *The Power of Impossible Thinking*. Upper Saddle River, NJ: Wharton School.

Wind, Y., and V. Mahajan (2001). *Convergence Marketing*. Financial Times Prentice Hall, New York.

Zott, C., and R. Amit (2009). The business model as the engine of network-based strategies. In P. R. Kleindorfer and Y. Wind, eds., *The Network Challenge: Strategy, Profit and Risk in an Interlinked World*. Upper Saddle River, NJ: Wharton.

9. On the Role of Insurance Brokers in Resolving the Known, the Unknown, and the Unknowable

Neil A. Doherty and Alexander Muermann

Insurance transfers risk, and knowledge of the level of risk is important to the parties in deciding whether to engage in this activity. Without knowledge of the underlying loss distribution, the insurer will find it difficult to set a price and the policyholder is unable to tell whether he is getting a good price from the insurer. It is also difficult for both parties to see what impact the policy will have on the insurer's overall book of business and its ability to keep its promised payment. Here we show that brokers play an important role in completing markets that otherwise might "fail" through lack of knowledge. In particular, we show three important functions for brokers. Absent brokers, there is a tendency for insurers to be unwilling to acquire costly information on the policyholder's loss distribution and therefore unwilling to tender for new insurance contracts. Brokers can avoid this problem if their own loss information can be credibly signaled to bidding insurers. Second, where information on losses is asymmetric (i.e., adverse selection), intervention by brokers can lead to Pareto improvements in the equilibrium set of insurance contracts. Again, the condition is that brokers can credibly signal loss information to insurers. And, third, when complete insurance contracts cannot be written because the parties are unable to even identify the types of risk which might occur, brokered relationships can lead to implicit risk transfers.

These three functions span closely, but not perfectly, the classification of knowledge in the conference title: the known, the unknown, and the unknowable, or *KuU*. Various taxonomies of knowledge (or the lack thereof) have been offered. For example, the known (*K*) can be usefully defined as a circumstance in which the distribution of an event is known. In Frank Knight's language "known" is thus equated with "risk." Likewise, the unknown (*u*) might describe an unknown distribution. The fact that we ask questions about the distribution reveals a level of awareness of the event we are contemplating—we simply cannot ascribe probability and/or magnitude. This is the same as Knight's "uncertainty."

The known and the unknown thus describe present knowledge of a probability distribution, or the lack thereof. A different characterization of knowledge is the inherent ability of circumstances to become known. We call these knowable. The known are obviously knowable, but the unknown might also be knowable insofar as there exist mechanisms that allow transforming the unknown into the known. These mechanisms can be either known or unknown. The unknowable (*U*) then refers to circumstances of inherent impossibility to become known.

It is often unknown whether a circumstance is a "knowable unknown" or an "unknowable unknown." However, new phenomena occasionally occur and insofar as such events become imprinted in our minds for the future they are revealed to be knowable unknowns. Thus, if it is accurate to say the events of the type and scale of 9/11 were not imagined, then they were not known to be knowable or unknowable. But since that day, we are all too sadly aware of the future exposure to such events and mega-terrorism might be a knowable unknown.

This distinction of the knowable and unknowable parallels the distinction of decidable and undecidable set-theoretic statements. Kurt Goedel in his famous paper, "On Undecidable Propositions of Principia Mathematica and Related Systems," published in 1931, proved that "there are statements that can be formulated within the standard axiom system for arithmetic but which cannot be proved true or false within that system." One of the first undecidable statements is the continuum hypothesis, which states that no set has a cardinality greater than that of the natural numbers but less than that of the reals. Goedel showed in 1937 that this hypothesis cannot be proved from the axioms of set theory, and Paul J. Cohen demonstrated in 1964 that neither can it be disproved.

But all this begs the secondary question as to *who* does, does not, or cannot even contemplate, a distribution. By default, we normally use terms like known, unknown, and unknowable to refer to humankind in general. Thus, a known fact is known to someone, thus it is accessible to others. Similarly, the unknown is outside all human knowledge, and the unknowable is beyond human capacity. But for decision-making, we need also to look at the ownership of knowledge. Information and imagination may be asymmetrically distributed; some may know the probability distribution and other may not; some may be able to image novel events that are beyond the ken of others.

We will show how brokers play a crucial role in the acquisition of information (conversion of the unknown but knowable into the known), the transmission of information between asymmetrically informed parties, and the creation of risk sharing facilities for unknown events where complete contracts cannot be written.

We start by noting that the unknown but knowable can be converted into the known by an appropriate investment in information. Risk mapping, actuarial, statistical, and economic analysis of past loss data and loss modeling are examples of techniques that can help specify loss distributions. However, these techniques are costly and will be undertaken by a rational being only if the benefits from having the loss information exceed the costs of its assembly. Clearly, insurers would like such information in order to underwrite policies. But, there is an underinvestment problem in a competitive market. Insurers may be reluctant to bid on a new insurance contract without an acceptable estimate of the loss distribution. This is an illustration of the "winner's curse." However, insurers may be unwilling to make the costly investment in information if they are competing for the business and have only a small chance of winning. We will show that, when brokers are compensated by profit-based contingent commissions, they can credible signal loss information to bidding insurer and thereby avoid the winners curse and stimulate bidding.

The second role we ascribe to brokers is in resolving problems of adverse selection. The classic solution to such problems is for the insurer to offer a menu of contracts to all policyholders. The menu will include policies with costly signaling devices such as deductibles. Because the cost of bearing the deductible is higher the greater the probability of loss, the parties will sort into risk types in their menu selection, with low risks choosing the deductible. We will show that when brokers intermediate the contracts, this costly signaling can be avoided. If brokers can credibly reveal policyholders loss types, insurers can target different policies to the known risk types. However, there is a cost associated with the credible signal: brokers are paid a profit-based contingent commission that aligns their interests with those of the insurers. We will show that, in a market with both contingent commission insurers and noncontingent commission insurers, together with brokered and nonbrokered insurance sales, the equilibrium policy set is Pareto superior to that under the self-selection menu.

The third role we provide for brokers is to cope with the unknowable. The extreme case is where the events that might cause loss cannot even be identified. These might be unanticipated losses from new technologies, new laws, or the unforeseen consequences of new social–economic interactions. Thus, certain cyber risks could not have been known a few years ago, the health and legal implications of toxic mold were a complete surprise to insurers and policyholders alike, and arguably, mega-terrorism, the likes of 9/11, was something that was totally unanticipated. If risks are not anticipated, it is difficult to write and price insurance formal contracts. Thus, transferring such risks would seem to be a problem. We will show that in brokered markets, insurers might be quite willing to pay for surprise losses that are not covered by the policy to preserve the goodwill of the broker and the value that relationship offers. It is true that insurers might be willing to make such *ex gratia* payments to valued individual policyholders to preserve their business. However, the presence of brokers, and the greater value to the brokers' books, significantly expands this informal insurance market and also allows an interested third party to arbitrate between legitimate *ex post* risk transfers and pure "holdup." Thus, brokers are a repository for the reputation of insurers and use this role to expand insurance markets. As with the other roles described above, brokers are motivated to play this role by receiving a profit-based contingent commission from the insurers.

The common driver of these three broker roles is a particular compensation structure: profit-based contingent commissions. This feature is of topical interest, since the brokerage industry has recently been attacked for its use of contingent commissions. The attack was spearheaded by the New York attorney general, Elliot Spitzer, who argued that such commissions made the broker beholden onto the insurer who paid the commissions. Allegedly, this created a conflict of interest since brokers were supposed to owe a fiduciary to their policyholders. Our analysis shows that, by redressing some of the *KuU* problems, such commissions play an important role in expanding insurance markets to the benefit of policyholders and insurers alike.

9.1. UNDERINVESTMENT IN LOSS INFORMATION IN A COMPETITIVE INSURANCE MARKET WITH SYMMETRIC INFORMATION

9.2.1. WITHOUT BROKERS

Our starting point is an individual or firm (we will simply call this party a policyholder) that wishes to buy insurance for a risk. The policyholder invites

n identical insurers to bid for the contract. None of these insurers knows the loss distribution, nor does the policyholder. Denoting the rent to an insurer from winning the contract as R and $f(n)$ as the probability of winning, then the expected rent is $f(n)R$. Thus, any insurer will invest in information if

$$f(n)R \geq c$$

where c is the cost of risk modeling, or any related technique for measuring the distribution. Alternatively, we can state the minimum risk premium the insurer needs, conditional on receiving the contract, to invest in information as

$$R^{\text{INS}} = \frac{c}{f(n)}$$

The policyholder in turn, will have some reservation price on insurance. We assume that the policyholder will accept or reject any offer to supply insurance after the loss distribution is revealed; therefore, we can express the reservation price as a risk premium, R^{POL}.

Thus, if no insurer will bid without information, then the condition for the insurance contract to be closed with one of the insurers is

$$R^{\text{POL}} \geq R^{\text{INS}} \geq \frac{c}{f(n)}$$

So, for example, if $f(n) = 1/n$, then the policyholder's risk premium must exceed cn. So, at most, only $n^{\text{MAX}} = R^{\text{POL}}/c$ insurers can be invited to compete in the auction. Thus, there is a trade-off. With more insurers in the auction, there is a danger that none will find it worthwhile to incur the costs of information and, fearing the winner's curse, will not bid. But even if $n < n^{\text{MAX}}$ then it is not clear that the increasing competition will lead to lower prices; rather it will bid up the bidding insurer's reservation prices. This is depicted in figure 9.1.

9.1.2. With Brokers

The problem is that the costs of information are repeated by all bidding insurers. Consider now another competition in which the policyholder seeks a broker to place the business on its behalf. Since brokers are not risk takers, it is not crucial for the brokers to know the loss distribution to bid for this business. Brokers more likely will offer and promote their placement, risk management, modeling, and various service skills as well as their compensation structure and the policyholder will choose accordingly. The successful broker will map the risk and possibly estimate the loss distribution. Suppose this is the case. Now, when conducting an auction to place the risk with an insurer, can the broker credibly transmit the loss information to bidding insurers?

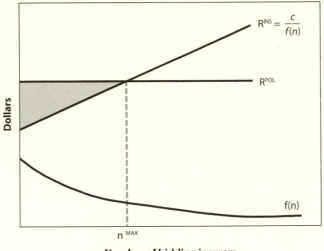

Figure 9.1. Insurers competing in an auction.

The simplest mechanism to generate credible signals to bidding insurers is the broker's compensation structure. If the broker's pay is scaled to the winning insurer's profit, then clearly the broker will wish insurer's to be fully informed of the risk so that the successful bidder can anticipate a profitable contract. Thus, in principle, a profit-based compensation should align the incentives of brokers and insurers and lead to the transmission of truthful loss information in the insurance auction. Are the incentive compatibility conditions likely to be met in practice?

In practice, broker compensation has several elements. The main form of compensation is a premium commission that is paid by the insurer on each contract. The commission is usually a flat percentage of the premium that varies according to the particular insurer and to the line of business. Sometimes, the policyholder and broker will negotiate a fee and the premium commission will be declared and offset against the fee. How the fee is negotiated may vary from case to case, but it is common for fees to be based on work done and/or some metric for the value added by the broker's services.

For current purposes, the most interesting element of broker compensation is the contingent commission.[1] In addition to premium commissions and/or fees, brokers will often receive an additional commission from the insurer, which is based on some metric of the book of business the broker places with the insurer.

---

[1] The following information is taken from Cummins and Doherty (2006).

Most commonly, these commissions are based on either the volume of business placed with the insurer or its profitability. The profit-based commissions are more common but the volume-based structures are more usual with the mega-brokers. The commissions are usually progressive; that is, the marginal commission rate increases with profit and/or volume. Typically, these contingent commissions account for 1–2% of premiums compared with 9–11% for premium commissions. However, the incentive compatibility feature of the profit-based commissions does suggest that the insurers might be willing to trust loss information given by the broker and thereby willing to bid without a full loss survey and estimation.

The landscape has recently changed as a result of investigations into the brokerage industry by the former New York attorney general Elliot Spitzer. He launched an attack on brokers based mostly on the supposed conflict of interest posed by the payment of contingent commissions and on alleged rigging of the bids made by insurers in the auction to place the business. The conflict of interest was based on a simple legal notion that the broker is an agent of the policyholder and would not service the policyholders interests if paid by the insurer. Our analysis challenges that notion. The policyholder might be well served if the broker does transmit credible loss information. It will lower the bidding insurers' reservation prices insofar as it avoids the replication of information costs and will thereby encourage more vigorous bidding.

However, Elliot Spitzer's enquiry has changed the landscape. Several of the largest brokers, including Marsh and Aon, have abandoned contingent commissions. But since these were mainly volume, rather than profit, based, the change has less bearing on the current issue. Moreover, the numerous profit-based commissions of the smaller brokers seem to be largely unaffected by Spitzer's enquiry.

A comparison of figures 9.1 and 9.2 shows the impact of brokers. In figure 9.1, insurers fear the winner's curse and will not bid without a costly loss survey. This raises the insurer's reservation price in proportion to the number of bidders and caps the number of bids at n^{MAX}. Moreover, competition will tend to squeeze surplus to be allocated between the winning insurer and the policyholder and will not necessarily lower the price. If brokers can transmit credible loss information the reservation prices of insurers are de-linked from the number of bidders and potentially more surplus can be allocated. Of course, this expanded surplus must now include the broker's contingent commission.

9.2.2. ADVERSE SELECTION: THE ROLE OF BROKERS

We now switch to a situation in which the policyholder knows its loss distribution, or risk type, but the insurer does not.[2] This is a classic adverse selection

---

[2] This section builds on analysis in Cummins and Doherty (2006).

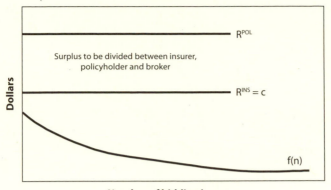

Number of bidding insurers

Figure 9.2. The role of brokers.

setup. We consider a single period in which insurers can offer menus of price–quantity contracts. In other words, the insurer can offer any policyholder the choice from a menu of contracts, each of which specifies both the price and the quantity of insurance (i.e., a deductible or coinsurance rate) offered.

This situation has been the subject of considerable analysis, starting with Rothschild and Stiglitz (R-S) in 1976. In their analysis there are two types, high and low risks, each of which knows its type, but this information is unknown to the insurer. The insurer does know the proportion of each type in the population and the expected loss for each type; it simply does not know who is high risk and who is low risk. R-S showed that, with a sufficient proportion of high-risk types, a Nash equilibrium exists in which high risks purchase a full insurance policy with a high price, and low risks purchase a partial insurance policy with a low price. Even though they are risk averse, the low risk are willing to accept partial insurance to signal their type. Knowing their risk type, the high risks find the policy with the deductible unattractive because they realize they have a large chance of a claim and thus bearing the deductible.

The Nash equilibrium of Rothschild and Stiglitz is shown in figure 9.3. The menu offered is H and L. High risks are indifferent because these both lie on the high-risk indifference curve, I_H. However, if L is shifted very slightly southwest down the low-risk price line, the high risks will strictly prefer H. For the low risks, however, L is preferred to H (the latter lying above the low-risk indifference curve I_L).

Now we can introduce a broker and recognize that different insurers might be competing for business. Now, one insurer offers a profit-based contingent commission to the broker. As argued above, this commission is incentive

202DOHERTY AND MUERMANN

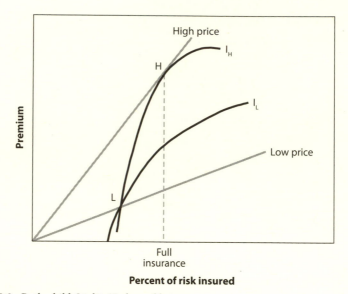

Figure 9.3. Rothschild-Stiglitz Nash equilibrium.

compatible between the broker and insurer and motivates the broker to reveal the policyholders risk types truthfully. Noting that the commission must be paid, the premiums charged by the insurer are no longer actuarially fair. Figure 9.4 shows the higher premiums for the different risk types in bold (the gray lines represent the original R-S situation depicted in figure 9.3). With these higher prices and truthful revelation of risk types, the insurer can offer policy H_1 to the high-risk types and policy L_1 to the low-risk types. Note that H_1 is the welfare maximizing policy for high risks on the new high-risk price line. Policy L_1 lies on the new low-risk price line anywhere under the indifference curve I_L.

Now the policy pair H_1 and L_1 is not a Pareto improvement over the R-S situation without the broker depicted by policies H and L. Compared with R-S, the high risks are strictly worse off but the low risks are better off. However, suppose that two (or more) insurers are competing. Insurer 1 does not offer contingent commissions but offers the R-S pair H and L in direct sales to the policyholder. Insurer 2 offers H_1 only to high risks and L_1 only to low risks. With these choices, the high risks can select policy H, from the nonbroker insurer 1, whereas the low risks can go to the broker and obtain policy L_1 from insurer 2. Thus, the Nash equilibrium is the policy pair H and L_1, which is Pareto superior to the nonbroker market pair H and L.

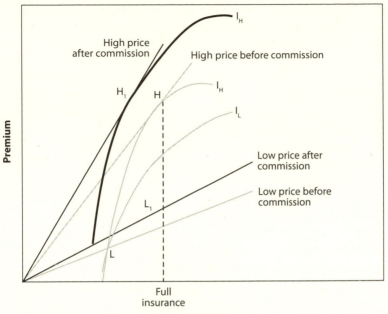

Figure 9.4. Premia for different risk types.

9.3. INCOMPLETE CONTRACTING OF THE "UNKNOWN": THE ROLE OF BROKERS AS A COORDINATION DEVICE

We now consider risk-sharing mechanisms in circumstances in which events are unknown to either party.[3] This situation not only includes unknown events that are unknowable but also unknown events that are knowable. If the cost of transforming the unknown into the known outweighs the benefit then it is optimal for both parties to not invest in such transformation and thereby leave knowable events unknown. Nevertheless, policyholders might have an interest in spreading risks of those events. How can insurance markets then be organized to implicitly offer coverage for unknown events? What role do brokers play in expanding coverage beyond known events?

Many insurance contracts are incomplete. A reinsurance contract is typically not as detailed in its wording as the primary policy it is based on. At the same time it is understood that the relationship between an insurer and reinsurer

---

[3] This section builds on analysis in Doherty and Muermann (2005).

lasts over many years. This arrangement gives flexibility to deal with unknown events. The reinsurer can extract future rents from an ongoing relationship with the insurer and might therefore be willing to cover unknown events that go beyond the precise wording of the contract. It is interesting that brokers play an important role in the reinsurance market. By owning a large book of business, brokers can sanction reinsurers who do not behave according to market expectations in dealing with unknown events; they can move the entire book of business to a rival reinsurer. This leverage facilitates implicit risk sharing of unknown risks within the relationship.

A second example of incomplete insurance policies involves companies such as Chubb, which have gained a reputation of not precisely sticking to a contract's wording. This again allows for dealing with the occurrence of unknown events and their implicit coverage. How does Chubb credibly gain and maintain its reputation while charging a relatively expensive rate on their policies? Chubb operates with a network of independent agents and brokers who own the renewal rights of the policies placed with Chubb. Those agents and brokers pose a large potential threat to Chubb as they might move the business away to a rival insurer. But by purposefully creating this threat, Chubb ensures to credibly gain and maintain its reputation and charge for the implicit coverage offered.

9.3.1. INCOMPLETE CONTRACTS CAN BE GENERATED IN A BILATERAL RELATIONSHIP WITHOUT A BROKER

For events that are known, and ideally can be measured, insurance contracts can be written. However, there are other events that are not, or cannot be, anticipated and are therefore not written into the insurance coverage. Had we known about such events, insurance may well have been desired. But, to the extent that they were unforeseen, insurance is not formally arranged. We will show that an orderly mechanism to transfer these unanticipated risks does exist and that brokers play an important role in completing this market. The key to understanding this market is the concept of "holdup."

Suppose that a relationship exists between the insurer and policyholder and that the insurer expects future rents from the expected continuation of the relationship. The future rents create bargaining power for the policyholder. Should some event arise that is not covered by the policy, the policyholder can threaten to cancel the policy, with loss of future rents, unless the insurer makes a payment for the uninsured event. Even though the insurer has no legal obligation to make a payment, the insurer has an incentive to implicitly cover unknown events as long as future expected profits from continuing the relationship are greater than the transfer.

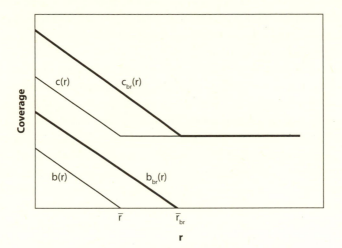

Figure 9.5. Optimal amount of implicit and explicit coverage.

In short, the policyholder can hold up the insurer for a payment to cover the otherwise uninsured loss. The holdup is backed by the threatened cancellation of the policy and, over time, by the renewal of the policy when the insurer makes a payment. In each period, the policyholder pays a premium that covers the expected payment for events that are formally covered by the contract plus a loading with the expectation that the future rents implicitly generate coverage for unknown events. If an unknown event occurs and the insurer pays such transfer then the policyholder stays with the incumbent. If, however, the insurer collects the additional loading but does not pay the transfer then the policyholder switches to a rival insurer.

It can be shown that it is optimal for policyholders to pay such rents and implicitly generate partial coverage of unknown events if the discount rate is not too high. Full coverage is not optimal for either the covered or unanticipated events, because the premium is loaded. Furthermore, it is optimal to provide more explicit coverage of known events than implicit coverage for unknown events. Figure 9.5 plots the optimal amount of implicit and explicit coverage, $b(r)$ and $c(r)$, as a function of the interest rate.

There are two problems with this bilateral mechanism to provide implicit coverage for unknown events. The first is that the amount of implicit coverage might be too small to be useful. The amount of holdup is limited by the future rents from that particular relationship, that is, the discounted value of the future loadings. The second problem is that the holdup power might be exercised by the policyholder for extortion rather than to indemnify a loss. The trouble is that the holdup power of the individual policyholder is independent of the actual loss. In principle, both these problems could be resolved if all policy-holders' actions are coordinated.

Suppose that individual losses could be observed without cost by all poli-cyholders. If one individual policyholder has an unanticipated loss and the insurer does not pay an appropriate amount, then all policyholders receive a negative signal about the insurer's performance. This lowers their priors as to whether the insurer will make future transfers for such losses. With the lower priors, policyholders cancel their policies and switch to competing insurers. Thus, the penalty to the insurer for not paying, is that the nonpayment is public information and leads to a loss of the combined rents of all its policyholders. Contrary to that, if the insurer makes a payment to the individual suffering the loss, then the insurer's reputation is enhanced and all policyholders renew.

Policyholder coordination also addresses the extortion problem. If policy-holders see that no loss was suffered and the policyholder was simply black-mailing the insurer, or if the policyholder was otherwise undeserving, (e.g., the policyholder did not try to mitigate the loss once it occurred) then policyhold-ers might support the insurer in its refusal to make a payment. In this case, policyholders would renew their policies anyway (with only the extortioning policyholder making the cancellation threat). In this way, the enhanced holdup power of the policyholder community, can be exercised with some retroactive judgment about whether transfer payments are actually deserving.

This more efficient mechanism requires strong assumptions on the informa-tion available to all policyholders and their coordination of actions. In fact, each policyholder must be able to observe all unknown events and transfers from all insurers to all policyholders. As long as those unknown events are not mega-events that are widely covered by the media, it is doubtful that policy-holders would observe unknown events and transfers of other policyholders. This is where brokers can provide a coordination device for policyholders to increase their leverage against the insurer without having to observe all events and transfers.

9.3.2. BROKERS AND INCOMPLETE CONTRACTS

Rather than rely on the separate actions of all policyholders to exercise holdup, the actions can be coordinated through a broker. The key to the broker's role lies in its ownership of the renewal rights to its book of business with each insurer; brokers are thus said to "own a book of business." This means that the insurer concedes its rights to market directly to the policyholders who have placed with that broker. Thus, the broker can recommend to its policyholders to switch business from a nonperforming insurer without that insurer being able to make a side deal directly with the policyholder. The insurer purposefully gives up those rights to credibly commit to cover unknown events.

Initially, the policyholder chooses a broker who places the policy with an insurer. If a policyholder incurs an unknown event and the insurer makes an appropriate transfer (conditioned by the future rents), the policyholder stays with the broker who renews the policy with the incumbent insurer. If the insurer does not pay a transfer, the policyholder will stay with the incumbent broker as long as the broker moves the book of business to a rival insurer; otherwise, the policyholder will go to a rival broker. Thus, competition to retain business, both by brokers and insurers, gives the insurer an incentive to make transfer payments for unknown losses and also gives the broker an incentive to discipline the insurer who fails to do so. We will say a little more about the broker's motivation shortly when we discuss compensation.

The intervention of the broker also provides an arbiter to evaluate the policyholders' claims for transfers for unknown losses. If the claim is phony and if the broker judges that such payments are not appropriate, then the broker can choose to support the insurer in its refusal to pay. In this way, the broker can discriminate between the types of events for which *ex post* transfers do provide an appropriate risk spreading and those that do not. For example, consider the rash of toxic mold claims that hit the industry recently, which arguably were not explicitly covered by the policies. Many would argue that *ex post* payments were inappropriate because this type of loss could be avoided by proper maintenance and it is also difficult to verify the actual losses alleged. With this reasoning, insurers might have refused to pay and been backed up by policyholders. Moreover, policyholders (excluding those making a claim) might support this refusal rather than having their premiums increased in the future for losses that they could easily avoid by their own actions.[4] Contrast this with some of the cyber risks that have given rise to liabilities of those holding or managing data. Some of these risks would have been *ex ante* insurable had they been known in advance; there was limited moral hazard and they had low correlation. So, such events, when newly revealed would be candidates for *ex post* transfers.

It can be shown that the increased leverage of brokers, who derive holdup power from their entire book, will provide more efficient risk sharing of unknown events as long as the broker's commission is not too high. Figure 9.5 shows the optimal amounts of implicit and explicit coverage with the broker,

---

[4] In fact, this issue was ambushed by the courts who often enforced coverage and in some states by regulators who restricted insurer choice in whether to include mold coverage going forward.

$b_{br}(r)$ and $c_{br}(r)$. It is not optimal only to generate more implicit coverage for unknown events over a wider range of interest rate values, but also to buy more explicit coverage for known events. In this sense, brokers not only expand the market for implicit insurance on unanticipated events, but also lower the transaction costs for explicit insurance.

The key to the brokers role in expanding the formal insurance market to cover unanticipated events, is its compensation structure. To motivate them to do this, they need to share in the value created from this activity. Moreover, when one of their policyholders has a unanticipated loss, then the broker must be motivated to execute its holdup in an appropriate way. These considerations suggest that the broker share in the rents that are actually created. Indeed, they point to exactly the same type of compensation structure described in the earlier sections of the paper—a profit-based contingent commission.

9.4. CONCLUSION

We illustrated the importance of insurance brokers in addressing potential inefficiencies caused by lack of knowledge about underlying probability distributions. If obtaining information about a risk is costly, competition in bidding for a policy may lead to inefficient underinvestment in loss, which in turn will deter insurers from bidding on new insurance risks. Brokers, as non-risk takers, may resolve this "winner's curse" by investing in information themselves and then stimulating bidding on policies by truthfully revealing this information to insurers. The incentive compatibility conditions for truth telling are built into the broker's compensation, which is scaled to insurer rents.

We next addressed a situation in which loss information is asymmetrically (un)known, that is, an adverse selection problem. Without brokers, the asymmetric information issue might be resolved by policyholders self-selecting from contract menu. But this solution is costly because low risk must signal their type. We have shown that competition between directly transacted and brokered insurance contracts leads to a Pareto improvement of the Rothschild-Stiglitz separating equilibrium. A necessity of this result is that brokers are paid contingent on the insurers' profit. Only then can brokers credibly signal to transmit true information about the risk type to insurers.

Last, we explored the role of brokers in expanding the insurance market beyond contractible events. The provision of brokers with the renewal rights on policies and thus with leverage against insurers facilitates implicit risk sharing of unanticipated, noncontractible events. Again, the alignment of brokers' with insurers' incentives through profit-based contingent commission is important.

Of particular topical interest is that all three broker roles are promoted with the use of profit-based contingent commissions. This feature directly challenges the recent adverse publicity given to such compensation arrangements. Elliot Spitzer has criticized these arrangements as compromising the broker's fiduciary duty to act on behalf of the policyholder. Our analysis suggests that contingent commissions can indeed benefit the policyholder.

In summary, we have shown that insurance brokers play an essential role in transforming the knowable unknown into the known, in transmitting the known to parties for whom risks are unknown, and in organizing risk sharing of the unknowable.

REFERENCES

Cummins, J.D., and N.A. Doherty (2006). The economics of insurance Intermediaries. *Journal of Risk and Insurance* 73, 359–96.

Doherty, N.A., and A. Muermann (2005). Insuring the uninsurable: Brokers and incomplete insurance contracts. Center for Financial Studies working paper Nr. 2005/24.

Rothschild, M., and J. Stiglitz (1976). Equilibrium in competitive insurance markets: an essay on the economics of imperfect information. *Quarterly Journal of Economics* 90, 629–49.

10.   Insuring against Catastrophes

Howard Kunreuther and Mark V. Pauly

The terrorist attacks of 9/11 and the hurricanes in the Gulf Coast have raised a number of questions regarding the role that insurance can or should play in providing protection against catastrophic risks.[1] This chapter focuses on the role that information about potential adverse events plays in both the supply and demand for insurance where there is considerable uncertainty regarding the likelihood of the event occurring and the resulting consequences. Our focus will be on how insurers and those at risk react to events that can cause catastrophic losses to them.

Natural hazards are an example of a known risk (K) which have the potential of causing catastrophic losses to insurers and where there are considerable data to estimate the likelihood and consequences of these events for those residing in hazard-prone areas. Terrorism illustrates an unknown (u) event, which also has the potential to cause severe losses to insurers but where the likelihood of a terrorist attack and its consequences are not well specified because there are limited data available. In neither case is the probability distribution well

[1] We would like to thank Neil Doherty for helpful comments on a previous version of this paper. Support from the Wharton Risk Management and Decision Processes Center and a grant from the Federal Emergency Management Agency Preparedness Policy, Planning and Analysis Division in the National Preparedness Directorate, U.S. Department of Homeland Security (Grant 2008-GA-T8-K004) is acknowledged. The views and opinions expressed are those of the authors and should not be interpreted as representing those of the United States Government or FEMA.

specified; however, the degree of uncertainty with respect to the risk and the ways to reduce the likelihood and magnitude of future losses differ between the two cases.

An unknowable (U) risk is one where the probability cannot be determined through past data and scientific information, so that individuals are not able to form any beliefs (other than the "insufficient reason" default) about probabilities.[2] Insurers often refuse to cover such risks if they focus their attention on them; however, if they are not on their radar screen, they may fail to exclude them explicitly, and the policyholder may be protected by default. Thus, an insurer might consider excluding a risk such as a war or insurrection because it is difficult to estimate either the premium or its consequences, but the insurer might not exclude an event such as an out-of-control sports celebration, in which case the policyholder will be financially protected against damages caused by it.

In some situations, one can draw a fine line between an unknowable and unknown risk. With respect to the events of 9/11, to our knowledge there was not an insurer or reinsurer in the world who had conceived of the possibility that a plane crashing into the World Trade Center could cause the structure to collapse. In this sense, such a risk would be considered unknowable. However, by writing contracts that promised coverage for perils not excluded, insurers were agreeing to provide coverage against losses from unknowable events, for at least the first time they occur—after which they presumably become knowable, and then may be explicitly priced or explicitly included or excluded from coverage. This seems to be what happened with the type of terrorism risk associated with 9/11.

This paper focuses on known (K) and unknown risks (u) facing insurers, using natural hazards and terrorism as illustrative examples of these two cases. With respect to natural disasters, Hurricane Katrina is the most costly disaster in the history of the insurance industry to date, with total claims at $46.3 billion. The previous year's hurricanes Charley, Frances, Ivan, and Jeanne that hit Florida in the fall of 2004 produced a combined total loss of $29 billion. Each of these disasters was among the top 20 most costly insurance losses in the world from 1970 to 2008 (Kunreuther and Michel-Kerjan 2009).

Regarding terrorism, the attacks of September 11, 2001 killed over 3000 people from more than 90 countries and injured about 2250 others. These attacks inflicted damage estimated at nearly $80 billion, approximately $32.4 billion of which was covered by about 120 insurers and reinsurers. Of the total insured

---

[2] This case is termed complete ignorance by Camerer and Weber (1992) in their classification of risks.

losses, those associated with property damage and business interruption are estimated at $22.1 billion (Wharton Risk Center 2005). The insured losses from 9/11 illustrate the high degree of risk correlation between different lines of insurance coverage. Indeed, these attacks not only affected commercial property and caused business interruption, but also led to significant claims from other lines of coverage: workers' compensation, life, health, disability, and general liability insurance.

This chapter proceeds as follows. The next section examines conditions of insurability so that one can better understand why it is difficult to insure catastrophic events in general, and why some pose more severe and longer-lasting problems than others. Section 10.2 shows how catastrophic losses from hurricanes, earthquakes, floods, and terrorism have impacted insurers' willingness to provide coverage against these risks. Section 10.3 examines the demand for coverage against these risks so that one has a better understanding as to the challenges in providing protection against catastrophic losses. Section 10.4 then examines the types of private–public partnerships for reducing losses and providing protection against low-probability, high-consequence events. The concluding section suggests future research in this area.

10.1. FACTORS INFLUENCING THE SUPPLY OF INSURANCE

Insurance markets function best when the losses associated with a particular risk are independent of each other and the insurer has accurate information on the likelihood of the relevant events occurring and the resulting damage. By selling a large number of policies for a given a risk, the insurer is likely to have an accurate estimate of claim payments it expects to make during a given period of time. To illustrate this point with a simple example, consider an insurer who offers a fire insurance policy on a set of identical homes each valued at $100,000. Based on past data, the insurer estimates there is a 1/1000 chance that a home will be destroyed by fire. Assuming this is the only event that can occur during the year, the expected annual loss for each home would be $100 (i.e., $1/1000 \times \$100,000$).

If the insurer issued only a single policy to cover the full loss from a fire, then there would be a variance of approximately $100 associated with its expected annual loss. As the number of policies issued, n, increases, the variance of the expected annual loss per exposure, or the mean loss per policy, decreases in proportion to n. Thus, if $n = 10$, the variance of the mean loss will be approximately $10. When $n = 100$ the variance decreases to $1, and with $n = 1000$ the variance is $0.10. It is thus not necessary to issue a very large number of policies to significantly reduce the variability of expected annual losses per policy if the risks are independent. This model of insurance works well for risks such as fire, automobile and loss of life since the assumptions of independence and ability to estimate probabilities and losses are satisfied. Risks that can cause catastrophic losses normally do not satisfy the above conditions, so they are more difficult to insure.

Before insurance providers are willing to offer coverage against an uncertain event at premiums anywhere close to the risk of loss they expect, they must be able to identify and quantify, or at least partially estimate, the chances of the event occurring and the extent of losses likely to be incurred. (An unreasonable premium for a buyer here would be one that is very close to the maximum value of the loss the buyer might experience.) Such estimates can be based on past data (e.g., loss history of the insurer's portfolio of policyholders, loss history in a specific region) coupled with data on what experts know about a particular risk through the use of catastrophe mdels.

Catastrophe models were introduced in the mid-1980s but did not gain widespread attention until after Hurricane Andrew hit southern Florida in August 1992, causing insured losses of over $23.7 billion (in 2007 prices) (Kunreuther and Michel-Kerjan 2009). Until 9/11 this was the largest single loss in the history of insurance. Nine insurers became insolvent as a result of their losses from Hurricane Andrew. Insurers and reinsurers felt that they needed to estimate and manage their natural hazard risk more precisely, and turned to the modelers of catastrophe risks for decision support. Obviously, the data they had before the event was insufficient to protect them.

10.1.1. USE OF EXCEEDANCE PROBABILITY CURVES

Based on the outputs of a catastrophe model, the insurer can construct an exceedance probability (EP) curve that specifies the probabilities that a certain level of total losses will be exceeded.[3] The losses can be measured in terms of dollars of damage, fatalities, illness, or some other unit of analysis. To illustrate with a specific example, suppose one were interested in constructing an EP curve for an insurer with a given portfolio of residential earthquake policies in Long Beach, California. Using probabilistic risk assessment, one would combine the set of events that could produce a given dollar loss and then determine the resulting probabilities of exceeding losses of different magnitudes. Based on these estimates, one can construct the EP curve depicted in figure 10.1. Suppose the insurer focuses on a specific loss L_i. One can see from figure 10.1 that the likelihood that insured losses will exceed L_i is given by p_i.

---

[3] The material in this subsection draws on chapter 2 in Grossi and Kunreuther (2005).

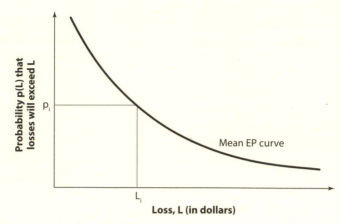

Figure 10.1. Example of an exceedance probability curve.

The x axis measures the loss to the insurer in dollars and the y axis depicts the probability that losses will exceed a particular level.

One can also incorporate uncertainty in the analysis by constructing confidence intervals around the mean EP curve, as shown in figure 10.2. The curve depicting the uncertainty in the loss shows the range of values, $L_i^{.05}$ and $L_i^{.95}$ that losses can take for a given mean value, L_i, so that there is a 95% chance that the loss will be exceeded with probability p_i. To illustrate, suppose that experts were asked to estimate a 95% confidence interval characterizing the losses from a hurricane hitting New Orleans with probability p_i. Their analysis might reveal that $L_i^{.05}$ = $40 billion and $L_i^{.95}$ = $200 billion with L_i = $90 billion. In a similar vein, one can determine the range of probabilities, $p_i^{.05}$ and $p_i^{.95}$ so that there is 95% certainty that losses will exceed L_i. Using the above illustrative example, experts might conclude that $p_i^{.05}$ = 1/5000 and $p_i^{.95}$ = 1/300 that a hurricane would hit New Orleans where damage would exceed L_i = $90 billion.

It is much easier to construct an EP curve for natural disasters than it is for terrorist activities. But even for these more predictable events, there may be considerable uncertainty regarding both the likelihood of their occurrence and the resulting damage. For low-probability, high-consequence risks, the spread between the three curves depicted in figure 10.2 shows the degree of indeterminacy of these events. Providing information on the degree of uncertainty associated with risk assessments should increase the credibility of the experts producing these figures. The uncertainty arises largely from the experts' lack of confidence in the models they used to generate the curve. If they feel very uncertain about the models, the confidence interval will be large.

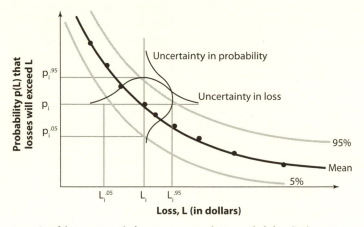

Figure 10.2. Confidence intervals for a mean exceedance probability (EP) curve.

10.1.2. Insurability Conditions

Consider a standard insurance policy where premiums are paid at the start of a given time period to cover losses during this interval. Two conditions must be met before insurance providers are willing to offer coverage at reasonable premiums against an uncertain event. One must first be able to identify and quantify, or estimate at least partially, the chances of the event occurring and the extent of losses likely to be incurred. Such estimates can be based on past data or catastrophe loss modeling, coupled with data on what experts know about a particular risk. For example, the data might tell us that experts know almost nothing about this particular risk, but that they know a great deal about some other risks. The insurer can then construct an EP curve that depicts the probability that a certain level of loss will be exceeded on an annual basis.[4] The second condition is the ability to set different premiums for each potential customer or class of customers facing different probabilities of suffering a loss and/ or the magnitude of that loss.

If both conditions are satisfied, a risk is considered to be insurable. But it still may not be insured (even if it is theoretically insurable) because it is not profitable to do so. In other words, it may be impossible to specify a rate at

---

[4] It is not necessary to have a precise estimate of the probability for a risk to be covered by insurance (Eeckhoudt and Gollier 1999). For example, the first U.S. satellite launch (Explorer I in 1958) was covered despite the lack of historical data and the difficulty of calculating the risk of failure (Doherty 1987).

which some customers will buy insurance for which there is sufficient demand and incoming revenue to cover the development, marketing, operating, and claims processing costs of the insurance and yield a net positive profit over a prespecified time horizon. In such cases, the insurer will opt not to offer coverage against this insurable risk.

10.1.3. Determining Whether to Provide Coverage

In his study on insurers' decision rules as to when they would market coverage for a specific risk, Stone (1973) develops a model whereby firms maximize expected profits subject to satisfying a constraint related to the survival probability of the firm.[5] Even if insurance against a particular risk is assumed to yield a positive expected profit, the insurer will decide not to add this coverage to its portfolio if by doing so the *survival constraint* is violated.[6]

An insurer satisfies its *survival constraint* by choosing a portfolio of risks with an overall expected probability of total claims payments greater than some predetermined amount (L^*) that is less than some threshold probability, p_1. This threshold probability is affected by the trade-off between the expected benefits of another policy and the costs to the insurer of a catastrophic loss that reduces its surplus by L^* or more. This threshold probability does not necessarily bear any relationship to what would be efficient for society or what would prevail in capital markets. The value of L^* is determined by concerns with insolvency and/or a sufficiently large loss in surplus, perhaps based on the fear that the insurer's credit rating will be downgraded, making it more costly for the insurer to raise capital in the future.

A simple example illustrates the method by which an insurer that pays attention to its survival constraint would determine whether a particular portfolio of risks is insurable with respect to hurricanes. Assume that all homes in a hurricane-prone area are equally resistant to damage so that the insurance premium, z, is the same for each structure. Furthermore, assume that an insurer has A dollars in current surplus and wants to determine the number of policies it can write and still satisfy its survival constraint. Then, the maximum number of policies, n, satisfying the survival constraint is given by

[5] Stone also introduces a constraint regarding the stability of the insurer's operation. However, insurers have traditionally not focused on this constraint in dealing with catastrophic risks.

[6] The survival constraint is rather similar to the concept of value-at-risk (VaR), widely used in the risk management of banks and insurance companies. The VaR is a tolerance level set on the possible loss of capital. For example, a VaR of $100 million at the 1% level means that there is a 99% certainty that the capital loss will not exceed $100 million.

$$\text{Probability [Claims payments } (L^*) > (n\,z + A)] < p_1 \qquad (10.1)$$

The insurer will use the survival constraint to determine the maximum number of policies (n^*) it is willing to offer. It can also make an adjustment in premiums and/or a transfer of some of the risk to others in the private sector (e.g., reinsurers or capital markets) or rely on state or federal programs to cover catastrophic losses. It will still offer coverage against this risk only if (n^*) yields a positive expected profit.

Following the series of natural disasters that occurred at the end of the 1980s and in the 1990s, insurers may have focused on the survival constraint given by equation 10.1 to determine the amount of catastrophe coverage they were willing to provide. Rating agencies, such as A.M. Best, focused on insurers' exposure to catastrophic losses as one element in determining credit ratings, so insurers paid attention to the likelihood of a large loss that might threaten their current standing.

10.1.4. Setting Premiums

For an insurer to want to offer coverage against a particular risk it needs to determine a premium that yields a positive expected profit and avoids an unacceptable probability and level of loss. State regulations often limit insurers in their rate-setting process, and competition can play a role in what may be charged in a given marketplace. Even in the absence of these influences, there are two other issues that an insurer considers in setting premiums for catastrophic losses: uncertainty in loss and highly correlated risks.[7]

Uncertainty in Loss. Catastrophic risks pose a set of challenging problems for insurers because they involve potentially high losses that are extremely uncertain. Figure 10.3 illustrates the total number of loss events from 1950 to 2000 in the United States for three prevalent natural hazards: earthquakes, hurricanes, and floods. Events were selected that had at least $1 billion of economic damage and/or over 50 deaths.

---

[7] There are two other problems insurers face with respect to setting premiums with respect to risks: adverse selection and moral hazard. Neither appears to be a major problem with respect to catastrophic risks such as natural disasters. Adverse selection occurs when the insurer cannot distinguish (or does not discriminate through price) between the probabilities of a loss for different categories of risk, while the insured, possessing information unknown to the insurer, selects a price/coverage option more favorable to the insured. Moral hazard refers to an increase in the probability of loss caused by the behavior of the policyholder.

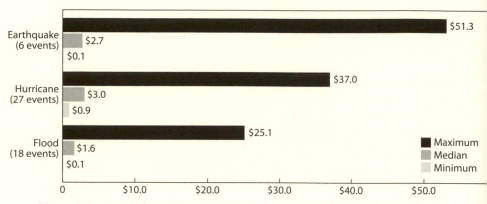

Figure 10.3. Historical economic losses in $ millions versus type of significant U.S. natural disaster 1950–2000. *Source:* American Re (2002).

Looking across all the disasters of a particular type (earthquake, hurricane, or flood), for this 50-year period, the median loss is low while the maximum loss is very high. The 2004 and 2005 seasons have already dramatically changed the upper limits in figure 10.3. Hurricane Katrina is estimated to have caused between $150 billion and $170 billion in economic losses, more than four times that of the most costly hurricane between 1950 and 2000. Given this wide variation in loss distribution, it is not surprising that there is a need for catastrophe models to aid insurers and reinsurers in estimating their potential claims from events that have not yet occurred but are scientifically credible.

Highly Correlated Risks. Catastrophic risks involve spatially correlated losses or the simultaneous occurrence of many losses from a single natural disaster event. For example, a major hurricane or earthquake can cause damage to many properties in a relatively small geographic area. If an insurer sells a block of residential policies in a neighborhood, it could potentially experience a large (spatially correlated) total loss should a disaster occur in the region.

The possibility of catastrophic losses due to high correlation of risks requires insurers to be highly capitalized to deal with the tail risk implied by equation 10.1. In particular, the prices charged for catastrophe insurance must be sufficient to cover the expected claims costs and other expenses, but also must cover the costs of allocating risk capital to underwrite this risk. Moreover, because the levels of risk capital needed to underwrite catastrophe risk are usually high relative to the expected liability, the capital cost built into the premium is high, often dominating the expected loss claim cost. Thus, insurers usually need to set prices that are high relative to the loss expenses, simply to earn a normal rate of return on equity and thereby maintain their credit rating (Merton and Perold 1993).

10.2. ROLE OF CATASTROPHIC LOSSES ON SUPPLY OF INSURANCE

There is considerable empirical evidence that, following a catastrophic disaster, insurers who suffered large losses are reluctant to continue providing coverage. In theory, one should treat these events as outcomes in the tail of a distribution of possible losses that require the insurer to replenish its surplus by going to the capital market for funds. In practice it is not so easy for insurers to raise large amounts of capital following a large-scale realized loss, presumably because the possibility of a similar event occurring in the future makes many investors reluctant to provide capital. Insurers have faced such difficulties following large-scale losses from natural disasters and the terrorist attacks of 9/11.

10.2.1. EMPIRICAL EVIDENCE FROM NATURAL DISASTERS

Insurers provided coverage against earthquakes, hurricanes, and floods without any public sector involvement until they suffered severe losses from major disasters. In the case of earthquakes, the Northridge, California earthquake of January 1994 caused $18.5 billion in private insured losses while stimulating considerable demand for coverage by residents in earthquake-prone areas of California. Insurers in the state stopped selling new homeowners' policies because they were required by state regulations to offer earthquake coverage to those who demanded it. This led to the formation of the California Earthquake Authority (CEA) in 1996, which raised the deductible from 10 to 15% and limited the losses that insurers can suffer from a future earthquake (Roth 1998).

Flood insurance was first offered in 1897 by a newly established stock company in Cairo, Illinois, but was discontinued in 1899 when flooding from the Mississippi and Missouri rivers completely wiped out the home office. It was not offered again until the mid-1920s when thirty American fire insurance companies issued flood coverage and were congratulated by the American insurance magazines on having placed this coverage on a sound basis. However, the losses experienced by insurers following the 1927 Mississippi floods and severe flooding in the following year led all companies to discontinue coverage by the end of 1928 (Manes 1938). Few private companies offered flood insurance over the next forty years.

In 1968, Congress created the National Flood Insurance Program (NFIP), making the federal government the primary provider of flood insurance for homeowners and small businesses. Private insurers market coverage and service policies under their own names, retaining a percentage of premiums to cover administrative and marketing costs. Communities that are part of the program are required to adopt land-use regulations and building codes to reduce future flood losses (Pasterick 1998). Private insurers provide coverage for larger commercial establishments.

Coverage from wind damage is provided under standard homeowners' and commercial insurance policies. Following Hurricane Andrew, some insurers felt that they could not continue to provide coverage against wind damage in hurricane-prone areas in Florida. Many felt that insurance rate regulation would prevent them from charging the high rates that would be required to continue writing coverage with a positive expected profit. Insurers who wrote sizeable amounts of coverage in Florida were also concerned about experiencing catastrophic losses following the next hurricane to make landfall in the area. For example, State Farm and Allstate Insurance paid $3.6 billion and $2.3 billion in claims, respectively, in the wake of Hurricane Andrew due to their high concentration of homeowners' policies in the Miami/Dade County area of Florida. Both companies and other insurers began to reassess their strategies of providing coverage against wind damage in hurricane-prone areas (Lecomte and Gahagan 1998).

This concern led to the formation of the Florida Hurricane Catastrophe Fund (FHCF) in November 1993, which reimburses a portion of insurers' losses following major hurricanes (Lecomte and Gahagan 1998). The FHCF is a state-run catastrophe reinsurance program, and participation is mandatory for every residential property insurer writing covered policies in the state of Florida. The purpose of the fund is to improve the availability and affordability of property insurance in Florida by providing reimbursements to insurers for a portion of their catastrophic hurricane losses. Each company is required to pay a premium into the fund based on its hurricane exposure.

In 2004, the total claims-paying capacity of the fund was expanded from $11 billion to $15 billion and increased to $27 billion in 2007 for a "temporary" period of three years. Losses associated with the 2004 and 2005 hurricane seasons left the FHCF with payment obligations of $8.45 billion. These loss payouts led to a funding shortfall that in turn led the FHCF to issue $1.35 billion in revenue bonds to cover the shortfall and $2.8 billion in pre-even notes to provide liquidity for the 2006 storm season (Florida Hurricane Catastrophe Fund 2007).

10.2.2. PROVISION OF TERRORISM INSURANCE

Prior to September 11, 2001, terrorism exclusions in commercial property and casualty policies in the U.S. insurance market were extremely rare (outside of ocean marine), presumably because losses from terrorism had historically been small and, to a large degree, uncorrelated. Attacks of a domestic origin were isolated, carried out by groups or individuals with disparate agendas. Thus, the United States did not face a concerted domestic terrorism threat, as did countries such as France, Israel, Spain, and the United Kingdom.

In fact, insurance losses from terrorism were viewed as so improbable that the risk was not explicitly mentioned or priced in any standard policy and it was never excluded from so-called "all-risk" policies, with the exception of some marine cargo, aviation, and political risk policies. Even the first attack on the World Trade Center (WTC) in 1993[8] and the Oklahoma City bombing of 1995[9] were not seen as being threatening enough for insurers to consider revising their view of terrorism as a peril worth considering when pricing a commercial insurance policy. Since insurers and reinsurers felt that the likelihood of a major terrorist loss was below their threshold level of concern, they did not pay close attention to their potential losses from terrorism in the United States (Kunreuther and Pauly 2005).

Following the terrorist attacks of 9/11, insurers warned that another event of comparable magnitude could seriously strain the capacity of the industry (U.S. GAO 2005). Furthermore, they contended that the uncertainties surrounding large-scale terrorism risk were so significant that the risk was uninsurable by the private sector alone. As a result, many insurers excluded terrorism damages from their "all causes" commercial policies. Those firms demanding insurance protection against such losses were forced to purchase a policy that added terrorism as a specific cause. They often had difficulty finding an insurer offering such coverage at a premium they were willing to pay, and sometimes could not find a seller who was willing to provide terrorism insurance at any price.

When coverage was offered, the prices were likely to increase significantly over what they were prior to 9/11 and coverage limits were reduced. For example, prior to 9/11, Chicago's O'Hare airport had $750 million of terrorism insurance coverage at an annual premium of $125,000. After the terrorist attacks, insurers offered the airport only $150 million of coverage at an annual premium of $6.9 million. The airport purchased this insurance as it was required to have insurance in order to operate (Jaffee and Russell 2003). Golden Gate Park in San Francisco, California was unable to obtain terrorism coverage and its nonterrorism coverage was reduced from $125 million to $25 million. Yet

---

[8] The 1993 bombing of the WTC killed 6 people and caused $725 million in insured damages. See Swiss Re (2002).

[9] Prior to September 11, 2001, the Oklahoma City bombing of 1995, which killed 168 people, had been the most damaging terrorist attack on domestic soil, but the largest losses were to federal property and employees and were covered by the government.

the premiums for this reduced amount of protection increased from $500,000 in 2001 to $1.1 million in 2002 (Smetters 2004).

The paradox is this: before 9/11, coverage against losses due to terrorism was indeed provided by insurers in the predominant "all perils" policy form, at apparently nominal additional premiums. Little or no attention was given by regulators to the impact that a terrorist loss would have on insurer reserves or viability. Six months after the terrorist attacks of September 11, forty-five states permitted insurance companies to exclude terrorism from their coverage, except for two types of coverage: workers' compensation insurance policies where occupational injuries are covered without regard to the peril that caused the injury, and fire policies in states that have a law where losses from fire are covered no matter what the cause.[10] The price of coverage for the few insurers that continued to offer terrorism protection went from almost zero to a very high level.

What accounts for this enormous shift? The most plausible explanation is that the events of 9/11 greatly increased insurer uncertainty about terrorism losses in additional to increasing the expected value. As described earlier, greater uncertainty leads to higher premiums, at least for a time. Terrorism also has features that make estimating the likelihood of catastrophic events more challenging than for other low-probability, high-consequence risks. In contrast to natural disasters, where the likelihood of an event is determined by natural forces, terrorists are likely to determine what actions to take based on what their adversaries are doing to protect themselves.

This harder private market led to a call for some type of federal intervention (U.S. Congress Joint Economic Committee 2002a). At the end of 2002, Congress passed the Terrorism Risk Insurance Act (TRIA) as a temporary measure to increase the availability of risk coverage for terrorist acts (U.S. Congress 2002b). TRIA is based on risk sharing between the insurance industry and the federal government. The Act expired on December 31, 2005, was renewed in a modified form for another two years, and then extended for another seven years in December 2007.

Under TRIA, with its requirement that insurers offer coverage to commercial firms, sufficient insurance coverage is available today at moderate cost for commercial and residential properties in most of the country where the threat of a terrorist attack is not viewed as extremely high, and/or where the resulting damage is not anticipated to be major. The principal problems related to demand remain for large metropolitan areas where insurers must manage their

---

[10] See section 10.4 for more details on the nature of workers' compensation insurance and fire policies as they relate to terrorism losses.

concentrations of risk so as not to expose their firm to a ruinous financial loss. Due to the unknown probabilities of terrorism losses, insurers determine the extent of coverage that they are willing to offer by determining their aggregate exposure under an assumed scenario (e.g., an explosion of a 5-ton truck bomb in New York City) that will not exceed a certain percentage of its policyholders' surplus.

10.3. DEMAND FOR INSURANCE PROTECTION

Individuals faced with the possibility of a catastrophic loss tend to ignore the event until after it occurs, at which point they are extremely interested in protecting themselves. This section discusses key factors that are important to homeowners in hazard-prone areas in deciding whether to purchase insurance and then develops a sequential model of choice to explain their behavior. Empirical evidence is presented in support of such a model from studies of homeowners' behavior with respect to natural disasters. We then turn to why firms might not purchase terrorism insurance and provide supporting evidence from surveys of firms following 9/11.

10.3.1. DETERMINING WHETHER TO INSURE YOUR HOME AGAINST NATURAL DISASTERS

Most residents in hazard-prone areas have limited probabilistic knowledge of the hazard. There is considerable evidence from field studies and controlled experiments that prior to a catastrophe, individuals underestimate the chances of such a disaster occurring. In fact, many potential victims perceive the costs of getting information about the hazard and costs of protection to be so high relative to the expected benefits that they do not obtain such information, and therefore do not consider investing in loss reduction measures or purchasing insurance (Kunreuther and Pauly 2004).

This reluctance to voluntarily invest in protection may be compounded by perceived short-term *budget constraints*. For lower-income individuals, insurance is considered a discretionary expense that should be incurred only if they have money left over after taking care of what they consider the necessities of life. In focus groups on the topic, a typical reaction of such a homeowner living in a hazard-prone area to the question "Why don't you have flood or earthquake insurance?" is "I live from payday to payday." That the homeowner could have purchased a less expensive house and saved enough to cover insurance premiums out of their paycheck is not considered. The above quote thus reflects how people think about insurance, not with the actual constraints on their resources. The riskiness of buying a more costly house than one can afford has, of course, been highlighted by the turmoil in housing markets during the 2008–2009 financial crisis.

Another factor that has been purported to limit homeowners from wanting to purchase insurance is the expectation of liberal disaster assistance following a catastrophic event. Federal disaster assistance creates a type of Samaritan's dilemma: providing assistance *ex post* (after hardship) reduces parties' incentives to manage risk *ex ante* (before hardship occurs).[11] To the extent that parties expect to receive government assistance after a loss—a form of free or low-cost insurance—they might have less incentive to engage in mitigation or buy insurance before a disaster occurs. Because less insurance is purchased, the government's incentive to provide assistance after a disaster is reinforced or amplified.

The empirical evidence on the role of disaster relief suggests that individuals or communities have *not* generally based their decisions on whether or not to invest in mitigation measures by focusing on the expectation of future disaster relief. Kunreuther et al. (1978) found that most homeowners in earthquake- and hurricane-prone areas did not expect to receive aid from the federal government following a disaster. Burby et al. (1991) found that local governments that received disaster relief undertook more efforts to reduce losses from future disasters than those that did not. This behavior seems counterintuitive and the reasons for it are not fully understood.[12]

10.3.2. A SEQUENTIAL MODEL OF CHOICE

One possible explanation for the lack of interest in insurance and ignoring the possibility of disaster relief is that individuals utilize a sequential model of choice when dealing with low-probability, high-consequence events. As a first stage in such a process, individuals relate their perceived probability of a disaster (p) to a threshold level of concern (p^*), which they may unconsciously set. If $p < p^*$ they do not even think about the consequences of such a disaster by assuming that the event "will not happen to me." In this case they do not take protective actions. Only if $p > p^*$ will the individual or family consider ways that they can reduce the risk of future financial losses.

---

[11] For more details on the relationship between *ex ante* protective behavior and *ex post* expectations of disaster assistance see Kunreuther et al. (1978), Kaplow (1991), Harrington (2000), Browne and Hoyt (2000), Ganderton et al. (2000), and Moss (2002).

[12] To our knowledge there is no empirical evidence about whether firms take into account the likelihood of receiving federal aid when determining whether or not to invest in protective measures and/or purchase insurance.

The contingent weighting model proposed by Tversky et al. (1988) provides a useful framework for characterizing individual choice processes with respect to this lack of interest in purchasing insurance voluntarily. In this descriptive model, individuals make trade-offs between the dimensions associated with alternatives such as probability and outcomes. The weights they put on these dimensions are contingent, because they may vary depending on the problem context and the way information is presented.

The decision to ignore events where $p < p^*$ may be justified if a homeowner claims that there is limited time available to worry about the vicissitudes of life, and a manager focuses on events that constitute a meaningful threat to the firm's operations. Residents and decision makers in firms need some way of determining what risks they should pay attention to. If they perceive the likelihood of some event to be sufficiently low that it is not on their radar screen, then only the occurrence of the disaster will cause the individual to address it seriously.

10.3.3. EMPIRICAL EVIDENCE FROM NATURAL DISASTERS

Data supporting such a sequential model of choice has been provided through homeowners' surveys of insurance purchase decisions in flood, hurricane and earthquake-prone areas undertaken over 25 years ago (Kunreuther et al. 1978). Data from surveys of homeowners in California lend further confirming evidence to such a process. Four mail surveys undertaken since 1989 examine the spatial and demographic characteristics of those homeowners who had purchased earthquake insurance. The findings indicate that insurance purchase is *unrelated* to any measure of seismic risk that is likely to be familiar to homeowners. Rather, past experience plays a key role in insurance purchase decisions (Palm 1990, 1995).

To illustrate, consider the Loma Prieta earthquake of 1989, which caused substantial damage to property in Santa Clara County, and to a lesser extent, Contra Costa County, California. In these counties, there were major differences in responses to the 1989 and 1990 survey. In 1989, prior to the earthquake, about 34% of the uninsured respondents in both counties felt that earthquake insurance was unnecessary. One year later, only about 5 percent gave this response. This finding suggests that a disaster causes individuals to think about ways they can protect themselves from the next event and that insurance now becomes an attractive option.

There is also empirical evidence that many homeowners who purchase insurance are likely to cancel policies if they have not made a claim over the course of the next few years (Kunreuther et al. 1985). In the case of flood insurance, this finding is particularly striking since the NFIP requires that homes located in special flood hazard areas (SFHAs) purchase insurance as a condition for federally backed mortgages. To determine the extent to which residents of these areas took advantage of the program, FEMA examined applications for disaster assistance from 1549 victims of a flood in August 1998 in northern Vermont and found that 84% in SFHAs did not have insurance, 45% of whom were required to purchase it. A study by *Geotrac* revealed that more than one-third of the properties damaged in a 1999 flood in Grand Forks, North Dakota were noncompliant with the mandatory insurance purchase requirement (Tobin and Calfee 2005).[13] With respect to earthquake insurance, eight years after the creation of the California Earthquake Authority (CEA) in 1996, the take-up rate for coverage was down from 30 to 15% (Risk Management Solutions 2004).

Insurance is thus likely to be treated by many individuals as an investment rather than a protective measure, so that those who purchase coverage and do not collect on their policies over the next few years may feel that their premium payments have been wasted. In the case of flood insurance, this finding also indicates that some banks that were expected to enforce the requirement that individuals in high-hazard areas purchase flood coverage looked the other way.

10.3.4. WHY FIRMS MAY NOT PURCHASE TERRORISM INSURANCE VOLUNTARILY

The choice not to purchase terrorism insurance may sometimes be considered rational from a corporate risk management perspective. Most large public companies are owned by investors who have diversified portfolios. These investors are unlikely to be severely affected financially if the terrorism loss affects only one or two firms in their holdings. Likewise, large firms own many assets, and they will have low demand for insurance against events that will affect only a small number of those assets. If the premium for insurance is well above their perceived expected loss, it may be cost-effective for them to forego purchasing coverage.

Another reason why firms may not purchase terrorism insurance is that their managers are not concerned about the risk. There is considerable empirical evidence on managerial decision-making that firms develop simplified decision rules to determine whether or not to undertake certain protective measures (Russo and Schoemaker 1990). The sequential model of choice discussed above

---

[13] With the passage of the 1994 National Flood Insurance Reform Act, lenders who fail to enforce the flood insurance requirement can be fined up to $350. Prior to that time no penalties were imposed.

implies that if the probability of a disaster that will seriously affect the firm financially is below a level of concern, it is not worth worrying about (Camerer and Kunreuther 1989). Data from a leading brokerage firm (Marsh) from 2007 reveals that four out of ten companies decided not to buy terrorism coverage, either because they think they are not at risk ("it will not happen to us") or because they have limited resources to spend on insurance other than standard property coverage, or for both reasons (Michel-Kerjan et al. 2009).

Finally, as elaborated in the work of Kydland and Prescott (1977) for which they received the Nobel Prize in economics, the federal government cannot credibly commit *ex ante* to refuse to bail out noninsured firms in the aftermath of an attack. If a firm believes that the government will provide financial relief to those in need after another attack, it will have less interest in purchasing insurance coverage than if it were on its own. This *Samaritan's dilemma* arises when society extends assistance to others and, by so doing, leads those at risk not to take appropriate *ex ante* actions that would have reduced their need for *ex post* assistance.

10.3.5. EMPIRICAL EVIDENCE ON TERRORISM

There are significant differences across industrial and retail sectors in the degree of diversification of risk across corporate assets and facilities. Figure 10.4 shows the differences in take-up rates for a sample of Aon accounts in 11 sectors that renewed their terrorism coverage (both TRIA and combined coverage) during the period October 1, 2003 to September 30, 2004. Sectors like entertainment, financial services/real estate, and health care exhibit high take-up rates, while basic materials, manufacturing, and pharmaceutical/chemical sectors exhibit much lower take-up rates.

Corporate demand for insurance depends on, among other things, the price of the coverage, the degree of risk aversion of firms in the sector, the buyer's expectations of losses, and the level of diversification of risks in a company's portfolio. In addition, other factors influence firms' decision processes, such as perceived responsibility for mitigating and responding to terrorist attacks, interdependencies with other actors, spillover effects from these sectors resulting in indirect losses, and synergies with other risks faced by competitors. For example, we see in figure 10.4 that the take-up rate for terrorism coverage among retailers in the consumer goods sector is more than 20% lower than for the financial/real estate sector. This is partly because the effects of diversification are more fully recognized in retailing, with its largely dispersed, low-rise structures, than in the real estate sector, which often faces loan covenants by its lenders that require terrorism coverage.

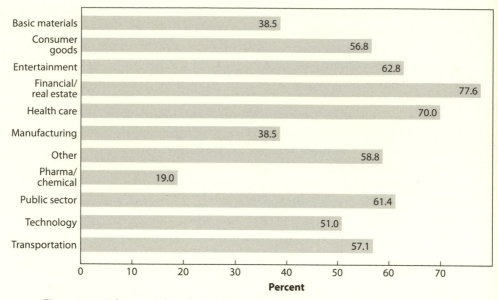

Figure 10.4. Take-up rate by industry. *Source:* Aon (2004).

The chemical sector is an interesting case. Given the hazards involved in this sector, one might expect a relatively high demand for terrorism coverage. The problem in the chemical sector is that hundreds of facilities in the United States already have nonterrorism worst-case scenarios that could cause death and injury to more than 100,000 people, thus exceeding any reasonable possibility of having private insurance at the corporate level provide coverage for these many possible events. According to the Aon (2004) report, the demand for terrorism insurance in the chemical sector has been minimal, largely because two decades of retrenchment for the larger companies toward self-insurance has already occurred. This explains the very low take-up rate of 19% for the pharma/chemical sector depicted in figure 10.4.

In interviews conducted as part of a study (Wharton Risk Center 2005), larger chemical companies claim that they have "owned" the risk from major accidents, whatever their cause, for some time and can provide cheaper risk-bearing capital to cover these risks than going to a pure outside solution. Some have portfolios of insurance placed with both outside insurers and captives. Smaller chemical companies cannot make this claim, and may well be going bare because they perceive an attack will not occur against them and/or they do not have sufficient resources to afford to buy the coverage. Should they suffer a large loss from a terrorist attack, they may be forced to declare bankruptcy and then start over again.

10.4. A PRIVATE–PUBLIC PARTNERSHIP FOR INSURING AGAINST CATASTROPHIC RISKS

In this section we sketch out the elements of an insurance program for dealing with catastrophic risks and suggest ways it can be combined with other public-private sector initiatives to reduce future disaster losses. This general framework applies both to known risks with ambiguous probabilities and to unknown risks (where by definition, the probabilities relevant to insurer decisions are ambiguous). We comment at the end on whether the unknown case is different in degree or kind from the known case.

10.4.1. SETTING RISK-BASED PREMIUMS

If one believes that those residing in hazard-prone areas should be responsible for bearing their own financial burden after suffering losses from a catastrophe, then insurance rates should reflect the risk. Such a pricing policy will promote more rational decisions on housing investment and mitigation. In the case of natural disasters, property owners residing along the Gulf Coast should pay considerably more for insurance against wind and water damage from hurricanes than in other parts of the country. Individuals residing in areas where floods, tornadoes and hurricanes are rare should pay next to nothing for insurance that covers these hazards. Those who face earthquake hazard should pay premiums that reflect this risk. Such a system of risk-based premiums encourages individuals in low-risk areas to buy coverage and prevents the problems of adverse selection.

The challenge in implementing a risk-based rating program for catastrophic events is that the premiums charged to those residing in the highest risk areas would likely be considerably greater than they are today. In fact, many states regulate rates so that premiums do not reflect the actual risks borne. In addition some residences in high-risk areas are owned by low-income families who cannot afford the costs of insurance or the costs of reconstruction should their house suffer damage from a disaster.[14] A risk-based insurance program with subsidies to low-income individuals would enable insurers to set the appropri-

---

[14] One could pose the following question regarding these uninsured low-income residents: "If you cannot afford the insurance, how can you afford the house? You could downsize your ownership of assets until you can protect those assets with insurance."

ate rates over time and still achieve fairness goals, unless they are prevented from doing so by state regulation.

Given the existing system of state rate regulation and the need for special treatment for low-income residents in high-hazard areas, there are political challenges in implementing the proposed program. The use of catastrophe models and exceedance probability curves can be extremely useful in this regard for legitimizing the types of rates that should be charged. An open question is whether regulators will use these models in determining what rates they are willing to approve.

10.4.2. A MULTILAYERED INSURANCE PROGRAM

To encourage those at risk to take protective measures while at the same time providing protection to private insurers against catastrophic losses we propose a multilayered program that involves both the public and private sectors. The *first level* of disaster losses would be borne by the victims themselves in order to encourage them to adopt safer measures and to avoid moral hazard problems that might otherwise occur if individuals behaved more carelessly because they knew they were fully protected against the risk. This form of self-insurance is equivalent to having a deductible on an insurance policy. The magnitude of the deductible could vary depending on the amount of coverage in place (e.g., a percentage deductible), the needs of those at risk and their willingness to trade off a lower price for less protection against small losses.

Losses in *layer 2* would be covered by private insurers with the amounts of coverage based on their surplus, their current portfolio, and their ability to diversify across risks. Firms with limited assets that insure policyholders in only one region of the country will want to take on a much smaller book of business than large insurers with policies written in many states and/or protect themselves through risk transfer mechanisms.

Layer 3 would consist of private sector risk transfer mechanisms that include reinsurance and catastrophe bonds with the proportion of funds allocated by insurers to each of them depending on the prices and the available coverage. The capital markets have recently emerged as a complement to reinsurance for covering large losses from disasters. Through new financial instruments known as catastrophe bonds, an insurer or reinsurer can access needed funds following a disaster. If the losses exceed a prespecified amount, then the interest on the bond, the principal, or both are forgiven. To justify the risks of losing their principal and/or interest, capital market investors demand a large enough risk-adjusted return to invest in these bonds. This comes in the form of a higher than normal interest rate when no disaster occurs.

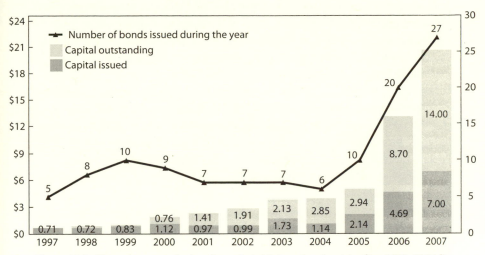

Figure 10.5. Natural catastrophe bonds: capital risk issued and outstanding 1997–2007 (in $ billion). *Sources:* Data from Swiss Re Capital Markets, Goldman Sachs, and Guy Carpenter.

Catastrophe bonds have been on the market since 1997. Figure 10.5 illustrates the evolution of risk capital issued and outstanding, and the number of bonds issued between 1997 and December 2007. The market recorded total issuance of over $4.7 billion in 2006 (twenty new issuances, almost twice as many as in 2005), a 125% increase over the $2.1 billion in 2005. This was a new record high, and a 75% increase over the $1.14 billion issued in 2004, and a 20% increase over the $1.73 billion issuance in 2003 (the previous record). The risk capital issued during 2005 and 2006 was equal to the total issued during the preceding five years. Bonds outstanding increased significantly as well, which reflects the issuance of multiyear bonds in previous years. At the end of 2006, outstanding risk capital continued to grow significantly, to $8.7 billion, with nearly $4.7 billion of that being issued. In 2007, twenty-seven new catastrophe bonds were issued, for a total of $7 billion in capital, and $14 billion was outstanding. The 2008 financial crisis had an impact on this market in the sense that no new cat bonds were issued between September and December 2008. Total cat bond volume for 2008 was $2.7 billion (Kunreuther and Michel-Kerjan 2009, chapter 8).

Regulatory, accounting, and tax issues are preventing the cat bonds from being used more widely. Another impediment to the widespread use of cat bonds is that it requires specialized knowledge and skills. Investors without these attributes are likely to allocate their funds elsewhere (Jaffee 2005).

Layer 4 would cover large-scale losses. It could take the form of multi-state pools for providing coverage in certain regions of the country subject to particular hazards, such as hurricanes in the Gulf Coast states. The federal government could also offer catastrophe reinsurance contracts and/or provide prefunded federal reinsurance for mega-catastrophes.

Lewis and Murdock (1996) proposed that the federal government offer catastrophe reinsurance contracts, which would be auctioned annually. The Treasury would auction a limited number of excess of loss (XOL) contracts covering industry losses between $25 billion and $50 billion from a single natural disaster. Another option is for the federal government to provide reinsurance protection against catastrophic losses that cannot be covered by the private sector. One advantage that the federal government has over private reinsurers is its financial ability through taxing and borrowing authority to cover a disaster that occurs in the next few years before sufficient funds are built up to cover these losses. There may be a special need for federal involvement for protection against terrorism where insurers cannot set rates based on risk and where coverage is required today for certain policies (e.g., workers' compensation in all states, fire following a terrorist attack in eighteen states).

10.4.3. LINKING INSURANCE WITH OTHER INITIATIVES

For a catastrophic disaster insurance program to reduce losses from future events it needs to be linked with other private–public sector initiatives. The importance of well-enforced building codes and land-use regulations to control development in hazard-prone areas becomes an important part of such a program. If some states and the federal government are providing protection against catastrophic losses, they can also require these risk-reducing measures as part of such a private–public partnership.

One way to encourage adoption of cost-effective mitigation measures is to have banks provide *long-term mitigation loans* that could be tied to the property. The bank holding the mortgage on the property could offer a home improvement loan with a payback period identical to the life of the mortgage. For example, a 20-year loan for $1500 at an annual interest rate of 10% would result in payments of $145 per year. If the annual premium reduction due to the adoption of the mitigation measure is greater than $145 per year, an insured homeowner would have lower total payments by investing in mitigation (Kleindorfer and Kunreuther 1999). For such a program to achieve its desired impact, insurance premiums must be risk-based so that the premium reduction for undertaking the mitigation measure exceeds the annual home improvement loan payment.

Building codes require property owners to meet standards on new structures but normally do not require them to retrofit existing structures. Often such codes are necessary, particularly when property owners are not inclined to adopt mitigation measures on their own due to their misperception of the expected benefits resulting from adopting the measure and/or their inclination to underestimate the probability of a disaster occurring. Cohen and Noll (1981) provide an additional rationale for building codes. When a structure collapses, it may create externalities in the form of economic dislocations and other social costs that are beyond the financial loss suffered by the owners. For example, if a poorly designed structure collapses in a hurricane, it may cause damage to other buildings that are well designed and still standing from the storm. Knowing this, an insurer may offer a smaller premium discount than it would otherwise have given to a homeowner investing in loss reduction measures.

Communities can also offer *tax incentives* to encourage property owners to adopt mitigation measures. The city of Berkeley has encouraged home buyers to retrofit newly purchased homes by instituting a transfer tax rebate. The city has a 1.5% tax levied on property transfer transactions; up to one-third of this amount can be applied to seismic upgrades during the sale of property. Qualifying upgrades include foundation repairs or replacement, wall bracing in basements, shear wall installation, water heater anchoring, and securing of chimneys. (Earthquake Engineering Research Institute 1998). Between fiscal years 1993–1994 and 2007–2008 the city of Berkeley provided $13.4 million in seismic rebates based on this tax incentive program.[15]

10.4.4. OPEN ISSUES

Voluntary or Required Coverage. In developing an insurance program for catastrophic losses, one of the open issues is whether all property owners should be required to have this insurance coverage (and whether such a requirement could be enforced). Since banks normally require homeowners' coverage and commercial insurance as a condition for a mortgage, a sizable number of property owners would indeed have catastrophic protection. Of course, this requirement presumably reflects a bank's judgment that the expected profitability of a mortgage at a lower interest rate coupled with a requirement to pay for coverage is greater than the profitability of a mortgage with no requirement but a higher interest rate to offset the possibility of default.

---

[15] Personal correspondence with Heather M. Murphy, City of Berkeley Finance Department, April 7, 2009.

There will be some individuals who either own their property outright or are not required by their bank to purchase insurance. They may decide to take their chances and not purchase coverage. If there are enough of these uninsured individuals and the past is a guide for the future, the federal government is likely to provide financial assistance following the next large-scale disaster. In this case, one would want to consider making insurance protection mandatory.

A related option would be for government at some level to levy a tax on all property in the United States with the payment based on the actuarial risk. The government would then cover the catastrophic losses from natural disasters. The local property tax would be the natural base to be surcharged, but the federal government often pays for the relief. If such a tax were imposed, then one would need to separate out the catastrophic portion of the loss from lesser damage that would continue to be covered by a homeowners' or commercial insurance policy.

Role of Regulation. If insurance is to provide the appropriate signals to residents in hazard-prone areas, risk-based premiums must be charged. State insurance departments need to give insurers freedom to charge these rates subject to solvency concerns that regulators may have if unduly low premiums are proposed by some insurers. One of the advantages of a risk-based system is that it rewards individuals who undertake mitigation measures by providing them with lower premiums. If premiums are subsidized in high-hazard areas, then the insurer has limited economic incentives to provide coverage to these property owners and no reason to reward them with a lower premium that fully reflects the expected benefit of adopting a loss reduction measure.

If one wants to encourage the use of capital market instruments to cover catastrophic losses, it would be useful to reexamine the current regulations and accounting practices that restrict the use of these instruments today. Jaffee (2005) has indicated three issues that deserve consideration. Accounting standards currently do not allow insurance firms to reflect the risk transfer achieved by nonindemnity catastrophe funds on their financial reports filed with state insurance regulators. A new Financial Accounting Standards Board proposal as it relates to special purpose vehicles (SPVs) used in issuing cat bonds may also have detrimental effects on the cat bond market. A third area is whether one can gain more favorable treatment for the SPVs issuing a catastrophe bond.

Special Treatment for Lower-income Families. There are likely to be a number of low-income residents who reside in high-hazard areas. These individuals may not be willing or able to afford the relatively high premiums that they would be charged on their disaster insurance policy. They also may not have funds available to invest in mitigation measures even if offered a home improvement loan. Serious consideration should be given to special treatment for this group by public sector agencies at the local, state, and/or federal levels on both equity and efficiency grounds. There needs to be a more detailed analysis as to what proportion of the homes in high-hazard areas are occupied by low-income residents and the types of subsidies that should be offered them so they can afford insurance and invest in cost-effective mitigation measures.

Unknown Risks. If insurance contracts continue to take the current form of promising coverage for all risks not specifically excluded (and therefore covering unknown risk), the framework we have proposed would still apply, with the various layers of coverage linked to the size of the loss. That is, the consumer might be expected to bear the full cost of a small loss from a previously unknown cause, the private market would cover the next layer, and government might play a role in covering losses that come from previously unknown causes and are catastrophic. Should insurers propose returning to an older form of contract in which only specified risks were covered, public policy issues might be raised, but thus far this has not happened.

10.5. CONCLUSIONS AND FUTURE RESEARCH

Modifying the demand side of catastrophe insurance is challenging but seems feasible. In contrast, modifying the supply side to deal with high loss but highly uncertain and unpredictable events is daunting, especially in a world in which the natural and political environments are unpredictable. Both the demand side and the supply side appear to be experiencing changes whose final impact is hard to predict. Market insurance can help with some risk pooling; in theory, government might help with other risks, but our expectations and optimism here need to be tempered with a realization that agents in both the public sector and private markets appear to have difficulty in correctly detecting, conceptualizing, and arranging ways to deal with the unknown. Further experimentation in this area is needed for us to gain more insight into what programs are likely to work in practice.

REFERENCES

American Re (2002). *Topics: Annual Review of North American Natural Catastrophes 2001.*

Aon (2004). *Terrorism Risk Management and Risk Transfer Market Overview*, December.

Browne, M. J., and R. E. Hoyt (2000). The demand for flood insurance: Empirical evidence. *Journal of Risk and Uncertainty* 20, 291–306.

Burby, R.J., B.A. Cigler, S.P. French, E.J. Kaiser, J. Kartez, D. Roenigk, D. Weist, and D. Whittington (1991). *Sharing Environmental Risks: How to Control Governments' Losses in Natural Disasters.* Boulder, CO: Westview.

Camerer, C., and H. Kunreuther (1989). Decision processes for low probability events: Policy implications. *Journal of Policy Analysis and Management* 8, 565–92.

Camerer, C., and M. Weber (1992). Recent developments in modelling preferences: Uncertainty and ambiguity. *Journal of Risk and Uncertainty* 5, 325–70.

Cohen, L., and R. Noll (1981). The economics of building codes to resist seismic structures. *Public Policy* (Winter), 1–29.

Doherty, N. (1987). Insurance, risk sharing and incentives for the commercial use of space. In M. K. Macauley, ed., *Economics and Technology in U.S. Space Policy.* Resources for the Future and the National Academy of Engineering.

Earthquake Engineering Research Institute (1998). *Incentives and Impediments to Improving the Seismic Performance of Buildings.* Oakland, CA: Earthquake Engineering Research Institute.

Eeckhoudt, L., and C. Gollier (1999). The insurance of low probability events. *Journal of Risk and Insurance* 66, 17–28.

Florida Hurricane Catastrophe Fund (2007). Fiscal Year 2005–2006 Annual Report, Tallahassee, FL.

Ganderton, P.T., D.S. Brookshire, M. McKee, S. Stewart, and H. Thurston (2000). Buying insurance for disaster-type risks: Experimental evidence. *Journal of Risk and Uncertainty* 20, 271–89.

Grossi, P., and H. Kunreuther (2005). *Catastrophe Modeling: A New Approach to Managing Risk.* New York: Springer.

Harrington, S. (2000). Rethinking disaster policy. *Regulation,* Spring, 40–46.

Jaffee, D. (2005). The role of government in the coverage of terrorism risks. In *Terrorism Risk Insurance in OECD Countries.* Paris: Organisation for Economic Cooperation and Development (OECD), chapter 7.

Jaffee, D., and T. Russell (2003). Market under stress: The case of extreme event insurance. In R. Arnott, B. Greenwald, R. Kanbur, and B. Nalebuff, eds., *Economics for an Imperfect World: Essays in Honor of Joseph E. Stiglitz.* Cambridge, MA: MIT Press.

Kaplow, L. (1991). Incentives and government relief for risk. *Journal of Risk and Uncertainty* 4, 167–75.

Kleindorfer, P., and H. Kunreuther (1999). The complimentary roles of mitigation and insurance in managing catastrophic risks. *Risk Analysis* 19, 727–38.

Kunreuther, H., and E. Michel-Kerjan (2009). *At War with the Weather: Managing Large-scale Risks in a New Era of Catastrophes.* New York: MIT Press.

Kunreuther, H., and M. Pauly (2004). Neglecting disaster: Why don't people insure against large losses? *Journal of Risk and Uncertainty* 28, 5–21.

Kunreuther, H., and M. Pauly (2005). Terrorism losses and all-perils insurance. *Journal of Insurance Regulation* 25, 1–18.

Kunreuther, H., R. Ginsberg, L. Miller, P. Sagi, P. Slovic, B. Borkan, and N. Katz (1978). *Disaster Insurance Protection: Public Policy Lessons*. Malden, MA: Wiley Interscience.

Kunreuther, H., W. Sanderson, and R. Vetschera (1985). A behavioral model of the adoption of protective activities. *Journal of Economic Behavior and Organization* 6, 1–15.

Kydland, F., and E. Prescott (1977). Rules rather than discretion: The inconsistency of optimal plans. *Journal of Political Economy* 85, 473–91.

Lecomte, E., and K. Gahagan (1998). Hurricane insurance protection in Florida. In H. Kunreuther and R. Roth, Sr., eds., *Paying the Price: The Status and Role of Insurance against Natural Disasters in the United States*. Washington, DC: Joseph Henry Press, 97–124.

Lewis, C., and K.C. Murdock (1996). The role of government contracts in discretionary reinsurance markets for natural disasters. *Journal of Risk and Insurance* 63, 567–97.

Manes, A. (1938). *Insurance: Facts and Problems*. New York: Harper & Brothers.

Merton, R., and A. Perold (1993). Theory of risk capital in financial firms. *Journal of Applied Corporate Finance* 6 (3), 16–32.

Michel-Kerjan, E.O., P.A. Raschky, and H.C. Kunreuther (2009). Corporate Demand for Insurance: An Empirical Analysis of the U.S. Market for Catastrophe and Non-Catastrophe Risks. Wharton Risk Center Working Paper #2009-04-06.

Moss, D. (2002). *When All Else Fails: Government as the Ultimate Risk Manager,* Cambridge, MA: Harvard University Press.

Palm, R. (1990). *Natural Hazards: An Integrative Framework for Research and Planning*. Baltimore: Johns Hopkins University Press.

Palm, R. (1995), *Earthquake Insurance: A Longitudinal Studies of California Homeowners*. Boulder, CO: Westview Press.

Pasterick, E.T. (1998). The National Flood Insurance Program. In H. Kunreuther and R.J. Roth, Sr., eds., *Paying the Price: The Status and Role of Insurance against Natural Disasters in the United States*. Washington, DC: Joseph Henry Press.

Risk Management Solutions (2004). The Northridge, California Earthquake: A 10-Year Retrospective. May.

Roth, R. Jr. (1998). Earthquake insurance in the United States. In H. Kunreuther and R. J. Roth, Sr., eds., *Paying the Price: The Status and Role of Insurance Against Natural Disasters in the United States*. Washington, DC: Joseph Henry Press.

Russo, J.E., and P. Schoemaker (1990). *Decision Traps*. New York: Simon & Schuster.

Smetters, K. (2004). Insuring against terrorism: The policy challenge. In R. Litan and R. Herring, eds., *Brookings-Wharton Papers on Financial Services*, 139–82.

Stone, J. (1973). A theory of capacity and the insurance of catastrophic risks, part I and part II. *Journal of Risk and Insurance* 40, 231–43 (part I) and 40, 339–55 (part II).

Swiss Re (2002). *Focus Report: Terrorism—Dealing with the New Spectre*. Zurich: Swiss Re, February.

Tobin, R., and C. Calfee (2005). The National Flood Insurance Program's Mandatory Purchase Requirement: Policies, processes, and stakeholders. Washington, DC: American Institutes for Research.

Tversky, A., S. Sattath, and P. Slovic (1988). Contingent weighting in judgment and choice. *Psychological Review* 95, 371–84.

U.S. Congress, Joint Economic Committee (2002a). *Economic Perspectives on Terrorism Insurance.* Washington, DC, May 2002.

U.S. Congress (2002b). *Terrorism Risk Insurance Act of 2002.* HR 3210. Washington, DC, November 26.

U.S. Government Accountability Office (GAO) (2005). *Catastrophe Risk, U.S. and European Approaches to Insure Natural Catastrophe and Terrorism Risks,* Appendix III, GAO-05-199, Washington, DC, February 28.

Wharton Risk Center (2005). *TRIA and Beyond: Terrorism Risk Financing in the U.S.*

11. Managing Increased Capital Markets Intensity

The Chief Financial Officer's Role in Navigating the Known, the Unknown, and the Unknowable

Charles N. Bralver and Daniel Borge

KuU—the known, the unknown and the unknowable—reminds us that decision makers usually face situations where hard facts and analytic models are, by themselves, insufficient descriptions of reality and that different people have different perceptions of present reality and future possibilities. The role of the chief financial officer of a modern corporation is an example of *KuU*s having substantive consequences in the practical world of finance. Differences in perceived *KuU* can lead to conflict between management and investors over how a company should be run, who runs it, and who owns it. In our view, the chief financial officer (CFO)'s mission is to lead management's efforts to detect and resolve such conflicts before they reach crisis proportions—by narrowing *KuU* differences between management and the capital markets. To be successful, the CFO must channel the intensity of the capital markets into financial disciplines that measure and manage value to the satisfaction of the capital markets. In other words, the CFO should be the agent of the company in the capital markets and the agent of capital markets discipline inside the company. In so doing, the CFO is providing critical underpinning to the chief executive officer (CEO)'s own credibility with the same stakeholders.

11.1. *KuU* AND THE DECISION MAKER

The *KuU* construct (known, unknown, unknowable) has implications for research but also for decision makers. Researchers can use the construct as a

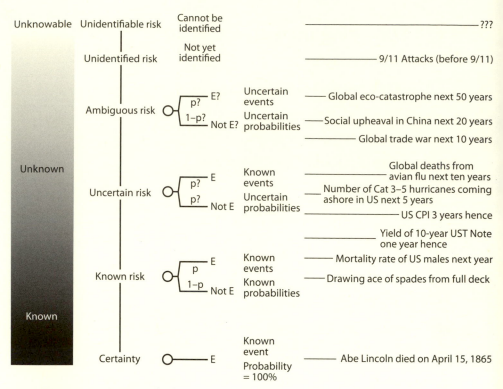

Figure 11.1. Six types of risk.

guide; as they accumulate new data and knowledge, *K* expands (and so does *u*). Decision makers have a different job: they must decide and when they do so, they explicitly or implicitly assess *K* and *u* and as much of *U* as they can imagine. They have no choice but to act on their beliefs about all the important variables, not just on the hard facts known to them.

To focus on the nature of risks relevant to a decision maker, we break the three broad categories of *KuU*—known, unknown and unknowable—into six distinct types of risk (see figure 11.1). *Certainty* is a known event with a 100% probability (Abe Lincoln died on April 15, 1865). *Known risk* presents known events with known probabilities (drawing the ace of spades from a full deck of cards). *Uncertain risk* presents known events with uncertain probabilities (the Yankees win the World Series next season). *Ambiguous risk* presents both uncertain events and uncertain probabilities (global eco-catastrophe within the next 50 years). *Unidentified risks* are risks not yet recognized by the decision

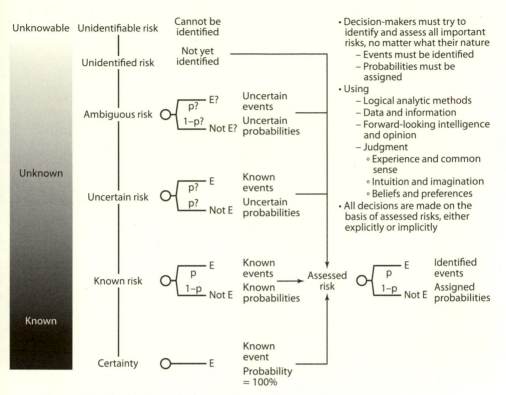

Figure 11.2. The decision maker's imperative.

maker but that are recognizable with further effort and imagination. *Unknowable risks* cannot be identified, by definition.

Because these distinctions focus attention on the elements of the decision problem that are known and unknown, they can guide the decision maker in how and where to gather more information. They can also help gauge how much weight to put on each element of the analysis in deciding what action to take.

Few business decisions of any importance present only certainties and known risks. Most present risks that range from uncertain to unknowable. But no matter what types of risk are present, the decision maker explicitly or implicitly converts them all into *assessed risks* with *identified events* and *assigned* probabilities. Ultimately, these are based on the decision maker's judgment and beliefs, hopefully supported by the best evidence and analysis available (see figure 11.2). Even the purely intuitive decision maker, by making a particular choice, has bet on an implicit risk assessment—but without

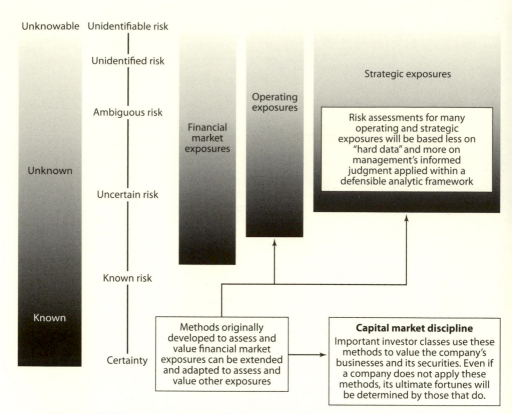

Figure 11.3. Company assessment and valuation of exposures.

knowing what it is. The field of risk management is based on the assumption that it is usually better to be as explicit and as logical as possible when assessing risks.

Since different people have different sets of knowledge (***KuU***s), they may come to different risk assessments when considering the same decision. This may lead them to disagree about the best course of action. The CFO's job is to detect and narrow these differences before they blow up into a crisis. To do so, the CFO must move well beyond the familiar "hard" numbers and accounting conventions and into the same areas of uncertainty that investors are weighing when valuing the company—known risks, uncertain risks, ambiguous risks, and unidentified risks (figure 11.3).

Assessing the full spectrum of uncertainties that face a company is a far cry from the traditional notion of the CFO and implies a much greater involvement with strategic and financial questions that necessarily require sound intuition and judgment rather than routine analysis or the accurate calculation of accounting recipes. Clearly, the task is different for the CFO of the nonfinancial corporate vs. a financial institution, as the nature of leverage, assets, cash flows, and exposure to systemic risk are different in the two cases. Our principal, though not exclusive focus is on the nonfinancial corporate.

11.2. *KuU*—THE EXAMPLE OF THE CFO

The role of the CFO has evolved and expanded since the early 1970s when the title first appeared. As our earlier research indicated, today's CFO oversees a sprawling empire than can include accounting, financial reporting, financial controls, regulatory compliance, tax accounting and policy, insurance, real estate management, corporate operating services, cost control and outsourcing, MIS, business analytics, internal consulting, performance measurement, business intelligence, budgeting, capital investments, project management, strategic planning, purchasing, cash management, financial market operations and exposure management, capital structure, debt and equity financing, M&A support, enterprise risk management, and investor relations—and possibly other functions as well. The CFO also sits at the table with the CEO and other senior managers when corporate policies and business strategies are set.

Even though there may have been good reasons for each role being added to the CFO's job, the overall impression might be that the CFO has become, since the late 1990s, the catchall for any function that does not fit elsewhere. The CFO has also been touted as the CEO's natural business partner, performing the role of portfolio manager of the company's businesses. This role has been reinforced by the many CFOs who have become chief executives.

But we urge a reconsideration of the notions that the CFO should be a superadministrator or the junior CEO. These notions arose before passage of the Sarbanes-Oxley Act (SOX) and before the parallel radical changes in institutional investor behavior had reached today's levels. Rising capital markets intensity will force a refocus on core financial functions organized around one principle: *The CFO is the agent of the company in the capital markets and the agent of capital markets discipline inside the company.* The CFO cannot afford to dissipate energy on any role that detracts from this mission. If the company runs afoul of the capital markets, it may result in the removal of management and the loss of the company's independence. This also raises issues of the CFO's partnership with the CEO, and how the CFO priorities set out here provide effective support of the CEO's own dialogue with the markets. We would characterize the division of responsibility as follows:

- The CEO has ultimate responsibility for satisfying many constituencies: investors, above all, but also the Board, employees, customers, suppliers, strategic partners, regulators/legislators, and the general public.

- In our view, the CFO should be tightly focused on interactions with the capital markets and as SOX is increasingly "bedded down" at major corporates, not divert major effort there or in other areas where capital market skills are less relevant. Again, this is contrary to the conventional wisdom that sees the CFO as superadministrator or junior CEO.

- Both the CEO and CFO have roles to play in preventing or reducing valuation gaps that could invite adverse capital market reactions—particularly from activist investors. Together they must persuade the capital markets that the company can be expected to earn attractive risk-adjusted returns over the long term and that no other strategy—or management team— offers significantly better risk-adjusted returns.

This division flows in turn into external communications, where overlapping and complimentary versions of the same message are important.

- *The CEO must tell a compelling story about the company's prospects.* It has to be a coherent, well-informed distillation of how the company sees its environment; its place in that environment; and how it will succeed in that environment. It is a vision not a spreadsheet. It appeals to all the constituents of the company, not just investors.

- *The CFO makes sure that the CEO's story is credible and appealing to the capital markets.* Presents believable evidence and analysis that builds the market's confidence in the CEO's story—and its risk/return profile. Helps the CEO avoid statements that will flop with savvy investors. Translates the broad strokes of the CEO's story into pragmatic financial terms that the market understands, including the financial resources and strategies needed to make the CEO's story come true. As financial results roll in, the CFO places them in the context of the CEO's story and the fundamentals of the business—helping investors distinguish the signal from the noise so they can value the company fairly.

Finally, this division cascades into decision-making and its cousin, decision support.

- *The CEO and business heads make business decisions.* They are responsible for producing the revenues and managing the costs. The CFO can help by providing financial resources and transactions, decision tools, performance measurement tools, and so on. The CFO must have no axe to grind for any particular business, only the company as a whole.

- *The CFO opposes strategies that will be poorly received in the capital markets and proposes strategies that will be well-received in the markets.* He or she uses capital market methods and standards to value strategies and businesses to prevent/cure valuation gaps. He or she uses capital market transactions to improve the risk/return of proposed strategies. The CFO is willing to stand up to the natural bullishness of business champions or the unwarranted timidity of those who don't realize how risks can be contained. The CEO understands this and prefers honest internal debate to market miscues.

11.3. CAPITAL MARKETS INTENSITY: WHAT IS IT?

So what exactly does "capital markets intensity" mean? We view it as the increasing complexity, velocity, and power of the forces that the capital markets can bring to bear on a company. Public companies have always depended on the capital markets to finance their operations and to monetize the franchise values they create—and those companies have always been subject, to some degree, to the market's judgment of incumbent management. Underperforming companies have always seen a penalty in the stock price when investors voted with their feet.

What is new is the quantum leap in the ability and willingness of the capital markets to exercise judgment *around the clock.* This fiercer discipline can now show up quickly in the values of the company's debt and equity securities, its ability to raise funds, and its ability to maneuver in the marketplace. This factor is particularly manifest in the arrival of activist investors who may force management to change its strategy and restructure its operations, persuade the board of directors to replace management, seek to replace board members, or catalyze the company's involuntary acquisition. It is also evident in the greater activism of many traditional institutional investors, such as pension funds, and in the growing number of boards that are acting more independently of management.

These challenges put management on a much shorter leash. To retain its freedom of action, management must understand and satisfy the requirements of the capital markets—just as those requirements are being more rigorously and rapidly enforced. The CFO is essential to making this happen.

Capital markets intensity has been building in recent years due to the combined effects of advances in financial engineering, the rapid evolution of global financial markets, and the rise of investor activism. Companies feel this intensity as the markets react more quickly and harshly to perceived changes in a company's prospects and as market participants use new techniques and strategies to put their views into action—often intruding on management's accustomed prerogatives to manage the company as it sees fit.

Advances in financial engineering have created powerful but complex techniques to identify, measure, value, and transform risks and other financial attributes. This has spawned new financial instruments, new ways of managing complex portfolios, and new ways of analyzing and valuing traditional securities. Financial engineering is driven by progress in financial theory, analytic methods, data availability, and computing power, which support many effective hedging and risk management techniques as well as the more esoteric or excessively complex products, which unraveled during the financial crisis. While the regulation and viability of several techniques and instruments have been constrained by the financial crisis of the last part of the current decade, indices such as the VIX, ABX, and CMBX were critical barometers of market sentiment during the height of the crisis, even if open to criticism that their levels could be manipulated. Indeed, financial engineering has become a distinct profession, with staff on both the banking side and among investors and corporate treasury staff. At this writing, there are more than 20 specialized graduate-level programs in financial engineering.[1]

Financial engineering began in the financial industry and continues as a factor in many disciplines—risk monitoring and control, pricing, product design, trading, portfolio management, balance sheet management, and many other areas. It is also apparent in the way that many financial institutions are now regulated. Banking and insurance supervisors use risk analytics to estimate how much risk an institution is taking and therefore how much capital it needs to buffer potential losses. Basel II, the most recent effort by banking regulators to do this, is well on the road to implementation. While new global accords are likely to attempt to rectify weaknesses revealed during the financial crisis, they will not change some of the core implications for corporate borrowers. This has significance beyond banks since it affects banks' appetite and capacity to provide credit to their customers. Capital-intensive, lower-margin forms of credit are being discouraged or repriced upward. The CFO looking for funding will need to understand what the risk/return of his financing proposal looks like to his banker. For example, concerns about potential withdrawal of credit to the "Mittelstand" (middle market) prompted German opposition to several aspects of the Basel accords.

---

[1] *Financial Engineering News*, March–April 2006.

Financial engineering enabled new products, regulatory policies, and management practices that have radically altered financial institutions' business strategies. Some have gone as fast as they arose, some will change radically, and some prove enduring. From 2004 to 2008, this included a substantial decrease in the fraction of commercial loans originated by large banks that are held in portfolio, as more loans were securitized and moved to open-market distribution and trading; the enormous growth in asset-backed securities, such as mortgages and credit card receivables; progressively finer tuning of credit analysis and pricing in consumer lending; new alternatives for small investors, such as protected equity notes; analytically driven trading and investment strategies made possible by real-time data and execution; better and cheaper operating services offered to institutional investors and corporations; a rise in proprietary positioning by many big financial players; and, not least, a huge new business based on financial engineering itself—risk management transactions and advice (once known as the derivatives business). Unfortunately, these developments were also accompanied by excessive leverage, flawed analysis, careless management, and a naïve belief in the continued availability of cheap and abundant credit.

The complexity of some of these activities is daunting and became more so as new ideas came onstream. Analyzing a complex derivative or hybrid security cannot be done on the back of an envelope. It requires deep mathematics, lots of good data, and powerful computers, not to mention, experienced judgment to sift the practical from the merely theoretical.

Analyzing a single complex transaction is hard enough, but analyzing and understanding the behavior of a portfolio of such transactions is much harder, since the transactions are likely correlated with each other along many dimensions, which creates an explosively large math problem. To make matters worse, these correlations may be poorly understood and difficult to predict, and the underlying modeling's logic or assumptions opaque and difficult for an outsider to assess. To grapple with complexities such as this, financial institutions and investors have invested enormous sums in risk experts, analytic software, management information systems (MIS), computing power, and data feeds. Spending on market news, data, and research alone was estimated at $12 billion in 2005 and growing near double-digit rates.[2]

Few nonfinancial companies aspire to master the more arcane reaches of financial engineering. Nor should they. But growing financial complexity is relevant to those companies' CFOs because it continually raises the threshold of minimal competence required of a user of the capital markets to manage risks and conduct transactions safely and effectively. We will return to this topic later.

---

[2] The market returns in 2005. *IMD Digest*, April 10, 2006.

But the essence of financial engineering is its power to design nearly any desired bundle of financial attributes to move a company or investor from an undesired risk/return profile to its desired risk/return profile. For a period, it appeared that the bearing of risk was optional and highly customizable. While in the case of subprime mortgages and their inclusion in related collateral debt obligation (CDO) and collateral loan obligation (CLO) products this led to catastrophic direct losses or distressed "mark to liquidation" pricing of securities, many exposures continue to be more manageable based on new techniques. Many commodity, weather, catastrophe, and other exposures are now more measurable and, in principle, manageable (when markets exist for the necessary transactions, as discussed below). For instance, if an airline regards its exposure to volatile jet fuel prices as excessive, it can reduce that exposure or cap it at tolerable level. Conversely, Mexico for example, hugely dependent on oil exports, sold forward its exports to mid-2010 at circa $75/bbl in early 2008, bridging much of the late 2008 market collapse. If a hedge fund is bullish on tech stocks but neutral on the S&P, it can lever up the tech stocks and hedge out the S&P. If an insurance company wants to protect its corporate bond portfolio from a looming recession, it can hedge the credit spread but stay long on treasury yields. If an oil company wants to limit its uninsured exposure to Gulf hurricanes, it can sign contracts that pay off if such a hurricane occurs.

These are only the simplest of examples. Name the desired bet, however nuanced and complex, and a financial engineer can probably design a strategy to accomplish it—but only where markets exist for the required transactions.

This new capability introduces difficulties of its own. As suggested above, complexity may overwhelm the user's capacity to understand or manage what has been done. A structure that fits in theory may not be doable in practice. Worst-case scenarios may turn out to be not the worst, by far. Exit strategies may not work when the time comes. Valuing, monitoring, and readjusting the positions over time may turn out to be much harder than anticipated. The intended results may be swamped by unexpected credit problems or liquidity crises, both in instrument liquidity and in overall market liquidity. These problems appeared in full force during the 2007–09 financial crisis.

Ironically, one difficulty is the direct result of having so many new choices: which of the plethora of available alternatives is the best? How are they to be evaluated and ranked? Conventional experience and traditional practices are poor guides to this new world. Accounting, in particular, confuses and obstructs more than it clarifies. As we discuss below, the CFO will need a comprehensive set of capabilities that is up to the task.

This greater ability to take only the desired mix and intensity of risks has special significance for the activist investors who may bedevil the corporate

CFO. An investor can now take a highly focused, precise, and leveraged bet that extracts maximum benefit from the target company with minimum risk exposure and minimum use of the investor's own capital. For example, the investor can buy a corporate bond to profit from triggering an overlooked prepayment clause but not be subject to the issuer's overall credit risk or to fluctuations in market interest rates. The unwanted exposures are eliminated with a customized package of hedges. A lender financing the investor's play may tolerate higher than normal leverage, knowing that the bet is more much limited and specific than simply holding the bond. But the effect on the company is undiminished. While such investor positions may not in all instances be fully within the spirit or letter of the securities laws, the CFO must consider the types of trades against the company's equity, debt, or credit default swaps (CDS) that an outsider may play, and be armed with the financial, legal, and regulatory tools to counter or expose such strategies.

This is only one of several ways in which hedge funds can use new and sometimes obscure financial techniques to magnify their influence at minimal risk. Hu and Black (2006)[3] describe others, including the use of borrowed shares or equity swaps to acquire shareholder votes without economic ownership. These transactions do not trigger existing disclosure rules, giving hedge funds a means to secretly acquire considerable voting power without taking any price risk on the shares. In fact, it is quite possible to acquire voting power while having an effective short position in the company, opening up the perverse possibility of profiting from voting *against* other shareholders' interests. This can also be true of CDS holders lacking a bond holder's concern of whether a company goes bankrupt, and acting against creditors who might normally cooperate in debt restructuring.

Financial engineering has armed the activists with new weapons. Are target companies willing and *able* to use financial engineering to defend themselves? The CFO must be prepared.

Rapid evolution of global financial markets produced a plethora of new instruments, new marketplaces, and new players. Established markets, such as equities, became more efficient and aggregated additional pools of liquidity, while thinly traded new markets collapsed when liquidity became scarce. Public markets have been supplemented by versatile private markets like over-the-counter (OTC) derivatives, whose volumes have held in certain products and maturities and shrank dramatically in others. Instant communication continues to tie markets to each other: cash, financial claims, and information flow with

[3] Hu, H.T.C. and B. S. Black, (2006). The new vote buying: Empty voting and hidden (morphable) ownership. *Southern California Law Review* 79, 811–908.

fewer impediments from market to market and country to country, whether on the upside or the downside. Technology and greater competition reduce the operational component of transaction costs.

Nonfinancial corporates have benefited from this fusion of financial engineering and more versatile and efficient FX , interest rate, and commodity hedging, and, for most periods, the high-grade debt markets. Even after the financial crisis, they have more financing, investment, and risk management alternatives; greater ability to customize their finances to fit their particular needs; the ability to adjust their financial strategies more quickly and at lower costs; more timely and accurate information about the values of their positions; and so on.

An important example of the potent fusion of financial engineering with financial market evolution is the credit derivatives market. Outstanding credit derivative contracts rose from about $4 trillion at year-end 2003 to an estimate of over $17 trillion at year-end 2005, and their value now exceeds that of stock of corporate bonds and loans. Credit derivatives, in their various forms, allow the transfer of credit risks from one party to another. For example, an owner of a corporate bond may, for a price, enter into a derivative contract to transfer a defined portion of the bond's default risk to another party who wishes to take that risk at that price. Beginning as a financial engineering concept in the late 1980s, credit derivatives developed into an actively functioning and fast-growing market involving financial institutions and institutional investors—especially hedge funds—that allow the packaging, pricing, and reallocation of credit risk among the parties. Banks have used credit derivatives to transfer a portion of the credit risk on their lending activities to insurance companies, hedge funds, and other asset managers. Had they not done so, their notional credit exposure in 2004 would have been more than $400 billion higher than it was. This has given banks another way to reduce the amount and concentration of their credit exposures and the appearance of freeing up capital for other activities. This depended, however, on swapping diffuse credit risks for very concentrated counterparty exposures to the small number of firms writing CDS (as credit insurance) in large volumes. Again, the corporate CDS market continued to function even as the parallel market in CDS against CDO and CLO exposures collapsed during 2007 and 2008.

But the successful use of credit derivatives requires a high degree of skill. Even the best models rely on assumptions that may not hold in the future, such as the correlations of defaults among the various names in a given structure or in a portfolio of credit derivatives. And what if the user wants to change course? How do you unwind the transaction and at what cost? Credit derivatives, like most new financial products, require new skills and tools to use successfully.

So why should the CFO of a nonfinancial company care about credit derivatives? Nonfinancial companies are not very active in those instruments. One reason is that the company may appear as a name in a credit derivative structure. If so, its credit quality will be analyzed and valued every day by the participants in that market. The CFO needs to know what this forward-looking market is saying about the company's perceived financial strength, just as a CFO needs to know how the company's bonds are rated and traded. Another reason to care is that many nonfinancial companies have significant credit exposures to customers or business partners that may be managed better through the use of credit derivatives at some point. The CFO must also be aware that credit derivatives are another tool that an activist investor might use to maximize pressure on the company at minimum risk to the investor. We highlight credit derivatives as an example not because they are the most important thing the CFO needs to know about but because they are a good cautionary tale about capital markets intensity—that relentless innovation fueled by financial engineering and financial market evolution will present the CFO with challenges that require a much more disciplined approach to interacting with the capital markets.

The capital markets now provide a multitude of ways for corporations to buy, sell, unbundle, and repackage financial attributes into a more desirable risk/return profile. These include commodity futures, equity options, and interest rate swaps, and the new and challenging, such as credit derivatives, insurance derivatives, and weather derivatives. Some of these are standardized contracts traded on exchanges and some are highly customized structures negotiated between the counterparties in the OTC market.

The OTC derivatives market is important for its size and as the place where the most customized and complex risk structures are created. Major financial institutions are capable of closely matching the unique package of financial attributes that a particular user needs. This gives a company new alternatives to shed unwanted risks and to seize attractive new opportunities whose risks can now be contained and managed. Used wisely, these transactions can support the specific needs of a company's business strategy in order to maximize the upside while staying within the company's appetite for taking risk. Of course, high levels of customization come at a cost. Financial institutions must be compensated for their design and execution skills and for managing any residual risks they take. OTC structures also create counterparty credit risks. Longer-term, more exotic structures cannot easily be undone so lack of liquidity may make for difficult and costly exit strategies. The valuation of the contract over its life can be difficult and contentious. The financial crisis revealed the heavy costs of neglecting to identify and limit these potential problems.

The combination of financial engineering and more highly evolved capital markets now provides a vast array of opportunities for users to actively manage their risk/return profiles to achieve their specific strategic and financial objectives. Passive, naïve risk-taking is no longer excusable. Here are a few examples of how these techniques are being used (and sometimes misused):

- When four private equity firms—Blackstone Group, Hellman & Friedman LLC, Kohlberg Kravis Roberts & Co., and Texas Pacific Group—bought Texas Genco, they used derivatives transactions arranged by Goldman Sachs to protect themselves from falling energy prices. In 2005, Cerberus Capital bought paper and timber operations from Mead-Westvaco. Goldman arranged hedges for Cerebus to reduce its exposure to big fluctuations in prices of pulp, natural gas, and currencies.[4]

- Oil refiners and large agribusiness companies use commodity hedges of corn futures linked to ethanol production, which in turn is tied to gasoline futures prices.

- Southwest Airlines runs a fuel hedging program that provided substantial relief from surging energy costs during 2001 to 2006. And Southwest was not the only airline benefiting from fuel hedges.[5] By contrast, China Aviation Oil lost $550 million on oil options and derivatives in 2005, underscoring the dangers of inadequate risk management and capital market skills.

At this point, we must admit that much of the existing apparatus for actively managing risks using financial engineering and new market instruments is devoted to a limited range of market-traded risks (interest rates, currencies, traded debt and equity securities, commodities, etc.), not the operating and strategic risks that are more important to a nonfinancial company. You can't yet go to the market to hedge your reputation risk. It has also become apparent that careless finanical engineering can be a cure worse than the disease. However, the immediate task of the CFO, who must deal successfully in the capital markets, is centered on these market-traded risks and the CFO must be skilled in managing them. Most important of all, he or she must parallel investors' efforts to assess all risks, including operating and strategic, when putting a value on the company as a whole. As time goes by, it may become more practical to

---

[4] Goldman builds ambitious role in buyout realm. *The Wall Street Journal*, October 31, 2006.

[5] Does hedging affect firm value? Evidence from the U.S. airline industry, D. A. Carter, D. A. Rogers, and B. Simkins. *Financial Management*, April 1, 2006.

directly address many operating and strategic risks and give companies more options for actively managing these risks as well. The successful CFO will see these opportunities before the competition sees them.

Increasing investor activism is making it much more difficult for incumbent management to insulate itself from the discipline of the capital markets. Along with SOX, the recent surge in activism follows the notorious corporate scandals of recent years where egregious incompetence or dishonesty by senior managers inflicted huge losses on investors. But it is also fueled by a growing conviction that activism can pay off for investors by pressuring management teams to perform better and to tend to investors' interests rather than their own. Hedge funds are the most conspicuous activist investors, but activism among pension funds and other institutional investors is growing too. Corporate boards are becoming more independent and that means that activist proposals have a much better chance of succeeding than in the not-long-ago days when boards were effectively rubber-stamping management's decisions.

Investor activism is what gives capital market intensity its new quantum of energy. Financial engineering and financial market evolution can proceed without posing much of an immediate threat to corporate management teams. Underperformance due to management's inattention to capital market requirements and opportunities may cause passive investors to sell the stock but not to knock on management's door. Manager's jobs are at risk from passive investors only if stock underperformance is prolonged and severe. But activist investors may knock the door down and insist on immediate changes in management behavior, or else. And they may do so by exploiting the powerful tools provided by financial engineering and financial market evolution.

Hedge funds are the most visible and aggressive activists. They are lightly regulated and can follow nearly any investment strategy that can be executed in the markets. They have gained access to large pools of capital that can be magnified further by high leverage. Many use the sophisticated tools of financial engineering and will exploit any financial instrument available in the markets that serves their objectives. They are driven by the single, clear objective of realizing large gains in the *market value* of their investments. They have been largely free of most of the bureaucratic and regulatory constraints that often prevent regulated firms from pursuing value-maximizing behavior. Hedge funds are certainly not infallible, as large numbers of them fail or shut down every year, sometimes in spectacular fashion—as did Amaranth Advisors, after losing more than $5 billion on natural gas prices in a few weeks during 2006. Moreover, 2000–2007 hedge fund performance numbers reflect survivor bias, which overstates the true average returns. Despite the shutting of hundreds of funds during the financial crisis and after the luxury of being net long- and short-term funded ended, successful hedge funds continued to attract funding from investors even in the depths of the crisis.

Not all hedge funds are activist investors, of course, but those that are have been busy. A few examples will illustrate:

- Using a 5.5% stake in H.J. Heinz, Nelson Peltz and his fund, Trian Capital, mounted a successful campaign to win two board seats in August 2006. In the process, he pressured the company to reduce costs and the stock price rose. Pelz and Trian also succeeded at Wendy's International by winning three board seats and pushing through operational changes and a spin-off.[6]

- Eric Knight, of Knight Vinke Asset Management, was a principal force behind persuading a reluctant Royal/Dutch Shell to merge its two boards in 2004. Knight also pushed Suez SA to acquire the 50% of Electrabel Power it didn't already own.[7]

- Burton Capital pressured Cenveo to replace the CEO and chairman with Robert Burton and led the company to put itself on the auction block.[8]

- TCI and Atticus Capital thwarted Deutsche Boerse's bid for the London Stock Exchange.[9]

- Two hedge funds, Pirate Capital and Barington Capital, won five seats on the board of Pep Boys in 2006.[10]

- Two "old timers," Carl Icahn and Kirk Kerkorkian, are in this game as well, armed with hedge fund backing. Icahn has launched activist campaigns at numerous companies including Blockbuster, Mylan Laboratories, Scandia Forsak, Kerr-McGee, Temple-Inland, VISX, and Time-Warner. Kerkorian famously won a board seat at GM, pushing it to restructure and to pursue strategic alliances. (His representative on the board subsequently resigned to protest GM's lack of responsiveness.[11])

A less anecdotal view of hedge fund activism is found in a recent paper[12] that studied all 13D filings (5% or greater holdings) of hedge funds for 2003 through

---

[6] Bigger than they look. *The Wall Street Journal*, October 9, 2006.
[7] Hedge funds hit rough weather but stay course. *The Wall Street Journal*, June 22, 2006.
[8] Hedge funds at the gate. *Citigroup Global Markets*, September 22, 2005.
[9] Hedge funds at the gate. *Citigroup Global Markets*, September 22, 2005.
[10] *BusinessWeek*, August 30, 2006.
[11] Hedge funds at the gate. *Citigroup Global Markets*, September 22, 2005.
[12] Hedge fund activism. A. Klein and E. Zur. Working paper, Stern School of Business, New York University, October 1, 2006.

2005. The researchers found that over 60% of the time, hedge funds were successful in getting management to accept their demands, whether it concerned a board seat (a 72% success rate), a change in strategy or operations, share repurchases, abandoning a merger, or allowing the firm to be acquired. Success was usually achieved by the credible threat of a proxy fight, even if the threat was not put into action. The study also showed that investors, on average, earned higher returns as a result of the hedge fund's intervention.

Traditional institutional investors may be becoming more active as well, although their incentives to do so are muted by diversification requirements that may discourage them from pursuing costly campaigns when their holdings of target companies are small fractions of their portfolios. However, they may be willing to support proxy campaigns mounted by others. A portfolio manager at a U.S. mutual fund put it this way: "We take this stuff extremely seriously. You don't want to be in *The Wall Street Journal* saying you voted for a management team that turned out to be a bunch of clowns."[13]

CALPERS, the huge California public employee pension fund, has long been a more active challenger of incumbent managements than most other institutional investors. A recent study[14] asserted that CALPERS' efforts to prod managements of underperforming companies in its portfolio produced significant gains in value for the fund. In addition, CALPERS has invested $4 billion with activist managers who focus on corporate governance issues. The fund reports that this has been one of its most effective strategies.[15]

The activism of institutional investors may also differ from that of hedge funds in that its focus is on promoting shareholder-friendly governance practices, including board independence, rather than on specific operating or strategic changes in the business.

Fickle debt markets. Investor activism is not confined to shareholders. Debt holders are becoming more assertive as well. One reason is that less debt is held by commercial banks and more is in the hands of hard-nosed investors who buy and sell debt on the open market or who hold credit risk in the form of credit derivatives. There was a time when a relationship with a commercial bank provided a borrower with considerable flexibility and forbearance in times of stress. Banks worked with their borrowers to resolve problems with a minimum of conflict and disruption because they valued continuing

---

[13] Corporate-governance concerns are spreading, and companies should take heed. *The Wall Street Journal*, April 12, 2006, p. A2, by A. Murray.

[14] Monitoring the monitor: Evaluating CALPERS' shareholder activism. B. Barber. UC Davis working paper, April 18, 2006.

[15] Corporate-governance concerns are spreading, and companies should take heed. *The Wall Street Journal*, April 12, 2006, p. A2, by A. Murray.

relationships with the borrowers. Those days are long gone. Commercial banks are now much tougher. They may value their relationships with the investors who purchase the loans they originate just as much as they value their relationships with borrowers. Indeed, they have obligations to their investors that prevent them from being overly accommodating to borrowers. Even more unsettling: the largest commercial banks have extremely profitable relationships with hedge funds and private equity firms—links that may be much more important than any lending relationship.

For their part, debt investors do not care about "relationships"—their concern is only for the market value of their holdings. It is true that many traditional corporate bond investors have been relatively passive, rousing themselves only when a default occurs. But there are more than enough opportunistic traders and activists around to ruin the day of a CFO. The trading desks of large banks, investment banks, and actively managed bond funds make markets in companies' debt instruments and set prices that are daily and very public barometers of their perceived financial health. Those prices have often been a better guide to the future than the company's debt rating, despite the above mentioned manipulation of CDS prices in some credits. As such, debt prices are something that CFOs must pay close attention to. It is also worth keeping an eye on the debt-rating agencies. They are trying to be more aggressive in credit monitoring of corporate bonds, having been stung too many times by falling bond prices well in advance of formal downgrades. For example, Moody's Investor Services purchased KMV, a market-value-driven credit assessment tool, to provide earlier warning of credit defaults. To the extent they are successful in this, it will mean that the agencies will have adopted and internalized many of the same criteria and methods used by the capital markets—as we are suggesting that CFOs do. The rating agencies' poor performance in the run up to the financial crisis only increases the presssure to reform their methods.

There are signs that some traditional bondholders are pressing harder to defend their interests. To cite one example, bondholders of retailer Neiman-Marcus forced changes in a leveraged buyout (LBO) structure that substantially reduced a cash dividend to shareholders, leaving the cash in the company for the protection of bondholders.[16]

Hedge funds, not surprisingly, are feared aggressors in the debt markets. Just as they do in equities, they take positions that give them maximum influence with minimum risk. For example, Whitebox Advisors took advantage of United

[16] *CFO Magazine*, February 6, 2006.

Heath Group's late SEC filing to exercise an overlooked debt covenant and demand the immediate payment, at par, of bonds that the fund had purchased at
a deep discount. The move promised Whitebox a large profit. (It is not known
if Whitebox actually had any economic exposure to the bonds or whether its
exposure had been hedged away.[17]) Even private equity firms are becoming
wary of hedge funds obstructing debt restructurings that involve their portfolio
companies. "It's not like the old days" when banks held most of the debt, says
John Danhakl, founding partner of Leonard Green & Partners, a private-equity
firm with $3.7 billion under management. "You don't know who the lenders are
and whether you can get waivers if you need them. Hedge funds can blow up
your company."[18]

Boards of Directors. A critically important development for all types of activist investors is the relatively recent shift in the behavior of corporate boards.
Spurred by regulatory changes and the public embarrassment and legal difficulties experienced by the boards of scandal-ridden companies, non-executive
directors are becoming more independent of management—and more willing to challenge and replace senior managers. Not long ago, most boards were
dominated by members who were chosen by and were loyal to the CEO. Board
members rarely knew more about the company than management wanted
them to know. Executives' proposals were rarely questioned and usually ap-
proved without significant changes; unwelcome shareholder proposals were
routinely rebuffed or ignored.

But that is definitely changing. SOX and the listing requirements of major
stock exchanges mandate certain changes, such as board nominations conducted solely by outside directors and regular meetings of directors held
without management present. Many boards are taking further steps, such as
meeting with employees and important investors, hiring outside consultants
to help them evaluate business plans and management proposals, and taking
more responsibility for running the board itself, often with an independent director taking the lead.

Their independence is showing up in the numbers. The percentage of boards
with a majority of independent directors went from 54% in 2000 to 83% in
2005. In parallel, the departure rate of U.S. CEOs increased from 10% in 2003
to 16% in 2005.[19] High-profile exits include chief executives at Disney, Bristol
Myers, Pfizer, Volkswagen, Deutsche Telekom, Airbus, Hewlett-Packard, AIG,

---

[17] Hedge funds play hardball with firms filing late financials. *The Wall Street Journal*, August 29,
2006.
[18] Debt buyers vs. the indebted. *The Wall Street Journal*, October 17, 2006.
[19] Drama in the boardroom. *The Wall Street Journal*, October 2, 2006.

and Merck. About 35% of the CEOs leaving U.S. companies were forced out in 2005, up from 12% in 1995.[20]

The challenge of capital markets intensity is that it involves familiar elements whose combined effect is easy to underestimate. In this case, familiarity breeds complacency. Because some elements of capital markets intensity have been growing and visible for a long time (aspects of financial engineering and market evolution, for example) it is tempting to dismiss them as "known" and miss the larger significance of the elements taken together as a mutually reinforcing whole. The stock-market bubble, corporate scandals, and the financial crisis of recent years have boosted investor concern about the prevalence of conflicts of interest and incompetence in corporate management. Parallel changes in the capital markets mean that these concerns manifest themselves in new and more powerful ways. For example, hedge funds that have a direct stake in a company's value are now armed with access to large and growing pools of capital, powerful analytics, and new financial techniques. They also are dealing with boards that are more anxious to demonstrate their independence from management. This gives hedge funds much more leverage over the corporate managers they judge to be underperformers. Capital markets intensity has increased by much more than the sum of its separate elements.

CFOs who have been understandably distracted by SOX compliance over the last few years may be further behind than they realize. Companies, and especially their CFOs, must respond to this challenge by acquiring and deploying the capital markets capabilities that we describe below—capabilities that directly relate to understanding and responding effectively to capital markets requirements. Accountants have had their day. A CFO's future success hinges on risk assessment, valuation, market execution, active portfolio management, and credibility with investors.

11.4. CAPITAL MARKETS INTENSITY: HOW DOES IT WORK?

Valuation is the process that drives capital markets discipline. The market acts every day to set a value on a company's debt and equity securities based on its assessment of the risk and expected return, over time, of the company's businesses and balance sheet, including the value of strategic options on future business opportunities.

Passive investors take management's strategy as a given and value the company accordingly. If the company does not meet the market's requirements for risk/return, passive investors will sell the stock and its price will fall. Activist

---

[20] Why corporate boardrooms are in turmoil. *The Wall Street Journal*, September 16, 2006, p. A7.

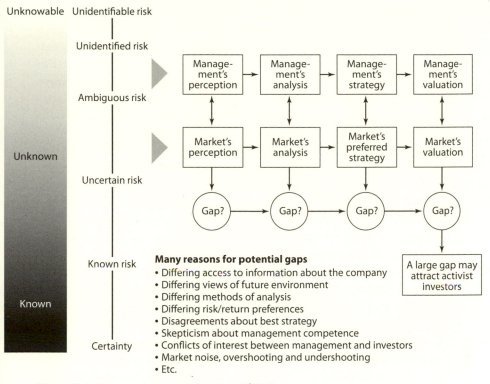

Figure 11.4. Management vs. investor views of *KuU*.

investors value the company under different business and financial strategies. If an alternative strategy would yield a higher value than management's strategy, the resulting valuation gap may cause activist investors to press management and the board to change strategy. If they meet resistance, the activists may rally other investors to the cause. Their pressure can result in the removal of management, the appointment of activists to the board, and intervention in company operations. It may even lead to the involuntary acquisition of the company. Even if the process does not get this far, the public spectacle of investors criticizing the company may hurt the reputations of management and the board.

In other words, starkly different views of *KuU* can precipitate a fierce battle between the management of a company and its investors (figure 11.4). Some of these differences in *KuU* arise from differences in perception, analysis, and preferred strategies. These differences arise because management sees a different set of "facts" than investors see. For example, management knows more about the internal operations of the company than investors do. But the market efficiently pools a vast array of knowledge about the business environment that management may not be fully aware of. So management's perception of the future business environment and the company's fitness to compete in that environment may differ greatly from the market's perception. There may also be differences in how management and the market analyzes the same set of facts. There could also be different agendas and risk appetites that lead to different preferred strategies. And so on. Narrowing the differences in *KuU* between management and investors reduces the potential for conflict.

If a battle between management and activist investors does break out, rising capital market intensity greatly increases the odds that investors will win this battle—unless management and the board preempt the process by bringing capital markets discipline inside the company to prevent significant valuation gaps from developing in the first place. That is why it is so important that the CFO focus on being the agent of the company in the capital markets and the agent of capital markets discipline inside the company.

While we refer primarily to publicly traded companies in this paper, capital markets intensity exerts great pressure on private companies too. Most companies taken private intend to go public again within three to five years, and they must meet equity market standards at that point. So management must anticipate that need and manage accordingly while the company is still private. Nor is there good reason to believe that private equity investors are any less demanding than public owners; in fact, they are likely to be more so. (Presumably they bought the company because they saw a value gap that was not being realized by public investors.) Most private companies carry substantial debt, and debt is certainly a potent source of capital market discipline. Private companies transact in the financial markets and must maintain credit lines and trading relationships, and play by the rules of those markets. So while they may get a temporary reprieve by meeting short-term reported earnings targets, they get no reprieve from capital markets discipline.

Whether public or private, a company that wants to minimize conflicts with investors over the company's management or strategies must be able to detect and narrow differences between how management and investors value the company—in other words, by bringing the *KuU*s of management and investors closer together. For management, this may require changes in disclosure policies, changes in how management communicates its outlook and strategies, better understanding of how markets set values, closer monitoring of market signals, greater agility in responding to market signals with tactical or strategic changes in business operations, better use of the markets in altering the company's risk/return profile, and so on.

Thanks to rising capital markets intensity, the option of defying investor sentiment is available only if management can be proved right before investors intervene. And that is a window that gets smaller with each passing day.

11.5. CFOS AT THE CROSSROADS

Just when capital markets intensity is applying pressure to align the company's financial disciplines and decision-making processes more closely with market valuations, many CFOs are preoccupied with reported earnings, not with broader measures of value creation. Among the primary drivers of their earnings fixation: SOX compliance and a fear of disappointing stock analysts and short-term investors.

In a revealing survey of 401 CFOs from a variety of industries, Graham et al.[21] found that generally accepted accounting principles (GAAP) earnings were ranked, by a wide margin, as the most important performance measure reported to outsiders. Eighty percent of the respondents said they would curtail value-enhancing activities, such as research and development, advertising, maintenance, and positive net present value (NPV) investments, to meet reported earnings targets. The reasons most frequently cited by CFOs for sacrificing value for earnings were to maintain or increase stock price; to improve the external reputation of the management team; and to convey future growth prospects since, they believed, failure to hit earnings benchmarks creates uncertainty about a company's prospects. A majority would sacrifice value for earnings even when earnings targets could be met instead by accounting changes *permitted by GAAP*. The authors conjectured that SOX had created a strong aversion to accounting changes of any kind.

Unfortunately for CFOs, one consequence of the stock bubble and corporate scandals was the regulatory backlash that produced SOX, which in turn has led to a preoccupation with the precision, if not the accuracy, of a company's accounting. Under penalty of jail time, the CFO has had to focus on numbers that were supposed to be known, but which too often turned out to be unknown: the company's actual accounting numbers.

For most CFOs, the good news is that SOX is moving from being an all-consuming fire drill to becoming an orderly process where most of the day-to-day effort is delegated to others. Of course, the CFO is still on the hook if things go wrong, so SOX compliance still requires alert supervision and occasional intervention.

---

[21] The economic implications of corporate financial reporting. J. R. Graham, C. R. Harvey, and S. Rajgopal. NBER Working Paper No. 10550, January 11, 2005.

The unwelcome news is that the legacy of SOX will linger on. We believe that SOX has created a firmer expectation in the capital markets that a company's disclosures will be not only truthful and numerically valid but relevant and useful to determining the company's value. Stated another way, investors expect senior managers to clearly communicate much more of what is known to them but unknown to investors. (Management may also be interested in the inverse: the market may collectively know much that is unknown to them.)

So the CFO is at a crossroads. The time requirements of SOX are winding down and most CFOs are looking forward to working on more substantive and strategically important matters. Lying ahead are some fundamental choices: between accounting-driven decisions and value-creating decisions; between empire-building and financial prowess; between spin and objective evaluation using capital market standards.

We stated earlier that the right choice for a CFO is to be the agent of the company in the capital markets and the agent of capital markets discipline inside the company. The role does not take the finance chief away from the decision-making table; if anything it makes him even more important. But it does mean that he will look at alternative strategies in a particular light: how will the capital markets judge this strategy? Is there another strategy that would be seen as more valuable by the markets? Will the markets have enough information to judge this strategy fairly? If not, what do we need to communicate so that the markets do not undervalue what we are doing? It would be terrific if *all* senior managers shared that viewpoint, but in practice they will not. Only the CFO has the neutrality, portfolio perspective, and capital market expertise to represent the market's view inside the company. It is only in this sense that the CFO can be the business partner of the CEO—by making sure the CEO does not make decisions that flop in the capital markets.

In saying that the CFO should be the agent of capital markets discipline inside the company, we are not saying that he or she takes on new or greater obligations to directly represent shareholders' interests. As a member of management, the CFO serves the CEO, who serves the board, which serves the shareholders. This indirect obligation is not new and does not change. The CFO's direct obligation is to the CEO and consists of helping the CEO and the management team understand and respond to capital markets requirements.

11.6. CAPABILITIES REQUIRED TO BRING CAPITAL MARKETS DISCIPLINE INSIDE THE COMPANY

Note that we make no mention of reported earnings even though we know that most CFOs have a maniacal focus on short-term reported earnings. But we firmly advocate taking the value road. We understand that even the CFOs who agree with us will still have to pay attention to reported earnings, but we hope to relegate such concerns to being a constraint rather than the objective. SOX is certainly no impediment to adopting value creation as the primary financial objective. SOX, after all, cares only that reported earnings are calculated according to the rules, not whether they go up or down or meet some target.

Warning to the reader: The following list of capabilities is ambitious. We are not aware of any company that has mastered them all. But some companies, in our experience, are much further along the path than others and we believe they will be fitter to compete than the laggards. These "idealized" capabilities should be seen as goals to reach for, even if falling short of them is likely.

We believe a company should have these capabilities if it is to successfully respond to capital markets intensity:

- A market-oriented risk/return decision framework

- Mark-to-market metrics (in liquid, two-way markets when available and economic value metrics when they do not)

- Capital market access and expertise

- Active portfolio management

- Credibility with investors

Although many of the capabilities we describe were developed within the financial industry, they apply, in principle, to any company. Yet the underlying framework is a good platform on which to build, particularly since it uses *changes in market value* to define risk and return. This is just what capital markets intensity requires. Of course, emphasis and implementation are different because financial companies specialize in taking financial risks and providing financial services. Nonfinancial companies need similar capabilities but tailored to a situation where (1) they are not in the business of providing financial services to others and cannot afford the same depth of capital market skills found in leading financial firms; and (2) their biggest risks are strategic and operating, not financial. The primary risks of nonfinancial companies tend to fall toward the "ambiguous risk" end of the spectrum rather than the "known risk" end. That means many of their risks must be assessed and modeled with more forward-looking judgment than the data-rich and less ambiguous financial risks that concern financial firms.

For example, deciding whether or not to bet on a new technology is not simply a statistical exercise using past data since data, on that particular technology do not exist. Drawing on relevant research, expert opinion, analytical tools, and

Exhibit 11.1
Market-oriented Risk/Return Decision Framework

1. Analytic framework testable, over time, against market outcomes:
   - Define "risk" in quantitative terms: changes in value
   - Identify types of risk across enterprise
   - Apply consistently to all activities
   - Aggregate (not add) risks to portfolio and enterprise level
   - Establish risk/return objectives and total risk appetite
2. Risk information systems
   - Capture, track, and report risks by activity and in aggregate
   - Link risks and returns for all activities
3. Decision-making process that reflects risk/return judgments
   - Business-level analytics that incorporate risk framework
   - Risk-based policies, limits and authorities
   - Risk-based transfer pricing
   - Risk-based product pricing
   - Risk-based performance measurement
   - Risk-based incentives
   - Cultural buy-in to risk/return discipline
4. Financial engineering and MIS expertise at or above market standards

its own forward-looking judgment, management must identify and evaluate different scenarios for the success or failure of the new technology and assign probabilities, based on informed belief, to the scenarios.

Let us take a closer look at each of the required capabilities.

A market-oriented risk/return decision framework (exhibit 11.1). A company without a well-founded, market-oriented risk/return decision process is unlikely to detect dangerous valuation gaps, let alone do something to narrow them. A risk/return framework identifies, quantifies, and manages risk/return trade-offs to achieve a higher valuation. This framework operates throughout the company at both the tactical and strategic levels. It is an integral part of how a company does business, not something that touches only finance.

The framework should be based on explicit and measurable definitions of risk and return—changes in market value (or economic value when market values are clearly unreliable)—corresponding to the capital markets view of risk and return. (Earnings junkies are permitted to add earnings constraints, if they must.) This measure should be used for all types of activities and all important activities should be covered by the framework. The framework should provide for the aggregation (not summation) of risks to the corporate consolidated level, taking into account any important correlations among risks. Management should also develop and adopt explicit risk/return objectives, including its appetite for total risk.

Once in place, the framework provides clear guidance to the entire organization. It also establishes a common language and consistent methods that everyone uses to analyze and debate risks arising in any area of the company's business. Of course, populating the entire framework with actual numbers may be a long journey, but we have observed that large payoffs can occur long before the process is complete.

Implementing this framework requires information systems that capture, track, and report risks and returns for activities and for the consolidated company. In the early days, these "systems" will be a patchwork of existing sources of information cobbled together on a best-efforts basis. Sleek and seamless automation is not something to wait for.

However illuminating, all of this is wasted effort unless the framework is actually used to inform risk/return trade-offs in the company's decision-making and governance processes: performance measurement, incentives, strategic planning, budgeting, capital investments, mergers and acquisitions (M&A), pricing, balance sheet management, control systems, and so on. Insuring that risk/return discipline is actually applied in practice requires that the culture embrace it. This happens only when management leads the way.

Typical gaps (exhibit 11.2). The most glaring gap is that very few nonfinancial companies are even trying to implement an explicit risk/return framework. Some are now moving toward *enterprise risk management*—a good start. Unfortunately, too many regard ERM as nothing more than a control system to limit risk-taking rather than a decision tool for maximizing the upside while staying within the company's appetite for total risk. Focusing solely on limiting the downside may lead to the upside going to activist investors.

A gap that may be faced by many nonfinancial firms is a failure to invest sufficiently in the costly talent necessary to build and maintain the analytical aspects of the risk/return framework. Risk experts are employed by the hundreds in financial firms and are highly paid.

A gap observed even in many financial firms with years of risk management experience is that the analytical process is not effectively connected to the decision-making process. Highly sophisticated risk experts produce reports that

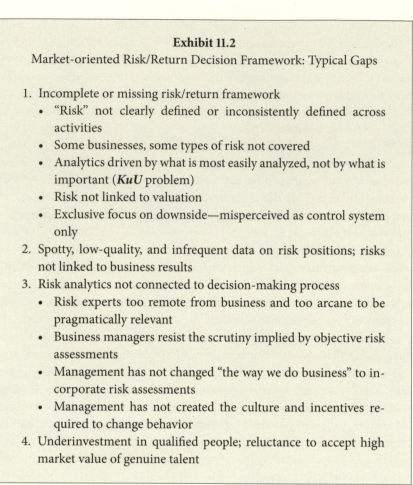

Exhibit 11.2
Market-oriented Risk/Return Decision Framework: Typical Gaps

1. Incomplete or missing risk/return framework
   - "Risk" not clearly defined or inconsistently defined across activities
   - Some businesses, some types of risk not covered
   - Analytics driven by what is most easily analyzed, not by what is important (*KuU* problem)
   - Risk not linked to valuation
   - Exclusive focus on downside—misperceived as control system only
2. Spotty, low-quality, and infrequent data on risk positions; risks not linked to business results
3. Risk analytics not connected to decision-making process
   - Risk experts too remote from business and too arcane to be pragmatically relevant
   - Business managers resist the scrutiny implied by objective risk assessments
   - Management has not changed "the way we do business" to incorporate risk assessments
   - Management has not created the culture and incentives required to change behavior
4. Underinvestment in qualified people; reluctance to accept high market value of genuine talent

business managers don't understand or use. Risk experts may have only superficial knowledge of the businesses they are trying to model. Business managers may not have received even the most basic training in the assessment of risks. Risk experts and business managers may rarely communicate. Worst of all, business managers may not have an incentive to use the risk/return framework because their performance is still being measured by old risk-insensitive measures. These are all symptoms of management's failure to change the culture of the company to support risk/return discipline in the way the company does business.

Mark-to-market metrics (exhibit 11.3). Once prospective risks and returns are assessed, management can estimate values for businesses, transactions,

---

Exhibit 11.3
Mark-to-Market Metrics

1. Acquisition or synthesis of relevant market comparables
2. Analytic framework to apply comparables to internal activities
3. Process to validate methodology and verify data

---

portfolios, and the company as a whole. But the senior managers must also compare the company's valuation to the market's valuation to see if a gap exists and if so, they have to examine *why* it exists. For a publicly traded company, the market's valuation as a whole is directly observable, but the market's valuations of the company's components are not—they must be inferred from how the market values other traded entities that, in some synthetic combination, are comparable to the business or activity carried out inside the company. This is not an easy or precise process, but it usually can be done to a reasonable approximation and it provides the basis for identifying components of the company that are judged more or less valuable by the market than by management.

The company's process of "marking itself to market," piece by piece, is not just an analytic exercise. It should be consistent with the company's risk/return framework and thus be the basis of measuring and rewarding business performance. It should also drive important decisions, such as pricing products and services, allocation of capital and resources, the restructuring, sale, or acquisition of businesses, and the choice of capital investments. The mark-to-market process also provides a healthy challenge to the company's strategic assumptions and its beliefs about the business environment, since the market's beliefs and assumptions may be quite different. A company that doesn't go through this valuation process may be blind to valuation gaps in some of its businesses—and open to intervention from activist investors.

Typical gaps (exhibit 11.4). The most glaring gap in mark-to-market capabilities may be that management does not accept its validity or relevance. An entrenched accounting mentality may trump the need to look at the company the way the market sees it. Many pharmaceutical companies trade well above their book values because accounting simply ignores one of their most valuable assets: the future value of new drugs in the pipeline, an asset that the market takes the trouble to estimate. Management may also reject the inevitable volatility of market-based valuations as not being "real." To that we can only

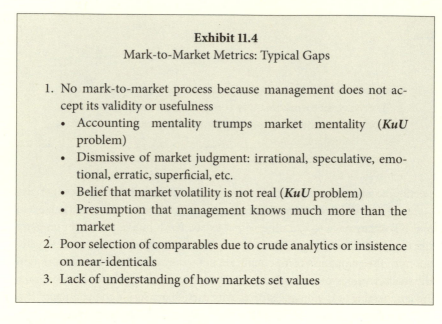

Exhibit 11.4
Mark-to-Market Metrics: Typical Gaps

1. No mark-to-market process because management does not accept its validity or usefulness
   - Accounting mentality trumps market mentality (*KuU* problem)
   - Dismissive of market judgment: irrational, speculative, emotional, erratic, superficial, etc.
   - Belief that market volatility is not real (*KuU* problem)
   - Presumption that management knows much more than the market
2. Poor selection of comparables due to crude analytics or insistence on near-identicals
3. Lack of understanding of how markets set values

say that the market sets values that can be acted upon and accountants cannot make the same claim. Reality may be volatile. The financial crisis may tempt some to reject market prices out of hand because of the apparent divergence of panic pricing and fundamental values. This would be to mistake a temporary disequilibrium for a general rule.

Capital market access and expertise (exhibit 11.5). Once the company has a desired strategy rooted in risk/return and valuation disciplines, it must be able to put that strategy into action. The financial components of the strategy are executed in the capital markets by the CFO's team; they may include a multitude of instruments and markets. The team must master the mechanics and operational requirements of each. It must establish and maintain trading lines, credit lines, and working relationships with a diverse base of counterparties and financial service providers. It must be able to analyze transactions for suitability and pricing; to assess, monitor, and alter risk exposures; and to monitor markets and respond to events. The capital markets transactions must aggregate to a portfolio that fits the desired balance of risk/return in the company's business strategy.

To do all of this successfully requires, above all, talented market professionals who know the markets and have experience in dealing in them. Whenever it ventures into the markets, the company is up against bankers, dealers, traders,

Exhibit 11.5
Capital Markets Access and Expertise

1. killed transactors and position managers who can hold their own against dealers and other sophisticated players
2. Appropriate analytics to evaluate possible transactions and positioning strategies
3. Access to current market prices and market-moving news
4. Back-office systems that can handle desired volume, mix, and complexity of transactions
5. MIS that can accurately track current positions, P&L, and risk exposures
6. Risk-based controls—market, credit, liquidity, and regulatory compliance
7. Credit rating or credit support that provides sufficient access to willing counterparties
8. Ability to identify and execute market transactions that fit the company's desired risk/return profile
9. Recognition and avoidance of markets, transactions, and positions that are beyond the company's capabilities to evaluate and manage

and investors who are highly skilled, superbly equipped, and advantageously positioned in the market's transaction and information flow. These financial players are also driven by *market values* since they are subject to mark-to-market accounting and incentives. It is not only hedge funds that can take advantage of a company that is inattentive to market values. Clever traders can extract a heavy price for helping a company achieve accounting results that are not related to value. The company must be able to use the services of some of these players, but pay no more than a fair price for doing so.

Typical gaps (exhibit 11.6). Capital markets professionals are even more expensive than risk experts. A company may underinvest to the point that it does not reach the threshold of minimum competence required for safely operating in the markets. Attaining a good balance of expense versus competence is a management challenge to be taken very seriously. Nonfinancial companies may not have enough experience in the financial markets to appreciate the

---

Exhibit 11.6
Capital markets access and expertise: Typical Gaps

1. Underinvestment in qualified people; reluctance to accept high market value of genuine talent
2. Underinvestment in necessary MIS and operating systems
3. Lack of appreciation for liquidity, credit, and operating risks (**KuU**)
4. Misjudgment of the true market risks of complex instruments (**KuU**)
5. Poor preparation for entering unfamiliar markets (**KuU**)
6. Failure to defend against potentially conflicting agendas of bankers, dealers, and other sophisticated players
7. Inadequate supervision by management
   - Lack of independent, qualified risk oversight and audit functions
   - Inadvertent creation of perverse incentives to take undesirable risks
   - Failure to harmonize capital market operations with the strategy, objectives, and risk appetite of the company

---

treacherous credit, liquidity, and operating risks of some financial instruments and markets. These risks may not arise often, but when they do, disaster can ensue. The financial crisis of 2007–09 was a vivid demonstration that a deficit in financial market skills can be costly.

Inadequate supervision of the capital markets team exposes a particularly dangerous gap. It is not enough to hire a good team and build a modern, fully wired trading room. An isolated team left to run itself can easily stray into transactions that are, at best, irrelevant to the company's strategy or, at worst, dangerously risky. Management must provide for qualified oversight and audit functions that can monitor what is happening to be sure that activities are suitable and within preestablished risk limits. But most important is that management create incentives that are aligned with the company's strategy and risk appetite. The financial industry has learned this the hard way after numerous disasters involving poorly supervised rogues or incompetents in their trading rooms.

Exhibit 11.7
Active Portfolio Management

1. Portfolio view of businesses and company as a whole
   - Consistent financial and risk MIS across businesses/activities that is compatible with risk/return framework
   - Assessment of correlations or linkages among businesses/activities
   - Understanding of specific factors driving business performance
   - Active intelligence-gathering to detect threats/opportunities
2. Frequent valuation of all businesses/activities
   - Value based on internal view of prospective risk/return, AND
   - Estimate of current market values
   - Reconcile and explain differences between internal and market views
     - Differing risk assessments
     - Differing return expectations
     - Differing valuation methodologies
3. Incorporation of valuations into strategic decision-making processes
   - Corporate planning and budgeting
   - New business evaluation/approval
   - Business line strategy formulation
   - Capital investments: R&D, new technology, new capacity, brand, etc.
   - Acquisitions/divestitures
   - Restructurings and reorganizations
   - Capital structure: leverage, dividends, stock issuance/buyback, debt composition, strategic hedges, etc.

Active portfolio management (exhibit 11.7). Senior managers must not let significant valuation gaps persist. So they must put in place a recurring cycle of valuation, valuation gap analysis, strategy formulation, and execution—both tactical and strategic. This does not mean that management should try to react in a knee-jerk fashion to every blip of market noise and to faddish trends that can sometimes cause market valuations to temporarily depart from well-founded values. But the capital markets cannot be ignored for too long. As the cliché goes, "the market can stay irrational longer than you can stay solvent." When management learns that one of its businesses has a low valuation in the market, it must take action either to change the business to increase its market value, exit the business, or evangelize about the true nature of the business so the market raises its valuation. The same applies to the company's business mix and capital structure. Active portfolio management uses risk/return criteria to judge businesses both individually and as part of the company's portfolio. Business entry/exit and resource allocation are calculated to achieve the best risk/ return for the portfolio as a whole. Management must always be alert to market feedback and adjust its strategies accordingly over time, or risk finding activist investors doing the adjusting.

Adjustments in strategy or tactics may include both financial market trans-actions and operating changes in the business itself. As the capital market evolves, there will more opportunities to use financial instruments that can be tailored to the particular business needs of the company, but operating a busi-ness day-to-day with risk/return discipline will be the most effective way to prevent significant valuation gaps.

Typical Gaps (exhibit 11.8). Some businesses manage themselves, either ex-plicitly or implicitly, as holding companies. Business lines are independently run and evaluated on a stand-alone basis. This may be appropriate when the business lines really are economically independent. But, in that case, we won-der why they would not better off as separate entities. More often, business lines are related to one another either through direct interactions with each other or by being correlated through their mutual dependence on a common set of busi-ness drivers. But assessing correlations is hard and therefore often neglected— and the potential benefits (freeing up capital, reducing volatility) from actively exploiting these correlations are forgone.

Some companies have a "me too" strategy for entering and exiting businesses, aping whatever their competitors do rather than doing their own hard-headed risk/return analysis based on their particular situations. Other companies ac-quire businesses simply to get bigger, particularly if management is rewarded for empire building rather than value creation. This may present a particularly attractive target for activist investors.

A common bureaucratic failure is to allocate resources arbitrarily rather than by an assessment of risk/return. Arbitrary allocations can be the result of political favoritism, habit, ("last year plus 5%"), or cash cows being al-lowed to reinvest their own cash flows even when they have no good way to invest them.

Exhibit 11.8
Active Portfolio Management: Typical Gaps

1. No portfolio-level strategy; implicit holding-company mentality
2. Business entry/exit driven by short-term accounting or herding instincts
3. Resources allocated arbitrarily
   - Political favoritism
   - Bureaucratic inertial extrapolation
   - Hostage-taking by cash cows
4. M&A driven by empire-building or defensive "me-too-ism"
5. Hoarding of investors' capital to minimize need to tap capital markets

---

A particularly tempting target of activist investors is a company that hoards excess capital that is invested poorly or that is not needed to support the actual risks of its business portfolio. Activists move in to lever up the company and/or repatriate cash to investors.

Credibility with investors (exhibit 11.9). All of the above will go for naught unless important investors have confidence in what management says and what management will do. Without that confidence, they will discount the stock heavily and possibly seek to replace top managers. They will not have confidence in management if the company's financial reports are frequently restated; if investors regard its financial disclosures and management statements as confusing, misleading, or unnecessarily opaque; if they believe management is feathering its own nest at the expense of shareholders; if they believe management is committed to an inferior business strategy; if they believe management is too reckless or too timid in taking risks; or if they believe management is simply not up to the task of running the company efficiently and effectively. Many financial companies have learned this the hard way during the financial crisis. Investor confidence in management is built over time based on a track record of honesty, clarity, and achievement of results. Investors come to believe that there is not a serious *KuU* gap between them and management; they learn to see that if a gap opens up, it can be closed. Once confidence in a management team is lost, it is very difficult to restore.

Exhibit 11.9
Credibility with Investors

1. Informed assessment of debt and equity investor base
   - Current information on who are the principal investors in the company
   - How different investors think and behave
   - Which investors have the most influence on market prices
   - What investors know and don't know about the company
2. Effective communication channels
   - Direct dialogue with key investors to discover objectives, views, and intentions
   - Public channels of disclosure and management commentary
     - Coherent disclosure policies that minimize confusion, error, and surprises
     - Track record that inspires confidence in what management says
3. Avoidance of "imperial" management
   - Independent, competent, and informed directors
   - Display of respect for investor rights and due consideration of investor proposals
   - Management compensation that is reasonable and linked to shareholder results
4. Clear and coherent articulation by management of
   - Financial objectives, including risk-taking practices and risk appetite
   - Company business strategy and reasons for choosing it
   - Principal drivers of business performance and the outlook for those drivers
   - Most important risks and opportunities and what the company will do about them
   - Explanation of current financial results, within context above
5. Convincing debunking of beliefs/assumptions that could lead investors to undervalue company

---

Exhibit 11.10

Credibility with Investors: Typical Gaps

1. Fixation on GAAP earnings not value creation
2. Inadequate disclosure of factors relevant to valuation and risk assessment
3. Management agenda conflicts with investor agenda

Typical gaps (exhibit 11.10). A pervasive problem, discussed earlier, is the iron grip that GAAP earnings targets have on so many management teams. They fear nothing more than facing hostile stock analysts who apparently can take 5% off the stock price for missing earnings expectations by 10 cents a share. And here we are, telling them that investors care about value, not earnings. We have no easy solution to this problem; it is probably true that petulant analysts can jerk around the stock price in the short run—and managements need to survive the short run to enjoy the long run. But chasing GAAP earnings without regard to value creation is not a reliable recipe for lasting success. Opening up a valuation gap may attract activist investors who care nothing for earnings targets if they can make $500 million by extracting value that management has left on the table.

Management teams are often reluctant to release information that would be useful to investors on the grounds that it would help the competition or that it would create a never-ending stream of requests for even more information. That may well be true, but it is putting the cart before the horse. What is more important than investors being able to fairly value the company and buy into its strategy and management? Poorly conceived disclosure that obscures the risk/return of the company creates opacity that may force investors to heavily discount the stock—perhaps unnecessarily. It also raises suspicions that management may not be managing risk/return in an intelligent fashion.

Most troublesome is that some management teams have a genuine, irreconcilable conflict with investors. They are more interested in their own enrichment than in creating value for investors, and they exploit lax corporate governance and sleepy boards to do so. They will not be interested in our recommendations. We are confident that increasing capital markets intensity will eventually bring them down.

11.7. CONCLUSION

A company must satisfy itself that it truly maintains capital markets discipline within its business portfolio and that those businesses apply the same discipline in their subportfolios. The company must be continually attuned to and responding to what the market is telling it. If it does not, management is at greater risk than ever of being second-guessed and perhaps replaced. Board members risk embarrassment and tarnished reputations. Those scenarios will only become more urgent as capital markets intensity continues to increase.

The CFO is the one who most closely supports the CEO in making this happen by being the agent of the company in the capital markets and the agent of capital markets discipline inside the company. The CFO must focus attention on this above all else. This requires a dispassionate assessment of the capabilities required and the gaps that must be filled—and a commitment to filling those gaps over time.

Successful CFOs will help the company identify and choose strategies that will be well received by the various players in the capital markets—strategies that improve the risk/return balance of the company's entire portfolio of activities. Those finance chiefs will expertly tap the capital markets for funding, risk mitigation, and other transactions that support the chosen strategies; they will clearly and credibly communicate the company's strategies and outlook to investors; they will detect and narrow disagreements with investors about valuation of equity or debt instruments.

This role will be far more valuable than being the superadministrator of a sprawling empire of disparate functions. We firmly believe that it redefines what it means to be the business partner of the CEO.

12. The Role of Corporate Governance in Coping with Risk and Unknowns

· ·

Kenneth E. Scott

The concern of this book is with financial risk management: the known, the unknown and the unknowable. There may not be complete agreement on what that encompasses. For my purpose, I would define *risk* as the possible occurrence of a future event (state of nature) that has a significant financial consequence for a decision maker. Depending on your particular position, your primary focus might be on the management of risk by financial institutions, or on the oversight of that management by government agencies regulating financial institutions, or on businesses in their operations or dealings with financial institutions and transacting partners. My perspective will mostly be centered on the latter.

Further, the book's theme is the utility of classifying risks as known (K), unknown (u) and unknowable (U). The use of those terms varies among authors. In the absence of full consensus, one can only make clear his own usage. I view those risks in terms of a probability distribution, with the KuU classes lying along a continuum of knowledge about the density function and how it is generated. The polar K example might be an honest roulette wheel, while the polar U example would be an event that no one is even thinking about. There is no sharp definitional line to be drawn, but we can have varying degrees of confidence in our understanding of the mean and variance (and other parameters) of the distribution in question.

Most of the chapters in this book deal with aspects of addressing risks directly—classifying them, examining their origins and generating processes, calculating their probabilities of occurrence and density functions and tails, estimating the losses associated with different magnitudes and circumstances, and considering individual perceptions and responses to those risks (cognitive biases and tendencies). Corporate governance per se does not address those matters as its focus. (Corporate governance, as I am using it, is not limited to corporations, but is concerned with the decision-making structure of any form of firm or organization.) In most of the legal and economic literature, it centers on "agency costs": conflicts among shareholders (controlling and minority), directors and management, or more broadly between principals (who hold some type of ownership or residual stake) and agents (through whom they must act) in administering the affairs of the firm or organization. Principals can utilize assistants to aid in the internal monitoring of management: directors, accountants, counsel, consultants. But they too are agents, imposing costs. The extent of residual agency costs is one of the risks investors bear.

There are some who define corporate governance so broadly as to include every force or factor that bears on the decision-making of the firm, which can be so all-encompassing as to thwart productive analysis. In this chapter, I consider how the firm can try to manage the postulated three categories of risk in the context of the various agency costs that shape their responses.

12.1. THE ROLE OF CORPORATE GOVERNANCE IN RISK MANAGEMENT

In those terms, the corporate governance issue is how to design the decision and incentive structure of the firm. But from whose point of view? To accomplish what?

1. Shareholders, in general, seek to maximize the equity value of the firm and their risk-adjusted returns. That means, in Clive Granger's terminology, that their concerns are not limited to d-risk of loss but include u-risk of gain—in other words, total risk. That, of course, is not the goal of central banks or financial regulators, or the taxpayers whom they hopefully represent. Nor is it the perspective of insurers, who seek to understand the extent and variance of expected losses so they can set premiums and their capital levels accordingly.

2. Managers have a primary interest in their compensation and job security, and in protecting their firm-specific human capital. Therefore, they are usually modeled as risk averse, unlike risk-neutral shareholders holding diversified portfolios, and hence may be markedly more sensitive to d-risk than to u-risk. For that reason, their compensation generally includes performance-based

incentives, so that they will accept more risk. The devil, as usual, is lurking in the details of the incentive scheme, as suggested by corporate collapses such as Enron or WorldCom, or more recently by the process of mortgage debt securitization and the behavior of firms like Citigroup and AIG. The objective is not to make managers indifferent to risks transferred to others, or turn them into risk seekers, or tempt them into fraudulent manipulation of accounting results to obtain short-term bonuses.

The divergence of interest between owners and managers can be affected by the choice of legal form and status for the firm. It is widest in the public corporation owned by outside and largely passive investors, where reliance on bounding agency costs and managerial opportunism is largely committed to outside directors and what is left of the hostile takeover market. It can be reduced in general or limited partnerships and limited liability companies (LLCs), where there can be greater identity between managers and investors, and managers' human and investment capital can be tied more closely to the survival of the firm. And it can be minimized in private firms, as, for example, when private equity funds transform previously public companies.

3. Central banks and government regulators place a heavy emphasis on d-risk. If they are dealing with a (government-insured) bank, their focus in the first instance is on the probability of incurring losses to the point of loss of confidence or insolvency, and then to the likelihood of contagion or knock-on losses to other banks and counterparties rising to the level of systemic risk and financial collapse. For that process, we do not have any generally accepted and well-defined model.

But this conference is not limited to risk management by banks. Systemic risk concerns can be seen as posed by the failure of any very large financial institution (witness LTCM or Lehman) or even any very large business firm. From a political point of view, there are strong incentives to invoke, however loosely, systemic risk as justification for bailouts ("guarantees") for any large enterprise, such as Chrysler (or General Motors).

So for central bankers and financial regulators, the problem has a number of dimensions. First, what is the size threshold of the firms and losses on which their attention should be concentrated? That threshold could be defined politically, as no doubt it often is, or economically, as by the size of an insurance fund or its replenishment capacity, or by the triggering of a financial collapse and its effects on the real economy. Second, what is an acceptable level of probability that the threshold will not be reached? Do we seek a confidence interval of nonfailure out to 95, 99, 99.9%, or what? In the operation of private firms, there are very significant costs to trying to cover the extreme tail. Third, how do they impose their views on these matters on the decision-making of the firm? The mere enactment of laws or regulations does not necessarily produce compliance or achieve their objective.

12.2. THE ROLE OF MANAGEMENT IN COPING WITH RISK

My assumption is that management in the typical firm will have considerable discretion in charting a course among these three points of view. And under all three, it will generally make sense for management to try to better understand the risks confronting its line of business. But that does not provide an answer to the questions of how much expenditure to devote to what aspect and how to organize the decision-making structure of the firm. In looking at risks in terms of the three broad categories of this book, we necessarily abstract from the specific assets and lines of business of actual firms.

12.2.1. KNOWN RISKS (K)

If the density function of a certain type of risk is reasonably well known, what problems remain? Shareholder, and societal, interests are advanced by risk-neutral decision making, on the basis of estimated net cash flows, discounted to present value at an appropriate rate. That raises several issues:

1. Devising the right incentives to lead risk-averse managers to make risk-neutral decisions is far from a simple undertaking in compensation design. Beyond the familiar concern over "excessive" compensation awarded by a chief executive officer (CEO)-dominated board, the *form* of the compensation may easily induce risk-preferring behavior and short-term maximization or even accounting manipulation. Immediate large bonuses, or stock options that vest early and may be quickly cashed out, do not align managers' interests with those of shareholders. More subtly, managers may make riskier choices toward a reporting period end in hopes of overcoming earlier poor performance for which they are responsible, or choose among acceptable accounting treatments that which smoothes earnings to create a perception of lower volatility.

2. Because of the difficulty of achieving precise alignment through incentive compensation, a "corporate culture" of the independence of risk analysts can be an important secondary safeguard. If risk analysis is conducted at the division or business unit level in a firm, there can be explicit or implicit pressure to reflect the desires of managers promoting a particular project or investment. Further, from the point of view of the firm, the relevant risk is not that of the individual investment but its marginal impact on the aggregate risk of the firm

as a whole—a portfolio, rather than a stand-alone, perspective. Both considerations suggest that risk management may be most effective if carried out as a staff function under a chief risk officer at the top level of an M-form firm, reporting to the CEO and also to the board.

There has been a discernible trend toward consideration and adoption of comprehensive enterprise risk management plans over the last decade. No doubt it has been driven in some part by concerns over possible legal liability. The Delaware Chancery Court decision in *Caremark* (1996) discussed at length the directors' fiduciary obligation to attempt in good faith to assure that a company's information and reporting system is in concept and design adequate to assure the board that appropriate information will come to its attention in a timely manner. Then the Sarbanes-Oxley Act of 2002 placed additional emphasis on the adequacy of a company's internal controls and the importance of the role of the audit committee, though its focus was on financial statement fraud, which is only one element of risk management.

But there are also positive incentives to develop an enterprise risk management plan, because there are potential competitive advantages if it is done well. Better handling of risk not only improves the prospects for survival of the firm in the face of negative events (d-risk), but also enhances its debt capacity and ability to take advantage of investment opportunities that may materialize (u-risk) even in bad times.

An enterprise risk management plan would systematically try to identify and quantify an array of different material risks in terms of their timing, probability, and severity, to develop mitigation and hedging strategies, and to set capital allocations to correspond to some acceptable probability of nonfailure (given the firm's financial distress costs). Audit committees of New York Stock Exchange (NYSE)-listed companies are now required by its rules "to discuss policies with respect to risk assessment and risk management." Involvement of the board in risk management requires top executives to articulate and defend their estimates and strategy to a group including outside directors who were not involved in their creation. That function could be performed most effectively if the directors included a few who were financially sophisticated, or had at least a passing acquaintance with such esoterica as extreme value theory or Bayesian probability analysis.

12.2.2. Unknown Risks (u)

If the density function is from management's viewpoint not well defined or well understood, the firm confronts several possible courses. It can undertake to transfer the risk to counterparties who are more expert on that type of risk or better able to bear it in a more diversified portfolio. Or it can seek to better understand the risk itself. Both have costs, and can be seen as investment decisions.

1. Risk transfer, through derivatives of many forms, has been the major financial innovation of recent decades and created rapidly growing markets and new institutions. Firms can transfer general economic risks (such as movements in interest rates or foreign currency rates) and be left with idiosyncratic or firm-specific risk, focusing on the business activity that is their own expertise.

In the process, corporate governance also changes. The role of equity (and shareholders) as the all-purpose risk bearer is to some extent reduced, and counterparties (investment banks, hedge funds, prime brokers) become external monitors of the firm—a demanding function which they are only beginning to fully comprehend. In its most concentrated form, private equity funds and venture capitalists and hedge funds in leveraged buyouts (LBOs) become themselves the bulk of the equity holders in the firm, reversing the separation of ownership and control which Berle and Means deplored.

2. Another course for the firm is to increase expenditures on trying to achieve itself a better understanding of the risk by acquiring more information. Viewing *KuU* as a continuum, not a set of discrete classes, the challenge for management is to move the uncertainties confronting the firm from right to left, from *U* to *u* to *K*, insofar as feasible. How? Taking up external events first, the quest would be for more information—more data points in *K* to reduce variance, more occurrences in *u* to flesh out the form of a distribution. How is that information to be acquired? One can do research outside the firm, drawing on data from trade associations or government. But one can also attend to assembling and sharing information within the firm. In law, firms are sometimes held to "know" what their various agents and employees know, which can come on occasion as an unpleasant surprise to top management. The quest for "first-order knowledge" is dependent on systems designed for that purpose. In the realm of *u*, management does have considerable knowledge of the risks; they have been identified, so management can set about instituting acquisition and reporting mechanisms for the additional data it needs to collect.

There are also internal sources of risk in any firm. Some arise out of instances of employee behavior—for example, theft, kickbacks, bribes, concealing trading losses, harassment, environmental infractions—of which top management is unaware. These categories seem to me to fall more in *K* than *u*, and are largely insurable (if with caps). They are in the domain of internal controls to detect and prevent, which received a lot of attention in the Sarbanes-Oxley Act of 2002 (SOX) and its requirement (§302) of certification as to their effectiveness by the chief executive officer (CEO) and chief financial officer (CFO) of the firm, with attestation (§404) of that assessment by the firm's auditors. Control systems are investments, and §404 was widely criticized as requiring extensive (and expensive) detail and procedures not particularly related to the material accuracy of the firm's financial statements or overall risk exposure. In response, the Securities and Exchange Commission (SEC) and Public Company Accounting Oversight Board (PCAOB) have recently adopted new standards that would give auditors more discretion to focus on controls in areas of greater risk and financial statement relevance, but the scope of internal controls and their audit would still be a subject of regulatory mandate rather than an investment decision left to the top management which bears the potential liability (§906).

No doubt, part of the reason for a mandate is that risks can also come from the behavior of top management itself, as in the wave of public firm collapses from accounting fraud, where internal controls may be in place but rendered inoperative, or accounting discretion is stretched to show profits and meet or beat analyst forecasts. SOX tried to address that possibility by enhancing the flow of information to the audit committee (which must be composed of independent directors) from not only the outside auditors (§204) but also internal whistleblowers (§§806, 1107) and attorneys (§307). It has often been argued that the level of independent directors plays a significant role in effective corporate governance and monitoring management, and some studies do show a corresponding reduction in earnings management and accounting fraud. But it may be more effective to make the gains reaped by top executives under circumstances of misconduct subject to forfeiture or recapture (§304). The Office of Federal Housing Enterprise Oversight (OFHEO) made an effort to claw back some $115 million in bonuses from three executives of Fannie Mae fired for earnings manipulation in connection with a $6 billion restatement, but in the end settled for their making $2 million in charitable donations.

12.2.3. BANK FAILURE

Returning to the area of bank failure and systemic risk, part of the problem is that the systemic consequences and costs of failure may appear to be an externality from the standpoint of the initial bank in a knock-on chain. But systemic risk is u, not U, for the other banks in the potential chain; it is foreseeable and recognized, though the probability may be highly uncertain and thought to be low. Counterparties have reasons to monitor the risk profile and solvency of the banks and institutions with whom they deal, a point driven home forcefully by LTCM and the subprime mortgage debacle. But those reasons are somewhat reduced by the favored position given counterparties in certain derivatives contracts to engage in closeout netting if an obligor goes into receivership. That has advantages in terms of maintaining "orderly" financial markets, and disadvantages in terms of the lessened incentives for monitoring and self-protection among counterparties. And when an obligor is bailed out by a government fearful of the consequences of its failure, those reasons are rendered irrelevant.

Putting aside contagion cascades, there is the difference in perspective already noted between the concern of a bank's management and shareholders with return as much as risk and the concern of bank regulators with failure above all else. Bank management has incentives to assess and manage risk, but also to balance it off against return, which is less important for bank regulators. The regulators have an arsenal of tools to try to impose their views, many of them intended to affect management decision-making long before reaching the point of insolvency.

The Basel Committee has been working for most of the last two decades on capital requirements based on ever more refined models of banking risk. The Basel I requirements have been in full effect since 1992; the more elaborate Basel II proposals permit certain banks to rely on their own internal ratings, in recognition of the fact that the operations of large international banks are too complex and fluid for supervisors to master or control with confidence. The covariances of the loans and positions constituting a bank's portfolio would be very difficult to measure or estimate, particularly in the case of a large complex institution. This seems to be leading to more emphasis on fair value accounting (which can bring with it greater exposure to management manipulation) and disclosure of disaggregated information (as in the SEC's extensible business reporting language [XBRL] proposals), to enable the market (Basel's Pillar 3) to play a more salient part in bank oversight.

Perhaps more important than the levels generated by the different models and formulae is the concept of "prompt corrective action," calling for increasingly severe supervisory intervention in management as a bank's capital descends toward minimum required levels. Provided that the supervisors are getting reasonably accurate measures of the bank's economic capital, decision-making authority is shifted away from management and toward the supervisors' risk preferences as capital declines. At this point, it is not easy to know just how effective this prompt corrective action approach, adopted in the United States in 1991, will be when subjected to stresses as in the current financial crisis.

12.2.4. THE UNKNOWABLE (U)

By definition, little can be done to learn about or manage U. The timing and distribution function, or even the existence of the risk in the polar case, is a mystery. How then, even ignoring any externalities that may be involved, should a firm cope with such possible random shocks? Primarily, by limiting its leverage and having enough capital and liquidity to absorb unknowable losses if they should occur (or take advantage of unknowable investment opportunities if one is so fortunate). How much of a liquid capital margin is sufficient or appropriate for this purpose? Sufficient is, again, by definition, unknowable. Appropriate is a matter of your perspective, as discussed in section 12.2. From the managers' point of view, it depends on their "risk-sensitivity" function— how safe they want to be—and that is affected by the incentive structure under which they are operating. Shareholders, as noted, presumably wish a risk-neutral assessment to be reflected in the market value of the equity. If the safety margin is perceived as being too large, or "excess capital," then that will hurt the market value of the stock and may thus induce a takeover, but that ought not to be the case if the market assesses the firm's safety margin as appropriate.

That returns us to the prior subject of management incentives. The most promising approach may be to make sure that management has a large stake in the long-run survival and value of the firm, beyond just their jobs—that is to say, a substantial investment that cannot be readily withdrawn (directly or indirectly). There are various ways to try to achieve this: compensation plans that involve restricted stock, stock option plans that do not permit sale (or hedging) until a significant period after exercise, bonus plans that require banking and adjustment for subsequent years' performance.

How would such an incentive scheme operate? By heightening sensitivity to the possible existence of U, several consequences might follow. Management might formally create a structure for periodically considering what U risks could impend. And management could create a capital margin that went well beyond the goals of covering expected losses, the appropriateness of which would ultimately be judged by the market.

13. Domestic Banking Problems

Charles A. E. Goodhart

Problems in the banking sector are primarily caused by losses. A profitable bank is, by and large, one without problems. So in table 13.1 there is a matrix of the conditions under which losses are incurred and the resulting nature of the loss, and then a (brief) record of the reaction by three segments of private sector agents: accountants, the individual bank, and the capital market. The final row indicates how the public sector might respond.

The first point to make is that the three-way split (i.e., *KuU*) proposed by the organizers of this book is insufficient. The distribution has to be four-way, as shown in table 13.1. Whether one regards mean expected (but not yet realized) losses (EL) as a subset of *K*, or a part of *u*, is perhaps a matter of taste. What is crucial is to separate EL from unexpected losses (UL), and UL covers both losses that are unknown, but whose probability distribution is believed to be known, or at least is capable of estimation (i.e., *u*), and those for which no prior (subjective) probability distribution can be reasonably established (i.e., *U*). If we call the element of UL for which the probability distribution is known *K*, then we could describe the framework as *REKU*, where losses are, in turn, realized, expected, subject to a known probability distribution, and unknowable.

Many of the elements in the cells of the matrix of table 13.1 are so well known and self-evident as to need little, or no, discussion. I have, however, marked with (?) those elements, or cells, where some additional discussion may be useful.

TABLE 13.1
Nature of Banking Losses

	R	E	K	U
Condition	(1) Past Actual	(2) Mean expected	(3) Known probability distribution	(4) Unknowable
Nature of loss	Realized	Expected	Unexpected	Unexpected
Response by				
Accountants	Historic cost	Mark to market Mark to model (?)	Forward-looking Risk assessment statement (?)	None
Bank	Provisioning	Interest margin Dynamic preprovisioning collateral	VaRs, credit risk models, liquidity, diversification, internal risk control, insurance, hedging	Backup Internal risk control Excess capacity Liquidity, flexibility, professional advice, prayer
Market	Corporate governance	Corporate governance	Corporate governance (?)	None (?)
Authorities	Accountancy regulations Bankruptcy laws Tax laws Leverage ratios (FDICIA) Penalties for failures (?)	Accountancy (IAS 39, FASB 133) Tax (?) Entry regulations Glass-Steagall Interest rate limits Basel I	Basel II IMF FSAP Stress Tests Liquidity ratios Systemic models (?) LOLR Remuneration controls (?)	Liquidity injections LOLR Nationalization

Let us, however, begin (briefly) with column 1, under **R**. Accountants have traditionally preferred to deal with hard facts, unquestionable data on actual past losses, against which banks need to provide by specific provisions and write-offs. The market responds to data on (past) losses by adjusting prices. When equity prices fall, it becomes easier to arrange for a transfer of ownership by takeover, merger, or buyout. If the losses are so large that the bank becomes insolvent, the relevant bankruptcy codes then apply. So, the nature of the response to large realised losses in the banking system depends on the relevant bankruptcy laws. These differ from country to country,[1] and as between banks and other nonbank corporations. A good guide is Bliss and Kaufman (2006). Such international differences in bankruptcy codes can cause problems in managing cross-border financial crises, but this is a specialized subject, which I have written about elsewhere; see Krimminger (2004) and Goodhart (2005).

Like accountants, tax inspectors, and the Inland Revenue generally, prefer to relate tax payments to actual hard data on past, known profits and losses. They fear that relating tax to expected cash flows will enable tax payers to manipulate such figures to reduce net payments. Economists have argued that, by the time losses have crystallized, the data are of historical interest only, and do not represent a "true and fair" account of the current position of the company. But the concern of the accountant to be able to justify every figure (in a court of law) and the suspicion of the tax authorities that estimation will lead to manipulation militate against moving accounting onto a more up-to-date basis.

In so far as accounting, and provisioning, is on a historic cost basis, then it also follows that simple leverage ratios (relating capital to assets/liabilities), such as mandated by the Federal Deposit Insurance Corporation Improvement Act (FDICIA) will also be on a historic basis.

Perhaps the most interesting element in this column relates to the final entry, on the question of the penalties for failure, and the (legal) costs of bankruptcy. The authorities can influence the proclivity of the private sector to take risk by varying the penalty for failure. For example, if the penalty for a bank default was to be the execution of anyone who had been a director or officer during the three previous years, there would be fewer such defaults. But that would lead

---

[1] Most countries treat an insolvent firm (bank) operating in multiple jurisdictions as a *single entity*, whereby one court takes the lead in guiding the resolution, but in which all creditors of a particular class are treated equally, irrespective of geographical location (the universal approach), but others, such as Australia and the United States in the case of banks, have the courts in their own jurisdiction conduct separate proceedings using the assets under its control of the benefit of local creditors (the territorial or specific entity approach). For an account of how such national depositor preference came into existence, somewhat accidentally, in the United States in 1993, see Kaufman (1997).

to banks taking virtually no risks, and society does not want that. How do we decide what is the optimal degree of riskiness for banks to take? Are banks in our respective countries too risk-loving, or insufficiently so? How might we try to assess what the optimal degree of risk-taking might be? At least in this case there is an instrument, in the shape of (legal) penalties on failure, bankruptcy laws, directors' liabilities (e.g., for the design of internal risk control procedures, as in New Zealand), and so on.

A frequent assertion is that a toughening of penalties on those held responsible for failure or negligence (directors, auditors, etc.) will lead to an offsetting decrease in the number/quality of those applying for such a position. There must surely be such a tendency, and in the limit if such penalties should become draconian, no sensible person would apply for such a role. Whereas there have been many studies of the effect of legal penalties on the number of transgressions (murder, bankruptcy, etc.), I am not aware of empirical studies of the effects of legal penalties on the number/quality of applicants for positions subject to such potential legal penalty. This is probably because it is difficult to get the necessary data.

Decisions, for example, on risk-taking, depend not only on the penalties for failure, but also on the rewards for success. Much of the blame for recent corporate governance failures has been attributed to the desire of executives to manipulate earnings so as to drive market prices to levels that would generate higher option prices. Decision makers inside banks (and other companies) are just as, or more, likely to be swayed by the implications of their actions for their own returns, as they are by the imposition of capital adequacy regulations (CARs). Yet the authorities intervene in great detail over banking CARs, and barely at all over the form, and consequent incentive effects, of remuneration packages. Yet the effect on key decisions and behavior of executive remuneration packages is probably much greater than that of CARs. What exactly then is the rationale for interference in CARs but not in remuneration? For example, suppose there were a requirement that the CEO of any bank (firm) must have his pension invested as to 90% in the stock of his own firm (and not be allowed to sell puts, etc.) up to (n) years after leaving the bank. Would such a requirement do as much to safeguard banks as the whole of Basel II? But, harking back to a previous question, might that make banks too risk averse?

Turning next to column 2, *R*, a second key point is that there is currently considerable tension between placing more emphasis on past actual realized as compared with mean expected losses in accountancy and tax treatment, and probably other fields as well. Accountants and revenue officials have, at least in the past, preferred to base accounts and taxes on known, verifiable past data, feeling that markets are often unreliable and models can be manipulated. In contrast, economists, and others, have argued that past data are accurate, but out-of-date and so incapable of giving a "true and fair" view of present conditions.

A problem is that the present state of play in the system (IAS 39, FASB 133) is an uncomfortable mix of the two (i.e., historic cost and expected values), so much so that hedge accounting may sometimes lead to "artificial" volatility. The whole question of what involves proper hedging (e.g., Fannie Mae) has become, as a result, complex and worrisome. Similarly, there is a problem with the tax authorities, at least in Europe. The IR (Inland Revenue) is quite reluctant to accept schemes such as the countercyclical Spanish dynamic preprovisioning, against expected but unrealized losses, as an acceptable offset against profits. Similarly whether the IR will accept valuations based on "mark-to-model" estimates of the values of assets remains uncertain, since they may regard these as a subjective way of deferring taxes. There is a continuing problem of ensuring joined-up regulation, whereby the accountants, the tax authorities, private sector firms, and the government all move together at the same pace (in the process of putting more weight on expected losses relative to past realized losses).

The proper protection against EL should be an interest rate margin with a sufficient risk premium built into it. When the interest margin is insufficient, risk is not being correctly priced. No amount of initial capital can make up for incorrect pricing. Not only will the capital become eroded, but it is being used inefficiently, so corporate governance should bring about a change in ownership. Risk premia may be insufficient because of "excess" competition, or misjudgment, or myopia owing to a run of years of good fortune and success, as appeared to be the case at the outset of 2007. Much of the blame for the banking crisis in the United States in the 1930s was placed at the time on "excess" competition, and many of the controls then introduced, for example, controls on interest rates, such as Reg Q and Glass-Steagall were intended to restrain such competition. Whereas concern about "excess" competition has been soft-pedaled in recent decades, one of the facets of the opposition to public-sector banks is that their subsidization and lower capital ratios tend to drive interest margins below a level that can support a healthy private banking sector; examples are the Landesbanken in Germany and the Post Office in Japan.

One of the main, if not the main, purposes of Basel I was to limit international competition from the publicly owned French banks and from the (then) low-margin Japanese banks. Thus, I regard the main thrust of Basel I as having been to control the banks' handling of EL. The treatment of risk in Basel I was anyhow so primitive that it can hardly be counted as an appropriate response to UL.

Absent subsidized competition from public sector banks (and mispriced deposit insurance), would an uncontrolled private sector system reach a socially optimum equilibrium where interest margins would incorporate an appropriate risk margin (at all times); would a "free banking" system be desirable? My own view is that a combination of externalities (potential contagious systemic collapses) and myopia (exaggerated swings in confidence) make that unlikely, but this remains a contentious issue. If I am right, the authorities have a hard task in trying to prevent both insufficient competition and "excessive" competition; how does one discern the optimal extent of competition for a banking system? Is the extent of such competition in (parts of) the United States, or the United Kingdom, or Japan, or France, now optimal? If not, how might one move the system toward the optimum (and do we know enough to try such social engineering anyhow?)

Next, turning to column 3, how far should the audit of any (banking) firm opine upon the perceived forward-looking riskiness of a firm? What should the regular audit statements report, if anything, about the main risks facing a company? If such a statement were to be incorrect, would there be any legal liability, and under what circumstances? If no legal liability, what would be the point? How far should banks be required to report, if at all, on their (historical) value-at-risk (VaR) values, the outputs of their credit risk models, stress tests, hedges and other forms of insurance, etc., etc.?

In the United Kingdom a ruling had been made that all major companies should publish an operating and financial review (OFR) as part of their annual report, which should outline the main risks attending each firm's future development. Just before this was due to come into effect, in November 2005, the Chancellor of the Exchequer canceled this requirement, as part of an exercise to limit the extent of externally required reporting burdens on private sector firms. There was a somewhat muted round of criticism of this step, on the grounds that it would reduce a valuable source of information. An example can be found in the following letter to the *Financial Times*, (Monday, December 19, 2005) by Mr. M. Goyder; the *F.T.* was the only newspaper to become involved in discussing the pros and cons of OFRs.

"Sir, So the scrapping of the statutory operating and financial review eight months after its introduction (and after seven years of preparation) is a "minor recalibration."

Over the next five years forward-looking statements will become universal round the world. We need rigour in measuring and reporting on the values and behaviours that are essential to the creation of enduring shareholder value. Investors need to have their finger on the pulse of relationships with customers, employees and suppliers. The OFR standard offers a clear, understandable framework for moving into this new generation of reporting.

The irony of the "recalibration" is that companies are left with most of the work to comply with a European Union directive, but with added uncertainty and fewer of the benefits that come from focusing on the future.

The market can price expected, and past actual, returns well, when the information becomes available, and changes in market prices can lead to the usual mechanisms of corporate governance, such as takeovers of underperforming companies. There does remain some question whether markets do price uncertainty, in the guise of the probability distributions of future returns, well in all circumstances, for example, the tech bubble and the recent housing bubble and bust. Moreover, it is difficult to see how it is conceivably possible to price the unknowable. No doubt this is discussed elsewhere in this book.

The distinction between K, known probability distribution, and U, unknowable, is also fuzzy, particularly in the case of low-probability, but high-impact, events. The frequency of hurricanes, and the ease of observing them, is sufficiently high to put them in the K category, but how about terrorist attacks, meteors hitting the earth, or fraud? The latter is particularly important for banks. Many banking problems (Barings, BCCI) have been instigated by fraud. How reliable are the data? Do banks have an incentive to hush up frauds that are small enough to survive without external notice?

Basel II has included a category, operational risk, against which capital is to be held. It is far from clear why holding capital is an appropriate safeguard against a low-probability, high-risk event (e.g., should Japanese banks hold more capital than, say, German banks because Tokyo has a higher earthquake risk than Frankfurt?). Holding more capital will not reduce the incidence of fraud; rather the reverse, since the need to earn a decent return on capital may lead to attempts to cut corners. Obviously, the more capital, the larger the loss (from fraud, or anything else) that can be absorbed, but that is an argument for higher capital ratios overall, not for relating them to operational risk. For a further critique of the Basel II imposition of operational capital requirements, see Goodhart (2001) and Instefjord et al. (1998).

My final main query relates to the need to develop models for assessing the systemic risk of the banking sector in any country. Virtually all the models, and mechanisms, for identifying banking risk have been primarily designed for, and applied to, the *individual* bank. But the regulators should be concerned with the banking *system* as a whole, not the individual bank within that.

Trying to develop a (systemic) model(s) that might enable regulators to make such an assessment has been one of my areas of work in the last couple of years. My colleagues and I have completed a number of papers on this subject in recent years (e.g., Goodhart et al. 2004a, b, 2005b, 2006; Goodhart and Zic-chino 2005), and more are in prospect, as the work program continues.

In practice, however, bank regulators, as represented, for example, by the Basel Committee of Banking Supervisors (BCBS), have sought to discover how the most sophisticated banks *individually* seek to assess and to control risk for their own purposes, and then introduce regulation to encourage (all) other banks to follow suit. I interpret the claim of the BCBS that Basel II seeks to bring regulatory capital more closely into line with bank economic capital in this manner. When economic conditions worsen, nonperforming loans rise, ratings decline, and asset prices fall; the economic situation has worsened. Under such conditions, banks will become more cautious, and perceived (economic) capital ratios will rise. Under Basel II regulatory capital will rise too. Regulation is inherently procyclical. The more such regulation is made risk sensitive, the more procyclical it will become.

Empirical work has shown that the best forward-looking indicator of future financial crises is a prior combination of asset price bubble and surge in bank lending (see the work of Borio et al. (BIS) 1994; Borio and Lowe 2002; Goodhart et al. 2004c, 2005a). Such bubbles/lending surges occur when economic conditions appear good, and both economic and regulatory capital requirements do not constrain. There was a hope that the greater awareness of the need for risk management brought about by the introduction of Basel II would, of itself, restrain banks from overexpansion in (asset price) booms, but there has been no evidence of this, rather the reverse. As revealed by the apparent decline in CARs evidenced in the QIS IV carried out in the United States, formal capital requirements will decline under Basel II more during booms than heretofore under Basel I.

It is possible that greater risk awareness among individual banks will outweigh the greater procyclicality that enhanced risk sensitivity in capital regulation will bring to the system as a whole. But it would be optimistic to rely on that. The greater likelihood would seem to be that our present regulatory proposals may amplify cyclical effects.

Does it matter if the formal effect of regulation is to lessen restraint in booms and to tighten during downturns? This is what individual banks are always likely to do on their own. Now this tendency is to be reinforced by official regulation.

A problem is that the attempts of each individual bank to cut back during downturns and to maintain/gain share during good times (dancing while the music plays) has external effects on the system as a whole, and hence on other banks. Cutbacks in loan extension and sales/realizations of assets may serve to strengthen the individual bank in the event of a depression, but at the expense of worsening economic conditions more broadly, and hence weaken other banks.

It is difficult to assess such interactive effects through the kind of stress and scenario tests currently undertaken. These inquire of each individual bank how they might fare under certain simulated adverse conditions. Almost by definition such exercises cannot easily, if at all, take account of interactive, cumulative effects. As a result such stress tests may give an overoptimistic indication of the strength of the system as a whole. It is one of the purposes of the previously noted modeling work, on which I have been engaged, to try to estimate such potential interactive effects. There is a long way to go yet.

This general line of thought suggests that the desideratum is to design state-varying regulations that tighten during bubbles/booms, and revert to some appropriate minimum during recessions, when banks will anyhow become cautious on their own account. While regulators tend to applaud tightening regulatory controls yet further during booms, they get nervous at any suggestion of relaxation during depressions! Moreover, concern about maintaining a level playing field, a major objective of the BCBS, and about possible disintermediation, act as disincentives to the discretionary adoption in individual countries of state-varying regulations. Nevertheless, there have been some moves in this direction. The combination of a property/housing price asset boom with a bank lending surge has been a common forerunner of systemic financial crises. State-varying loan to value ratios have been adopted in Hong Kong, South Korea, and, most recently (December 2005), Estonia. The Spanish preprovisioning exercise has already been mentioned. In my view this is the way to go.

To conclude, it is not easy to try to estimate the optimal degree of either competition or of risk-taking in banking (or elsewhere), or indeed where we stand now relative to that elusive optimum. In any case it is difficult to devise instruments that could move us toward the optimum. It is, therefore, not so surprising that public policy regulation has tended to be reactive, waiting until some disaster strikes and then trying to shut the stable door after the horse has bolted.

REFERENCES

Bliss, R. R., and G. G. Kaufman (2006). US Corporate and Bank Insolvency Regimes: A Comparison and Evaluation. Work in progress, drafted October 23; a shorter version has appeared in Federal Reserve Bank of Chicago Economic Perspectives, 44 (2006).
Borio, C., N. Kennedy, and S. Prowse (1994). Exploring aggregate asset price fluctuations across countries: Measurement, determinants and monetary policy implications, BIS Economic Paper 40.
Borio, C., and P. Lowe (2002). Asset prices, financial and monetary stability: Exploring the nexus. BIS Working Paper 114.

Goodhart, C.A.E. (2001). Operational Risk, Financial Markets Group Special Paper, no. 131, London School of Economics (September).

Goodhart, C.A.E. (2005). Multiple Regulations and Resolutions. In *Systemic Financial* · *Crises: Resolving Large Bank Insolvencies* (Federal Reserve Bank of Chicago).

Goodhard, C.A.E., and L. Zicchino (2005). A model to analyse financial fragility. *Bank of England financial Stability Review*, 106–115 (June).

Goodhart, C.A.E., P. Sunirand, and D. P. Tsomocos (2004a). A model to analyse financial fragility: applications. *Journal of Financial Stability* 1, 1–30.

Goodhart, C.A.E., P. Sunirand, and D. P. Tsomocos (2004b). A time series analysis of financial fragility in the UK banking system. Oxford Financial Research Centre Working Paper No. 2004-FE-18.

Goodhart, C., B. Hofmann, and M. Segoviano (2004c). Bank regulation and macroeconomic fluctuations. *Oxford Review of Economic Policy* 20, 591–615.

Goodhart, C., B. Hofmann, and M. Segoviano, (2005a). Default, credit growth and asset prices. Paper presented at IMF Conference on Financial Stability, September 6/7, 2005, Washington, DC.

Goodhart, C.A.E., P. Sunirand, and D.P. Tsomocos (2005b). A risk assessment model for banks. *Annals of Finance* 1, 197–224.

Goodhart, C.A.E., P. Sunirand, and D.P. Tsomocos (2006). A model to analyse financial fragility. *Economic Theory* 27, 107–42.

Instefjord, N., P. Jackson, and W. Perraudin (1998). Securities fraud. *Economic Policy* 27, 587–623.

Kaufman, G.G. (1997). The New Depositor Preference Act: time inconsistency in action. *Managerial Finance* 23(11), 56–63.

Krimminger, M.H. (2004). Deposit insurance and bank insolvency in a changing world: Synergies and challenges. International Monetary Fund Conference, Washington, DC, May 28.

14. Crisis Management

The Known, the Unknown, and the Unknowable

Donald L. Kohn

In pursuing its policy objectives, a central bank must make decisions in the face of uncertainty related to incomplete knowledge about the evolving condition of the economy and the financial system as well as about the potential effects of its actions. This uncertainty implies that the central bank must incorporate into its decisions the risks and consequences of several alternative outcomes. That is, it needs to assess not only the most likely outcome for a particular course of action but also the probability of the unusual—the tail event. And it needs to weigh the welfare costs of the possible occurrence of those tail events.

This risk management approach has been articulated by Chairman Greenspan for monetary policy, and it is equally applicable to a central bank's decisions regarding crisis management, the topic I focus on in this chapter.[1] Crises are themselves tail events, and the policy response to them is focused on the possibility and cost should the outcome be especially adverse.

Knowledge—reliable information—is essential to managing risks. In a financial crisis, however, information inevitably will be highly imperfect. The very nature of a crisis means that the ratio of the unknown and unknowable will be especially large relative to the known, and this, in turn, can influence how policymakers judge risks, costs, and benefits.

[1] Alan Greenspan (2004). Risk and uncertainty in monetary policy. *American Economic Review* 94 (May), 33–40.

Although the subject of this chapter is crisis management, I want to emphasize at the outset that the far-preferable approach to financial stability is to reduce the odds on such crises developing at all. To this end, central banks seek to foster macroeconomic stability, encourage sound risk-taking practices by financial market participants, enhance market discipline, and promote sound and efficient payment and settlement systems. In this arena, an ounce of prevention is worth many pounds of cure. Before going further, I should say that the views I express here are my own and not necessarily those of other members of the Board of Governors or its staff.[2]

14.1. COSTS, BENEFITS, AND POLICY OPTIONS

But even prevention has costs that must be weighed along with its benefits. No financial system that is efficient and flexible is likely to be completely immune from episodes of financial instability from time to time, and policymakers will be forced to make judgments about the costs and benefits of alternative responses with very incomplete information.

In a financial crisis, the potential cost of inaction or inadequate action is possible disruption to the real economy, which would damp activity and put undesirable downward pressure on prices. Such disruptions can come about because crises heighten uncertainty about the financial status of counterparties and about the eventual prices of assets. In an especially uncertain environment, lenders may become so cautious that credit supplies are cut back more than would be justified by an objective assessment of borrowers' prospects; concerns about counterparty risk can impair the smooth functioning of payment and settlement systems, interfering with a wide variety of markets; asset prices can be driven well away from equilibrium values; and confidence can be undermined. These types of tail events could depress economic activity for a time and, if prolonged, could also adversely affect efficiency and productivity by impairing the ability of financial markets to channel savings into the most productive investments.

Although policy action may be able to reduce the odds of adverse effects or alleviate their impact, some policy responses to a crisis can themselves have important costs that need to be balanced against their possible benefits. In short, intervening in the market process can create moral hazard and weaken market discipline. If private parties come to believe in the possibility of policy actions that will relieve them of some of the costs of poor decisions or even just bad

---

[2] Edward C. Ettin, Myron L. Kwast, and Patrick M. Parkinson, of the Board's staff, provided valuable ideas and comments.

luck, their incentives to appropriately weigh risks in the future will be reduced and discipline of managers watered down. Weaker market discipline distorts resource allocation and can sow the seeds of a future crisis.

The possible real costs of policy actions imply that they should be taken only after the determination that, in their absence, the risk is too high that the crisis will disrupt the real economy. Once that judgment is reached, the central bank and other authorities have a variety of instruments to use, and the degree of potential moral hazard created will depend on the instrument chosen.

Approaches that work through the entire market rather than through individual firms run a lower probability of distorting risk-taking. Thus, a first resort to staving off adverse economic effects is to use open market operations to make sure aggregate liquidity is adequate. Adequate liquidity has two aspects: First, we must meet any extra demands for liquidity that might arise from a flight to safety; if they are not satisfied, these extra demands will tighten financial markets at exactly the wrong moment. This was an important consideration after the stock market crash of 1987, when demand for liquid deposits raised reserve demand; and again after 9/11, when the destruction of buildings and communication lines impeded the flow of credit and liquidity.

Second, we must determine whether the stance of monetary policy has to be adjusted to counteract the effects on the economy of tighter credit supplies and other consequences of financial instability. Policy adjustments also can help head off some of those effects in that, by showing that the central bank recognizes the potential seriousness of the situation, they bolster confidence. As a consequence, meetings of the Federal Open Market Committee (FOMC)—often in conference calls if the situation is developing rapidly—have been an element in almost every crisis response. Those meetings allow us to gather and share information about the extent of financial instability and its effects on markets and the economy as we also discuss the appropriate policy response.

Some critics have argued that the FOMC's policy adjustments in response to financial instability encourage undue risk-taking in the financial markets and the economy. However, to the extent that the conduct of policy successfully cushions the negative macroeconomic effects of financial instability, it genuinely lowers risk and that fact should be reflected in the behavior of private agents. Other instruments to deal with instability—discount window lending, moral suasion, actions to keep open or to slowly wind down ailing financial institutions—are much more likely than monetary policy adjustments to have undesirable and distortionary effects on private behavior. By making credit available to individual firms on terms more favorable than would be available in the market, or by affording a measure of protection to existing creditors, these other instruments carry substantial potential for moral hazard. Hence, they are and should be used only after a finding that more generalized instruments, like open market operations, are likely to be inadequate to stave off significant economic disruption.

If it is determined that actions to support the credit of specific firms are necessary, such actions should be designed to minimize moral hazard. Sometimes moral suasion will be sufficient—simply by calling attention to the potential consequences of withholding payments or credit, private parties may be persuaded that avoiding such an outcome is in their self-interest. But central banks must be careful that moral suasion is not perceived as coercion or an implied promise of official indemnification for private losses. If the central bank concludes that it must lend to individual depository institutions to avoid significant economic disruption, in most situations any such loans should be on terms sufficiently onerous to discourage reliance on public-sector credit.

The Federal Reserve tries to find the approach that reduces the odds on economy-wide spillover effects while interfering as little as possible with the market and allowing people and institutions to suffer the consequences of decisions that turn out to be bad. Nearly every major bout of financial instability has called for some degree of monetary easing—most often only temporarily until the threat of the low-probability but high-cost economic disruption has passed. Other tools have been used occasionally, and an assessment of their costs and benefits has depended on the nature of the crisis.

Moral suasion was an element in dealing with the panicky private-sector actions associated with the sharp and apparently self-feeding market price breaks of 1987 and 1998. Lending through the discount window helped to promote an orderly unwinding of distressed institutions in the period of prolonged and widespread problems among important intermediaries in the late 1980s and early 1990s. And such lending was crucial in getting liquidity to the right places after the disruption of 9/11. In each case, the nature of the response has depended on the state of the economy and financial markets before the event. When the economy is strong and financial systems robust, a shock to the financial system is less likely to feed back on the economy.

14.2. INFORMATION FLOWS IN A CRISIS

Clearly, judgments in a crisis must balance a number of difficult considerations in rapidly changing circumstances in which up-to-date, accurate, information is scarce.

Our experience suggests some of the key questions that might arise when confronting a crisis: How large is the financial disruption—how many firms or market participants are involved and how large are they? What is the potential for direct and indirect contagion, both domestic and international? Who are the counterparties and what is their exposure? Who else has similar exposures and might be vulnerable to further changes in asset prices that could be triggered by a firm's failure and unwinding of positions? How long are the financial disruptions likely to last? Are substitute providers of financial services available, and how easily and quickly can they be employed? And, critically, what are the initial and expected states of the macroeconomic and financial environments under various scenarios?

Coming to grips with these questions requires a considerable amount of detailed, up-to-the-minute information—more than can be known ahead of time. Even in the best of circumstances, much of the information on variables relevant to decisions about whether or how to intervene will be unknown (especially if a crisis materializes quickly) or unknowable. Published balance sheets and income statements—or old examination reports—give only a starting place for analysis when asset prices and risk profiles are changing rapidly and in ways that had not been anticipated. In addition, crises invariably reveal previously unknown interdependencies among financial intermediaries and among intermediaries and the ultimate suppliers and demanders of funds.

Central banks and others that might be involved in crisis management must take steps to push back the frontiers of the "unknown" before a crisis hits and to develop procedures for obtaining the "knowable" quickly when needed. More information is not just "nice to have." Policymakers want to choose the path with the lowest moral hazard consequences. But they are in a difficult position in a crisis. The costs of not acting forcefully enough will be immediate and obvious—additional disruption to financial markets and the economy. The costs of acting too forcefully—of interfering unnecessarily in markets and creating moral hazard—manifest themselves only over a longer time and may never be traceable to a particular policy choice. The natural tendency to take more intrusive actions that minimize the risk of immediate disruptions is probably exacerbated by ignorance and uncertainty; the less you know, the easier it is to imagine bad outcomes and the more reliant you may be on people in the market whose self-interest inevitably colors the information they are giving you.

Each episode of financial instability is different and teaches us something new about what information is useful and who needs to call whom to share information. For example, clearing mechanisms for futures and options were an issue in the 1987 crash; capital impairment of depositories, its effect on lending, and the response of regulators took center stage in the late 1980s and early 1990s; the importance of market liquidity came to the fore in 1998 when even the prices of off-the-run Treasury securities took a beating; and physical infrastructure issues dominated developments after the terrorist attacks on 9/11.

Although a knowledge base is helpful, the answers to the questions I posed earlier will depend critically on a free flow of new information. In a world of financial institutions with a presence in many lines of business crossing national boundaries, obtaining such information and developing cogent analysis requires widespread cooperation among many agencies. The Federal Financial Institutions Examination Council—in which all U.S. depository institution regulators participate—is a forum for developing information and relationships within the regulatory community. The President's Working Group itself was a product of the 1987 stock market crash, which revealed a need for better communication and coordination among all financial regulators. In addition, we build bilateral relationships with foreign authorities through participation in various international groups, such as the Basel Committee on Banking Supervision, the Committee on Payment and Settlement Systems, the Financial Stability Forum, and so on. A number of the phone calls I made and received in the hours and days after 9/11 were with people in other central banks with whom I had established working relationships on monetary policy groups or in international preparations for Y2K. But although agency-to-agency communication is important, it is in a sense only a secondary source of information. The primary and best sources are the contacts we all develop with major financial participants as we carry out our daily operations and oversight responsibilities.

Whatever the origin of the crisis, the Federal Reserve has usually found itself near the center of the efforts to assess and manage the risks. To be sure, we have some authorities and powers that other agencies do not. But, in addition, we bring a unique perspective combining macro- and microeconomic elements that should help us assess the likelihood of disruptions and weigh the consequences of various forms of intervention. Because of our responsibility for price and economic stability, we have expertise on the entire financial system and its interaction with the economy. Central banks need to understand—to the limited extent anyone can—how markets work and how they are likely to respond to a particular stimulus. Our role in operating and overseeing payment systems gives us a window into a key possible avenue for contagion in a crisis. At the Federal Reserve, our supervisory responsibilities provide us with knowledge of the banking system and the expertise to interpret information we get from other agencies. We have people at the Board and Reserve Banks who are expert in macroeconomics, in banking, in payment and settlement systems, and in various financial markets, and all have market contacts; our colleagues at the Federal Reserve have proven to be our best source and filter of information in the midst of a crisis.

Despite our efforts, much will still be unknown and some things will be unknowable as we make decisions in a crisis. Financial instability is by definition a tail event, and it is the downside possibilities of that tail event that concern the authorities. Market participants are reacting under stress, on incomplete and often false information, in situations they have not faced before. Uncertainty—in the Knightian sense of unquantifiable risk—is endemic in such situations. Uncertainty drives people to protect themselves—to sell the asset whose price is already declining, to avoid the counterparty whose financial strength might conceivably be impaired, to load their portfolios with safe and liquid assets. Market mechanisms are tested in ways that cannot be modeled ahead of time.

Contagion is always a key underlying issue in trying to assess the potential for sustained disruption of the financial system and the economy. Contagion, in turn, is partly a question of psychology—how will people react under conditions of stress? So, too, is moral hazard—once the stressful situation passes, how will people adapt their behavior as a consequence of any intervention? Thus, much of the most desirable information is unknowable in any quantitative sense. The authorities must rely, therefore, on judgment, based on experience and on as much information as can be gathered under adverse circumstances.

14.3. THE CHANGING FINANCIAL SYSTEM AND THE KNOWN, THE UNKNOWN, AND THE UNKNOWABLE

The evolution of financial markets and institutions over recent years was thought for some time to have made the financial system more resilient and reduced the need for intervention. The lowering of legal and regulatory barriers across financial services and geography, the development of derivative markets, and the securitization of so much credit has enabled intermediaries to diversify and manage risk better, reduced the number of specialized lenders who would be vulnerable to sector- or area-specific shocks, and seemed to have left borrowers far less dependent on particular lenders and consequently the economy much less vulnerable to problems at individual or even classes of institutions.

We now know that was not the case; the financial system was more resilient to a range of shocks but more vulnerable to highly unusual events, like a widespread decline in house prices for the first time since the Great Depression. Finance had become increasingly dependent on securities markets—in part through the originate-and-distribute model of credit flows. This trend was reinforced by financial engineering, which had built new ways to distribute risk in securities markets. But the resulting instruments were complex and opaque. They were based on sophisticated modeling of the knowns in the behavior of asset prices and were more vulnerable to unknowns and unknowables. Users had become complacent after years of relative economic stability marked, for the most part, by infrequent and relatively mild recessions. Against what appeared to be a stable economic background, returns were bolstered by increasingly thin capital and higher leverage in the financial sector.

In this environment, adverse developments that began in the housing market spread quickly to both securities markets and banks as well as to other financial intermediaries. Those developments revealed weaknesses in both the origination of credits and their distribution. The process of reducing leverage and becoming safer resulted in a sharp widening of many spreads in financial markets and a tightening of credit conditions just as the economy weakened. Increasing risk aversion undermined market making and liquidity. And new and complicated interdependencies in markets made the financial system much more vulnerable to weaknesses at several types of institutions that previously had not been thought to be central to systemic stability. The risk management systems of many important market participants had not adapted to the growing complexity of modern financial firms or to the different characteristics of structured credit products, and the actual management of risk was highly dependent on being able to transact in liquid markets.

The crisis has also revealed serious inadequacies in the regulatory oversight of the financial system. Regulators too did not understand well enough the vulnerabilities of the evolving financial structure, and where they understood, they did not demand action that was sufficiently rapid and forceful to head off problems. Gaps appeared in oversight, especially of systemically important firms. New choke points appeared in the intermediation process. Crisis management was forced into highly difficult and unusual actions to stem the damage to the financial sector and the economy.

The task ahead is to build a regulatory system that better serves economic welfare by insisting on a more robust financial system. We must fill the gaps: Every systemically important intermediary should be subject to oversight; the more systemically important the intermediary is, the stronger the oversight and the greater the insistence on capital, liquidity, and risk management to match its role in the economy. And someone should be looking at the system as a whole, the interactions among markets and participants that might reveal a vulnerability that a focus on individual participants could miss. Finally, we must have a better way of dealing with a systemically important institution that finds itself in trouble and could threaten the financial system. If we are to avoid a repetition of the financial crisis that began at the end of 2007, the private sector and the regulators must find a better way for the financial system to deal with the unknowns and the unknowables that are the inevitable consequence of an innovative and adaptable market-based financial system and economy.

15. Investing in the Unknown and Unknowable

Richard J. Zeckhauser

David Ricardo made a fortune buying bonds from the British government four days in advance of the Battle of Waterloo.[1] He was not a military analyst, and even if he were, he had no basis to compute the odds of Napoleon's defeat or victory, or hard-to-identify ambiguous outcomes. Thus, he was investing in the unknown and the unknowable. Still, he knew that competition was thin, that the seller was eager, and that his windfall pounds should Napoleon lose would be worth much more than the pounds he'd lose should Napoleon win. Ricardo knew a good bet when he saw it.

This essay discusses how to identify good investments when the level of uncertainty is well beyond that considered in traditional models of finance. Many of the investments considered here are one-time only, implying that past data will be a poor guide. In addition, the essay will highlight investments, such as real estate development, that require complementary skills. Most readers will not have such skills, but many will know others who do. When possible, it is often wise to make investments alongside them.

Though investments are the ultimate interest, the focus of the analysis is how to deal with the unknown and unknowable, hereafter abbreviated uU. Hence,

---

[1] An earlier version of this paper appeared as "Investing in the Unknown and Unknowable," *Capitalism and Society* 1(2), 2006, Berkeley Electronic Press, www.bepress.com/cas/vol1/iss2/art5.

I will sometimes discuss salient problems outside of finance, such as terrorist attacks, which are also unknown and unknowable.

This essay takes no derivatives, and runs no regressions.[2] In short, it eschews the normal tools of my profession. It represents a blend of insights derived from reading academic works and from trying to teach their insights to others, and from lessons learned from direct and at-a-distance experiences with a number of successful investors in the *uU* world. To reassure my academic audience, I use footnotes where possible, though many refer to accessible internet articles in preference to journals and books. Throughout this essay, you will find speculations and maxims, as seems called for by the topic. They are labeled in sequence.

This informal approach seems appropriate given our present understanding of the topic. Initial beliefs about this topic are highly uncertain, or as statisticians would phrase it: "Prior distributions are diffuse." Given that, the judicious use of illustrations, and prudent attempts to provide taxonomies and sort tea leaves, can substantially hone our beliefs, that is, tighten our future predictions.

Section 15.1 of this chapter talks about risk, uncertainty, and ignorance, the last carrying us beyond traditional discussions. Section 15.2 looks at behavioral economics, the tendency for humans to deviate in systematic ways from rational decisions, particularly when probabilities are involved, as they always are with investments. Behavioral economics pervades the *uU* world. Section 15.3 addresses the role of skilled mathematical types now so prevalent in finance. It imparts a general lesson: If super-talented people will be your competitors in an investment arena, perhaps it is best not to invest. Its second half discusses a dispute between math types on money management, namely how much of your money to invest when you do have an edge. Section 15.4 details when to invest when you can make more out of an investment, but there is a better informed person on the other side of the transaction. Section 15.5 tells a Buffett tale, and draws appropriate inferences. Section 15.6 concludes the discussion.

15.1. RISK, UNCERTAINTY, AND IGNORANCE

15.1.1. Escalating Challenges to Effective Investing

The essence of effective investment is to select assets that will fare well when future states of the world become known. When the probabilities of future states of assets are known, as the efficient markets hypothesis posits, wise investing

---

[2] Ralph Gomory's (1995) literary essay on the unknown and unknowable provided inspiration. Miriam Avins provided helpful comments. Nils Wernerfelt provided effective research assistance.

involves solving a sophisticated optimization problem. Of course, such probabilities are often unknown, banishing us from the world of the capital asset pricing model (CAPM), and thrusting us into the world of uncertainty.[3]

Were the financial world predominantly one of mere uncertainty, the greatest financial successes would come to those individuals best able to assess probabilities. That skill, often claimed as the domain of Bayesian decision theory, would swamp sophisticated optimization as the promoter of substantial returns.

The real world of investing often ratchets the level of nonknowledge into still another dimension, where even the identity and nature of possible future states are not known. This is the world of ignorance. In it, there is no way that one can sensibly assign probabilities to the unknown states of the world. Just as traditional finance theory hits the wall when it encounters uncertainty, modern decision theory hits the wall when addressing the world of ignorance. I shall employ the acronym uU to refer to situations where both the identity of possible future states of the world as well as their probabilities are unknown and unknowable. Table 1 outlines the three escalating categories; entries are explained throughout the paper.

This essay has both dreary and positive conclusions about investing in a uU world. The first dreary conclusion is that unknowable situations are widespread and inevitable. Consider the consequences for financial markets of global warming, future terrorist activities, or the most promising future technologies. These outcomes are as unknowable today as were the 1997 Asian meltdown, the 9/11 attacks, or the NASDAQ soar and swoon at the end of the century, shortly before they were experienced.

These were all aggregate unknowables, affecting a broad swath of investors. But many unknowables are idiosyncratic or personal, affecting only individuals or handfuls of people, such as: If I build a 300-home community ten miles to the west of the city, will they come? Will the Vietnamese government let me sell my insurance product on a widespread basis? Will my friend's new software program capture the public fancy, or, if not, might it succeed in a completely different application? Such idiosyncratic uU situations, I argue below, present the greatest potential for significant excess investment returns.

The second dreary conclusion is that most investors—whose training, if any, fits a world where states and probabilities are assumed known—have little idea of how to deal with the unknowable. When they recognize its presence, they tend to steer clear, often to protect themselves from sniping by others. But for all but the simplest investments, entanglement is inevitable—and when investors do get entangled they tend to make significant errors.

---

[3] The classic description of uncertainty, a situation where probabilities could not be known, is due to Frank Knight (1921).

TABLE 15.1.
Escalating Challenges to Effective Investing

	Knowledge of States of the World	Investment Environment	Skills Needed
Risk	Probabilities known	Distributions of returns known	Portfolio optimization
Uncertainty *U*	Probabilities unknown	Distributions of returns conjectured	Portfolio optimization Decision theory
Ignorance *uU*	States of the world unknown	Distributions of returns conjectured, often from deductions about other's behavior; complementary skills often rewarded alongside investment	Portfolio optimization Decision theory Complementary skills (ideal) Strategic inference

The first positive conclusion is that unknowable situations have been and will be associated with remarkably powerful investment returns. The second positive conclusion is that there are systematic ways to think about unknowable situations. If these ways are followed, they can provide a path to extraordinary expected investment returns. To be sure, some substantial losses are inevitable, and some will be blameworthy after the fact. But the net expected results, even after allowing for risk aversion, will be strongly positive.

Do not read on, however, if blame aversion is a prime concern: The world of *uU* is not for you. Consider this analogy. If in an unknowable world none of your bridges falls down, you are building them too strong. Similarly, if in an unknowable world none of your investments looks foolish after the fact, you are staying too far away from the unknowable.

Warren Buffett, a master at investing in the unknowable, and therefore a featured player in this essay, is fond of saying that playing contract bridge is the best training for business. Bridge requires a continual effort to assess probabilities in, at best, marginally knowable situations, and players need to make hundreds of decisions in a single session, often balancing expected gains and losses. But players must also continually make peace with good decisions that lead to bad outcomes, both one's own decisions and those of a partner. Just this peacemaking skill is required if one is to invest wisely in an unknowable world.

15.1.2. THE NATURE OF UNKNOWABLE EVENTS

Many of the events that we classify as unknowable arrive in an unanticipated thunderclap, giving us little or no time to anticipate or prepare. But once they happen, they do not appear that strange. The human mind has an incredible ability to find a rationalization for why it should have been able to conjecture the terror attack of 9/11; or the Asian tsunamis of 1997 and 2005, respectively caused by currency collapse and underwater earthquake. This propensity to incorporate hindsight into our memories—and to do so particularly when Monday morning quarterbacks may attack us—hinders our ability to anticipate extreme events in the future. We learn insufficiently from our misestimates and mistaken decisions.

Other unknowable events occur over a period of time, as did the collapse of the Soviet Union. Consider most stock market swings. Starting in January 1996, the NASDAQ rose fivefold in four years. Then it reversed field and fell by two-thirds in three years. Similarly, the 50% collapse in the broad stock market from May 2008 till March 2009 was a fairly steady progression, with only a brief period of truly steep decline in fall 2008. Such developments are hardly thunderclaps. They are more like blowing up a balloon and then dribbling out the air. In retrospect, these remarkable swings have lost the flavor of an unknowable event, even though financial markets are not supposed to work that way. If securities prices at any moment incorporate all relevant information, a property that is usually posited, long-term movements in one direction are hardly possible, since strong runs of unanticipated good news or bad news will be exceedingly rare. Similarly, the AIDS scourge now seems familiar territory, though 25 years ago—when there had been only 31 cumulative deaths in the United States from AIDS—no one would have predicted a worldwide epidemic killing tens of millions and vastly disrupting the economies of many poor nations.

Are uU events to be feared? Warren Buffett once noted that virtually all surprises are unpleasant. Most salient uU events seem to fall into the left tail of unfortunate occurrences. This may be more a matter of perception than reality. Often an upside unknowable event, say the diminution of terror attacks or recovery from a dread disease, is difficult to recognize. An attack on any single day was not likely anyway, and the patient still feels lousy on the road to recovery. Thus, the news just dribbles in, as in a financial market upswing. B. F. Skinner, the great behavioral psychologist, taught us that behavior conditioned by variable interval reinforcement—engage in the behavior and from time-to-time the system will be primed to give you a payoff—was the most difficult to extinguish. Subjects could never be sure that another reward would not be forthcoming. Similarly, it is hard to discern when a string of inconsistently spaced episodic events has concluded. If the events are unpleasant, it is not clear when to celebrate their end.

Let us focus for the moment on thunderclap events. They would not get this title unless they involved something out of the ordinary, either good or bad. Casual empiricism—judged by looking at local, national, and international headlines—suggests that thunderclap events are disproportionately adverse. Unlike in the old television show, *The Millionaire*, people do not knock on your door to give you a boatload of money, and in Iraq terror attacks outnumber terrorist arrests manifold.

The financial arena may be one place with an apparently reasonable ratio of upside to downside *uU* events, particularly if we include events that are drifts and not thunderclaps. By the end of 2004, there were 2.5 million millionaires in the United States, excluding housing wealth (money.cnn.com/2005/06/09/news/world_wealth/). Many of these individuals, no doubt, experienced upside *uU* events. Some events, such as the sustained boom in housing prices, were experienced by many, but many upside events probably affected only the individual and perhaps a few others. Such events include an unexpected lucrative job, or having a business concept take a surprisingly prosperous turn, or having a low-value real estate holding explode in value, and so on.

We hear about the lottery winner—the big pot, the thunderclap, and the gain for one individual makes it newsworthy. In contrast, the tens of thousands of *uU* events that created thousands of new real estate investment millionaires are mostly reported in dry aggregate statistics. Moreover, contrary to the ads in the back of magazines, there is usually not a good way to follow these "lucky folks," since some complementary skill or knowledge is likely to be required, not merely money and a wise choice of an investment. Thus, many favorable *uU* financial events are likely to go unchronicled. By contrast, bad news financial events, such as the foreclosure explosion of 2008–09, like other bad news events, such as murders and fires, tend to get media attention. In drawing inferences about the distribution of financial *uU* events, it is dangerous to rely on what you read in the papers.

To return to the Pollyannish side, it is worth noting the miracles of percentage symmetry given extreme events. Posit that financial prices move in some symmetric fashion. Given that negative prices are not possible, such changes must be in percentage rather than absolute terms.[4] We will not notice any

---

[4] This is sometimes expressed that things move geometrically rather than arithmetically, or that the logarithm of price has a traditional symmetric distribution. The most studied special case is the lognormal distribution. See "Life is log-normal" by E. Limpert and W. Stahel, http://www.inf.ethz.ch/personal/gut/lognormal/brochure.html, for an argument on the widespread applicability of this distribution.

difference between percentage and absolute if changes are small relative to the mean. Thus, if a price of 100 goes up or down by an average of 3 each year, or up by a ratio of 103/100 or down by 100/103 hardly matters. But change that 3 to a 50, and the percentage symmetry helps a great deal. The price becomes 100(150/100) or 100(100/150), which has an average of 117. If prices are anything close to percentage symmetric, as many believe they are, then big swings are both enemy and friend: enemy because they impose big risks, friend because they offer substantial positive expected value.

Many millionaires have made investments that multiplied their money 10-fold, and some 100-fold. The symmetric geometric model would expect events that cut one's stake to 1/10 or 1/100 of its initial value to be equally likely. The opportunity to get a 10 or 100 multiple on your investment as often as you lose virtually all of it is tremendously attractive.

There is, of course, no reason why investments must yield symmetric geometric returns. But it would be surprising not to see significant expected excess returns to investments that have three characteristics addressed in this essay: (1) *uU* underlying features, (2) complementary capabilities are required to undertake them, so the investments are not available to the general market, and (3) it is unlikely that a party on the other side of the transaction is better informed. That is, *uU* may well work for you, if you can identify general characteristics of when such investments are desirable, and when not.

These very attractive three-pronged investments will not come along everyday. And when they do, they are unlikely to scale up as much as the investor would like, unlike an investment in an underpriced New York Stock Exchange (NYSE) stock, which scales nicely, at least over the range for most individual investors. Thus, the *uU*-sensitive investor should be constantly on the lookout for new opportunities. That is why Warren Buffett trolls for new businesses to buy in each Berkshire-Hathaway annual report, and why most wealthy private investors are constantly looking for new instruments or new deals.

15.1.3. Uniqueness

Many *uU* situations deserve a third *U*, for unique. If they do, arbitrageurs—who like to have considerable past experience to guide them—will steer clear. So too will anybody who would be severely penalized for a poor decision after the fact. An absence of competition from sophisticated and well-monied others spells the opportunity to buy underpriced securities.

Most great investors, from David Ricardo to Warren Buffett, have made most of their fortunes by betting on *uUU* situations. Ricardo allegedly made 1 million pounds (over $50 million today)—roughly half of his fortune at death—on his Waterloo bonds.[5] Buffett has made dozens of equivalent investments. Though he is best known for the Nebraska Furniture Mart and See's Candies, or for long-term investments in companies like the Washington Post and Coca Cola, insurance has been Berkshire Hathaway's firehose of wealth over the years. And insurance often requires *uUU* thinking, and careful analysis of when to proceed and when to steer clear. Buffett and Berkshire know when the unknowables in a situation make clear steering the wise course. No insurance of credit default swaps for them. However, a whole section below discusses Buffett's success with what many experts saw as a *uUU* insurance situation, so they steered clear; but he saw it as offering excess premium relative to risk, so he took it all.

Speculation 1: *uUU* investments—unknown, unknowable, and unique—drive off speculators, which creates the potential for an attractive low price.

Some *uU* situations that appear to be unique are not, and thus fall into categories that lend themselves to traditional speculation. Corporate takeover bids are such situations. When one company makes a bid for another, it is often impossible to determine what is going on or what will happen, suggesting uniqueness. But since dozens of such situations have been seen over the years, speculators are willing to take positions in them. From the standpoint of investment, uniqueness is lost, just as the uniqueness of each child matters not to those who manufacture sneakers.

15.1.4. Weird Causes and Fat Tails

The returns to *uUU* investments can be extreme. We are all familiar with the bell curve (or normal distribution), which nicely describes the number of flips of a fair coin that will come up heads in a large number of trials. But such a mechanical and controlled problem is extremely rare. Heights are frequently described as falling on a bell curve. But, in fact, there are many too many people who are extremely tall or extremely short, due, say, to glandular disturbances or genetic abnormalities. The standard model often does not apply to observations in the tails. So too with most disturbances to investments. Whatever the

---

[5] Ricardo's major competitors were the Baring Brothers and the Rothschilds. Do not feel sorry for the Rothschilds. In the 14 years from 1814 to 1828 they multiplied their money 8-fold, often betting on *UU* situations, while the Baring Brothers lost capital. www.businessweek.com/1998/49/b3607071.htm. Analysis based on Niall Ferguson's House of Rothschild.

explanation for the October 1987 crash, it was not due to the usual factors that are used to explain market movements.[6]

More generally, movements in financial markets and of investments in general appear to have much thicker tails than would be predicted by Brownian motion, the instantaneous source of bell curve outcomes. That may be because the fundamental underlying factors produce thicker tails, or because there are rarely occurring anomalous or weird causes that produce extreme results, or both. The uU and uUU models would give great credence to the latter explanation, though both could apply.[7]

15.5.5. COMPLEMENTARY SKILLS AND uU INVESTMENTS

A great percentage of uU investments, and a greater percentage of those that are uUU, provide great returns to a complementary skill. For example, many of America's great fortunes in recent years have come from real estate. These returns came to people who knew where to build, and what and how. Real estate developers earn vast amounts on their capital because they have complementary skills. Venture capitalists can secure extraordinary returns on their own monies, and charge impressive fees to their investors, because early stage companies need their skills and their connections. In short, the return to these investments comes from the combination of scarce skills and wise selection of companies for investment. High tech pioneers—Bill Gates is an extreme example—get even better multiples on their investment dollars as a complement to their vision and scientific insight.[8]

---

[6] Hart and Tauman (2004) show that market crashes are possible purely due to information processing among market participants, with no new information. They observe that the 1987 crash—20% in a day—happened despite no new important information becoming available, or negative economic performance after the crash. Market plunges due to ordinary information processing defies any conventional explanation, and is surely a UU event.

[7] Nassim Taleb and Benoit Mandelbrot posit that many financial phenomena are distributed according to a power law, implying that the relative likelihood of movements of different sizes depends only on their ratio. Thus, a 20% market drop relative to a 10% drop is the same as a 10% drop relative to a 5% drop (www.fooledbyrandomness.com/fortune.pdf). Power distributions have fat tails. In their empirical studies, economists frequently assume that deviations from predicted values have normal distributions. That makes computations tractable, but evidence suggests that tails are often much thicker than with the normal (Zeckhauser and Thompson 1970).

[8] Complementary skills can also help the less affluent invest. Miriam Avins, a good friend, moved into an edgy neighborhood in Baltimore because the abandoned house next door looked like a potential community garden, she knew she had the skills to move the project forward, and she valued the learning experience the house would bring to her family. Her house value doubled in 3 years, and her family learned as well.

Alas, few of us possess the skills to be a real estate developer, venture capitalist, or high-tech pioneer. But how about becoming a star of ordinary stock investment? For such efforts an ideal complementary skill is unusual judgment. Those who can sensibly determine when to plunge into and when to refrain from uUU investments gain a substantial edge, since mispricing is likely to be severe.

Warren Buffett's unusual judgment operates with more prosaic companies, such as oil producers and soft drink firms. He is simply a genius at everyday tasks, such as judging management capability or forecasting company progress. He drains much of the unknowable in judging a company's future. But he has other advantages. A number of Buffett's investments have come to him because companies sought him out, asking him to make an investment and also to serve on their board, valuing his discretion, his savvy, and his reputation for rectitude—that is, his complementary skills, not merely his money. And when he is called on for such reasons, he often gets a discounted price. Buffett flubbed it when he invested heavily in companies like Goldman Sachs and General Electric in fall 2008, but his pain was surely diminished because he had a 10% preferred coupon in both companies, quite apart from the now well-out-of-the-money options he received. Those like Buffett who can leverage complementary skills in stock market investment will be in a privileged position of limited competition. But that will accomplish little if they do not show courage and make big purchases where they expect high payoffs. The lesson for regular mortals is not to imitate Warren Buffett; that makes no more sense than trying to play tennis like Roger Federer. Each of them has an inimitable skill. If you lack Buffett capabilities, you will get chewed up as a bold stock picker.

Note, by the way, the generosity with which great investors with complementary skills explain their successes—Buffett in his annual reports, any number of venture capitalists who come to lecture MBAs, and the highly successful investors who lecture my executive students about behavioral finance.[9] These master investors need not worry about the competition, since few others possess the complementary skills for their types of investments. Few uU investment successes come from catching a secret, such as the whispered hint of "plastics" in the movie *The Graduate*. Mayer Amschel Rothschild had five sons who were bright, disciplined, loyal, and willing to disperse. These were the complementary skills. The terrific investments in a uU world—and the Rothschild fortune—followed.

---

[9] They speak to my Investment Decisions and Behavioral Finance executive program at Harvard. The first was Charlie Munger, Buffett's partner, in the 1980s. The two most recent were Jeremy Grantham of GMO and Seth Klarman of the Baupost Group. Some investment wizards do have a "magic sauce" that they will not reveal. Thus, the unbelievably successful Renaissance Technologies hedge fund, which relies on mathematical and computer models, reveals nothing.

Before presenting a maxim about complementary skills, I present you with a decision problem. You have been asked to join the Business Advisory Board of a company named Tengion. Tengion was founded in 2003 to develop and commercialize a medical breakthrough: "developing new human tissues and organs (*neo-tissues* and *neo-organs*) that are derived from a patient's own cells . . . [this technology] harnesses the body's ability to regenerate, and it has the potential to allow adults and children with organ failure to have functioning organs built from their own (*autologous*) tissues." (www.tengion.com/)

This is assuredly a *uU* situation, doubly so for you, since until now you had never heard the term neo-organ. A principal advantage of joining is that you would be able to invest a reasonable sum on the same basis as the firm's insiders and venture capitalists. Would you choose to do so?

I faced this decision problem because I had worked successfully with Tengion's president on another company many years earlier. He was an individual of high capability and integrity. I was delighted with the *uU* flavor of the situation, and chose to join and invest because I would be doing so on the same terms as sophisticated venture capital (VC) firms with track records and expertise in relevant biotech areas. They would undertake the due diligence that was beyond my capability. This was an investment from which virtually everyone else would be excluded. In addition, it would benefit from the complementary skills of the VCs.

15.1.6. SIDECAR INVESTMENTS

Such undertakings are "sidecar investments"; the investor rides along in a sidecar pulled by a powerful motorcycle. Perhaps the premier sidecar investment ever available to the ordinary investor was Berkshire Hathaway, many decades back. One could have invested alongside Warren Buffett, and had him take a ridiculously low compensation for his services. (In recent years, he has been paid $100,000, with no bonus or options.) But in 1960 who had heard of Warren Buffett, or knew that he would be such a spectacular and poorly compensated investor? Someone who knew Buffett and recognized his remarkable capabilities back then was in a privileged *uU* situation.

Maxim A: Individuals with complementary skills enjoy great positive excess returns from *uU* investments. Make a sidecar investment alongside them when given the opportunity.

Do you have the courage to apply this maxim? It is January 2006 and you, a Western investor, are deciding whether to invest in Gazprom, the predominantly government-owned Russian natural gas giant in January 2006. Russia is attempting to attract institutional investment from the West; the stock is sold as an American depository receipt (ADR), and is soon to be listed on the over-the-counter (OTC) exchange; the company is fiercely profitable, and it is selling gas at a small fraction of the world price. On the upside, it is generally known that large numbers of the Russian elite are investors, and here and there it is raising its price dramatically. On the downside, Gazprom is being employed as an instrument of Russian government policy; for example, gas is sold at a highly subsidized price to Belarus, because of its sympathetic government, yet the Ukraine is being threatened with more than a fourfold increase in price, in part because its government is hostile to Moscow. And the company is bloated and terribly managed. Finally, experiences, such as those with Yukos Oil, make it clear that the government is powerful, erratic, and ruthless.

This is clearly a situation of ignorance, or *uU*. The future states of the world are simply not known. Will the current government stay in power? Will it make Gazprom its flagship for garnering Western investment? If so, will it streamline its operations? Is it using foreign policy concerns as a device mainly to raise prices, a strong positive, and is it on a path to raise prices across the board? Will it complete its proposed pipelines to Europe? What questions haven't you thought of, whose answers could dramatically affect your payout? Of course, you should also determine whether Western investors have distinct disadvantages as Gazprom shareholders, such as unique taxes and secondary voting status. Finally, if you determine the investment is favorable given present circumstances, you should ask how quickly Russia could change conditions against outsiders, and whether you will be alert and get out if change begins.

You could never learn about the unknowables sufficiently well to do traditional due diligence on a Gazprom investment. The principal arguments for going ahead would be that speculation 1 and maxim A apply. If you could comfortably determine that the Russian elite was investing on its own volition, and that foreigners would not be discriminated against, or at least not quickly, this would make a sensible sidecar investment.[10]

15.2. BEHAVIORAL ECONOMICS AND DECISION TRAPS

Behavioral decision has shaken the fields of economics and finance in recent decades. Basically, this work shows in area after area that individuals systematically

---

[10] This investment was proposed when this chapter was presented as a paper at a conference sponsored by the Wharton School on January 6, 2006. The price was then 33.60. The stock peaked above 60 in spring 2008, but then collapsed with oil prices and the Russian stock market.

deviate from making decisions in a manner that would be admired by Jimmie Savage (1954) and Howard Raiffa (1968), pioneers of the rational decision paradigm. As one illustration, such deviators could be turned into money pumps: They would pay to pick gamble B over gamble A. Then with A reframed as A', but not changed in its fundamentals, they would pay to pick A over B.

That is hardly the path to prudent investment, but, alas, behavioral decision has strong descriptive validity. Behavioral decision has important implications for investing in *uU* situations. When considering our own behavior, we must be extremely careful not to fall prey to the biases and decision traps it chronicles. Almost by definition, *uU* situations are those where our experience is likely to be limited, where we will not encounter situations similar to other situations that have helped us hone our intuition.

Virtually all of us fall into important decision traps when dealing with the unknowable. This section discusses two, overconfidence and recollection bias, and then gives major attention to a third, misweighting differences in probabilities and payoffs. But there are dozens of decision traps, and some will appear later in this essay. The Nobel Prize-winning work of Daniel Kahneman and Amos Tversky (the latter was warmly cited, but died too soon to win),[11] and the delightful and insightful *Poor Charlie's Almanack*, written by Charles Munger (Warren Buffett's partner) respectively provide academic and finance-oriented discussions of such traps.

There are at least three major objections to behavioral economics: First, in competitive markets, the anomalies it describes will be arbitraged away. Second, the anomalies appear only in carefully crafted situations; they are much like optical illusions, intriguing but rarely affecting everyday vision. Third, they describe the way people do behave, but not the way they should behave. The first objection is tangential to this discussion; competitive markets and arbitrage are not present in many *uU* situations, and, in particular, not the ones that interest us. The second objection is relatively unimportant because, in essence, *uU* situations are those where optical illusions rule the world. A *uU* world is not unlike a fun house. Objection three I take up seriously below; this essay is designed to help people behave more rationally when they invest.

Let us first look at the biases.

15.2.1. OVERCONFIDENCE

When individuals are assessing quantities about which they know very little, they are much too confident of their knowledge (Alpert and Raiffa 1982).

---

[11] See nobelprize.org/nobel_prizes/economics/laureates/2002/public.html.

Appendix A offers you a chance to test your capabilities in this regard. For each of eight unknown quantities, such as the area of Finland, you are asked to provide your median estimate, then your 25th and 75th percentile estimates (i.e., it is one-quarter likely the true value will be more extreme than either of the two), and then your 1st and 99th percentiles, what are referred to as surprise points. In theory, an individual should have estimates outside her surprise points about 2% of the time. In fact, even if warned about overconfidence, individuals are surprised about 35% of the time.[12] Quite simply, individuals think they know much more about unknowable quantities than they do.

Speculation 2: Individuals who are overconfident of their knowledge will fall prey to poor investments in the *uU* world. Indeed, they are the green plants in the elaborate ecosystem of finance where there are few lions, like Warren Buffett; many gazelles, like you and me; and vast acres of grass ultimately nourishing us all.

15.2.2. RECOLLECTION BIAS

A first lesson in dealing with *uU* situations is to know thyself. One good way to do this is to review successes and failures in past decisions. However, since people do not have a long track record, they naturally turn to hypotheticals from the past: Would I have judged the event that actually occurred to be likely? Would I have made that good investment and steered clear of the other bad one? Would I have sold out of NASDAQ stocks near New Year 2001? Alas, human beings do not do well with such questions. They are subject to substantial recollection bias.[13]

Judging by articles in the *New York Times* leading up to September 11, 2001, there was virtually no anticipation of a major terrorist attack on the United States; it was a clear *uUU* event. But that is not what respondents told us one to three years later. They were asked to compare their present assessments of the likelihood of a massive terrorist attack with what they estimated that likelihood to be on September 1, 2001. Of more than 300 Harvard Law and Kennedy School students surveyed, 31% rated the risk as now lower, and 26% rated the risk as the same as they had perceived the 9/11 risk before the event.[14] We can

---

[12] Approximate average from Investment Decisions and Behavioral Finance, executive program, annually, fall 2001–2006, and API-302, Analytic Frameworks for Policy course. The former is chaired, the latter taught by Richard Zeckhauser, Kennedy School, Harvard University.

[13] See Gilbert (2006) for insightful discussions of the problems of rationalization and corrigibility.

[14] See Viscusi and Zeckhauser (2005).

hardly be confident that investors will be capable of judging how they would have assessed *uU* risks that occurred in the past.

15.2.3. Misweighting Probabilities and Preferences

The two critical components of decision problems are payoffs and probabilities. Effective decision requires that both be carefully calibrated. Not surprisingly, *prospect theory*, the most important single contribution to behavioral decision theory to date, finds that individuals' responses to payoffs and probabilities are far from rational.[15] To my knowledge, there is no tally of which contributes more to the loss of expected utility from the rational norm. (Some strong supporters of behavioral decision theory, however, think it is our norms that are misguided, and that the way the brain naturally perceives outcomes, not the prescriptions of decision theorists and economists, should be the guideline.) Whether drawing from prospect theory or observation, it seems clear that individuals draw insufficient distinctions among small probabilities. Consider the experiment shown in table 15.2, in which an individual is asked to pick A or B.

A rational, risk-averse individual should opt for B, since it offers a higher expected value—$25 versus $20—and less risk. Yet past experiments have shown that many individuals choose A, since in accordance with prospect theory they do not distinguish sufficiently between two low-probability events. We speculate further that if we used named contingencies—or example, the Astros or the Blue Jays win the World Series—alongside their probabilities, the frequency of preference for A would increase. The contingencies would be selected, of course, so that their likelihood of occurrence, as indicated by odds in Las Vegas, would match those in the example above.

This hypothetical experiment establishes a baseline for another one that involves *uU* events. This time the prizes are based on events that are as close to the spectrum of *uU* events as possible, subject to the limitation that they must be named.[16] Thus, a contingency might be that a 10,000-ton asteroid passed within 50,000 miles of Earth within the past decade, or that more than a million mammals crossed the border from Tanzania to Kenya last year. To begin our experiment, we ask a random sample of people to guess the likelihood of these contingencies. We then alter the asteroid distance or the number of animals in

---

[15] Kahneman and Tversky (1979).

[16] This illustration employs events that may have happened in the past, but subjects would not know. The purpose is to make payoffs immediate, since future payoffs suffer from a different form of bias.

TABLE 15.2
Lottery Choice: Payoffs Versus Probabilities

	Payoff	Probability
A	$2000	0.01
B	$1000	0.025

TABLE 15.3
Lottery Choice: Payoffs versus Probability or *uU* Event

	Payoff	Required contingency
C	$2000	Draw a 17 from an urn with balls numbered 1 to 100
D	$1000	10,000-ton asteroid passed within 40,000 miles of Earth

the question until the median answer is 0.03. Thus, if 50,000 miles got a median answer of 0.05, we would adjust to 40,000 miles, and so on.

We now ask a new group of individuals to choose between C and D, assuming that we have calibrated the asteroid and mammal question to get to 0.03 (see table 15.3). Lotteries C and D should yield their prizes with estimated probabilities of 1 and 3%, respectively. Still, we suspect that many more people would pick C over D than picked A over B, and that this would be true for the animal movement contingency as well.[17]

A more elaborated version of this problem would offer prizes based on alternative *uU* contingencies coming to pass. For example, we might recalibrate the mammal-crossing problem to get a median response of 0.01. We would then have the choices shown in table 15.4. Here the values have been scaled so the median response is three times higher for the asteroid event than the animal crossing. We would conjecture again that E would be chosen frequently.[18] People do not like to rely on the occurrence of *uU* events, and choices based on distinguishing among their probabilities would be an unnatural act.

---

[17] The experiment is at a disadvantage in getting this result, since peoples' assessments of the contingencies' probabilities would vary widely. Some would pick D because they attached an unusually high probability to it. In theory, one could ask people their probability estimate after they made their choice, and then look only at the answers of those for whom the probability was in a narrow range. However, individuals would no doubt adjust their retrospective probability estimates to help rationalize their choice.

[18] This experiment and the choice between lotteries C and D above only approximate those with numerical probabilities, since they are calibrated for median responses and individuals' estimates will differ.

TABLE 15.4
Lottery Choice: Payoffs versus *uU* Events

	Payoff	Required contingency
E	$2000	Calibrated large number of animals crossed the Tanzania–Kenya border
F	$1000	10,000 ton-asteroid passed within 40,000 miles of Earth

Daniel Ellsberg (1961) alerted us to ambiguity aversion long before he created a *uU* event by publishing the Pentagon papers. In an actual experiment, he showed, in effect, that individuals preferred to win a prize if a standard coin flip came up heads, rather than to win that prize by choosing either heads or tails on the flip of a mangled coin whose outcome was difficult to predict.[19] Such ambiguity aversion may be a plausible heuristic response to general decisions under uncertainty, since so often there is a better-informed person on the other side—such as someone selling a difficult-to-assess asset.[20] Whatever the explanation, ambiguity aversion has the potential to exert a powerful effect. Extending Ellsberg one step further, it would seem that the more ambiguous the contingencies, the greater the aversion. If so, *uU* investments will drive away all but the most self-directed and rational thinking investors. Thus, speculation 1 is reinforced.

15.3. MATH WHIZZES IN FINANCE AND CASH MANAGEMENT

The major fortunes in finance, I would speculate, have been made by people who are effective in dealing with the unknown and unknowable. This will probably be truer still in the future. Given the influx of educated professionals into finance, those who make their living speculating and trading in traditional markets are increasingly up against others who are tremendously bright and tremendously well-informed.[21]

---

[19] In fact, Ellsberg's experiment involved drawing a marble of a particular color from an urn. Subjects preferred a situation where the percentage of winning marbles was known, even if they could bet on either side when it was unknown.

[20] Fox and Tversky (1995, page 585) found that ambiguity aversion was "produced by a comparison with less ambiguous events or with more knowledgeable people. . . . [it] seems to disappear in a noncomparative context." Ambiguity aversion is still relevant for investments, if alternative investments are available and contemplated.

[21] Paul Samuelson, who attends closely to most aspects of the finance field, attests to this challenge. He observed that Renaissance Technology, run by former Stony Brook math professor James Simons, is "perhaps the only long-time phenomenal performer [in traditional financial markets] on a risk-corrected basis." Private communication, June 15, 2006.

By contrast, those who undertake prudent speculations in the unknown will be amply rewarded. Such speculations may include ventures into uncharted areas, where the finance professionals have yet to run their regressions, or may take completely new paths into already well-traveled regions.[22] It used to be said that if your shoeshine boy gives you stock tips it's was time to get out of the market. With shoeshine boys virtually gone and finance Ph.D.'s plentiful, the new wisdom might be

> When your math whiz finance Ph.D. tells you that he and his peers have been hired to work in the XYZ field, the spectacular returns in XYZ field have probably vanished forever.

Similarly, the more difficult a field is to investigate, the greater will be the unknown and unknowables associated with it, and the greater the expected profits to those who deal sensibly with them. Unknowables can't be transmuted into sensible guesses, but one can take one's positions and array one's claims so that unknowns and unknowables are mostly allies, not nemeses. And one can train to avoid one's own behavioral decision tendencies, and to capitalize on those of others.

Assume that an investor is willing to invest where he has an edge in uU situations. How much capital should then be placed into each opportunity? This problem is far from the usual portfolio problem. It is afflicted with ignorance, and decisions must be made in sequential fashion. Math whizzes have discussed this problem in a literature little known to economists, but frequently discussed among gamblers and mathematicians. The most famous contribution is an article published 50 years ago by J. L. Kelly, an AT&T scientist. His basic formula, which is closely related to Claude Shannon's information theory, tells you how much to bet on each gamble as a function of your bankroll, with the probability of winning and the odds as the two parameters. Perhaps surprisingly, the array of future investment opportunities does not matter.

Kelly's Criterion, as it is called, is to invest an amount equal to $W - (1 - W)/R$, where W is your probability of winning, and R is the ratio of the amount you

---

[22] I saw such path blazing by my former business partner Victor Niederhoffer in the 1970s, when he ventured into commodity investing. His associates hand recorded commodity prices at 15-minute intervals. He lined up a flotilla of TRS-80 Radio Shack computers to parallel process this information. His innovative data mining, spurred by accompanying theories of how markets behave, gave him a giant advantage over major investment houses. Niederhoffer continues along unusual paths, now making a second fortune after losing his first in the collapse of the Thai baht in 1997. www.greenwichtime.com/business/scn-sa-black1jun18,0,3887361.story?page=5&coll=green -business-headlines

win when you win to the amount you lose when you lose.[23] Thus, if you were 60% likely to win an even money bet, you would invest $0.6 - (1 - 0.6)/1 = 0.2$ or 20% of your capital.

It can be shown that given sufficient time, the value given by any other investment strategy will eventually be overtaken by value following the Kelly criterion, which maximizes the geometric growth rate of the portfolio. That might seem to be definitive. But even in the mathematical realm of optimal dynamic investment strategies, assuming that all odds and probabilities are known, we encounter a *uU* situation.

Paul Samuelson, writing in a playful mood, produced an article attacking the Kelly criterion as a guide for practice. His article uses solely one-syllable words. His abstract observes: "He who acts in N plays to make his mean log of wealth as big as it can be made will, with odds that go to one as N soars, beat me who acts to meet my own tastes for risk."[24] In short, Samuelson shows that the Kelly criterion, though mathematically correct, does not tell us how much to invest when one has an edge, since it ignores the structure of preferences.

I lack both the space and capability to straighten out the sequential investment problem. But a few observations may be worthwhile: (1) Most *uU* investments are illiquid for a significant period, often of unknown length. Monies invested today will not be available for reinvestment until they become liquid. (2) Markets charge enormous premiums to cash out illiquid assets.[25] (3) Models of optimal sequential investment strategies tend to assume away the most important real-world challenges to such strategies, such as uncertain lock-in periods. (4) There are substantial disagreements in the literature even about "toy problems," such as those with immediate resolution of known-probability investments. The overall conclusion is that (5) money management is a challenging task in *uU* problems. It afflicts even those with a substantial edge when making such investments. And when the unknowable happens, as it did with the air-pocket plunge in the 1987 stock market or the 1997 Asian crisis, un-

[23] www.investopedia.com/articles/trading/04/091504.asp. In an interesting coincidence, Elwyn Berlekamp, a distinguished Berkeley math professor who was Kelly's research assistant, was an extremely successful investor in a brief stint managing a fund for James Simons. See endnote 14.

[24] Samuelson, P. A. (1979). "Why we should not make mean log of wealth big though years to act are long. *Journal of Baking and Finance* 3, 305–07.

[25] For example, in real estate, a limited partnership interest that will come due in a few years is likely to sell about 30% below discounted expected future value. The significant discount reflects the complementary skills of acquirers, who must be able to assess and unlock the value of idiosyncratic partnerships. Personal communication, Eggert Dagbjartsson, Equity Resource Investments, December 2005. That firm earns substantial excess returns through its combination of effective evaluation of *UU* situations, the ability to structure complex financial transactions, and the unusual complementary skill of being able to deal effectively with a great range of general partners. Experience with Dagbjartsson's firm—at which the author is a principal—helped inspire this paper.

foreseen short-term money-management problems—e.g., transferring monies across markets in time to beat margin calls—tend to emerge. These five points imply that even if it were clear how one should invest in a string of favorable gambles each of which is resolved instantaneously, that would help us little in the real world of *uU* investing, which presents a much more difficult task.

15.4. INVESTING WITH SOMEONE ON THE OTHER SIDE

One of the more puzzling aspects of the financial world is the volume of transactions in international currency markets. Average daily volume is $1.9 trillion, which is slightly more than all U.S. imports in a year. There are hedgers in these markets, to be sure, but their volume is many times dwarfed by transactions that cross with sophisticated or at least highly paid traders on both sides. Something no less magical than levitation is enabling all players to make money, or think that they are making money.

But let us turn to the micro situation, where you are trading against a single individual in what may or may not be a *uU* situation. If we find that people make severe mistakes in this arena even when there is merely risk or uncertainty, we should be much more concerned, at least for them, when *uU* may abound.

15.4.1. BAZERMAN-SAMUELSON EXAMPLE AND LESSONS

Let us posit that you are 100% sure that an asset is worth more to you than to the person who holds it—indeed, 50% more. But assume that she knows the true value to her, and that it is uniformly distributed on [0,100], that is, her value is equally likely to be 0, 1, 2, . . . , 100. In a famous game due to Bazerman and Samuelson (1983), hereafter BS, you are to make a single bid. She will accept if she gets more than her own value. What should you bid?

When asked in the classroom, typical bids will be 50 or 60, and few will bid as low as 20. Students reason that the item will be worth 50 on average to her, hence 75 to them. They bid to get a tidy profit. The flaw in the reasoning is that the seller will accept only if she will make a profit. Let's make you the bidder. If you offer 60, she will not sell if her value exceeds 60. This implies that her average value conditional on selling will be 30, which is the value of the average number from 0 to 60. Your expected value will be 1.5 times this amount, or 45. You will lose 15 on average, namely 60 − 45, when your bid is accepted. It is easy to show that any positive bid loses money in expectation. The moral of this story is that people, even people in decision analysis and finance classrooms, where these experiments have been run many times, are very poor at taking account of the decisions of people on the other side of the table.

There is also a strong tendency to draw the wrong inference from this example, once its details are explained. Many people conclude that you should never deal with someone else who knows the true value, when you know only the distribution. In fact, BS offer an extreme example, almost the equivalent of an optical illusion. You might conclude that when your information is very diffuse and the other side knows for sure, you should not trade even if you have a strong absolute advantage.

That conclusion is wrong. For example, if the seller's true value is uniform on [1, 2] and you offer 2, you will buy the object for sure, and its expected value will be 1.5 times 1.5 = 2.25. The difference between this example and the one with the prior on [0, 1] is that here the effective information discrepancy is much smaller. To see this, think of a uniform distribution from [100, 101]; there is virtually no discrepancy. (In fact, bidding 2 is the optimal bid for the [1, 2] example, but that the extreme bid is optimal also should not be generalized.)

15.4.2. DRAWING INFERENCES FROM OTHERS

The general lesson is that people are naturally very poor at drawing inferences from the fact that there is a willing seller on the other side of the market. Our instincts and early training lead us not to trust the other guy, because his interests so frequently diverge from ours. If someone is trying to convince you that his second-hand car is wondrous, skepticism and valuing your own information highly helps. However, in their study of the heuristics that individuals employ to help them make decisions, Tversky and Kahneman (1974) discovered that individuals tend to extrapolate heuristics from situations where they make sense to those where they do not.

For example, we tend to distrust the other guy's information even when he is on our side. This tendency has serious drawbacks if you consider sidecar investing—free riding on the superior capability of others—as we do below. Consider two symmetrically situated partners with identical interests who start with an identical prior distribution about some value that is described by a two-parameter distribution. They each get some information on the value. They also have identical prior distributions on the information that each will receive. Thus, after his draw, each has a posterior mean and variance. Their goal is to take a decision whose payoff will depend on the true value. The individuals begin by submitting their best estimate, namely their means. After observing each other's means, they then simultaneously submit their new best estimate. Obviously, if one had a tight (loose) posterior his estimate would shift more (less) toward that of his partner. In theory, two things should happen: (1) The two partners should jump over each other between the first and second submission half of the time. (2) The two partners should give precisely the same estimate for the third submission.

In practice, unless the players are students of Robert Aumann[26]—his article "Agreeing to Disagree" (1976) inspired this example—rarely will they jump over each other. Moreover, on the third submission, they will not come close to convergence.

The moral of this story is that we are deeply inclined to trust our own information more than that of a counterpart, and are not well trained to know when this makes good sense and when it inclines us to be a sucker. One should also be on the lookout for information disparities. Rarely are they revealed through carnival-barker behavior. For example, when a seller merely offers you an object at a price, or gets to accept or reject when you make a bid (as with BS), he will utilize information that you do not possess. You had better be alert and give full weight to its likely value, for example, how much the object is worth on average were he to accept your bid.

In the financial world one is always playing in situations where the other fellow may have more information and you must be on your guard. But unless you have a strictly dominant action—one that is superior no matter what the other guy's information—a maximin strategy will almost always push you never to invest. After all, his information could be just such to lead you to lose large amounts of money.

Two rays of light creep into this gloomy situation: First, only rarely will his information put you at severe disadvantage. Second, it is extremely unlikely that your counterpart is playing anything close to an optimal strategy. After all, if it is so hard for you to analyze, it can hardly be easy for him.[27]

15.4.3. ABSOLUTE ADVANTAGE AND INFORMATION ASYMMETRY

It is helpful to break down these situations into two components. First, a potential buyer's absolute advantage benefits both players. It represents the usual gains from trade. In many financial situations, as we observed above, a buyer's absolute advantage stems from her complementary skills. An empty lot in A's hands may be worth much less than it would be in B's. Both gain if A trades to

---

[26] Robert Aumann and Thomas Schelling won the 2005 Nobel Memorial Prize in Economics for their contributions to game theory.

[27] Given the potential for imperfect play, it is sometimes dangerous to draw inferences from the play of others, particularly when their preferences are hard to read. The Iraqi weapons of mass destruction provide a salient example. Many people were confident that such weapons were present not because of intelligence, but because they believed Saddam Hussein could have saved himself and his regime simply by letting in inspectors, who in the instance would find nothing.

B, due to absolute advantage. But such an argument would not apply if A was speculating that the British pound would fall against the dollar when B was speculating that it would rise. There is no absolute advantage in such a situation, only information asymmetries.

Second, if both parties recognize a pure asymmetric information situation, only the better informed player should participate. The appropriate drawing of inferences of "what-you-know-since-you-are-willing-to-trade" should lead to the well known no-trade equilibrium. Understanding this often leads even ordinary citizens to a shrewd strategem:

Maxim B: When information asymmetries may lead your counterpart to be concerned about trading with you, identify for her important areas where you have an absolute advantage from trading. You can also identify her absolute advantages, but she is more likely to know those already.

When you are the buyer, beware; seller-identified absolute advantages can be chimerical. For example, the seller in the bazaar is good at explaining why your special characteristics deserve a money-losing price—say it is the end of the day and he needs money to take home to his wife. The house seller who does not like the traffic noise in the morning may palter that he is moving closer to his job, suggesting absolute advantage since that is not important to you. Stores in tourist locales are always having "Going Out of Business Sales." Most swindles operate because the swindled one thinks he is in the process of getting a steal deal from someone else.

If a game theorist had written a musical comedy, it would have been *Guys and Dolls*, filled as it is with the ploys and plots of small-time gamblers. The overseer of the roving craps game is Nathan Detroit. He is seeking action, and asks Sky Masterson—whose good looks and gambling success befit his name—to bet on yesterday's cake sales at Lindy's, a famed local deli. Sky declines and recounts a story to Nathan:

On the day when I left home to make my way in the world, my daddy took me to one side. "Son," my daddy says to me, "I am sorry I am not able to bankroll you to a large start, but not having the necessary lettuce to get you rolling, instead I'm going to stake you to some very valuable advice. One of these days in your travels, a guy is going to show you a brand-new deck of cards on which the seal is not yet broken. Then this guy is going to offer to bet you that he can make the jack of spades jump out of this brand-new deck of cards and squirt cider in your ear. But, son, do not accept this bet, because as sure as you stand there, you're going to wind up with an ear full of cider."

In the financial world at least, a key consideration in dealing with *uU* situations is assessing what others are likely to know or not know. You are unlikely to have mystical powers to foresee the unforeseeable, but you may be able to estimate your understanding relative to that of others. Sky's dad drew an inference from someone else's willingness to bet. Presumably Ricardo was not a military expert, but just understood that bidders would be few and that the market would over discount the *uU* risk.

15.4.4. COMPETITIVE KNOWLEDGE, UNCERTAINTY, AND IGNORANCE

Let us assume that you are neither the unusually skilled Warren Buffett nor the unusually clear-thinking David Ricardo. You are just an ordinary investor who gets opportunities and information from time to time. Your first task is to decide into which box an investment decision would fall. We start with the unknown probabilities shown in table 15.5.

The first row is welcome and relatively easy, for two reasons: (1) You probably have a reasonable judgment of your knowledge relative to others, as would a major real estate developer considering deals in his home market. Thus, you would have a good assessment of how likely you are to be in box B or box A. (2) If you are in box B, you have the edge. Box A is the home of the typical thick financial market, where we tend to think prices are fair on average.

The second row is more interesting, and brings us to the subject matter of this paper. In section 15.5, we will see Buffett sell a big hunk of reinsurance because he knew he was in box D. His premium was extremely favorable, and he knew that it was exceedingly unlikely that the other side possessed private information that would significantly shift the odds. Box C consists of situations

TABLE 15.5
Investing with Uncertainty and Potential Asymmetric Information

	Easy for others to estimate	Hard for others to estimate
Easy for you to estimate	Tough markets	They're the sucker
Hard for you to estimate	Sky Masterson's dad, you're the sucker	Buffett's reinsurance sale California Earthquake Authority

where you know little, and others may know a fair amount. The key to successfully dealing with situations where you find probabilities hard to estimate is to be able to assess whether others might be finding it easy.

Be sensitive to telling signs that the other side knows more, such as a smart person offering too favorable odds. Indeed, if another sophisticated party is willing to bet, and he can't know that you find probabilities hard to estimate, you should be suspicious. For he should have reasonable private knowledge so as to protect himself. The regress in such reasoning is infinite.

Maxim C: In a situation where probabilities may be hard for either side to assess, it may be sufficient to assess your knowledge relative to the party on the other side (perhaps the market).

Let us now turn to the more extreme case, situations where even the states of the world are unknown, as they would be for an angel investment in a completely new technology, or for insuring infrastructure against terrorism over a long period (see table 15.6).

In some ignorance situations, you may be confident that others know no better. That would place you in box F, a box where most investors get deterred, and where the Buffetts of this world, and the Rothschilds of yesteryear have made lots of money. Investors are deterred because they employ a heuristic to stay away from uU situations, because they might be in E, even though a careful assessment would tell them that outcome was highly unlikely. In addition, both boxes carry the Monday morning quarterback (MMQ) risk; one might be blamed for a poor outcome if one invests in ignorance, when it was a good decision that got a bad outcome; might not have allowed for the fact that others might have had better knowledge when in fact they didn't; or might not have allowed for the fact that others might have had better knowledge, when, in fact, they did, but that negative was outweighed by the positive of your absolute advantage. The criticisms are unmerited. But since significant losses were incurred, and knowledge was scant, the investment looks foolish in retrospect to

TABLE 15.6
Investing with Ignorance and Potential Asymmetric Information

	Known to others	Unknown to others
Unknown to you	Dangerous waters Monday morning quarterback risk	Low competition Monday morning quarterback risk

all but the most sophisticated. An investor who could suffer significantly from any of these critiques might well be deterred from investing.

Let us revisit the Gazprom lesson within this thought in mind. Suppose you are a Russia expert. It is still almost inevitable that real Russians know much more than you. What then should you do? The prudent course, it would seem, would be first to determine your MMQ risk. It may actually be reduced due to your largely irrelevant expertise. But if MMQ is considerable, steer clear. If not, and Russian insiders are really investing, capitalize on box E, and make that sidecar investment. You have the additional advantage that few Westerners will be doing the same, and they are your prime competition for ADRs.[28]

Speculation 3: *uU* situations offer great investment potential given the combination of information asymmetries and lack of competition.

Boxes E and F are also the situations where other players will be attempting to take advantage of us and, if it is our inclination, we might take advantage of them. This is the area where big money changes hands.

A key problem is to determine when you might be played for a sucker. Sometimes this is easy. Anyone who has small oil interests will have received many letters offering to buy, no doubt coming from people offering far less than fair value. They are monopsonists after all, and appropriately make offers well below the market. They may not even have any inside knowledge. But they are surely taking advantage of the impulsive or impatient among us, or those who do not understand the concepts in this paper.

Being a possible sucker may be an advantage if you can gauge the probability. People are strongly averse to being betrayed. They demand much stronger odds when a betraying human rather than an indifferent nature would be the cause of a loss (Bohnet and Zeckhauser 2004). Given that, where betrayal is a risk, potential payoffs will be too high relative to what rational decision analysis would prescribe.

15.4.5. INVESTING IN *UU* WITH POTENTIALLY INFORMED PLAYERS ON THE OTHER SIDE

Though you may confront a *uU* situation, the party or parties on the other side may be well informed. Usually you will not know whether they are. Gamblers opine that if you do not know who the sucker is in a game that you are the

---

[28] In January 2006, Gazprom traded in the west as an ADR, but soon became an over-the-counter stock.

sucker. That does not automatically apply with *uU* investments. First, the other side may also be uninformed. For example, if you buy a partially completed shopping center, it may be that the developer really did run out of money (the proffered explanation for its status) as opposed to his discovery of deep tenant reluctance. Second, you may have a complementary skill, such as strong relations with WalMart, that may give you a significant absolute advantage multiple.

15.4.6. THE ADVANTAGE MULTIPLE VERSUS SELECTION FORMULA

Let us simplify and leave risk aversion and money management matters aside. Further posit, following BS, that you are able to make a credible take-it-or-leave-it offer of 1. The value of the asset to him is v, an unknown quantity. The value to you is av, where a is your absolute advantage. Your subjective prior probability distribution on v is $f(v)$. The mean value of your prior is $m < 1$.[29] In a stripped-down model, three parameters describe this situation: your advantage multiple, a; the probability that the other side is informed, p; and the selection factor against you, s, if the other side is informed.[30] Thus, s is the fraction of expected value that will apply, on average, if the other side is informed, and therefore sells only when the asset has low value to her. Of course, given the *uU* situation, you do not know s, but you should rely on your mean value of your subjective distribution for that parameter.

If you knew $p = 0$, that the other side knew no more than you, you would simply make the offer if $am > 1$. If you knew there were selection, that is, $p = 1$, you would invest if your multiple more than compensated for selection, namely if $ams > 1$. The general formula is that your return will be

$$am[ps + (1 - p)1] \qquad (15.1)$$

Maxim D: A significant absolute advantage offers some protection against potential selection. You should invest in a *uU* world if your advantage multiple is great, unless the probability is high that the other side is informed and if, in addition, the expected selection factor is severe.

Following maxim D, you should make your offer when the expression in (15.1) exceeds 1.

---

[29] It is important that $m < 1$. Otherwise the seller would refuse your offer if he were uninformed.
[30] In health care, this process is called adverse selection, with sicker people tending to enroll in more generous health plans.

In practice, you will have a choice of offer, t. Thus, s will vary with t, that is, $s(t)$.[31] The payoff for any t will be

$$am[ps(t) + (1 - p)1] - t \qquad (15.2)$$

If, at the optimal offer t^*, this quantity is positive, then you should offer t^*.

15.4.6. PLAYING THE ADVANTAGE MULTIPLE VERSUS SELECTION GAME

Our formulation posited a take-it-or-leave-it offer with no communication. In fact, most important financial exchanges have rounds of subtle back-and-forth discussion. This is not simply cheap talk. Sometimes real information is provided, such as accounting statements, geological reports, antique authentications. And offers by each side reveal information as well. Players on both sides know that information asymmetry is an enemy to both, as in any agency problem.

It is well known that if revealed information can be verified, and if the buyer knows on what dimensions information will be helpful, then by an unraveling argument all information gets revealed.[32] Consider a one-dimension case where a value can be between 1 and 100. A seller with a 100 would surely reveal, implying that the best unrevealed information would be 99. But then the 99 would reveal, and so on down through 2.

When the buyer is in a uU situation, unraveling does not occur, since he does not know the relevant dimensions. The seller will keep private unfavorable information on dimensions unknown to the buyer. She will engage in signposting: announcing favorable information, suppressing unfavorable.[33]

The advantage multiple versus selection game will usually proceed with the seller explaining why she does not have private information, or revealing private

---

[31] Let $\underline{x}$ be the conditional mean of $x < v$. The value of s will be constant if $\underline{x}/v = $ positive k for all v. This will be the case if $f(v)$ is homogeneous, i.e., $f(kv) = k_n f(v)$, as with the uniform or triangular distribution starting at 0.

[32] See Grossman (1981) on unraveling. If information is costly to reveal, then less favorable information is held back and signposting applies (Zeckhauser and Marks 1996).

[33] To be sure, the shrewd buyer can deduce: "Given the number of unknown dimensions I suspected, the seller has revealed relatively few. Hence, I assume that there are a number of unfavorable dimensions," etc. When seller revelation is brief, only high m buyers will make exchanges. The doubly shrewd buyer may be informed or get informed on some dimension without the seller knowing which. He can then say: "I have unfavorable information on a dimension. Unless you reveal on all dimensions, this information will stay private, and I will know that you are suppressing information." The triply shrewd buyer, knowing nothing, will make the same statement. The shrewd seller has countermeasures, such as insisting on proof that the buyer is informed, e.g., by third party attestation, and if evidence is received, then revealing some but not all, hoping to hit the lucky dimension.

information indicating that m and a are large. Still, many favorable deals will not get done, because the less-informed party cannot assess what it does not know. Both sides lose *ex ante* when there will be asymmetry on common value information, or when, as in virtually all uU situations, asymmetry is suspected..

15.4.7. AUCTIONS AS UU GAMES

Auctions have exploded as mechanisms to sell everything from the communications spectrum to corporate securities, and, in 2009, toxic assets. Economic analyses of auctions—how to conduct them and how to bid—have exploded alongside. The usual format is that an informed seller faces a group of less-knowing buyers. The usual prescription is that the seller should reveal his information about elements that will affect all buyers' valuations, such as geologic information on an oil lease or evidence of an antique's pedigree, to remove buyers' concerns about the winner's curse. The winner's curse applies when an object, such as an oil lease, is worth roughly the same to all. The high bidder should be aware that every other bidder thought it was worth less than he did. Hence, his estimate is too high, and he is cursed for winning.

Real-world auctions are often much more complex. Even the rules of the game may not be known. Consider the common contemporary auction phenomenon, witnessed often with house sales in hot markets, and at times with the sale of corporations.[34] The winner, who expected the final outcome to have been determined after one round of bidding, may be told there will be a best and final offer round, or that now she can negotiate a deal for the item.

Usually the owner of the object establishes the rules of the game. In theory, potential buyers would insist that they know the rules. In practice, they often have not. When Recovery Engineering, makers of PUR water purifiers, was sold in 1999, a "no one knows the rules" process ensued, with Morgan Stanley representing the seller. A preliminary auction was held on an August Monday. Procter and Gamble (P&G) and Gillette bid, and a third company expressed interest but said it had difficulties putting its bid together. Gillette's bid was $27 per share; P&G's was $22. P&G was told by the investment banker that it would have to improve its bid substantially. Presumably, Gillette was told little, but drew appropriate inferences, namely that it was by far high. The final auction was scheduled for that Friday at noon. Merrill Lynch, Gillette's investment banker, called early on Friday requesting a number of additional pieces of due diligence information, and requesting a delay till Monday. Part of the information was released—Gillette had had months to request it—and the auction was

---

[34] See Subramanian and Zeckhauser (2005), who apply the term "negotiauctions" to such processes.

delayed till 5 p.m. Friday. The P&G bid $34. At 5 p.m., Merrill Lynch called, desperate, saying it could not get in touch with Gillette. Brief extensions were granted, but contact could not be established. P&G was told that it was the high bidder. Over the weekend a final deal was negotiated at a slightly higher price; the $300 million deal concluded. But would there have been a third round of auction if Gillette had bid $33.50 that Friday? No one knows.

The Recovery board puzzled over the unknowable question: What happened to Gillette? One possibility was that Gillette inferred from the fact that it was not told its Monday bid was low that it was in fact way above other bidders. It was simply waiting for a deal to be announced, and then would propose a price perhaps $2 higher, rather than bid and end up $5 higher.[35] Gillette never came back. A while later, Recovery learned that Gillette was having—to that time unreported—financial difficulties. Presumably, at the moment of truth Gillette concluded that it was not the time to purchase a new business. In short, this was a game of unknowable rules, and unknowable strategies.[36] Not unusual.

At the close of 2005, Citigroup made the winning bid of about $3 billion for 85% of the Guangdong Development Bank, a financially troubled state-owned Chinese bank. As the *New York Times* reported the deal, Citigroup "won the right to negotiate with the bank to buy the stake." If successful there, its "control might allow Citigroup to install some new management and have some control over the bank's future . . . one of the most destitute of China's big banks . . . overrun by bad loans."[37] Citigroup is investing in a uU situation, and knows that both the rules of the game and what it will win are somewhat undefined. But it is probably confident that other bidders were no better informed, and that both the bank and the Chinese government (which must approve the deal) may also not know the value of the bank, and were eager to secure foreign control. Great value may come from buying a pig in a poke, if others also cannot open the bag.

15.4.8. IDEAL INVESTMENTS WITH HIGH AND LOW PAYOFFS

In many uU situations, even the events associated with future payoff levels—for example, whether a technology supplier produces a breakthrough or a new

---

[35] Recovery created a countermeasure to raise any postdeal bid by inserting a breakup fee in its deal with P&G that declined (ultimately to 0) with the price premium paid by a new buyer.

[36] Details confirmed by Brian Sullivan, then CEO of Recovery Engineering, in personal communication, January 2006. Zeckhauser was on the Recovery board due to a sidecar privilege. He had been Sullivan's teacher, and had gotten him the job.

[37] *New York Times*, December 31, 2005, B1 and B4. Citigroup had several Chinese state-owned companies as partners, but they probably gave more political cover than knowledge of the value of the bank.

product emerges—are hard to foresee. The common solution in investment deals is to provide for distributions of the pie that depend not on what actually happens, but solely on money received. This would seem to simplify matters, but even in such situations sophisticated investors frequently get confused.

With venture capital in high tech, for example, it is not uncommon for those providing the capital to have a contractual claim to all the assets should the venture go belly up. Similarly, "cram down" financings, which frequently follow when startups underperform, often give venture capitalists a big boost in ownership share. In theory, such practices could provide strong incentives to the firm's managers. In reality, the managers' incentives are already enormous. Typical VC arrangements given bad outcomes cause serious ill will, and distort incentives—for example, they reward gambling behavior by managers after a bleak streak. Worse still for the VCs, they are increasing their share of the company substantially when the company is not worth much. They might do far better if arrangements specified that they sacrifice ownership share if matters turn out poorly, but gain share if the firm does particularly well.

Maxim E: In uU situations, even sophisticated investors tend to underweight how strongly the value of assets varies. The goal should be to get good payoffs when the value of assets is high.

No doubt Ricardo also took maxim E into account when he purchased the "Waterloo bonds." He knew that English money would be far more valuable if Wellington was victorious and his bonds soared in value, than if he lost and the bonds plummeted.

15.4.9. A uU Investment Problem

Now for a harder decision. Look at the letter in exhibit 15.1, which offers you the chance to make a modest investment in an oil well. You have never heard of Davis Oil and the letter came out of the blue, and without letterhead. You inquire, and find out that it is the company previously owned by the famous, recently deceased oilman Marvin Davis. Your interest is offered because the Davis Company bought the managing partner's interest in the prospect from a good friend and oil man who invited you into his prospect.[38] Davis is legally required to make this offer to you. Decide whether to invest or merely wait for your costless override before you read on.

---

[38] That man was Malcolm Brachman, president of Northwest Oil, a bridge teammate and close friend. Sadly, Malcolm had died in the interim. One consequence was that he could not advise you.

Exhibit 15.1

September 19, 2005

WORKING INTEREST OWNER: Richard Zeckhauser
Re: Well Proposal
         David Petroleum Corp.
         Devlin #1-12
         Section 12-T8N-R19W
         Washita County, Oklahoma

Gentlemen:

Davis Petroleum Corp. ("Davis") proposes the drilling of a 17,000´ Sub-Thrusted Springer test at a surface location of 660´ FNL and 1980' FWL and a bottom hole location of 1,650´ FNL and 990´ FWL of Section 12-T8N-R19W, Washita County, Oklahoma. Enclosed for your review is our AFE reflecting estimated dry hole costs of $6,869,100.00 and estimated completion costs of $2,745,400.00. As a working interest owner within the referenced unit and per the terms and conditions of that certain Order 450325, Cause CD 200100725-T, dated March 29, 2001, Davis respectfully requests that you elect one of the afforded options as follows:

1. Participate in the drilling and completing of said well by paying your proportionate share of well costs as stipulated by Order 450325;
2. Elect not to participate in the proposed test well, electing to farmout your unit interest delivering to Davis your interest at a proportionate 75% net revenue interest.

Per the terms of Order 450325 you have **15 days** upon receipt of this proposal to make your election as outlined above. Failure to respond within the 15 day period will evidence your election not to participate thus relinquishing your interest under paragraph 2, above.

   Please indicate the option of your choice by signing below and returning one copy of this letter to my attention. This proposal may be terminated without further notice. Should you have any questions, please contact me at (713) 439-6750 or Bill Jaqua at (405) 329-0779.

Sincerely,
Davis Petroleum Corp.

Alan Martinkewiz
Landman

THE UNDERSIGNED HEREBY ACCEPTS OPTION NO. ____, THIS ____ DAY OF _____, 2005
By: _____
Title: _____
Company: _____

Here is what your author did. He started by assessing the situation. Davis could not exclude him, and clearly did not need his modest investment. The letter provided virtually no information, and was not even put on letterhead, presumably the favored Davis approach if it were trying to discourage investment. Davis had obviously spent a fair amount of effort determining whether to drill the well, and decided to go ahead. It must think its prospects were good, and you would be investing as a near partner.

Bearing this in mind, he called Bill Jaqua—a contact Davis identified in the letter—and asked about the well. He was informed it was a pure wildcat, and that it was impossible to guess the probability of success. Some geologic technical discussion followed, which he tried to pretend he understood. He then asked what percentage of Davis wildcat wells had been successful in recent years, and got a number of 20–25%. He then asked what the payoff was on average if the wells were successful. The answer was 10 to 1. Beyond that, if this well was successful, there would be a number of other wells drilled in the field. Only participation now would give one the right to be a future partner, when presumably the odds would be much more favorable. This appeared to be a reasonably favorable investment, with a healthy upside option of future wells attached. The clinching argument was that Jaqua courteously explained that Davis would be happy to take his interest and give him the free override, thus reinforcing the message of the uninformative letter not placed on letterhead. (It turned out that the override would have only been 1% of revenue—an amount not mentioned in the letter—as opposed to 76% if he invested.)[39] In short, the structure of the situation, and the nature of Davis's play made a sidecar investment imperative. The well has not yet been started.

Davis was in a tough situation. It had to invite in undesired partners on favorable terms when it had done all the work. It reversed the usual ploy where someone with a significant informational advantage tries to play innocent or worse, invoke some absolute advantage story. Davis tried to play up the uU aspect of the situation to discourage participation.

15.4.10. REVIEW OF THE BIDDING

You have been asked to address some decision problems. Go back now and grade yourself first on the overconfidence questionnaire. The answers are in the footnote.[40] You were asked about three investments: Tengion, Gazprom, and

---

[39] Not mentioned in the letter was that 24% went off the top to priority claims, and that Davis charges 75% if you take the free override.

[40] (1) 173,710, (2) 2716, (3) 2,007,901, (4) 130,119, (5) 13, (6) 12,212,000, (7) $259B, (8) 13.45%, (9) 853,000.

Davis Oil. Go back and reconsider your choices, and decide whether you employed the appropriate principles when making them, and then assess the more general implications for investment in *uU* situations. Though this essay pointed out pitfalls with *uU* investing, it was generally upbeat about the potential profits that reside in *uU* arenas. Hopefully, you have been influenced, at least a bit.

15.5. SOME CAUTIONS: HERDING, CASCADES, AND MELTDOWNS

Understanding the *uU* world presents great opportunity, but it also suggests some cautions. We shall focus on just three: herding, cascades, and meltdowns.

15.5.1. HERDING

Animals gather together because there is safety in numbers. Investors cluster as well. That may help them fend off criticism, but it will not protect them from meltdowns in value, be they for individual assets or for the market as a whole. There are two main ingredients in such meltdowns: information cascades and fat-tailed distributions. A cascade is experienced when the information from one individual spills over to inform another individual, and when large a whole group gets informed. Fat tails, as we mentioned above, refers to the fact that financial assets have more big movements in price than experience with small movements would suggest, including some movements so large they would seem nearly impossible.

15.5.2. INFORMATION CASCADES

Information cascades occur when individuals draw inferences about the information that others possess from the actions they take. Thus, one individual's information cascades to affect the action of another. The danger with an information cascade is that it is very difficult for the players to know how much information is possessed in total. When the total possessed is much less than the total assessed, prices can be well out of line. Just such a situation may be responsible for the meltdown in housing prices in the United States in 2008. Each family purchasing a house looks to comparable sales for guidance. Using that basis, it seems sensible to pay say $300,000 for this home, since other equivalent homes nearby sold for as much as $320,000. The trouble is that all the other home buyers were also relying on the market price. In effect, there was herding on the information. Everyone would be happy to know that they bought close to the correct price, namely what others would buy for in the future. But, unfortunately, there was no hard basis to determine that correct price. One possibility would be to rely on the prices in equivalent nearby towns, but this just raises the herding on information issue one level. A whole region or nation can find its housing prices inflated.

Economists would say that there are multiple equilibria in such markets, at least one high priced and one low priced. The high-priced equilibrium of late 2007 proved to be unstable. A moderate shock knocked it away from that equilibrium, and prices spiraled downward to what will ultimately be a lower-priced equilibrium. People who bought houses in 2007 were unlikely to have thought about either information cascades or fat tails. That is, they did not contemplate that current house prices were based on little reliable information, and that big price movements, down as well as up, were quite possible.

In some circumstances, although there is abundant information in the system, and individuals closely monitor and behave in response to the actions of others, little of the information gets shared. Take a situation where each of 100 people gets a signal on whether housing prices are going down or up. The signal is not fully reliable. If prices are going down, it is 70% likely someone will get a down signal and 30% an up signal, and vice versa when the market is going up. Individuals choose whether to buy a house in numerical order, and will buy a house if, on the basis of what they know, they think prices are going up, though a small group buys because they desperately need a house. They draw inferences from the actions of others. Person 1 gets an up signal and buys a house. Person 2 can't be sure that 1 did not buy because he was desperate for a house, so his information would outweigh 1's action as a signal. Person 2 would not buy if he got a down signal, but he got an up signal. He too buys a house. Person 3 gets a down signal, but reasons that 1 and 2 probably for up signals, so his signal is outvoted; prices are likely to go up. Beyond that, everyone, whatever his signal, will buy. That is what we call an information cascade. Almost certainly, the aggregate information from all 100 people would indicate a down market, but the cascade of information from the first two individuals is what dominates the market.

15.5.3. MELTDOWNS

We are most likely to get prices far from equilibrium in those markets where prices rose rapidly. Individuals within might reason as follows: "Prices went up by roughly 8% each of the last three years. Thus, the price I should pay should depend not only on some multiple of rent—a normal metric—but must incorporate how much prices will go up next year. Others think that $300,000 is an appropriate price for such a house. That price builds in consensus expectations." This reasoning may be correct, but it represents a fragile situation. If prices do not go up by 8%, the price will not merely soften; it will collapse, since rapid appreciation was the basis for its high price.

Matters would be far different in unglamorous cities, say Indianapolis or Buffalo. House prices hardly budged in them for a long time. They were set in relation to rental rates, and did not rely on future expectations. In short, there was much more information in the system. People could make decisions on whether it was cheaper to rent or buy.

Experience with the NASDAQ and California home prices is instructive. From 1995 to 2000 the NASDAQ had multiplied more than six times in value before peaking in March 2000. It then fell by 60% in a year.[41] The median price of an existing detached home in California had tripled in eight years before mid-2007, and then fell in half in one year.[42]

In each case there was a dramatic run up before the big run down. Investors in the first case, and home buyers in the second were trying to guess how prices would move in the future. All participants were watching and taking comfort from the decisions of others. They moved with the herd as prices moved up. Once prices stopped their rapid ascent, they could not be sustained, since current values anticipated rapid appreciation. The participants were victims of the fat-tail phenomenon. Meltdowns were experienced.

Maxim F: When there may be herding on information, beware. Be doubly beware if the information comes from extrapolating a successful past to a successful future.

Some very major financial players ignored maxim F, to their peril. Many of our most prestigious investment houses lost many billions of dollars because they went with the herd to get a little extra kick by buying mortgage-backed securities. Perhaps more surprising, Fannie Mae and Freddie Mac effectively collapsed because they failed to examine their own markets.

The implication of maxim F is that effective decision makers must—as a recent insightful book for business and financial executives puts it in its first lesson—"Go to the Source," namely engage in the "relentless pursuit of information from the field." It tells the story of Bill George, the newly appointed president of medical equipment giant Medtronic, who went into the operating room where he witnessed the dreadful performance of the company's catheter during an angioplasty. By starting at the source, he discovered that the company's information system systematically covered up information about low quality: "People do not want to pass on bad news, and engineers [or any

---

[41] Yahoo! Finance.
[42] California Association of Realtors, 2008.

other group] can be in denial about a problem."[43] That last sentence distills our findings about much in the recent collapse of mortgage markets and financial institutions.

Maxim G: Be triply beware of herding when there is evidence that there have been significant changes in the basic structure of markets, however stable they have been in the past.

The mortgage market, a stable and successful market for decades, had undergone dramatic changes in the decade or so before it collapsed. Mortgages, originally the obligations of the banks that wrote them, had evolved into derivative products, with large numbers of mortgages packaged together and sold as a unit. That dramatically reduced the incentives for the banks that wrote them to scrutinize their safety. It also meant that no one really understood the risk characteristics of any package. A second major development, no doubt pushed along by the derivative developments, was that mortgages had come to be written with extraordinarily low down payments. Indeed, looking back four years from 2007, 25% of mortgages on new houses were written with down payments of 2% or less.[44]

Investment houses often warn us that past performance is not necessarily indicative of future results. Maxim G would tell us that past performance is particularly unreliable if basic assumptions from the past have been overturned. Our big losers among investment houses ignored their own warning when it came to mortgage-backed securities, and maxims F and G as well.

While issuing cautions, consider a final word about statistical inference. In the classroom, we are used to drawing inferences from multiple trials. Thus, to determine whether a new drug offers benefits, we might give it to 100 people and an existing drug to another 100, and see which performs better, say, in lowering cholesterol. This mental model of independent trials may not carry over to financial markets. The excess performance of 100 firms investing in mortgage-backed securities in a particular year is far from 100 independent trials. They will all do well if housing markets rise, but if such markets plummet, they will all be in trouble. A single year with 100 firms is closer to 1 observation than 100 independent observations. Hedge funds announced their ability to

---

[43] See Zeckhauser and Sandoski (2008), pages 7–43. The book's second lesson (pages 44–72) is also instructive if one wishes to elicit information from all and to avoid herding. It is "Fill a Room with Barbarians." The central finding is that "Seeking and fostering dissent provides two advantages. . . . [participants must] expose their opinions to a wide range of counterarguments . . . [and] diverse, well-founded arguments can reframe a problem so that everyone sees it in a new way."

[44] *American Housing Survey for the United States: 2007.*

do well in up or down financial markets, and from 1987 to 2007 they averaged almost a 14% return. But they were not really tested till 2008, when they were down on average 19.83% for the year.[45]

15.6. A BUFFETT TALE

Let us conclude with a happier tale. The following story encapsulates the fear of *uU* situations, even by sophisticated investors, and the potential for shrewd investors to take great advantage of such situations. In 1996, I was attending a National Bureau of Economic Research (NBER) conference on insurance. One participant was the prime consultant to the California Earthquake Authority. He had been trying to buy a $1 billion slice of reinsurance—to take effect after $5 billion in aggregate insured losses—from the New York financial community. The Authority was offering five times estimated actuarial value, but had no takers. It seemed exceedingly unlikely that the parties requesting coverage had inside information that a disastrous earthquake was likely. Hence, there was a big advantage, in effect $a = 5$, and p was close to 0. Maxim D—weigh absolute advantage against informational disadvantage—surely applied.

My dinner table syndicate swung into action, but ended up $999.9 million short. A couple days later, we learned that Buffett had flown to California to take the entire slice. Here is his explanation.

> ... we wrote a policy for the California Earthquake Authority that goes into effect on April 1, 1997, and that exposes us to a loss more than twice that possible under the Florida contract. Again we retained all the risk for our own account. Large as these coverages are, Berkshire's after-tax "worst-case" loss from a true mega-catastrophe is probably no more than $600 million, which is less than 3% of our book value and 1.5% of our market value. To gain some perspective on this exposure, look at the table on page 2 and note the much greater volatility that security markets have delivered us.
> —Chairman's letter to the shareholders of Berkshire Hathaway, 1996, www.ifa.com/Library/Buffet.html

Reinsurance for earthquakes is certainly a venture into the unknown, but had many attractive features beyond its dramatic overpricing. Unlike most insurance, it was exceedingly unlikely that the parties taking insurance had inside

---

[45] Data from the Hennessee Group's Hedge Fund Index (see www.hennesseegroup.com/indices/index.html)

knowledge on their risk. Thus, Buffett—despite attention to money management—was willing to take 100% of a risk of which Wall Street firms houses rejected taking even part. Those fancy financial entities were not well equipped to take a risk on something that was hard for them to estimate. Perhaps they did not recognize that others had no inside information, that everyone was operating with the same probability. And perhaps they were just concerned about Monday morning quarterbacking.

It is also instructive to consider Buffett's approach to assessing the probabilities in this uU situation, as revealed in the same annual report:

> So what are the true odds of our having to make a payout during the policy's term? We don't know—nor do we think computer models will help us, since we believe the precision they project is a chimera. In fact, such models can lull decision-makers into a false sense of security and thereby increase their chances of making a really huge mistake. We've already seen such debacles in both insurance and investments. Witness "portfolio insurance," whose destructive effects in the 1987 market crash led one wag to observe that it was the computers that should have been jumping out of windows.

Buffett was basically saying to Wall Street firms: "Even if you hire 100 brilliant Ph.D.s to run your models, no sensible estimate will emerge." These are precisely the types of uU situations where the competition will be thin, the odds likely favorable, and the Buffetts of this world can thrive.

As Buffett has shown on repeated occasions, a multibillionaire will rush in where mathematical wizards fear to tread. Indeed, that explains much of his success. In 2006 hurricane insurance met two Buffett desiderata, high prices and reluctant competitors. So he plunged into the market: Buffett's prices are as much as 20 times higher than the rates prevalent a year ago, said Kevin Madden, an insurance broker at Aon Corp. in New York. On some policies, premiums equal half of its maximum potential payout, he said. In a May 7, 2006, interview Buffett said: "We will do more than anybody else if the price is right . . . We are certainly willing to lose $6 billion on a single event. I hope we don't" (seekingalpha.com/article/11697).

At least two important lessons emerge from thinking about the "advantage-versus-selection" problem, and observing Warren Buffett.

Maxim H: Discounting for ambiguity is a natural tendency that should be overcome, just as should be overeating.

Maxim I: Do not engage in the heuristic reasoning that just because you do not know the risk, others do. Think carefully, and assess whether they are likely to know more than you. When the odds are extremely favorable, sometimes it pays to gamble on the unknown, even though there is some chance that people on the other side may know more than you.

Buffett took another bold financial move in 2006, in a quite different field, namely philanthropy. He announced that he would give away 85% of his fortune or $37.4 billion, with $31 billion going to the Bill and Melinda Gates Foundation. Putting money with the Gates Foundation represents sidecar philanthropy. The Foundation is an extremely effective organization that focuses on health care and learning. It is soon to be led by Bill Gates, a fellow with creativity, vision, and hardheadedness as strong complementary skills, skills that are as valuable in philanthropy as they are in business.

15.7. CONCLUSION

This essay offers more speculations than conclusions, and provides anecdotal accounts rather than definitive data. Its theory is often tentative and implicit. But the question it seeks to answer is clear: How can one invest rationally in uU situations? The question sounds almost like an oxymoron. Yet clear thinking about uU situations, which includes prior diagnosis of their elements, and relevant practice with simulated situations, may vastly improve investment decisions where uU events are involved. If they do improve, such clear thinking will yield substantial benefits. For financial decisions, at least, the benefits may be far greater than are available in run-of-the-mill contexts, since competition may be limited and prices well out of line.

How important are uU events in the great scheme of financial affairs? That itself is a uU question. But if we include only those that primarily affect individuals, the magnitude is far greater than what our news accounts would suggest. Learning to invest more wisely in a uU world may be the most promising way both to protect yourself from major investment errors, and to significantly bolster your prosperity.

Appendix A

Assessing Quantities

· ·

1. Democratic votes in Montana, 2004 Presidential election*
2. Length of Congo River (in miles)
3. Number of subscribers to *Field and Stream*
4. Area of Finland (in square miles)
5. Birth rate in France per 1000 population
6. Population of Cambodia
7. Revenues of Wal-Mart stores (largest in U.S.), 2003
8. Annual percent yields on 30-year treasury bonds in 1981
    (This year had the highest rate over the 1980–1998 period.)
9. Number of physicians in the United States, 2002
10. Number of electoral votes going to the Republican presidential candidate in 2008 (out of 538)
11. Value of Dow Jones Average on December 31, 2006 (on 6/30/06 closed at 11,150)
12. Value of the NASDAQ on December 31, 2006 (on 6/30/06 closed at 2172)

* Question 1, www.uselectionatlas.org/RESULTS/state.php?f=0&year=2004&fips=30; questions 2–6, *1995 Information Please Almanac*; question 8, *1999 Wall Street Journal Almanac*; questions 7 and 9, *World Almanac 2005*.

TABLE 15.7

	1st %ile	25th %ile	50th %ile	75th %ile	99th %ile
Democratic votes MT 2004 presidential election					
Congo River (length in miles)					
Field & Stream (number of subscribers)					
Finland (area in square miles)					
Birth rate of France (per thousand)					
Population of Cambodia					
Revenues of Wal-Mart stores, 2003					
% Yields on 30-year bonds, 1981					
Number of physicians in U.S., 2002					
Number of electoral college votes, Republican presidential candidate in 2008					
Dow Jones Average 12/31/06 (on 6/30/06 closed at 11,150)					
Value of NASDAQ 12/31/06 (on 6/30/06 closed at 2172)					

REFERENCES

Alpert, M., and H. Raiffa (1982). A progress report on the training of probability assessors. In Judgment Under Uncertainty: Heuristics and Biases. D. Kahneman, P. Slovic, and A. Tversky, eds., New York: Cambridge University Press, pp. 294–305.

Aumann, R. (1976). Agreeing to disagree. Annals of Statistics 4, 1236–39.

Bazerman, M., and W. Samuelson (1983). I won the auction but don't want the prize. Journal of Conflict Resolution 27, 618–34.

Bohnet, I., and R. Zeckhauser (2004). Trust, risk and betrayal. Journal of Economic Behavior and Organization 55, 467–84.

Ellsberg, D. (1961). Risk, ambiguity, and the savage axioms. Quarterly Journal of Economics 75: 643–69.

Fox, C., and A. Tversky (1995). Ambiguity aversion and comparative ignorance. *Quarterly Journal of Economics* 110, 585–603.

Gilbert, D. (2006). *Stumbling on Happiness.* New York: A. A. Knopf.

Gomory, R. (June 1995). An assay on the known, the unknown and the unknowable. *Scientific American* 272, 120.

Grossman, S. J. (1981). The informational role of warranties and private disclosure about product quality. *Journal of Law and Economics* 24, 461–83.

Hart, S., and Y. Tauman (2004). Market crashes without external shocks. *Journal of Business* 77, 1–8.

Kahneman, D., and A. Tversky (1979). Prospect theory: An analysis of decision under risk. *Econometrica* 47, 263–91.

Knight, F. (2001). *Risk, Uncertainty and Profit.* Boston: Houghton Mifflin.

Munger, C. (2005). *Poor Charlie's Almanack: The Wit and Wisdom of Charles Munger.* Order from www.poorcharliesalmanack.com/index.html.

Raiffa, H. (1968). *Decision Analysis.* Reading, MA: Addison-Wesley.

Samuelson, P. (1979). Why we should not make mean log of wealth big though years to act are long. *Journal of Banking and Finance* 3, 305–07.

Savage, L. J. (1954). *The Foundations of Statistics.* New York: Wiley.

Subramanian, G., and R. Zeckhauser, (2005). "Negotiauctions": Taking a hybrid approach to the sale of high value assets. *Negotiation* 8(2), 4–6.

Tversky, A., and D. Kahneman (1974). Judgment under uncertainty: Heuristics and biases. *Science* 185, 1124–31.

U.S. Census Bureau, Current Housing Reports, Series H150/07, *American Housing Survey for the United States: 2007.* Washington, DC: U.S. Government Printing Office.

Viscusi, W. K., and R. Zeckhauser (2005). Recollection bias and the combat of terrorism. *Journal of Legal Studies* 34, 27–55.

Zeckhauser, B., and A. Sandoski (2008). *How the Wise Decide: The Lessons of 21 Extraordinary Leaders.* New York: Crown Business.

Zeckhauser, R. (2006). Investing in the unknown and unknowable. *Capitalism and Society* 1(2), Berkeley Electronic Press, www.bepress.com/cas/vol1/iss2/art5.

Zeckhauser, R., and D. Marks (1996). Signposting: The selective revelation of product information. In Wise Choices: Games, Decisions, and Negotiations. R. Zeckhauser, R. Keeney, and J. Sebenius, eds., Boston: Harvard Business School Press, pp. 22–41.

Zeckhauser, R., and M. Thompson (1970). Linear regression with non-normal error terms. *Review of Economics and Statistics* 52, 280–86.

LIST OF CONTRIBUTORS

. . . .

Ashok Bardhan is a Senior Research Associate at the Fisher Center for Real Estate and Urban Economics, Haas School of Business, University of California, Berkeley. He has an MS in physics and mathematics from Moscow, Russia, an MPhil in international relations from New Delhi, India, and a Ph.D. in economics from UC Berkeley. His work experience has involved stints with the Reserve Bank of India and the Bhabha Atomic Research Center, Bombay, and as a foreign trade consultant. His recent research includes papers on the impact of global financial integration on real estate; housing finance and real estate in emerging economies; business process outsourcing and offshoring of R&D; management challenges of globalization of innovative activity; on US labor markets and external shocks; co-authorship of a book, *Globalization and a High-Tech Economy: California, U.S. and Beyond*; and the impact of the Internet on real estate. His current research projects include the impact of global capital flows on U.S. interest rates, and global sourcing and urban agglomerations.

Daniel Borge is a risk management consultant, an advisor to Oliver Wyman, and the author of *The Book of Risk* (Wiley). He was a senior managing director and head of corporate strategy for Bankers Trust, where he was the principal designer of RAROC, the first enterprise risk management system used in the financial industry. He is co-author, with Charles Sanford, of "The Risk Management Revolution," published in *Proceedings of Symposia in Pure Mathematics*, Volume 60 (American Mathematics Society, 1997); co-author, with Eleanor Bloxham, of "Enterprise Risk Management: What Directors Need to Know Now," *Corporate Board Member* (February 27, 2007); and author of "Risk Management and the CFO: A Risk or an Opportunity?," *Corporate Finance Review* (January/February 2006).

Charles N. Bralver is executive director of the International Business Center at the Fletcher School of Tufts University. He is responsible for the Master of International Business program and the affiliated Center for Emerging Markets Enterprises. Previously, Bralver was a founding partner of Oliver, Wyman & Co., managing director for Europe and vice chairman, and head of the firm's Strategic Finance practice. During this time he led strategy and risk management work in all major financial sectors for investment and commercial banks, insurance companies, regulators, and private equity firms in North America, Europe, and Asia. He is the author of several publications and his works have been cited in recent articles in a range of publications including the *Financial Times*, *The Economist*, and *Newsweek*. Bralver's articles on the economics of trading businesses have been published in the *Journal of Applied Corporate Finance* and are utilized in numerous business school course materials. Additional work on the CFO role includes "How CFOs Are Managing Changes in Roles and Expectations" (2006), co-published by Mercer Oliver Wyman and Russell Reynolds Associates. Bralver is active on numerous corporate and educational advisory groups and boards, including as a strategic advisor to Warburg Pincus and, from August 2007, the Senior Advisory Board of Oliver Wyman. He currently sits on Fletcher's Board of Overseers and Dartmouth's Board of Visitors of the Dickey Center for International Affairs. Mr. Bralver holds an A.B. in history and international relations from Dartmouth College, where he was a Rufus Choate Scholar, and an MALD from the Fletcher School.

Riccardo Colacito is assistant professor of finance at the University of North Carolina at Chapel Hill, Kenan-Flagler Business School. His research focuses on the econometrics of high-frequency data, on the optimal behavior of monetary authorities amid model uncertainty, and on the joint behavior of international stock markets and the U.S. dollar. His research has been published in peer-reviewed journals, including the *Journal of Business and Economic Statistics* and the *Journal of Money Credit and Banking*. He received his Ph.D. in economics from New York University, and his bachelor's and master's degrees in economics from Bocconi University, Italy. He has been a visiting scholar at the University of California, San Diego on several occasions.

Francis X. Diebold is Paul F. and Warren S. Miller Professor of Economics, professor of finance and statistics, and co-director of the Financial Institutions Center at the University of Pennsylvania and its Wharton School, and faculty research associate at the National Bureau of Economic Research. Diebold works in econometrics, forecasting, finance, and macroeconomics. He has published extensively and has served on the editorial boards of numerous journals, including *Econometrica* and *Review of Economics and Statistics*. He is an elected fellow of the Econometric Society and the American Statistical Association, and the recipient of Sloan, Guggenheim, and Humboldt awards. A prize-winning teacher and popular lecturer, Diebold has also held visiting appointments in economics and finance at Princeton University, the University of Chicago, Cambridge University, and New York University. Diebold is also active in corporate and policy circles, serving on numerous boards and consulting regularly with financial firms, central banks, and policy organizations. From 1986 to 1989 he served as an economist under Paul Volcker and Alan Greenspan at the Board of Governors of the Federal Reserve System in Washington, DC. He received his B.S. from the Wharton School in 1981 and his Ph.D. in 1986, also from the University of Pennsylvania.

Neil A. Doherty is a Ronald A. Rosenfeld Professor and professor of insurance and risk management at the Wharton School. A principal area of interest is in corporate risk management, focusing on the financial strategies for managing risks that traditionally have not been insurable. He has written several recent papers and three books in this area: *Corporate Risk Management: A Financial Exposition* (1985), *The Financial Theory of Insurance Pricing* (1987, with S. D'Arcy), and *Integrated Risk Management* (2000). A related area of interest is the economics of risk and information; he has written several papers on topics such as adverse selection, the value of information, and the design of insurance contracts with imperfect information. His papers have appeared in journals such as the *Journal of Risk and Insurance, Journal of Risk and Uncertainty, Journal of Political Economy, Journal of Public Economics, Quarterly Review of Economics,* and *Journal of Finance.*

Robert H. Edelstein joined the University of California at Berkeley in 1985 and is active in the fields of real estate economics and finance. He is a prodigious researcher and writer with work that addresses the major issues facing the real estate industry today. He has been published widely in prestigious economics and business journals topics related to commercial and residential financial analysis and real estate markets. He has testified before the United States Congress on many real estate finance issues. He brings a set of refreshing viewpoints, as well as an indomitable energy to the real estate and financial field, and is widely sought after for speaking engagements and as a consultant by both government agencies and private sector clients. He has been president of the American Real Estate and Urban Economics Association and has served on the board of directors of the American Real Estate and Urban Economics Association. He currently serves on the editorial boards of *Journal of Housing Economics, International Real Estate Review, Journal of Property Research,* and the *Journal of Real Estate Research,* and is a member of the board of the Asian Real Estate Society. He is also a member of several prestigious corporate boards. Dr. Edelstein received an A.B., A.M., and Ph.D. in economics from Harvard University.

Robert F. Engle is the Michael Armellino Professor of Finance at the New York University Stern School of Business, as well as the Chancellor's Associates

Professor of Economics at the University of California, San Diego. He is a fellow of the American Academy of Arts and Sciences, the Econometric Society, the American Statistical Association, and the American Finance Association. He is a member of the U.S. National Academy of Sciences. Professor Engle has recently given the invited Fisher-Schultz Lecture, as well as the William Phillips, Pareto, and Frank Paish lectures. In 2003 Professor Engle was honored with the Nobel Prize in Economic Sciences for his work in methods of analyzing economic time series with time-varying volatility (ARCH). In addition to ARCH, his research has introduced some of the most influential concepts in modern econometrics—GARCH models, cointegration, weak exogeneity, band spectrum regression, common features, autoregressive conditional duration (ACD), and, most recently, the CAViaR model. In four books and well over 100 academic journal articles, Professor Engle has applied these methods to analyze equities, options, currencies, and interest rates; his current research also includes an investigation of empirical market microstructure. He is a frequent speaker and consultant for financial institutions. He holds a Ph.D. in economics and a M.S. in physics from Cornell University, and is principal of Robert F. Engle Econometric Services. Before UCSD, he was an associate professor of economics at MIT.

Charles A. E. Goodhart, CBE, FBA, is a member of the Financial Markets Group at the London School of Economics and was deputy director 1987–2004. Until his retirement in 2002, he had been the Norman Sosnow Professor of Banking and Finance at LSE since 1985. Previously, he had worked at the Bank of England for seventeen years as a monetary adviser, becoming a chief adviser in 1980. In 1997 he was appointed one of the outside independent members of the Bank of England's new Monetary Policy Committee until May 2000. Earlier he had taught at Cambridge and LSE. Besides numerous articles, he has written a couple of books on monetary history; a graduate monetary textbook, *Money, Information and Uncertainty* (2nd ed., 1989); two collections of papers on monetary policy, *Monetary Theory and Practice* (1984) and *The Central Bank and The Financial System* (1995); and several other studies relating to financial markets and monetary policy and history. In his spare time he is a sheep farmer (loss-making).

Sir Clive W. J. Granger (1934–2009) sadly passed away while this book was in production. He published widely in the areas of statistics and econometrics, forecasting, finance, and demographics. For more than three decades, he developed methods for understanding the properties of time series data. In the 1960s, he pioneered spectral analysis, a technique for decomposing series into their component parts. In the 1970s, building upon work in physics, he developed the *Granger Test* for causality, a method for identifying "what causes what" when two series move together. The test is now routinely used by applied economists. In the 1980s, he pioneered cointegration, a methodology that can help us understand the long-run relationship between pairs of economic variables, such as change in the money supply and inflation. Over his long and productive career, Granger received numerous awards and honors for his work. In January 2003 he was named a Distinguished Fellow of the American Economic Association and at the end of that year was awarded the Nobel Prize in Economics. He received a knighthood in 2005 and later in the year became an Honorary Fellow of Trinity College, Cambridge. He authored ten books and over 200 papers and was a featured speaker at academic conferences throughout the world. Granger studied at the University of Nottingham, graduating in 1955, and received his Ph.D. in 1959. He joined the University of California, San Diego, in 1974 and helped build its Department of Economics into one of the world's top centers for econometrics.

Richard J. Herring is Jacob Safra Professor of International Banking and director of the Lauder Institute of International Management Studies at the University of Pennsylvania, and co-director of the Wharton Financial Institutions Center. Dr. Herring, an expert on financial institutions and international finance, was founding director of the Wharton Financial Institutions Center, which received two generous grants from the Sloan Foundation to establish an academic center of expertise on the financial services industry. Dr. Herring has advised numerous U.S. government agencies as well as several multilateral lending institutions. He is a member of the Shadow Financial Regulatory Committee, co-chair of the Biennial Multinational Banking Seminar, and has been a fellow of the World Economic Forum in Davos, Switzerland. He is currently a member of the Joint Task Force of the IMF, World Bank, and Basel Financial Stability Institute on Bank Insolvency. Dr. Herring is the author of more than 75 articles and books. His most recent book (with Robert E. Litan of the Brookings Institution) is *Financial Regulation in the Global Economy*. He serves on the editorial boards of several leading journals and is co-editor of the *Brookings–Wharton Papers on Financial Services*. Before coming to Wharton in 1972, Dr. Herring taught at Princeton University. He received his A.B. from Oberlin College (1968), and his M.A. (1970) and Ph.D. (1973) from Princeton University.

Paul R. Kleindorfer is Distinguished Research Professor at INSEAD (Fontainebleau) and the Anheuser-Busch Professor (Emeritus) of Management

Science at the Wharton School of the University of Pennsylvania. Dr. Klein-dorfer graduated with distinction (B.S.) from the U. S. Naval Academy in 1961. He studied on a Fulbright Fellowship in Mathematics at the University of Tübingen, Germany (1964/65), followed by doctoral studies at Carnegie Mellon University, from which he received his Ph.D. in 1970 in systems and communication sciences at the Graduate School of Industrial Administration. Dr. Kleindorfer has held university appointments at Carnegie Mellon University/GSIA (1968/9), Massachusetts Institute of Technology (1969/72), The Wharton School (1973–2006), INSEAD (2006–), and several universities and international research institutes. Dr. Kleindorfer is the author or co-author of many books and research papers in the areas of decision sciences, managerial economics, and risk management.

Donald L. Kohn is vice chairman of the Board of Governors of the Federal Reserve System. He was born in November 1942 in Philadelphia, Pennsylvania. He received an A.B. in economics in 1964 from the College of Wooster and a Ph.D. in economics in 1971 from the University of Michigan. Dr. Kohn is a veteran of the Federal Reserve System. Before becoming a member of the Board, he served on its staff as adviser to the Board for Monetary Policy (2001–02), secretary of the Federal Open Market Committee (1987–2002), director of the Division of Monetary Affairs (1987–2001), and deputy staff director for Monetary and Financial Policy (1983–87). He also held several positions in the board's Division of Research and Statistics: associate director (1981–83), chief of capital markets (1978–81), and economist (1975–78). Dr. Kohn began his career as a financial economist at the Federal Reserve Bank of Kansas City (1970–75). Dr. Kohn has written extensively on issues related to monetary policy and its implementation by the Federal Reserve. These works were published in volumes issued by various organizations, including the Federal Reserve System, the Bank of England, the Reserve Bank of Australia, the Bank of Japan, the Bank of Korea, the National Bureau of Economic Research, and the Brookings Institution.

Howard Kunreuther is the Cecilia Yen Koo Professor of Decision Sciences and Public Policy at the Wharton School, University of Pennsylvania and co-director of the Wharton Risk Management and Decision Processes Center. He has a long-standing interest in ways that society can better manage low-probability–high-consequence events as they relate to technological and natural hazards and has published extensively on the topic. Kunreuther is currently a member of the National Research Council (NRC) Board on Radioactive Waste Management, was a member of the NRC Board on Natural Disasters, and chaired the H. John Heinz III Center Panel on Risk, Vulnerability and True Costs of Coastal Hazards. He is a distinguished fellow of the Society for Risk Analysis and received the Society's Distinguished Achievement Award in 2001. Kunreuther has written or co-edited a number of books and papers, including *Catastrophe Modeling: A New Approach to Managing Risk* (with Patricia Grossi) and *Wharton on Making Decisions* (with Stephen Hoch). He is a recipient of the Elizur Wright Award for the publication that makes the most significant contribution to the literature of insurance.

Andrew Kuritzkes is a managing director of Mercer Oliver Wyman. He has consulted on a broad range of strategy, risk management, regulatory, and organizational issues for financial institutions and regulators in the United States, Canada, the United Kingdom, Switzerland, Germany, the Netherlands, Hong Kong, and Singapore. He has worked extensively with organizations, at the board and senior executive levels, on developments in finance and risk management, including the link between risk measurement and strategy, the impact of regulation, Basel II implementation, active portfolio management, and the evolution of wholesale lending. Mr. Kuritzkes has written and spoken widely on risk, financial structuring, and regulatory topics. His articles have appeared in *Strategic Finance, Risk, Die Bank, Banking Strategies, Journal of Applied Corporate Finance, Journal of Risk Finance, Journal of Financial Services Research*, and *the Brookings–Wharton Papers on Financial Services*. Mr. Kuritzkes serves on the advisory boards of the Harvard Law School Program on International Financial Systems and the *Journal of Risk Finance*. Before joining Oliver, Wyman & Company, Mr. Kuritzkes worked as an economist and lawyer for the Federal Reserve Bank of New York. He holds a J.D. degree from Harvard Law School, an M. Phil. degree in economics from Cambridge University, and a B.A. degree from Yale College.

Robert H. Litzenberger is currently an executive director at Azimuth Asset Management, LLC where he manages the Select fund. He previously was a partner at Goldman Sachs where he served as firmwide risk manager. He was responsible for the development, implementation, and monitoring of Goldman's global risk management system, setting and monitoring risk limits as well as meeting with Goldman's trading leaders and making comprehensive recommendations regarding his findings to Goldman's Risk Committee. Prior to this, Bob served as director of Derivative Research and Quantitative Modeling in the fixed income division at Goldman. Previously, he served as director of research and chief economist at AIG-Financial Products. Bob is co-author of *Foundations of Financial Economics* (1988) and has published more than 50 articles in leading academic finance journals. Since 1986, he has been on the finance faculty at the Wharton School of the University of Pennsylvania, where he held the Edward Hopkinson Chair in investment banking and is currently a professor emeritus. Before joining the Wharton faculty, Bob was the C.O.G. Miller Distinguished Professor of Finance at the Stanford Graduate School of Business. He is a former president of the American Finance Association. Bob holds a Ph.D. from the University of North Carolina, an M.B.A from the University of Pennsylvania, and a B.A. from Wagner College.

Benoit B. Mandelbrot is Sterling Professor Emeritus of Mathematical Sciences at Yale University and IBM Fellow Emeritus (Physics) at the IBM Research Center. He is author of *Les Objets Fractals*, 1975, 1984, 1989, and 1995 (translated into Basque, Brazilian, Bulgarian, Chinese, Czech, Italian, Portugese, Rumanian, and Spanish) and *The Fractal Geometry of Nature*, 1982 (translated into Chinese, German, Japanese, Korean, Russian, and Spanish). His *Selecta* include with *Fractals and Scaling in Finance: Discontinuity, Concentration, Risk* (1997), *Fractales, hasard et finance* (1997), *Multifractals and 1/f Noise: Wild Self-Affinity in Physics* (1999), *Gaussian Self-affinity and Fractals: Globality, The Earth, 1/f Noise and R/S* (2002), and *Chaos and Fractals: the Mandelbrot Set and Beyond* (2004). He co-authored with M. L. Frame *Fractals, Graphics, and Mathematics Education* (2002) and with R. L. Hudson *The (Mis)behavior of Markets: A Fractal View of Risk, Ruin, and Reward* (2004). He is a fellow of the American Academy of Arts and Sciences; a member of the U.S. National Academy of Sciences, and the American Philosophical Society; and a foreign member of the Norwegian Academy of Science and Letters. His awards include the 1993 Wolf Prize for Physics and the 2003 Japan Prize for Science and Technology, the 1985 F. Barnard Medal for Meritorious Service to Science (*Magna est Veritas*) of the U.S. National Academy of Sciences, the 1986 Franklin Medal for Signal and Eminent Service in Science of the Franklin Institute of Philadelphia, the 1988 Charles Proteus Steinmetz Medal of IEEE, the 1988 (first) Science for Art Prize of Moet-Hennessy-Louis Vuitton, the 1989 Harvey Prize for Science and Technology of the Technion in Haifa, the 1991 Nevada Prize, the 1994 Honda Prize, the 1996 Médaille de Vermeil de la Ville de Paris, the 1999 John Scott Award, the 2000 Lewis Fry Richardson Award of the European Geophysical Society, the 2002 William Procter Prize of Sigma Xi, the 2004 Prize of Financial Times/Deutschland, the 2005 Orlicz Medal of Poznan University, the 2005 Waclaw Sierpinski Prize in Mathematics of Warsaw University, and the Casimir Funk Award of PIASA. He also received a Distinguished Service Award for Outstanding Achievement from the California Institute of Technology, and a Humboldt Preis from the Alexander von Humboldt Stiftung.

David M. Modest is a managing director at JP Morgan Chase, where, within the firm's Proprietary Positioning Business, he runs the global effort in quantitative-research-driven trading strategies. Dr. Modest graduated from M.I.T. with S.B. and Ph.D. degrees in economics. Upon graduating from M.I.T., he joined the Columbia Business School faculty before becoming a tenured member of the faculty at the Haas School of Business at the University of California at Berkeley. At Berkeley, Dr. Modest was chairman of the finance group and received campus-wide and Haas School teaching prizes. Dr. Modest has also taught at the Stanford Business School and at the Sloan School of Management at M.I.T. Dr. Modest's life as a full-time practitioner began as a founding member of LTCM, where he was responsible for building the firm's relative-value equity businesses, including warrant, convertible, and single-stock option arbitrage; and quantitative long/short equity strategies. Subsequent to LTCM, Dr. Modest joined Morgan Stanley as a managing director, where he built and oversaw proprietary capital structure arbitrage and long/short equity trading groups. He was also extensively involved in enhancing Morgan Stanley's internal risk management capabilities and the firm's ability to provide state-of-the-art risk management services to its institutional and retail clients.

Alexander Muermann is assistant professor of insurance and risk management at the Wharton School of the University of Pennsylvania. He holds a Diplom in mathematics from the University of Bonn and a Ph.D. in economics from the London School of Economics. Prior to his current position, Alexander Muermann was a research assistant at the Financial Markets Group, a temporary lecturer in economics at the London School of Economics, and a quantitative analyst at Warburg Dillon Read of UBS AG. His research focuses on economic aspects of risk allocation and management. Current research projects include the impact of anticipated regret on decision-making under uncertainty and equilibrium analysis of risk allocation in the context of incomplete contracting, market power, insolvency, and externalities.

Mark V. Pauly is Bendheim Professor, vice dean, and chair of the Health Care Systems Department in the Wharton School at the University of Pennsylvania. He teaches courses on health care, public policy and management, insurance and risk management, and economics. Dr. Pauly was previously a professor at Northwestern University for sixteen years. He has also consulted for a number of organizations including the Greater New York Hospital Association, the Urban Institute, various pharmaceutical companies, and National Economic Research Associates. Dr. Pauly's books include *Health Benefits at Work: An*

Economic and Political Analysis of Employment-related Health Insurance, as well as *Supplying Vaccine: An Economic Analysis of Critical Issues* and *Financing Long Term Care: What Should Be the Government's Role?* His recent journal publications include "Structural Incentives and Adoption of Medical Technologies in HMO Fee-for-Service Health Insurance," "The Future U.S. Health Care System: Who Will Care for the Poor and Uninsured?," and "The Effects of Health Insurance Access to New Medical Technologies." Dr. Pauly received his Ph.D. in economics from the University of Virginia, his M.A. in economics from the University of Delaware, and his A.B. from Xavier University.

Til Schuermann is research officer at the Federal Reserve Bank of New York's research department, where he focuses on risk measurement and management in financial institutions and capital markets. Recent topics include integrated risk management and credit risk diversification. He is also a Sloan Research Fellow at the Wharton Financial Institution Center and teaches at Columbia University. Prior to joining the New York Fed in May of 2001 he spent five years at the management consulting firm Oliver, Wyman & Company, where he was a director and head of research. Til spent 1993 to 1996 at Bell Laboratories working on techniques from statistics and artificial intelligence to build models for bad debt prediction as well as developing risk-based management decision support tools. Til has published in the *Journal of Financial Economics, Journal of Banking & Finance, Journal of Money, Banking and Credit, Journal of Financial Services Research*, as well as *Risk Magazine*, and has edited a book, *Simulation-based Inference in Econometrics*. He received his Ph.D. in economics in 1993 from the University of Pennsylvania.

Kenneth E. Scott is a senior research fellow and the Ralph M. Parsons Professor of Law and Business Emeritus, Stanford University Law School. He is an expert in public regulation of banking institutions, corporation law, and securities law. His current research focuses on legislative and policy developments related to bank regulation and deposit insurance reform. He is also exploring the application of new economic perspectives to corporate law and governance issues. Scott's major work has been in the fields of law and regulation of corporations, securities and banking, and the fast-changing area of financial services. He is a member of the state bar in New York, California, and the District of Columbia. Scott is the author of two books: (with R. Posner): *Economics of Corporation Law and Securities Regulation* (Little, Brown, 1980) and (with W. Baxter and P. Cootner) *Retail Banking in the Electronic Age: The Law and Economics of Electronic Funds Transfer* (Allanheld, Osmun, 1977). He has been a member of the editorial board of *Financier* since 1994 and was a member of the editorial board of the *Journal of Financial Services Research* from 1992 to 2001. He is a prolific author of articles for legal and financial journals. Scott is currently a member of the board of directors of American Century Mutual Funds. He earned an A.B. in economics in 1949 from the College of William and Mary, where he was class valedictorian and a member of Phi Beta Kappa. He attended Princeton University as a Woodrow Wilson fellow, receiving an M.A. in political science in 1953. He graduated from the Stanford University Law School in 1956 with an LLB.

Nassim Nicholas Taleb held senior positions with major banks, focusing on the trading and risk management of complex derivatives (CSFB, UBS, BNP-Paribas, and Bankers Trust, among others) and worked independently on the floor of the Chicago exchanges. He founded Empirica Capital LLC in 1998 mainly to protect portfolios against extreme events. He is currently co-director of the Decision Science Laboratory and visiting professor at the London Business School. He was the Dean's Professor in the Sciences of Uncertainty at the University of Massachusetts at Amherst, and he taught derivatives modeling at the Courant Institute of Mathematical Sciences of New York University. He has an M.B.A. from Wharton and a Ph.D. from the University of Paris. Taleb is the author of *The Black Swan: The Impact of the Highly Improbable* (New York: Random House and London: Penguin, 2007), *Fooled by Randomness* (2nd ed. rev., Random House, 2005 [1st ed., Texere, 2001]), and *Dynamic Hedging: Managing Vanilla and Exotic Options* (Wiley, 1997). His work has been translated into 23 languages.

Richard J. Zeckhauser is Frank Plumpton Ramsey Professor of Political Economy and the Kennedy School of Government, Harvard University. Much of his conceptual research examines possibilities for democratic, decentralized allocation procedures. Many of his policy investigations explore ways to promote the health of human beings, to help markets work more effectively, and to foster informed and appropriate choices by individuals and government agencies. His joint papers in 2004 to 2005 include "Social Comparisons in Ultimatum Bargaining," *Scandinavian Journal of Economics*; "Racial Profiling," *Philosophy and Public Affairs*; "Informational Strategy and Regulatory Policy Making," *Minnesota Law Review*; "How Individuals Assess and Value the Risks of Climate Change," *Climatic Change*; "Eliciting Honest Feedback in Electronic Markets," *Management Science*; and "Aggregation of Heterogeneous Time Preferences," *Journal of Political Economics*. Zeckhauser's current research projects are directed at pharmaceutical pricing, deception, and reputations, bad apples, and bad bets in social policy, trust in Islamic and Western nations, information economics and Italian Renaissance art, the blending of negotiations and auctions, and collaborative undertakings between the public and private sectors.

INDEX

· ·

uncertainty (*continued*)
    186; ignorance and, 305–15, 327–29;
    improving acuity and, 187–88; insuf-
    ficient reason and, 211; insurance and,
    210–19 (*see also* insurance); invest-
    ment and, 305–15; Kappa class and,
    40; Knightian, 32, 164–81, 306n3;
    leanness and, 186–87; legitimation
    and, 172, 188; long-term vision and,
    187–88; meta-models and, 170–71;
    Omega concept and, 40; opportunism
    and, 186–87; prediction theory and,
    165–66, 169, 171, 179, 185; probability
    and, 33; randomness and, 47–58, 171–
    72, 176, 178; redeployable competen-
    cies and, 186; resilience and, 186–87;
    resource-based view (RBV) approach
    and, 186; responsiveness and, 186–87;
    shocks and, 12; subjectivity and, 38,
    165–68, 170–73, 175n14, 178–79, 189;
    supply chains and, 184–85; terrorism
    and, 210–14, 219–23, 226–29, 232;
    upper-tail, 3–4; wild randomness and,
    49–53; World War I era and, 164–65
unexpected losses (UL), 286, 290
uniqueness, 310–11
United Health Group, 257
United Kingdom, 82, 221, 291, 304
United States, 293; banking crisis of, 59;
    bank risk and, 122 (*see also* bank risk);
    bankruptcy laws in, 117; budget defi-
    cit of, 59; Chinese debt of, 59; d-risk
    and, 36; Federal Financial Institutions
    Examination Council and, 301; Great
    Depression and, 122–23, 136; housing
    market and, 155; international cur-
    rency market and, 323; millionaires
    in, 309; northeastern blackouts and,
    184; Prompt Corrective Action and,
    20n7; real estate and, 156, 312; savings
    and loan crisis of, 74, 118; terrorism
    insurance and, 220–23
United States Congress, 222
University of Chicago, 164
unknowable (*U*): auctions and, 332–33;
    bank risk and, 103–5, 112, 114, 117,
    120; complementary skills and,

312–14; concept of, 2; corporate gov-
    ernance and, 284–85; crisis mitigation
    and, 27–29; crisis preventions and,
    21–27; decision-making and, 240; ex
    ante quantification and, 104; fat tails
    and, 311–12; Gödel and, 159, 166n3,
    195; Heisenberg and, 159; holdup and,
    16–17; informed players and, 329–30;
    insurance and, 195–96; investment
    and, 305–43; nature of, 308–10; real
    estate and, 151, 157, 159, 162; recol-
    lection bias and, 317–18; risk and, 44;
    scientific approach to, 159–60; struc-
    tural flexibility and, 11–12; terrorism
    and, 104–5; transfer and, 11–12; Tur-
    ing and, 159; uniqueness and, 310–11;
    weird causes and, 311–12
unknown (*u*): auctions and, 332–33;
    bank failure and, 14–15; bank risk
    and, 103–5, 112, 114, 120; Basel II
    and, 104; better measurement and,
    6–7; complementary skills and,
    312–14; concept of, 2; conjecture and,
    3; corporate governance and, 277–85;
    credit crisis and, 105; crisis mitigation
    and, 27–29; crisis preventions and,
    21–27; decision-making and, 240; ex
    post wealth distribution for, 10–11;
    fat tails and, 311–12; holdup and,
    16–17; hypothesis and, 3; ignorance
    and, 305–15, 327–29; incentives and,
    14–15; incomplete contracting and,
    203–8; informed players and, 329–30;
    insurance and, 194–214 (*see also*
    insurance); investment and, 304–43;
    known and, 43; quantification and,
    104; real estate and, 152, 155, 162; rec-
    ollection bias and, 317–18; risk and,
    43–44 (*see also* risk); scenario analysis
    and, 25–26; stress testing and, 25–26;
    structural flexibility and, 11–12; ter-
    rorism and, 210–11 (*see also* terror-
    ism); transfer and, 11–12; uncertainty
    and, 2, 31 (*see also* uncertainty);
    uniqueness and, 310–11; weird causes
    and, 311–12
UPS, 182